The Voter's Dilemma and Democratic Accountability

MONA M. LYNE

THE VOTER'S DILEMMA AND DEMOCRATIC ACCOUNTABILITY

LATIN AMERICA AND BEYOND

THE PENNSYLVANIA STATE UNIVERSITY PRESS
UNIVERSITY PARK, PENNSYLVANIA

Library of Congress Cataloging-in-Publication Data

Lyne, Mona M., 1960–
The voter's dilemma and democratic accountability : Latin America and beyond /
Mona M. Lyne.
p.   cm.
Includes bibliographical references and index.
Summary: "Presents evidence that under certain widespread structural conditions, democratic accountability falls prey to the same N-person prisoner's dilemma that plagues any other decentralized attempt to procure collective goods. Examines four prominent democracies: postwar and contemporary Brazil and pre-Chavez and contemporary Venezuela"—Provided by publisher.
ISBN 978-0-271-03387-7 (pbk : alk. paper)
1. Elections—Brazil.
2. Elections—Venezuela.
3. Democracy—Brazil.
4. Democracy—Venezuela.
I. Title.

JL2492.L96 2008
324.981—dc22
2008012391

Copyright © 2008 The Pennsylvania State University
All rights reserved
Printed in the United States of America
Published by The Pennsylvania State University Press,
University Park, PA 16802-1003

The Pennsylvania State University Press is a member of the
Association of American University Presses.

CONTENTS

LIST OF TABLES AND FIGURES
vii

ACKNOWLEDGMENTS
xi

LIST OF ACRONYMS
xv

Introduction:
Theories of Democratic Accountability and
Development in Brazil and Venezuela
1

1
The Voter's Dilemma:
Collective or Clientelistic Goods?
21

2
Are Voters in Brazil and Venezuela
Opting for Policy-Based or Quid Pro Quo Voting?
63

3
Party Behavior:
Policy-Based or Quid Pro Quo Appeals to Voters?
99

4
Internal Party Organization:
Align Individual and Collective Goals to Build a Policy
Reputation or to Ensure Efficient Vote Buying?
147

5
Legislative Organization:
Governing Majority Agenda Control or Mutual Veto?
175

6
Policy Choice:
Generate Sustained Growth or Maximize Quid Pro Quo?
209

Conclusion
259

APPENDIXES
265

REFERENCES
273

INDEX
289

TABLES AND FIGURES

Tables

1	Fourfold typology of political goods	26
2	Democratic accountability as collective choice	37
3	Alignment of individual and collective goals within the party	47
4	Clientelistic exchange and partisan tides	84
5	Party vote share at time t, pooled model, Federal Chamber of Deputies, Brazil, 1945–1964, 1990–2006	86
6	Municipal dominance of presidential candidates in Brazil, by election year	91
7	Percentage of deputies with given level of dominance, Federal Chamber of Deputies, Brazil, 1946–1962	92
8	Percentage of deputies with given level of dominance, Federal Chamber of Deputies Brazil, 1986–2006	93
9	Determinants of party vote share, Federal Chamber of Deputies, Venezuela, 1958–1988	94
10	Effective number of parties, Federal Chamber of Deputies, Brazil, 1945–1962	102
11	Seat shares per party, Federal Chamber of Deputies, Brazil, 1946–1963 (%)	102
12	Seat shares per party, Federal Chamber of Deputies, Brazil, 1991–2007 (%)	103
13	Roll call voting, Federal Chamber of Deputies, Brazil, 1946–1964	106
14	Party composition of Executive Cabinet, Brazil, 1946–1964	108
15	Party composition of Executive Cabinet, Venezuela, 1959–1998	112
16	Clientelistic versus policy-based appeals in legislative voting	116
17	Party voting on executive-initiated economic development legislation, Federal Chamber of Deputies, Brazil, 1946–1963	120

18	Roll call voting, Federal Chamber of Deputies, Brazil, 1990–2007	130–131
19	Party composition of Executive Cabinet, Brazil, 1990–2007	135
20	Electoral alliances, federal legislative elections, Federal Chamber of Deputies, Brazil, 1950–1962	137
21	Electoral alliances, federal legislative elections, Federal Chamber of Deputies, Brazil, 1986–2006	139
22	Party switching within and across coalitions, within and between legislative sessions, Federal Chamber of Deputies, Brazil, 1989–2007	141
23	Seat shares per party, Federal Chamber of Deputies, Venezuela, 1958–1998 (%)	152
24	Determinants of seat assignments, Finance and Budget Committee, Federal Chamber of Deputies, Brazil, 1945–1964	159
25	Receipt of budget amendment funds, Federal Chamber of Deputies, Brazil, 1996–2001	172
26	Party distribution of committee presidents, Federal Chamber of Deputies, Brazil, 1948–1963 (%)	179
27	Party membership on the Finance and Budget Committee, Federal Chamber of Deputies, Brazil, 1948–1963	181
28	Party membership on the Constitution and Justice Committee, Federal Chamber of Deputies, Brazil, 1948–1963	182
29	Party membership on the Economics Committee, Federal Chamber of Deputies, Brazil, 1950–1963	182
30	The determinants of committee presidents, Federal Chamber of Deputies, Brazil, 1948–1963	183
31	The determinants of high-externality committee presidents, Social Democratic Party (PSD), Federal Chamber of Deputies, Brazil, 1948–1963	184
32	Legislative organization in clientelistic and policy-based systems	191
33	Roll rates on project and agenda-setting votes, by cabinet period and party, Federal Chamber of Deputies, Brazil, 1990–2007 (%)	201–202

34	Roll rates on project and agenda-setting votes, by cabinet period and party, Federal Chamber of Deputies, Brazil, 1947–1963 (%)	205
35	Policy choice and response to crisis in clientelistic and policy-based systems	228

Figures

1	Roll call voting unity (Rice indices), government coalition, Federal Chamber of Deputies, Brazil, 1945–1964 and 1989–2006	132
2	Roll call voting unity (Rice indices), opposition coalition, Federal Chamber of Deputies, Brazil, 1945–1964 and 1989–2006	133
3	Index of likeness, Federal Chamber of Deputies, Brazil, 1945–1964 and 1989–2006	133
4	Party seat shares, Federal Chamber of Deputies, Brazil, 1991–2006 (%)	143

ACKNOWLEDGMENTS

Anyone who has shared my good fortune to have spent considerable time in a developing country is soon struck by a paradox: although there seems to be great neglect of the public sphere in most of these countries, generosity and hospitality are abundant in personal relations. The kindness and consideration I experienced in Latin America prompted and reinforced my belief that the shortcomings in the public realm could not be adequately accounted for with an individual-level explanation. In the spirit of that benevolence, which helped to both inspire and sustain this project, I would like to first express my heartfelt thanks to the many friends, colleagues, and professionals in Brazil who shared so much so generously with me.

Raquel Horowicz was my Brazilian mother, a woman very much younger than her years, always ready to listen to my woes with a sympathetic ear and always game for some adventure. Arilton Teixeira was my guide to the beauty and exuberance of Brazilian culture, to Chico Buarque's genius, and to a better understanding of myself. Arilda Teixeira was a great friend, my samba partner in Salgueiro, and literally a lifesaver as she found a doctor who found a hospital when I really needed it and nursed me back to health after my release. Aridelmo Teixeira was my guide to Rio nightlife when Arilton was indisposed. Hilda Teixeira took care of me in the hospital and in her home. Beth Cobra provided friendship, many laughs, and her washing machine, all of which contributed greatly to my superb experience in Brazil. I could always call on Leandro Piquet Carneiro for advice, conversation, and succor, and he was equally perspicacious as a colleague, a friend, or a fellow street-corner anthropologist in Brazil. Alzira Macedo generously shared her home and her love of life and provided indispensable support during moments when I was truly at the end of my rope. Robert and Lienne, Nilton and Alexandre were always up for *umazinha* and great conversation at the corner *pé sujo* or the Mercado São Jose. Fabiano Guilherme dos Santos, Carlos Pio da Costa Filho, Wanderley Guilherme dos Santos, Maria Regina de Soares Lima, David Fleischer, and Rogério Schimdt were friends and colleagues who provided essential help and guidance. Winston Fritsch allowed me to audit his course at Pontifícia Universidade Católica–Rio, assisted me in lining up interviews with major Brazilian industrialists, and advised me as the manuscript developed. Antonio Otávio Cintra provided guidance, advice, and data from the Câmara dos Deputados. Márcio Rabat provided friendship and orientation in Brasília and in the Câmara. The staff in the Documents Section of the Câmara dos Deputados kindly provided me with space and Xeroxed thousands of pages of the *Diário do Congresso*. The staff of the Secretário-Geral da Mesa of the Câmara sat for interviews and provided data. The Consultoria do Orçamento e Fiscalização Financeira kindly provided data on release of budget amendment funds in the Câmara. The staff of the Electoral Archives of the National Electoral Tribunal was extremely solicitous and assisted me in combing through their bins of data for many weeks. Barry Ames, Octavio Amorim Neto, Fabiano Guilherme dos Santos, Argelina Figueiredo, and Fernando Limongi kindly shared their data on election results and roll calls.

Although I spent much less time in Venezuela, both academics and politicians were generous with their time and assistance. Steve Ellner, Naudy and Silvia Suarez, Ángel Álvarez, Ricardo Combellas, Herbert Koeneke, and Luis Gómez kindly shared their views on Venezuelan politics and provided logistical assistance. Paciano Pacheco, Carlos Canache Mata, Marco Tulio Bruni Celli, and Nelson Chitty generously shared their insider's views of Venezuelan politics.

Paul Drake and Peter Cowhey were my advisors and mentors at the University of California, San Diego. Their intellectual guidance, encouragement, and near-infinite patience were invaluable, as were their examples of the kind of professor I hope to emulate. Neal Beck was a latecomer to this project, but his keen analytic eye, frank advice, and genuine concern for my progress were indispensable to my ability to bring it to a close. Peter Smith provided cogent comments and helped with contacts across Latin America throughout this project. I thank Royce Carroll, Scott Morgenstern, Heather Hawn, and James Kruse for reading the entire manuscript and providing insightful comments and suggestions. Herbert Kitschelt deserves extra-special mention for his continual support, encouragement, and generous interest in my work, not to mention reading the entire manuscript several times. Two colleagues and dear friends deserve extra-extra-special mention for the many, many times they read and challenged my arguments and encouraged me to forge ahead: Mike Tierney and Octavio Amorim Neto. Words cannot express what their belief in and enthusiasm for the idea of the voter's dilemma has meant to me. Without their unflagging support and constructive criticism, great sense of humor, and innumerable engaging discussions of politics and political science, this project would never have come to fruition.

I wish to thank Melissa McMurray, Andrea Waddle, Ivan Esquiva, Christina Petrides, Jung Hwa Lee, Will Jennings, Julie Loggins, Cesar Zucco, Susanne Schorpp, Heather Hawn, Kelly O'Reilly, Acir Almeida, Francisco Junqueira Moreira da Costa, Lauro Stucco, Raul Sanchez Urribarri, and Chenghong Li for excellent research assistance. Mary Allison Joseph deserves special mention for her superb assistance with every aspect of field research in Venezuela: the nuts and bolts of setting up interviews, formulating interview questions, and interpreting the results.

I thank Sanford Thatcher for his efforts to move the manuscript through the process smoothly and swiftly.

Finally, I want to thank my grandparents W. H. and Mary Ann for sharing their love of Brazil. I thank my father, Henry; my mother, Elaine; and my brother, Bill, for their understanding, encouragement, and support as I changed careers and brought that change to fruition in this book. I thank Amy Cahill, Lisa Baldez, Susan Puglia, Martha Sandy, and Jill Frank for encouraging me to believe in myself.

ACRONYMS

General

ECLA — United Nations Economic Commission for Latin America
ISI — Import Substitution Industrialization

Brazilian Parties and Bureaucracies Second Republic (Segunda República), 1945–1964

CACEX — Foreign Trade Desk of the Bank of Brazil (Carteira de Comércio Exterior do Banco do Brasil)
CCJ — Constitution and Justice Committee in the Chamber of Deputies (Comisão de Constituição e Justiça da Câmara dos Deputados)
PDC — Christian Democratic Party (Partido Democrata Cristão)
PR — Republican Party (Partido Republicano)
PSD — Social Democratic Party (Partido Social Democrático)
PSP — Progressive Social Party (Partido Social Progresista)
PTB — Brazilian Labor Party (Partido Trabalhista Brasileiro)
UDN — National Democratic Union (Uniao Democrática Nacional)

Brazilian Parties, Military Rule, 1964–1985

ARENA — National Renewal Alliance Party (Associação Renovadora Nacional)
MDB — Brazilian Democratic Movement (Movimento Democrático Brasileiro)

Brazilian Parties, Contemporary 1985–2008

DEM — Democrats (Democratas), former PFL
PCdoB — Communist Party of Brazil (Partido Comunista do Brasil)

PDT	Democratic Labor Party (Partido Democrático Trabalhista)
PFL	Liberal Front Party (Partido da Frente Liberal)
PMDB	Brazilian Democratic Movement Party (Partido do Movimento Democrático Brasileiro)
PP	Progressive Party (Partido Progresista), former PPB
PPB	Brazilian Progressive Party (Partido Progresista Brasileira)
PPR	Republican Progressive Party (Partido Progresista Republicana)
PPS	Socialist People's Party (Partido Popular Socialista)
PSB	Brazilian Socialist Party (Partido Socialista Brasileiro)
PSD	Social Democratic Party (Partido Democrático Social)
PSDB	Brazilian Social Democracy Party (Partido da Social Democracia Brasileira)
PT	Workers' Party (Partido dos Trabalhadores)
PTB	Brazilian Labor Party (Partido Trabalhista Brasileiro)

Brazil, Miscellaneous

PDS	Democratic Social Party (Partido Democrático Social)
FEF	Fiscal Stabilization Fund (Fundo de Estabilização Fiscal) previously the FSE
FSE	Social Emergency Fund (Fundo Social de Emergência)
RGPS	Private Sector Pension System (Regime Geral de Previdencia Social)
RJU	Public Sector Pension System (Regime Jurídico Único)

Venezuelan Parties, Movements, Organizations, and Bureaucracies

AD	Democratic Action (Acción Democrática)
CEN	National Executive Committee of the AD (Comité Executivo Nacional)
CN	National Committee of the COPEI (Comité Nacional)
COPEI	Political Electoral Independent Organization Committee (Comité de Organización Política Electoral Independiente)
COPRE	Presidential Commission for the Reform of the State (Comisión Presidencial para la Reforma des Estado)
CTV	Confederation of Venezuelan Workers (Confederación de Trabajadores de Venezuela)

MAS	Movement for Socialism (Movimiento al Socialismo)
MBR-200	Revolutionary Bolivarian Movement 200 (Movimento Bolivariano Revolucionario 200), initially clandestine movement of young military officers supporting Chávez, founded in 1983, later evolving into the MVR
MEP	People's Electoral Movement (Movimeinto Electoral del Pueblo)
MIR	Movement of the Revolutionary Left (Movimiento de Izquierda Revolucionaria)
MVR	Fifth Republic Movement (Movimiento V [Quinta] República)
PCV	Venezuelan Communist Party (Partido Comunista de Venezuela)
PDVSA	Venezuelan State-Owned Oil Company (Petróleos de Venezuela)
PODEMOS	For Social Democracy (Por la Democracia Social)
PPT	Homeland for All Party (Patria para Todos)
PSUV	United Socialist Party of Venezuela (Partido Socialista Unido de Venezuela)
URD	Republican Democratic Union (Unión Republicana Democrática)

INTRODUCTION:
THEORIES OF DEMOCRATIC ACCOUNTABILITY AND
DEVELOPMENT IN BRAZIL AND VENEZUELA

"Solid fundamentals are not what the world expected from Lula."[1] As the economic turmoil prior to Brazil's 2002 presidential election indicated, many doubted that a leftist government led by Lula's Workers' Party (Partido dos Trabalhadores [PT]) would continue with basic reforms. But distrust of Lula's commitment to sustain the development policies initiated by his predecessor, Fernando Henrique Cardoso, was not the only factor driving skepticism about Brazil's future. A leading newsweekly recapped most analysts' pessimistic conclusions about the adequacy of Brazil's institutions: "Brazil is a hard country to change—especially when no party has a majority in a fragmented Congress. The business of assembling congressional majorities . . . is painfully slow."[2] Even if Lula had the will to move forward, many doubted whether he could match Cardoso's political acumen in harnessing Brazil's unwieldy democratic institutions to enact further reforms.

Indeed, some observers would point to the scandals that plagued Lula's first administration to support the view that Brazil's institutions prohibit effective policy making and to underscore Lula's missteps in dealing with Congress. Yet what remains striking, despite alternation between a center-right and a leftist government, as well as damaging scandals, is that successive Brazilian administrations have continued to hew to a path of gradual reform. Two terms under Cardoso were marked by the elimination of inflation, refocusing development strategy on regional and international trade, constructing a more agile state bureaucracy, and initial social security reform. Lula's first government followed with a major and crucial overhaul of the public social security system, judicial reform, and the consolidation and

1. "Lula's Leap" 2006.
2. "The Magic of Lula" 2006.

amplification of novel antipoverty programs. In his second term, Lula is concentrating on massive investment in long-needed infrastructure goods and has shown no sign of deviating from sound macroeconomics and continuing structural reforms. Both the *Economist* and the World Bank concur that the combination of solid fundamentals and an aggressive approach to poverty eradication has contributed to Brazil's lowest level of inequality in the past thirty years.[3]

At least as unexpected as Brazil's relatively successful experience with reform over the past decade was the implosion of Venezuela's democracy, one of the most vaunted and long-standing in the region. After a forced devaluation in 1983, Venezuelan politicians repeatedly failed to adopt reforms that were widely believed to be essential to staunching a growing crisis. Even as Venezuelan politicians dithered through a decade, many remained confident that Venezuela's solid institutions would eventually facilitate the emergence of viable reforms. The actual outcome is now only too well known.

Venezuela's two major parties proved ultimately hapless in addressing declining per capita income and a steady increase in poverty rates over the decade of the 1980s. Moreover, the only serious attempt at reform in the early 1990s was torpedoed by the very parties previously viewed as effective stewards of Venezuela's polity and economy. After orchestrating the impeachment of Carlos Andrés Perez in 1993, the once dominant Democratic Action (Acción Democrática [AD]) and Political Electoral Independent Organization Committee (Comité de Organización Política Electoral Independiente [COPEI]) parties were superseded in 1998 by strongman Hugo Chávez as the central figure in Venezuelan politics.

It is too early to fully assess the ultimate effects of Chávez's transformation of Venezuela's political institutions and economy. Nevertheless, his concentration of power in the executive and his program to implement a "socialist revolution" through extensive nationalization and worker-owned cooperatives, and the consequent decline in investment and production, are all too familiar in the developing world. Chávez's adroit use of oil revenues to provide short-term benefits to the previously disadvantaged, while masking many of the underlying disequilibria created by his policies, is also a well-worn pattern. Although Chávez currently enjoys wide popularity as a result of these policies, and his rhetoric notwithstanding, most economists agree that just as with AD and COPEI before him, he is failing to "sow the

---

3. Ferreira, Leite, and Ravallion 2007; "Lula's Leap" 2006.

oil" in a way that will lead to sustained growth when oil prices eventually decline.

The surprising success with reform in contemporary Brazil and questionable results, at best, under two very different regimes in Venezuela become even more puzzling if we consider a fourth case: the democratic government in place in Brazil from 1945 to 1964. Brazil's postwar democracy not only was governed by institutions nearly identical to those currently in effect, but also was beset with a remarkably similar crisis. In the early 1960s as well as the early 1990s, Brazilian legislators were confronted with accelerating inflation; inefficient industries; a bloated bureaucracy; and a social security system that was regressive, exclusionary, and fiscally disastrous. In the earlier regime, however, the only legislation that could muster sufficient support to become law exacerbated these problems—boosting spending without increasing revenues, augmenting subsidies for inefficient producers, enlarging the public bureaucracy, and expanding underfunded pension benefits for the few while continuing to exclude the majority. In the wake of numerous failed reform attempts, the regime was overthrown by a coup in 1964.

These four cases are indicative of a larger paradoxical pattern; why such dramatic variation in elections' ability to discipline politicians' development policy choices? Intuitively, polling the citizenry to select political leaders should drive governments to adopt effective development policies. Considerable empirical data support this intuition: the wealthiest, most developed countries in the world are all democracies. Moreover, most scholars concur that electoral sanctions *are* what drive politicians to adopt welfare-enhancing policies in the advanced industrial states. Yet many other democracies, including pre-Chávez Venezuela and postwar Brazil, have mediocre records of development, at best. This democracy-development paradox remains poorly understood.

Recent scholarship has emphasized poverty, development, or institutions as the key factors undermining democratic accountability and effective public policy in some democracies. Yet these approaches cannot account for patterns in Brazil and Venezuela. Why didn't the lauded Venezuelan democracy, favored by strong institutions and rising per capita income, yield elections that could better discipline development policy? Why has Chávez chosen a path of change that has a long pedigree of failure despite his success in sweeping away the institutional constraints of the earlier period? And why have politicians in contemporary Brazil succeeded with reforms while those of the postwar failed, despite both being governed by strikingly similar institutions that are universally considered to be weak? Finally, why have some of the most economically developed of the developing democracies in a given period collapsed, as was the case with postwar Brazil and Argentina, and pre-Chávez Venezuela, rather than evolved into thriving democracies? A theory that can convincingly explain the democracy-development paradox must account for the anomalous patterns in these prominent regimes.

I argue that the key to explaining the democracy-development paradox lies in recognizing that voters face a heretofore underappreciated collective action problem in using elections to hold politicians accountable—what I call *the voter's dilemma*. The central insight of the voter's dilemma is that under certain structural conditions, holding elected leaders accountable for effective public policy is not as straightforward as it might appear. As a result of two inherent features of the voter-politician relationship—*collective accountability* and *asymmetry of excludability*—voters sometimes face high risks in using their vote to reward good public policy. Political accountability is inherently *collective*—the individual voter can neither elect nor remove his or her representative—the voter's representative is determined by electoral laws and vote counts in the district. Moreover, there is *asymmetry of excludability* between clientelistic and collective goods.[4] All voters receive the collective benefits of effective development policy, such as a professional bureaucracy, efficient property rights, and economic growth, or any other collective goods, whether they voted for them or not. By definition, however, clientelistic benefits are provided only if the vote is traded in a quid pro quo.

If we consider the possibility of widespread machine-style clientelistic benefits traded directly for votes, it becomes clear that under some conditions voting for good public policy presents voters with a strategic problem akin to a prisoner's dilemma. If elections result in clientelistic politicians' control of national office, citizens who voted for politicians advocating collectively beneficial development programs are left with nothing. Conversely, if elections result in collectively minded politicians' control of national office, citizens who trade their vote in a quid pro quo will still receive the benefits of public policy.

Strictly speaking, the logic of the voter's dilemma implies that a given voter is always better off defecting and opting for the clientelistic candidate, no matter what other voters do, as in the classic prisoner's dilemma. In

---

4. This felicitous turn of phrase to characterize the key difference between clientelistic and collective goods comes from Stokes (2007).

practice, whether it is risky for voters to cooperate and vote for the collectively minded politician depends on how structural conditions affect equilibrium electoral strategies. If structural conditions render valuable clientelistic offers viable on a national scale, then the equilibrium electoral strategy will be clientelism, and direct voter-politician links will predominate. If structural conditions rule out valuable clientelistic offers on a national scale, then the equilibrium electoral strategy will be collective goods provision, and indirect voter-politician links will predominate. When the equilibrium electoral strategy is clientelism, then voters face high risks in rejecting clientelism—delivered and monitored votes provide the only access to government benefits in these types of systems. The voter who votes against clientelism under these conditions receives the sucker's payoff of exclusion from most government-provided goods. When the equilibrium electoral strategy is collective goods provision, then the political goods a voter receives are unconnected to his or her individual voting behavior, and thus voters can vote for clientelism or collective goods with little impact on their enjoyment of government-provided goods. In other words, structural conditions also create *asymmetry in the voter's return on the same kind of vote.*

Linking structural conditions to the microfoundational logic of the voter's dilemma allows us to generalize our body of theory of democratic accountability in a fashion that subsumes many anomalies that plague currently predominant approaches. The new institutionalism has provided one of the most important recent generalizations of our understanding of democratic accountability. As with all other theories built upon the current positive theory of elections, however, the failure to consider ubiquitous direct exchange has limited the explanatory reach of the new institutionalism. New institutionalism predicts politicians' strategies based on how institutions shape winning electoral strategies, beginning with the baseline assumption that the equilibrium strategy is some level of collective goods provision. Institutions alter the degree to which pure collective goods provision will redound to individual politicians' electoral success and thus alter the mix of national and locally targeted collective goods that politicians will supply. Notably, the new institutionalism links institutions to variation in the *scope* of the goods provided (national or local *collective* goods), but has no analytic apparatus to capture variation in the directness of the exchange and the possibility of exclusion.

Yet if structural conditions determine the equilibrium electoral strategy to be clientelism, then the baseline assumption of this theory does not hold. To correctly understand the effects of institutions when the clientelist equilibrium prevails, we must theorize about how institutional variation alters the link between electoral success and efficient production of clientelistic goods, rather than the production of national collective goods. If we generalize our theory of how institutions shape politicians' strategies depending on which equilibrium electoral strategy prevails, we can greatly enhance our understanding of institutional effects and resolve the anomalies that plague the current version of the theory.

Developmentalist theories such as modernization theory posit a direct link between structural change and variation in democratic accountability, but these theories foundered on the failures of postwar Brazil and Argentina, as demonstrated by O'Donnell (1979) in his classic study. The logic of the voter's dilemma endogenizes structural conditions to a microfoundational logic of electoral sanctioning and thus resolves important anomalies that plague developmental theories. The voter's dilemma can explain cases in which economic and political modernization fail to foster more effective accountability, as well as cases in which very moderate development *is* associated with effective democratic accountability. Structural changes that accompany economic modernization (emergence of industry and a working class) do not in and of themselves alter voters' vulnerability to clientelism. In the absence of structural change that reduces the risk to rejecting clientelism, a very modern economy employing state-of-the-art technology will not be sufficient to shift voters' choices away from clientelism.

The voter's dilemma logic also introduces strategic interaction between voters and thus resolves key anomalies that plague poverty-based theories of weak democratic accountability. Area and development specialists have long emphasized the relationship between highly inegalitarian distribution of income and weak accountability. Poverty-based theories of democratic accountability, however, predict that rising income should reduce clientelism and that only the poorest democracies would be thoroughly penetrated by clientelism. Theories that rely exclusively on poverty thus can tell us little about weak democratic accountability in many middle-income countries, such as Venezuela; cannot explain why all poor countries are not clientelist; and finally, are confounded by rich countries that are dominated by quid pro quo politics.

The prisoner's dilemma logic of the voter's dilemma, however, demonstrates that it is often not the individual characteristics of a given voter, but the strategic context of the voting choice, that drives the outcome. If structural conditions favor the clientelist equilibrium, not just low-income voters, but *all* voters can potentially be harmed by exclusion from government-provided goods. Regardless of income, if the standard of living of voters depends on clientelist exchange, they run substantial risk in voting for effective collective development policy. If voters have alternatives that are comparable to but not dependent on the clientelistic bargain, then they lose little by opting for the developmentally oriented politician regardless of their income, even if other voters do not.

The combination of abundant resources and limited economic opportunities that were immune from clientelist control can explain why elections failed to discipline Venezuelan politicians' policy choices in the pre-Chávez era, despite rapidly rising per capita income and strong institutions. Oil-rich governments in Venezuela had considerable margin with which to increase the value of quid pro quo benefits, and thus elected leaders were able to make an anticlientelist vote risky for many, even as per capita income rose. A dynamic very similar to that in pre-Chávez Venezuela also played out in postwar Brazil—structural conditions meant options to clientelist offers were few, and politicians were able to maintain quid pro quo benefits that made policy-based voting risky for most citizens. The result in Venezuela was that despite strong institutions, rising GDP per capita, and the benefit of hindsight, development policy in the 1960s and 1970s had many of the same flaws as the import substitution industrialization (ISI) development policies followed by the Southern Cone countries in the 1940s and 1950s. As with postwar Brazil, Venezuelan governments subsidized any and all producers regardless of future potential for efficiency, and both countries failed to implement the second stage of an infant-industry policy: gradual reduction of subsidies and protection to induce maturation and the emergence of competitive producers.

The ISI policies adopted in both Brazil and Venezuela eventually led to chronic economic and political crisis in the 1980s. Yet only one of these countries has adopted coherent structural reforms that are fostering sustained and steady economic growth. Why is it that Brazil has moved to a path of viable and sustainable reform, whereas Venezuela has chosen policies that will likely provide only an apparent short-term reprieve and that will ultimately yield to an even more difficult future crisis?

If structural change alters the balance between resources and demands such that national politicians can no longer maintain clientelistic offers that voters find valuable, the electoral equilibrium shifts and politicians can compete on the basis of collective goods reform. If this balance shifts such that clientelistic politicians can no longer meet voters' demands, the risks of policy-based voting are reduced, and these structural changes create the conditions for effective democratic accountability. This is what has occurred in contemporary Brazil and this is why, in a case unique among the four examined in this book, Brazilian politicians have adopted viable reforms. Although Brazil's institutions remain unwieldy and continue to foster considerable localism in Brazilian politics, structural conditions now make it possible for voters to exercise policy-based sanctioning, and the equilibrium electoral strategy is collective goods provision. The result is that elections are now rewarding those politicians who succeed in steering Brazil's cumbersome politics in the direction of good public policy, particularly more effective development policy.

However, as Venezuela under Chávez and many other cases highlight, the key to the shift is not crisis—crisis *does not* necessarily lead to effective structural reform. Only when crisis is associated with the inability to continue making clientelist offers that voters find valuable will collective goods policy reform become electorally viable. If resources remain sufficient to continue making clientelist offers, even if at levels below pre-crisis offers, and as long as voters find them valuable, the risks associated with rejecting such offers will lead to a result in which the politician who can reorganize clientelism to address the crisis will be the new winner. As will be shown in subsequent chapters, this argument makes sense of many of what appear to be contradictory and self-defeating choices in Chávez's institutional and policy changes.

The Literature: The New Institutionalism and Poverty-Based Theories of Clientelism

Why do politicians in some democracies adopt policies capable of fostering steady long-term growth, while others do not? In the second half of the twentieth century, economic development was the overwhelming policy priority in most developing countries. Yet even under democratic rules stipulating that political authorities be chosen through polling the citizenry, most developing countries failed time and again to reach this goal. At the same time, this is not a general failing of democracy. Most observers concur that the same electoral constraints *do* drive politicians to adopt welfare-enhancing policies in the advanced industrial states.[5] Why are voters in some de-

---

5. The conclusion that the electoral fates of incumbent executives are linked to economic performance in the advanced industrial democracies is one of the most well established in political science. See Kramer 1971, 1983 and Lewis-Beck 1988.

mocracies able to hold their elected officials accountable for poor economic outcomes, whereas in others, voters appear impotent? We lack a theory of democratic accountability that can explain this democracy-development paradox.[6]

The current literature provides two valuable but incomplete approaches to this question. The institutionalist school argues that institutional variation alters the degree to which elections create incentives for politicians to provide national collective goods. A second approach emphasizes poverty and underdevelopment as the factors distorting electoral accountability in developing countries. Both of these perspectives have greatly advanced our understanding of political behavior and choice across democracies. At the same time, neither approach satisfactorily explains the democracy-development paradox.

All democracies use elections as their central accountability mechanism. There is great variation, however, in the precise shape of these and other democratic institutions, with important implications for how well politicians' individual incentives are aligned with the promulgation of effective public policy. According to rational-choice institutionalists, variation in executive-legislative relations and electoral law lead to variation in the degree to which politicians promulgating national collective goods policy will be rewarded with electoral success. Politicians' varying commitment to the public good is driven by how well these key institutions align their individual goal of reelection with the collective goal of promulgating broad national collective goods policies (Ramseyer and Rosenbluth 1993; Cox and Rosenbluth 1995; Shugart and Carey 1992; Cox and McCubbins 2001).

In brief, institutional rules that restrict voters' choices to higher levels of aggregation should better align politicians' incentives with the promulgation of effective national public policy. Thus, in comparison to presidentialism, parliamentarism provides voters with only one vote at the national level, and thus, voters in parliamentary systems are more likely to use that vote to exercise choice over the direction of national public policy (Cox and Rosenbluth 1995). Similarly, electoral rules that restrict voters to choices between parties (party-centered rules), rather than giving them choices both

---

6. Some might argue that the poor economic performance of developing democracies is driven by factors other than electoral politics. For a discussion of the weaknesses of the more common alternative theories applied to developing countries—dependency, statism, and rent seeking—see Lyne 1999. In this book I develop an argument to demonstrate that the two are indeed linked, if we consider a clientelist equilibrium and develop the implications of such an equilibrium for electoral incentives.

between and within parties (candidate-centered rules) should drive voters to use their legislative vote to give voice to their preferences for national policy (Shugart and Carey 1992; Cox and McCubbins 2001). Institutionalists combine these two logics to argue that parliamentary systems with party-centered rules will create the strongest alignment between individual politicians' goals and the collective goal of good public policy, whereas presidential systems with candidate-centered rules will have the weakest alignment.[7]

This theory has been validated in applications to advanced industrial democracies. New institutionalism has provided very powerful theoretical insight into variation in the scope of the goods that politicians will provide, whether they will emphasize broad national collective goods or locally targeted collective goods (pork), and the stability of the status quo policy (Ferejohn 1974; Cain, Ferejohn, and Fiorina 1987; Carey and Shugart 1995; Tsebelis 1995). This school of thought has also laudably advanced the development of a general theory of electoral accountability aimed at unifying patterns across all democracies. At the same time, institutional analysis leaves key questions unanswered. As discussed above, the institutions governing *both* democratic regimes in Brazil included presidentialism, bicameralism (a chamber of deputies and a senate), federalism, and open-list proportional representation, which new institutionalists argue are among the most inimical to the provision of broad collective goods in the world.[8] Elected politicians' response to similar crises, however, has been radically different.

Venezuela's record also raises important questions for institutional theory. Once widely regarded as one of Latin America's rare stable and successful democracies, the country's acclaimed political parties proved inadequate to the task of addressing the economic decline that began in the early 1980s.

---

7. This summary is necessarily extremely brief. I will treat the electoral rules portion of the argument in more detail in Chapter 4. I will also provide detailed definitions of the sometimes controversial terms *national collective policy, particularism* and *pork barrel, rents,* and *clientelism* in Chapter 1. For the purposes of reviewing institutional theory here, I wish only to draw a broad distinction between policies that maintain stability and long-term growth and those that blatantly fail to address a crisis, as in postwar Brazil and Venezuela in the 1990s.

8. For general discussions of the dysfunction of Brazilian politics and institutions in the earlier regime, see Schmitter 1971; Santos 1986; Skidmore 1967; Geddes 1994; and Ames 1987. On institutions in the current regime, see Shugart and Carey 1992; Geddes 1994; Geddes and Ribeiro Neto 1992; Mainwaring 1992, 1995, 1999; Mainwaring and Perez-Linán 1997; Ames 1995a, 1995b, 2001; and Weyland 1996a. For a comprehensive comparative analysis of institutions that includes Brazil as a paradigmatic case of inauspicious institutions, see Cox and McCubbins 2001. For an alternative view that argues that Brazilian democracy is weakened by clientelism, see Hagopian 1996.

Despite the fact that Venezuela's party-centered institutional rules are theorized to create strong incentives for politicians to provide broad national public policy, the only serious attempt at reform was cut short by the impeachment of the reformist president by his own party.[9] Since Chávez's ascendance in 1998, Venezuela's vaunted stability has been replaced with considerable political upheaval.

A more general survey of institutional variation across democracies underscores the gaps in institutional explanations illustrated by Brazil and Venezuela: institutional rules do not vary consistently with variation in the efficacy of key policies such as economic development. The executive-legislative relations and electoral laws that form the core of the institutional argument exhibit the full range of variation across all democracies and within both groups, developed and developing. In contrast, effective economic policies are heavily concentrated in the advanced industrial states. Both groups of countries include presidential and parliamentary regimes, and within each group there are many examples of pairing both forms of executive-legislative relations with each of the forms of electoral law—those that are argued to strengthen and to weaken parties.[10] In short, while institutional theory has greatly added to our knowledge of how institutions shape the scope of policy—emphasis on national versus local collective goods—and the propensity for movement from status quo policy, it appears less effective in explaining dramatic failures of accountability that are commonly seen in many developing countries.

A second problem for institutional approaches regards the longevity of such counterproductive institutions. As Douglass North (1990) forcefully argues, institutions are endogenous to politics. If institutions were the key variable driving the abysmal development policy outcomes commonly observed in many developing democracies, then would we not expect political entrepreneurs to challenge these choices? Why would parties that are credibly committed to reform of such institutional obstacles to good governance not become the new winners? The most obvious way an ambitious political

---

9. For laudatory studies of the general Venezuelan system, see Levine 1973, 1978; Levine and Kornblith 1995; and Martz 1977. For specifically institutional analyses of Venezuela, see Shugart and Carey 1992 and Crisp 2000. From the outset, institutionalists qualified their analyses of Venezuelan institutions, arguing that perhaps they were too party centered. These revisions have been more systematically developed in Shugart and Haggard 2001 and Shugart and Wattenberg 2001. I discuss the original theory and these revisions in detail in Chapter 4.

10. Large n cross-national tests of the electoral-system aspect of new institutional theory that include both developed and developing democracies have produced mixed results, at best. See Morgenstern and Potoff 2004.

party could capitalize on the accountability vacuum in many developing countries would be to change its own behavior and internal organization such that it could offer voters clearer and more coherent policy positions, thus facilitating voters' ability to hold them accountable. Ferejohn (1999), for example, argues that such an adaptation took place in the advanced industrial democracies, as winning parties gradually converged on a competition over a basic set of left versus right economic policies. As I will show in subsequent chapters, this was certainly an option open to all parties in Brazil and Venezuela, and even was attempted by some parties, but only emerged as a winning strategy in contemporary Brazil. Yet institutionalist theory provides little insight into why such solutions have so rarely emerged in developing democracies.

In contrast, scholars favoring a developmentalist perspective employ poverty-based theories of clientelism, as well as modernization theories of political organization, to explain why the effectiveness of electoral controls varies dramatically across cases. According to this school, individual voters' short time horizons, typically driven by substantive need, compel them to accept an immediate material reward in direct exchange for their vote. In contrast, if voters held politicians accountable for providing basic collective goods such as efficient property rights, a stable currency, and a professional bureaucracy, this would improve their ability to meet a range of needs over time. Higher-income voters do not typically suffer from dire immediate needs, and thus their valuation of different goods is not so heavily conditioned by the immediacy of the return. They have the luxury of choosing collective goods that are, in the absence of time-horizon considerations, more valuable.[11]

These low-income voters and their requirements are what drive politicians' strategies. Politicians who desire public office must adapt to the de-

---

11. Both the earlier clientelist literature (Scott 1969, 1972; Schmidt et al. 1977; Strickon and Greenfield 1972), as well as more recent work on the subject (Kitschelt 2000; Stokes 2000, 2005, 2007; Stokes and Medina 2007; Desposato 2001, 2006a; Mainwaring 1999) emphasize poverty as the key causal variable. Kitschelt (2000, 857), reviewing the earlier literature, unifies and makes explicit the micrologic that informed but often was not explicit in many of these studies. Several recent analyses of clientelism introduce the asymmetry of excludability between clientelist and collective goods to explain why voters opt for clientelism (Chandra 2004; Stokes and Medina 2007; Stokes 2000, 2005; Lyne 2006, 2007). Stokes (2007) relies on the diminishing marginal utility of income and excludability. Poor voters, who value the clientelist good highly, will choose to comply with the politician who can withhold benefits. This emphasis on poverty and underdevelopment as the cause of clientelism is also seen in the work of various versions of modernization theory (Huntington 1968; Sartori 1986).

mands of existing organizations: "given pressure to gain support, a party will emphasize those inducements that are appropriate to the loyalty patterns among its clientele" (Scott 1969, 1147). These loyalty patterns, in turn, are driven by the level of economic development. Group loyalties in underdeveloped economies are centered around parochial ethnic or kinship organizations that specialize in making parochial, individualistic claims on public authorities (Scott 1969; Almond and Coleman 1960; Lemarchand 1972; Landé 1973). At low levels of development, then, politicians' organizational and policy choices are channeled by voters' immediate needs, and the organizations that specialize in meeting those needs, through their articulation of demands for individualized exchange.

Changes in voters' loyalty patterns and group organization, which would drive politicians to collectively oriented organizational and policy choices, are assumed to occur simultaneously with capitalist development. Economic development raises incomes and thus reduces the number of voters who heavily discount the future. At the same time, the process of industrialization means that "new economic arrangements take hold and provide new foci of identification and loyalty" (Scott 1969, 1146–7). The transfer of loyalty from parochial to categorical or programmatic organizations occurs as part and parcel of economic growth itself. As economic development proceeds, "businessmen and laborers each [came] to appreciate their broader, longer run interest as a sector of society, [and] they increasingly required general legislation that met their interests in return for political support" (1149).

This work advanced our understanding of democratic accountability in two important ways. First, by treating clientelism as a systematic alternative to policy-based voting, this literature exposed the specific nature of assumptions about voter-politician links embedded in theories derived from the study of the advanced industrial democracies. Second, it rightly emphasized the relationship between structural variables, such as level of development and distribution of income, and poor democratic performance. However, a wide range of evidence contradicts the specific predictions about individual voter behavior and systemic outcomes.

Empirically, developmentalist theories are confronted with contradictory evidence at both the micro and the system levels. Many studies have indicated that income level is not the key variable that distinguishes voters opting for quid pro quo from those exercising policy-based sanctioning. An enormous literature documents the fact that middle-class, working-class, and rural/informal-economy voters have all often traded their votes in a quid pro quo for excludable benefits.[12] The conclusion that voters at all income levels in developing democracies often voted clientelist is corroborated by studies of interest-group and party behavior. Although the early research on postwar developing democracies provided little systematic work on voting behavior, these studies clearly demonstrated that categorical interest groups and programmatic parties do not emerge in lockstep with economic development.[13]

At the system level, a poverty-based theory of clientelism cannot account

---

12. Most of the evidence on voting behavior in the early studies of clientelism is presented in monographic or anecdotal form. Within these discussions there are many examples of institutionalized vote trading for the working and middle class. In Brazil, for example, the system of ex officio voter registration in place between 1945 and 1964 authorized private employers and national government agencies (in fact required them by law) to register their employees to vote en bloc. This system provided the link between votes and benefits (jobs) for organized labor and government employees and has been dubbed a "typical resource of urban clientelism." In 1945, the ex officio system accounted for 23 percent of the national vote in Brazil (Souza n.d., 27–28). A similar system in place in Chile from 1889 to 1924 allowed votes to be cast in absentia. Often, elected representatives themselves played the role of "boss" and would collect the voting certificates of their constituents and cast them for themselves! (Alexander 1977, 17). Other corroborating evidence for higher-income voters' clientelist voting includes the well-documented fact that state bureaucracies in most developing countries fail to provide even the most basic public services because virtually all jobs were provided to middle-class voters in exchange for political support. On the trading of votes for bureaucratic jobs in Latin America, see Geddes 1994; on developing countries in general, with further bibliography, see Roth 1968. Although most of the data substantiating that voters of all income levels often voted clientelist come from the postwar studies, recent empirical work by two preeminent scholars of democratic accountability supports a structurally driven prisoner's dilemma theory of clientelism. Both Stokes's work in Argentina (2006, 138), as well as Putnam's in Italy (1993, 99–101) show that income and other individual demographic characteristics are unrelated to voting clientelist; both scholars argue that variables characterizing *the voter's province* are the best predictor of clientelist voting (for Stokes, the socioeconomic structural conditions of the province; for Putnam, the level of civic culture of the province).

13. The work on interest groups is more comprehensive and systematic than that on parties. Pye (1958) argues that "new" interest groups (i.e., those associated with modern economic occupations) often maintained the practices of the "traditional informal associations" (481). Several large multicountry studies of interest-group behavior in developing democracies came to similar conclusions (Almond and Coleman 1960; Almond 1956; Scott 1972; Powell 1970; Landé 1973). These studies of interest-group behavior in the developing world, and in Latin America in particular, supported Schmitter's (1971, 1974) development of the concept of state corporatism, in which interest groups associated with a modern economy (labor unions, business associations) are manipulated from the top down by political leaders trading benefits for votes and resources, rather than organized from the bottom up to hold elected leaders accountable for public policy. Martz (1964) and Kaufman (1974) clearly highlighted a lack of correspondence between level of development and parties' programmatic policy commitments. An assessment of the historical work on the existence of programmatic parties, however, must proceed with some caution, as many scholars relied on high levels of internal unity as an indicator of a party's programmatic policy orientation. Yet this indicator is misleading, since clientelist parties are perfectly compatible with high internal unity (Kitschelt 2000).

for why all poor countries, such as those in Scandinavia in the nineteenth century, were not organized around clientelist politics, and why some rich countries, such as Middle Eastern oil exporters, with quite high per capita incomes, are organized around some version of quid pro quo politics (Kitschelt 2000). And as O'Donnell (1979) argued persuasively in his classic study, modernization theories of political development had trouble explaining why the most advanced developing economies of the postwar period, Brazil and Argentina, did not develop into flourishing democracies. Venezuela's political devolution in the 1980s and 1990s, despite its relatively developed economy and high per capita income, presents a similar anomaly for developmentalist theory.

In sum, institutional and poverty-based theories of democratic accountability leave many gaps in our understanding of the democracy-development paradox. The variables favored by institutionalists provide little purchase on differences such as those between postwar and contemporary Brazil—two countries with almost identical institutions but dramatic differences in policy outcome. Poverty-based theories assume that structural conditions affect only the low-income voter's ability to exercise policy-based voting and thus predict that democratic accountability will be seriously distorted in only the poorest democracies. These theories shed little light on why elections failed to discipline development policy in prominent cases of relatively high per capita income, such as postwar Brazil and Argentina and post-1958 Venezuela. I argue that we can provide a general explanation for the democracy-development paradox that resolves these anomalies if we more carefully consider the problems that derive from the collective nature of democratic accountability. The voter's dilemma highlights how collective accountability, under certain structural conditions, can alter the risks that *all* voters in *any* institutional environment face in using elections to hold politicians accountable.

Outline of the Book

The examination of Venezuelan and Brazilian democracy presented in subsequent chapters provides a test of institutional theory, poverty-based theory, and my alternative of the voter's dilemma in explaining the democracy-development paradox. The remainder of the book is organized as follows. In Chapter 1, I develop the theory of the voter's dilemma and discuss the general conditions of supply and demand (structural conditions) that influence whether clientelist or collective goods provision is the equilibrium strategy. I also develop the distinct electoral constraints created by clientelist competition and contrast them with the constraints that emanate from policy-based competition. First, in clientelist systems, the government and opposition very often compete on an uneven playing field, whereas policy-based competition levels the playing field considerably. Second, when politicians compete in the delivery of clientelist goods, the electoral bases of support of all individual politicians (even within the same party) are mutually exclusive, whereas with policy-based competition, the party platform creates a common element in the electoral appeal of all rank-and-file members. And third, although in both types of systems there is an individual-collective conflict within the party regarding the level of investment in different types of electoral strategies, the substance of this conflict is quite distinct, leading to distinct imperatives for internal party organization.

In Chapter 2, I examine the independent variable of voters' choices and provide evidence that voters were opting for quid pro quo in postwar Brazil and in both Venezuelan regimes and that voters are increasingly exercising policy-based voting in contemporary Brazil. I triangulate the question of the kinds of choices voters are making by examining four types of data: public opinion, structural variables that indicate trends in supply of resources and voters' demands, evidence of vote monitoring and benefit delivery, and two microlevel variables that yield distinct observable indicators of whether politicians are winning votes through quid pro quo or policy-based appeals.

In the succeeding chapters I turn to the dependent variables of political behavior: institutional design and policy choice. The analysis of outcomes will be focused on both institutions and development policy. A full understanding of public policy choices requires an analysis of the institutions that shape these choices. In the first sections of each chapter I demonstrate that theories based on indirect links between voters and politicians (a policy-based competition) cannot explain dominant patterns. The subsequent sections in each chapter reveal how these patterns fall into place as responses to electoral imperatives when clientelistic voter-politician ties dominate (clientelistic competition).

In Chapter 3, I examine data on legislative voting, governing cabinets, electoral coalitions (in Brazil), and party switching (in Brazil) in postwar Brazil and pre-Chávez Venezuela. The results indicate an accountability vacuum, in which party behavior failed to provide voters with information about policy position: low intraparty unity, low interparty difference, and grand coalition and strange-bedfellow alliances. Although we would expect this behavior to be selected out if parties were competing to provide voters with collective policy goods, a theory of clientelist competition can link it to an electoral imperative: this apparently dysfunctional party behavior was driven by politicians' need to demonstrate their access to resources and ability to deliver them in a quid pro quo. I also examine how Chávez's changes in patterns of interest intermediation, purportedly designed to create a "participatory" and "protagonist" democracy, are no more than a reorganization of clientelism in Venezuela. It is no accident that Chávez deemphasizes political parties and representative democracy—this allows him to further decimate and delegitimize the previously dominant actors' networks of clientelist exchange while casting a veneer of democratic legitimacy on the creation of his own personalist, direct networks of exchange, now organized around *consejos comunales* (community councils). In this chapter I also demonstrate that party behavior in contemporary Brazil now exhibits the patterns we would expect if parties must provide voters with information on policy positions to succeed electorally, these patterns being moderately high intraparty unity and interparty difference and ideologically consistent coalitions.

In Chapter 4, I analyze internal party organization and show that proportional representation (open-list PR) in Brazil and absolutely closed lists, party control of nominations, and the single-*tarjeta* (single-card) vote in Venezuela failed to effectively link individual party members' incentives to the maintenance of a national policy program in the historical cases. In a policy-based system, choices such as these would quickly be selected out by parties that organize to align individual and collective incentives in maintaining the party's reputation for providing collective policy goods. The distinct individual-collective conflict that characterizes parties competing in clientelist systems provides an explanation for the durability of these choices. Rank and file, who are most concerned with their own (re)election, often face incentives to spend more resources than necessary to win each vote, as when they face a bidding war. The party, by contrast, must ensure that each individual member spends resources as efficiently as possible, to maximize the number of votes won by the party overall. As I show, what appears to be a dysfunctional failure to align individual and collective goals in building a collective goods policy reputation is actually an electorally savvy choice to align individual and collective goals in expending resources for buying votes.

I reinforce this understanding of the role of open-list PR by employing econometric techniques to determine the criteria party leaders employ to distribute valuable legislative perks across the two periods in Brazil. In the earlier period, the criteria was consistent with the conclusion that resources for buying votes was the key currency of elections—racking up a high electoral quotient was the most significant predictor of receiving a valuable committee assignment, and loyal party voting had no effect on receiving such perks. In the current period in Brazil, however, the criteria have changed in precisely the manner we would expect if policy is now the key currency of elections: loyal party voting is now the best predictor of receiving locally targeted resources for one's district, whereas number of votes received has little to no effect on receiving such resources. In this chapter I also discuss how Chávez's current project to force the dissolution of all previous political parties and create the United Socialist Party of Venezuela (Partido Socialista Unido de Venezuela [PSUV]) can be understood to address this same problem that plagues all competitors in clientelistic regimes: ensure efficient use of resources in buying votes.

In Chapter 5, I examine legislative organization and demonstrate that in postwar Brazil and pre-Chávez Venezuela, legislative organization prohibited turning an electoral majority into a legislative majority, and instead created mutual vetoes for major contending parties in the lower chamber. Agenda power was not conferred on a governing party or coalition, through the distribution of committee seats and presidencies, but instead was distributed to allow the major parties to monopolize control of certain committees, even when out of government. This type of organization in fact prevents politicians from fulfilling their commonly assumed role in policy-based democracies, translating an electoral mandate into a legislative mandate and then into public policy. These organizational choices, however, allowed parties to insulate their own most important resource streams from reprogramming by any current or future government, which is essential to surviving in a clientelistic system. This organizational form serves to adjudicate the distribution of resources among the electorally successful parties and ensure their continued control over these resources. In contemporary Brazil, however, the legislature has been reorganized such that the governing majority that mobilizes consent in elections can assert control over the legislative agenda and reprogram resources to meet public policy goals. In the last section I discuss Chávez's request for and receipt of extraordinary decree powers, which allow him essentially to legislate by fiat, the absolute dream of any personalist clientelist leader.

Finally, in Chapter 6, I examine the critical outcome of economic development policy. I argue that in general, clientelist systems and policy-based systems create radically different incentives for policy choice. In the absence of unlimited resources, clientelist systems will face repeated economic crises (often accompanied by political crisis) because elections reward politicians who are adept at extracting and distributing resources, rather than politicians who promote welfare-enhancing policies. When fierce electoral competition revolves around maximizing the creation and distribution of clientelistic benefits, as is the case when structural conditions favor the clientelistic equilibrium, politicians who try to devote some resources and government machinery to the provision of collective goods will lose. If policy-based voting predominates, by contrast, policy will be designed to turn government resources into programs that produce general outcomes that voters will reward.

This chapter shows how clientelist constraints on policy choice can explain some of the most important and counterproductive choices for import substitution industrialization (ISI) policy in postwar Brazil as well as pre-Chávez Venezuela: extremely high and variable levels of protection, capital-intensive production, and no incentives for infant-industry maturation. The alternative of lower and more carefully managed protection, labor-intensive production, and incentives for infant maturation were fully possible within the rubric of ISI. This more economically efficient ISI, however, would have created diffuse, untargetable benefits in the form of lower-priced, higher-quality goods and rising standards of living. The inefficient version of ISI, in contrast, maximized the creation of production opportunities and jobs that could be controlled and exchanged directly for political support. Thus, despite the fact that the inefficient version was doomed to economic exhaustion, it was more electorally valuable when politicians were competing to provide clientelist goods.

I also examine politicians' responses to the crisis of ISI, as well as the reforms that have been adopted in contemporary Brazil. Politicians in postwar Brazil appeared bent on exacerbating the crisis, as they turned reform legislation into new unfunded benefits, even as the government deficit exploded and inflation soared. Politicians in Venezuela appeared indifferent to crisis, as they acted to crucify the one member of their ranks who offered a serious program of reform. The variation in these responses can be explained with a theory of how the candidate-centered (Brazil) or party-centered (Venezuela) nature of institutions alters the best strategy for maintaining electoral viability in clientelist systems in crisis. I also examine how Chávez's so-called socialist revolution is a reorganization of policy to serve his personalist clientelist network. Finally, I show how changes in the viability of policy-based voting can explain why politicians in contemporary Brazil have succeeded in providing an effective policy response to a crisis that was very similar to the one that led to the demise of the postwar regime, despite no change in key institutional rules.

THE VOTER'S DILEMMA:
COLLECTIVE OR CLIENTELISTIC GOODS?

> As Brazil approaches its October [2006] elections, political scandal dominates the headlines, crime still plagues the largest cities, the gap between rich and poor persists, and the business community grudgingly accepts that President Luiz Inácio Lula da Silva will win an easy reelection. But there is one very important cause for optimism in Brazil: Its current problems are the sort that plague mature free-market democracies, not emerging-market basket cases.
>
> —Ian Bremmer, "Lula's Silver Lining"

On the eve of Lula's election in 2002, the conventional wisdom held that a Lula presidency would be, at best, unremarkable in terms of progressing with much needed policy reforms. Many believed that a Lula administration would be nothing short of disaster, as Lula was thought to favor reversing Fernando Henrique Cardoso's reforms and placing Brazil on a trajectory much more akin to Venezuela's under Chávez. Since his reelection in 2006, however, there has been a growing consensus among scholars, journalists, and pundits, as articulated by Bremmer above, that outcomes have improved rather dramatically in Brazil from the time of return to full democracy in 1989.[1] We lack a theoretical explanation for this change.

A common puzzle raised in the popular and academic press is why Lula, the founder of a prominent national workers' union and current leader of the most important leftist party in Brazil, makes choices so distinct from another well-known leftist in Latin America, Hugo Chávez. The authors of most accounts, like Bremmer (2006), explain Brazil's turnaround by alluding to some form of enlightenment on the part of politicians or voters. Lula is a pragmatist, it is said, whereas Chávez is an ideologue. Alternatively,

---

1. It is not just academics like Bremmer that place Brazil in the same category as the United States and Western Europe as a mature free-market democracy. Pundits as prominent as op-ed columnists for the *New York Times* have also repeatedly characterized Brazil as now in a different category from most developing countries—as a durable mass democracy led by the astute pragmatist, Lula. See Cohen 2008.

Lula has come to understand that the statist policies advocated by his Worker's Party (PT) early in its political ascent would not produce steady growth and would likely only repeat a long history of cyclic crises. Either explicitly or by implication, the conclusion is that Chávez apparently does not understand the entire postwar history of statist-policy-driven crises in Latin America. Or alternatively, the Venezuelan populace is susceptible to populist rhetoric, whereas the Brazilian electorate has matured and is no longer hoodwinked by the false promises of the demagogue.[2]

As in the example above, leadership characteristics are typically employed only to explain one or two prominent cases. But for this logic to explain broad patterns of democratic accountability, we must accept the dubious proposition that some countries have a very high concentration of perspicacious leaders, while others have almost none. The rise of Chávez after the disastrous failure of the previous system, initially thought to be led by skilled elites, would suggest that Venezuela remains in the unfortunate group of countries lacking effective leaders. Contemporary Brazil's success under governments with very different orientations seems to indicate that it now enjoys an abundance of good leaders. Yet we have little in the way of causal explanation for either pattern.

Explanations that place a heavy emphasis on the quality of leadership also imply that voters and elections are epiphenomenal, yet the level of effort and treasure devoted to winning elections in developing democracies renders such a view highly implausible. Alternatively, if we admit the importance of voters and elections, but conclude that the explanation lies with voters' maturity, we are in effect rejecting Lincoln's maxim that all the people cannot be fooled all the time.[3] However, without a theory of why it is possible to dupe the majority of voters in some countries over long periods of time, but not in others, this form of explanation is less than satisfactory.

In this chapter I develop an explanation that does not rely on leadership or voter characteristics and that is consistent with Lincoln's adage. The disappointing collective outcomes that are commonly attributed to individual failures are in fact the result of a collective action problem that under some conditions drives voters of all income levels and in any institutional environment to relinquish their statutory right to pass judgment on politicians'

2. It is worth noting that Brazilian voters did not lack the opportunity to vote for what most observers would label as populist politicians. The presidential candidacies of Quércia and Brizola (1994), Ciro Gomes and Eneas (1998), Garotinho and Eneas (2002), and Ciro Gomes and Buarque (2006) provided them with ample populist choices.

3. "You may fool all the people some of the time, you can even fool some of the people all of the time, but you cannot fool all of the people all the time" (Abraham Lincoln, sixteenth president of the United States [1861–65]).

overall policy performance and opt for clientelistic goods. The general theory of voting choice developed here yields as special cases both the currently dominant model of electoral politics, in which politicians supply some mix of national and local collective goods, and an alternative, clientelist model of electoral politics.[4]

The development of how clientelistic competition at the national level constrains politicians' choices and behavior will provide a general theoretical explanation for the persistence of institutional and policy choices that repeatedly produce dismal collective outcomes. Specifically, this theory of clientelistic electoral politics will explain why politicians in postwar Brazil and pre-Chávez Venezuela failed to address policy failures and looming crises, why Venezuela under Chávez is likely to suffer the same fate, and why contemporary Brazilian politicians have adopted reforms and managed crisis far more effectively than those in each of the other three cases.

Distinguishing Clientelism: Direct Versus Indirect Exchange

Scholars have long recognized a distinction between particularism or pork barrel, as discussed in American politics, and clientelism.[5] Initial studies of

---

4. In the following section I will provide full definitions of these terms. The analytic dimension of interest is whether or not political goods are provided or withheld on the basis of voting choices.

The currently dominant view in the literature is that the vast majority of democracies produce a mix of all three types of goods: national and locally targeted collective goods (pork) and clientelism. Of course there are no systems that produce purely national collective goods. But the advanced industrial democracies are characterized by the routine provision of basic public goods such as a stable currency, a professional bureaucracy, and relatively efficient property rights, which suggests that no politician could maintain his or her career without providing these goods. These systems in which the vast majority of national political leaders are elected on the basis of national and local collective goods provision often exhibit considerable clientelism, and both strategies have been observed within a single party in contemporary democracies (Scheiner 2005; Stokes 2005). Yet pockets of poverty-driven clientelism are implausible as an explanation for the dramatic failures of accountability that are routinely observed in many middle-income democracies, as well as less wealthy developing countries, and we need a better theory for why some democracies appear to provide almost no public goods. The goal of this book is to fill that gap with a unified theory that can also explain the incentives and resulting patterns of behavior and choice that prevail in the many democracies in which these basic public goods are sorely and routinely lacking. The voter's dilemma yields two equilibrium electoral strategies—one in which politicians provide a mix of goods, but in which the provision of basic public goods are a sin qua non of electoral viability—and one in which politicians can apparently disregard how well their government performs these basic functions and remain viable.

5. I will use the term *particularism* to designate all the types of goods that are provided on the basis of a narrow scope but that are not exchanged in a quid pro quo. In other words, I used *particularism* as an overarching term encompassing what scholars have called *particularism, pork, rents,* and *patronage*. While these goods are provided only to voters in a

clientelism focused on characterizing clientelism itself, primarily as observed in developing countries, and rarely discussed its relationship to what might be called "ordinary" particularism: the roads, dams, and harbors that are often called "pork barrel" projects in American politics.[6] Similarly, a number of studies concerned with the difference between national policy goods and pork barrel, such as the classic work by Ferejohn (1974), limited themselves to advanced industrial democracies.

As comparativists have pursued comprehensive empirical tests of general theories of electoral incentives, local collective goods and clientelism have increasingly been conflated. Most electorally based theories of democratic accountability, including the new institutionalism, distinguish analytically between different types of political goods based on the geographic scope of the good: national versus local. With this emphasis, all localism is the same—both classic particularism and clientelism are typically lumped into a single category of "local" or "not national goods." This simplification has been useful for exploring the merits and limitations of institutional theories of democratic accountability. To build a theory of democratic accountability that can explain the democracy-development paradox, however, we must consider an additional analytic distinction: the directness of the exchange.

In addition to the emphasis on the scope of a given political good, an accurate classification of the variety of political goods requires considering an additional, independent dimension: the directness of the exchange.[7] National collective goods and ordinary particularism such as roads and harbors are nonexcludable: receipt of these goods, even those such as restricted-scope particularism, is not predicated on trading one's vote in return (Kitschelt 2000). Particularism may often be less efficient from a national social welfare standpoint than if these resources were distributed according to an economic logic, rather than a political one. The key point to emphasize here,

---

specific district, firms in a particular sector, or certain dedicated individuals who work for the party, no one is excluded from these goods *on the basis of how they voted*. Although many scholars include direct-exchange clientelist benefits within the rubric of particularism, I use *particularism* as a global term for narrowly targeted indirect exchange. Clientelism is distinct from all these forms of particularism and refers to direct, quid pro quo exchange.

Many of the ideas and presentation in this section of the chapter were developed in a paper coauthored with Royce Carroll. See Carroll and Lyne 2006.

6. The early clientelist literature is vast. Some of the major contributions include Scott 1969 1972; Strickon and Greenfield 1972; Powell 1970; Landé 1973; and Schmidt et al. 1977.

7. For the authoritative discussion that "only the procedural nature of exchange relations counts to separate clientelist from programmatic linkage" between voters and their representatives, see Kitschelt 2000, 853. It is also worth noting that the relative weight of national policy goods and localism can fluctuate from election to election depending on how satisfied voters are with overall outcomes.

however, is that nonexcludability at the level of the district means voters do not have to relinquish their ability to include overall performance in their evaluation of politicians to receive locally targeted nonexcludable collective goods. Regardless of the relative emphasis on national or locally targeted collective (particularistic) goods, when any combination of these two types of goods dominate voting choices, it means that the voters and politicians are linked through an *indirect exchange* and that voters can link their choices to overall outcomes without sacrificing access to more specialized or localized goods.[8]

Clientelism, in contrast, can be of any geographic scope and entails a quid pro quo exchange based on how individuals voted; clientelism is not limited to a unit, nor do its principal characteristics change depending on the geographic scope.[9] Indeed, most early analysts of clientelism in developing countries describe hierarchical networks that link politicians and voters from the base to the apex of the political system (Nunes Leal 1977; Landé 1973). In short, clientelism is a system of quid pro quo exchange that knows no geographic or functional limits. Clientelistic networks of exchange can be organized at any level of aggregation and around almost any type of good, including the classic ones of food and building materials, industrial jobs, apparently public services such as schools and hospitals, and property rights (Kitschelt and Wilkinson 2007). Clientelism is defined by a *direct* exchange relationship between voters and politicians, and when it predominates in a given system, it means that voters by necessity have relinquished the possibility of using their vote to pass judgment on overall policy (Stokes 2007). As a consequence, elections lose their ability to drive politicians to carefully attend to the overall social welfare implications of their policies. These relationships are illustrated in Table 1.

Given the many definitions of particularism and collective goods in the literature, I briefly review the definitions I am employing here. The feature that distinguishes all particularism (pork, rents, patronage) from all collective goods is the scope of the target beneficiaries. Particularistic goods may

---

8. In practice, collective and particularistic goods may exclude some based on means tests, to be discussed below. The critical difference once again is that means tests do not require that voters forgo their ability to include overall policy outcomes in their voting choice.

9. The main difference depending on the size of the geographical area covered is how the exchange is organized. The larger the geographical area, the more likely clientelism will be organized into blocs and tiers that assign intermediaries or lower-level politicians the task of aggregating the vote across subnational units. The quid pro quo exchanges that characterize clientelism may also be organized along functional lines, as through state-corporatist interest groups.

Table 1 Fourfold typology of political goods

	Type of exchange	
Scope	I. Direct	II. Indirect
A. Local/sectoral	I.A. Clientelist	II.A. Particularist (*particularism, pork, patronage, economic rents*)
B. National	I.B. Clientelist	II.B. Collective

or may not be welfare enhancing, as Ferejohn (1974) demonstrated. Many locally targeted projects in the United States provide benefits to some districts at the expense of others, and powerful legislators receive proportionally more of such goods. Collective goods, in contrast, are welfare enhancing (Arnold 1990; Ferejohn 1974; Cox and McCubbins 2001). Collective goods certainly have distributional consequences—labor prefers a high-employment policy and business prefers a low-inflation policy—but the key point in comparison with clientelism is that no workers or firms are excluded from the benefits of either one of these policies on the basis of how they voted or which politician they supported.

A second type of good that favors a narrow constituency but that does not typically connote quid pro quo exchange is an economic rent. Rents, defined as market intervention designed to favor certain producer groups, through tax breaks, subsidies, or regulatory favors, typically are not targeted at a geographic constituency, but rather an economic sector. As with geographically targeted particularism, classic rents as defined by Krueger (1974) and Buchanan, Tollison, and Tullock (1980) are nonexcludable in the relevant political group, in this case the economic sector. Thus, tariffs on textiles or steel benefit all firms that produce the given product, regardless of the political affiliation of the producers. Similarly, an economic regulation that gives specialty glass producers an edge will help all such firms.[10] As Kitschelt has noted, parties are not clientelist "as long as they disburse rents as matter of codified, universalistic public policy applying to all members of a constituency, regardless of whether a particular individual supported or opposed the party that pushed for the rent-serving policy" (2000, 850).

At the same time, policies aimed at assisting producers *can* be distributed

---

10. The term *club goods* is often used for these kinds of rents to indicate that while they benefit a subnational group, they are nonexcludable and constitute a collective good for that smaller group.

on a quid pro quo basis, and we need an additional category to designate individually excludable goods targeted at producers. I refer to benefits provided to firms on a quid pro quo basis as *sectoral clientelism*. As with the difference between pork and clientelism, analysts have often conflated ordinary rents and political goods that are ostensibly aimed at a sector but that are actually only distributed to those who trade political support directly in return.[11]

It should be emphasized that there is no necessary impediment to supplying a mix of collective policy goods and ordinary (nonexcludable) particularism and rents. Indeed, as many analysts argue, politicians in most advanced industrial democracies provide some mix of national policy and particularism. In systems with many veto players, particularism can be the grease that allows the collective goods policy wheels to turn (Cox and McCubbins 2001; Evans 2004; Tsebelis 1995). On the basis of this analytic distinction, I will use the terms *policy goods* to designate this *mix or package* of collective policy goods/pork/rents/patronage and to distinguish this package from *clientelistic,* or *quid pro quo goods.*

Further, to avoid confusion, it is important to underscore the difference between clientelistic goods and means-tested programs. Means-tested programs have a feature in common with clientelistic goods in that means-tested goods provide benefits to some and exclude others. The key difference is the criteria used for exclusion. Means-tested programs use general criteria unrelated to voting, and typically tied to a larger policy goal, in order to determine exclusion. Exclusion from clientelist goods, by contrast, is based on how an individual votes. Clientelist goods are delivered only to those who vote for the politician dispensing the goods. The critical result is that those receiving the means-tested goods are not required to relinquish their right to exercise policy-based voting to receive the good.

---

11. Weingrod (1977) provides some illustrative examples from Sardinia of policies ostensibly targeted at a sector that are actually delivered only to those providing political support in direct exchange: "The local manager of a national bank approves loans as favors to persons whose support he can count on in the next municipal election; . . . the local village council who are not members of the party in power are unable to enlist support for [a] village school; . . . landowners who belong to the parties in power receive loans administered by government agencies, while other landowners are not made aware of the loan programs; . . . an elected member of the regional assembly obtains tobacco and wine licenses for several families of his supporters" (327–28). I will argue in Chapter 6 that ISI policy in most developing countries was in fact designed to allow governments to target specific firms, rather than sectors. This characterization of ISI is consistent with Bates (2001) and de Soto (2001), both of whom argue that ISI development policy in developing countries was more akin to mercantilism, in which production rights are distributed directly by political authorities, than to classic rents as defined by Buchanan, Tollison, and Tullock (1980) and Krueger (1974).

An example will show why particularistic and clientelistic strategies and goods are easily conflated, as has been common in the literature. A legislator adopting either a particularistic or a clientelistic strategy may use his or her influence in Congress to secure funds for local projects in the legislator's district, such as a school, hospital, or an infrastructure project. What differentiates the two is what happens to these resources when they are distributed in the district and the impact this local action has on a national (or local) public policy goal. Inefficient particularism, as defined by Ferejohn (1974) and Cox and McCubbins (2001), means that powerful legislators receive proportionally more of these locally distributed funds than a national social welfare criterion would prescribe, but the resources *are* typically used in the district to provide a local nonexcludable good. Thus, particularistic goods such as ports, schools, and hospitals contribute to improved national social overhead and human capital, albeit less than would be the case in comparison with a distribution of these resources based on national welfare considerations alone.

When the legislator employs a clientelistic strategy, in contrast, these resources are exchanged directly for votes. If elections are won on the basis of quid pro quo exchanges, then infrastructure contracts, teaching jobs, and hospital positions are filled not through technical qualifications, but instead through vote-delivery criteria. Those who receive these jobs either can deliver votes themselves or provide some other advantage to intermediaries whose job it is to deliver votes. The result is typically that the infrastructure project is started but not completed, or is of such poor quality that the useable life is minimal, and thus public works funds do little to increase social overhead capital. The school is staffed on the basis of vote delivery rather than teaching qualifications, so education dollars do little to increase human capital. The hospital is staffed with doctors, but it has no budget to buy medicine, and thus public health budgets do little to improve social welfare indicators.[12] In sum, these two distinct strategies for the use of locally targeted funds may look quite similar when legislators are competing for such funds in the Congress, but their effects on national and local social welfare and human and on social overhead capital formation differ dramatically. Particularism means that these social goals are pursued in a somewhat less efficient fashion than would be the case absent political criteria that deter-

---

12. For discussions of hospitals with no medicine or equipment and public works departments with no spare parts to make their equipment operational in Latin America, see Geddes 1991. For other descriptions of illiterate teachers, janitors who never clean, and infrastructure projects that are never completed, see Greenfield 1972.

mine interdistrict distribution. Clientelism typically means that pursuit of these social goals, at worst, will be decimated and, at best, will only occur as an unintended consequence of clientelist politics.[13]

As discussed in Chapter 1, institutional theories have illuminated the factors driving the production of more particularistic (Table 1, cell IIA) versus collective goods (Table 1, cell IIB).[14] Since scholars have rarely considered generalized clientelism as a substitute for indirect exchange, rather than simply a local or regional phenomenon driven by poverty in a system otherwise characterized by indirect exchange, we know very little about what determines whether a polity falls in column I or column II of Table 1. In the following section, I show that clientelism can also be driven by strategic interaction among voters, and I make the case for two distinct equilibrium electoral strategies.

Democratic Accountability as an N-Person Prisoner's Dilemma: The Voter's Dilemma

Whenever you observe individuals in a conflict that hurts all of them, your first thought should be of the Prisoner's Dilemma.

—Eric Rasmusen, *Games and Information: An Introduction to Game Theory*

Most scholars of democracy assume that communities delegate to government representatives to reap the gains available from collective action.[15] Given this understanding of the role and function of government, clientelism is an aberration. Voters who trade their vote for a quid pro quo sacrifice valuable collective policy goods that only a central agent, typically a government, can efficiently provide—public goods such as efficient property rights, a stable currency, a professional bureaucracy, and large-scale infra-

---

13. For a clientelistic system to function, some basic infrastructure goods, such as roads, ports, and so on, must be supplied; but for a colorful account of how decisions about road building are completely divorced from economic considerations and instead driven by whether the votes are turned in to the reigning higher-level politician in Minas Gerais, Brazil, see Greenfield 1972.

14. The basic institutional argument linking electoral incentives to the production of these goods was discussed in the Introduction; a good summary can be found in Shugart and Haggard 2001. A vast literature has expanded on this basic logic, treating veto points in the process of government policy making as sources of policy inefficiency. An excellent summary and synthesis of this literature can be found in Cox and McCubbins 2001 and Tsebelis 1995.

15. If we exclude Marxists, this group includes most normative as well as positive theorists of democracy.

structure—in return for an individual material reward. From this point of view, the puzzle of clientelism is why voters would make this apparently senseless trade-off.

The vast majority of explanations of clientelism are based on some variant of voter income as the driving factor, as discussed in the Introduction.[16] This view of clientelistic voting rests on the assumption that the key factor driving voting choices is the voter's individual circumstances. Such an assumption is quite reasonable when structural conditions yield collective policy goods provision as the equilibrium electoral strategy. Under these structural conditions, politicians must supply basic collective goods in order to get elected, and voters will enjoy the benefits of those collective goods regardless of how they vote. Under these conditions, voters can essentially ignore the choices of other voters and then in fact it *is* the voter's individual circumstances that will have the largest influence on his or her decision to vote clientelist. This conception of the link between voters and politicians, and the consequences of different voting choices, however, does not adequately consider all the ways in which problems of collective choice can hamstring voters.

Two key features of electoral exchange, under some conditions, can dramatically alter how we think about the voter-politician relationship and democratic accountability. First, democratic accountability is a problem of collective accountability. An individual voter cannot elect or remove his or her representative—electoral accountability is inherently a problem of *collective accountability*. The individual voter's representative is determined by vote counts and electoral rules, not his or her individual vote. In other words, the individual voter's ability to reward a good representative with reelection or punish a bad representative with electoral defeat depends on the actions of many other voters in the district. In short, electoral sanctioning is a problem of social, not individual, choice.

If we combine collective accountability with the difference in excludability between clientelistic and policy-based goods, we gain a more accurate picture of the obstacles the individual voter may confront in exercising policy-based voting and ensuring effective democratic accountability. The ac-

---

16. In this section I develop the theory of the voter's dilemma in detail. This theory illuminates the individual-level calculus that leads a given voter to either relinquish or exercise policy-based sanctioning. At the aggregate level of the election, supply-and-demand factors are key to determining whether elections will reward clientelist or policy-based strategies. I will develop the supply-and-demand aspects of the theory in the section "The Structural Conditions of Quid Pro Quo or Policy-Based Politics," this chapter, below.

tual election of a policy-based candidate requires that a winning coalition of voters opt for such a candidate. Yet each individual voter has no guarantee that other voters will in fact choose a candidate appealing to voters by means of policy commitments. Moreover, the difference in excludability that defines clientelistic versus policy goods means that under structural conditions that make widespread clientelistic offers viable, voters have sound reasons to doubt the policy commitments of other voters. The voter who opts for a policy-based candidate while a winning coalition chooses a clientelistic candidate receives neither collective policies nor clientelistic goods. At the same time, those in the clientelistic coalition have used their vote to secure their place in a system of exclusionary politics. Conversely, a voter who votes for a clientelistic candidate while a winning coalition elects a policy-based candidate still receives the collective policy goods.[17] In short, voting for a policy-based candidate presents the voter with an n-person prisoner's dilemma.

The difference in excludability, combined with collective accountability, means that a clientelistic vote provides the individual voter with an "insurance policy" that potentially protects him or her from the vagaries of other voters' choices. A clientelistic vote has the potential of providing protection against being excluded from political benefits should the voter's clientelistic candidate win. A policy-based vote does not.[18] Collective accountability coupled with the asymmetry of excludability is what renders voters at all income levels and in any institutional environment potentially vulnerable to clientelist appeals, despite the obvious failures of democratic accountability that result.

17. As the literature on voting has shown, voters are rationally ignorant and use a variety of cues and information shortcuts to assess their elected representatives' positions and performance (Berelson, Lazarsfeld, and McPhee 1954; Popkin 1991; Lupia and McCubbins 1998). Interest groups are one of the key institutions that provide information and perform an intermediary function in facilitating voters' ability to hold their elected representatives accountable. Yet voters face the same collective accountability problem in holding their group leaders accountable. Should the rank-and-file member of a labor union throw his or her weight behind the leader supporting categorical goods that benefit all workers, regardless of whether they vote for the pro-union policy-based candidate, or the leader who makes a deal with a clientelist candidate to trade its block of support directly for jobs that will be doled out to those who vote for the clientelist? The union that supports categorical benefits while all others make deals for clientelist benefits is in the same position as the voter who opts for collective policy goods while all others opt for quid pro quo. For reasons simplicity in exposition and the fact that the problem of collective accountability also plagues groups, I develop the argument here in terms of individual voters.

18. Of course, if the voter errs in selecting from among the available clientelist candidates, and votes for the loser, he or she also will not receive the clientelist goods. But if that voter votes for the collective goods candidate, while most other voters are choosing among clientelist candidates, his or her exclusion is assured.

This analysis reveals that under certain structural conditions the key variable driving the voter to choose either clientelist or policy goods turns not on a direct comparison of the two types of goods, nor on his or her income, but on the risks that voter faces in rejecting quid pro quo.[19] Some examples help illustrate the point. Middle-class voters who support a party with clear policy commitments rather than one that doles out government jobs in return for votes potentially risk a dramatic reduction in their standard of living. If they do not have sufficient private assets or comparable options immune from clientelist manipulation, and a majority in most districts finds the clientelist offer valuable, the result of their vote for the policy-based option will be a dramatic reduction in their standard of living, not the implementation of their preferred policies. Similarly, working-class voters who reject the state-corporatist (clientelist) union in favor of a class-based organization pursuing categorical benefits for the working class as a whole risk losing their jobs and being relegated to the informal economy if they lacks alternatives beyond clientelistic manipulation. If enough other voters in the district find the quid pro quo offer valuable, a vote for class-based representation results in the voter's loss of employment, not strong unions pursuing class interests.[20] In short, unless a voter has a means of livelihood comparable to the quid pro quo offer, yet beyond the reach of clientelistic manipulation, a vote against clientelism often carries great risks, regardless of income level.

To summarize, the theory of the voter's dilemma allows us to rule out two common intuitions about what drives voters to relinquish or exercise policy-based voting and pinpoint the causal variable as the risk the voter faces in rejecting clientelism. Collective accountability means that voters cannot choose and receive policy goods. This implies that the superior outcomes that result from collectively oriented policies are not necessarily suf-

---

19. This calculus will certainly be conditioned by other factors, for example, a normative preference for policy goods. Such factors may lead voters to apply some discount factor to the clientelistic offer. This does not alter the basic thrust of the argument. The voter's dilemma emphasizes the heretofore underrecognized risks associated with collective accountability when structural conditions favor the clientelistic equilibrium—that voters must consider the risks associated with rejecting the clientelistic offer in the instance when clientelism dominates national electoral politics.

20. In presidential systems, of course, the voter can make a separate choice for national executive and national legislator. Some scholars have suggested a hybrid system in which voters cast a policy-based vote for president and a clientelist or parochial vote for legislator (Shugart and Carey 1992). I believe that such a combination is unstable and will discuss this fully in Chapter 4. Moreover, as I will discuss below, in clientelist systems politicians can link a vote for both a legislative and a executive candidate to the delivery of one quid pro quo good.

ficient to sway the voter's choice. Asymmetry of excludability means that clientelists can withhold benefits but politicians providing collective policy goods cannot. This means that greater affluence does not necessarily imply independence from clientelism—it all depends on the value of the goods the clientelists can withhold. Even very high-income voters may face risks in rejecting clientelism, if they derive their wealth from, for example, production rights or a bureaucratic job conferred by the party in power in direct exchange for their support. The voter's dilemma reveals that elections provide a relatively costless instrument for holding politicians accountable for national collective goods only when structural conditions render clientelistic offers of negligible value to most voters.

The literature analyzing electoral accountability as a collective action problem has excluded the possibility of generalized clientelism by assumption, taking as its point of departure the view that voters are using *some* kind of policy metric in evaluating politicians. One branch of this scholarship has investigated the coordination problems voters face in agreeing on *which* policy metric to employ in evaluating elected officials (Ferejohn 1986, 1999; Weingast 1997). Another large body of literature has examined the problem of electoral accountability in terms of limits to voters' ability to monitor politicians' *deviation from a mandate to provide collective policy goods* (Downs 1957; Baron 1994; Lohmann 1998; Lupia and McCubbins 1998; Stokes 2001). Finally, some scholars have focused specifically on the problems associated with punishment of wayward politicians when the mechanism of enforcement is voting and elections (Barro 1973; Fearon 1999; Ferejohn 1986, 1999; Mueller 1989; Przeworksi, Manin, and Stokes 1999).

This body of literature has carefully delineated the problems voters face in holding politicians accountable for national policy goods when structural conditions render national-level clientelism inviable, and thus voters *actually cast* their votes for such nonexcludable goods. If most voters conclude that a clientelistic vote is their best choice, however, the assumptions underlying this literature do not hold. If most voters choose to vote for a clientelist, their ability to agree on some type of policy metric is moot. Similarly, if most voters choose to vote for quid pro quo, there is no policy mandate to monitor or for which to hold politicians accountable.

In game theoretical terms, this literature has treated the collective action problem associated with electoral accountability as one of coordination, as does Ferejohn (1986 1999) in his classic work. Coordination problems are characterized by a situation in which players have distinct preferences for the action on which all should coordinate, yet all players would prefer coordination on *some* action rather than no coordination at all.²¹ This characterization of the type of strategic interaction voters confront, however, is accurate only under the assumption that structural conditions eliminate the possibility of clientelism on a national scale, and thus that politicians must provide some basic level of collective, that is, *nonexcludable* goods in order to be elected. If voters do not face high risks in rejecting clientelism, then they will prefer to coordinate on *some* type of collective goods, even if not their first choice, rather than fail to coordinate and receive no collective goods at all. Voters may very well have distinct preferences for the package of nonexcludable policy goods they wish politicians to supply, but they all prefer some package of collective policy goods to none, because even if the winning policies are not their first choice, *they still enjoy whatever collective policy benefits are supplied*.

These assumptions regarding voting and voter-politician links, and the characterization of the key accountability problem as one of coordination, lead to the conclusion that most democracies, including most developing democracies, are characterized by the same types of voter-politician relationships and are driven by the same fundamental electoral dynamic. The implication is that in all except the extremely poor democracies, politicians compete to supply some mix of national and local collective goods as well as, perhaps, some clientelistic goods. According to this view, the key difference in the mix of goods supplied across all democracies is driven by variation on certain parameters such as executive-legislative relations (variation in nationalization of elections), electoral law (variation in scope of goods provided), number of poor voters (extent of clientelism), and other factors and that the mix of political goods is more heavily skewed toward clientelism in developing democracies because of the larger numbers of poor voters. The assumption that the same voter-politician relationships and the same underlying electoral dynamic prevail across democracies has been accepted relatively unquestioned despite the repeated failure of theories built on these assumptions to correctly predict process and outcome in developing democracies.²²

21. The classic example is the battle of the sexes, in which a couple faces a difference of opinion in how to spend their evening. The husband wishes to attend a boxing match while the wife prefers the ballet. Both would prefer to attend one or the other event together, however, more than they prefer to attend their more preferred event alone.
22. For example, the large number of scholars who went to the developing world to study the post–World War II second-wave democracies tested theories of interest-group behavior, party organization and behavior, and legislative organization that rested on the same assumptions that guided the study of the advanced industrial democracies. These studies thoroughly documented the near-total lack of empirical support in the developing democra-

Many analysts did not perceive the potential risks that all voters may face in rejecting clientelism, because clientelism was typically considered to be dominant only in some localities or regions or only in a few selected parties. Moreover, most analysts conceived of clientelistic goods in only two of its many manifestations. Scholars studying developing countries tended to emphasize the direct, easily observable exchanges of the relatively low-cost type provided to low-income voters. Those who studied machine politics in the United States highlighted the exchange of bureaucratic jobs for votes. But most scholars missed some of clientelists' most powerful tools for vote buying and exclusion: the manipulation of property rights and the justice system.[23] In short, clientelism was analyzed as isolated vote trading and as not much more than an appendage of a larger system in which politicians also had to provide basic national collective goods to remain electorally viable. In this scenario, even those voters opting for clientelism receive all the basic national and locally targeted collective goods supplied. In other words, most analysts considered clientelism to be a choice that some poor voters made as a result of immediate need and did not perceive the potential strategic interaction problem that all voters may confront, because the assumption was that basic collective goods were also being provided.[24]

---

cies for the expectations derived from these (advanced-industrial-based) theories. See, for example, Almond and Coleman 1960; Pye 1958; Agor 1971; and Kenworthy 1970.

23. Although he does not attribute the cause to clientelism, de Soto (2001) amply documents the exclusion of the majority from the formal system of property rights associated with creating, measuring, and alienating assets in many developing countries. And although there is ample evidence of the manipulation of production rights in direct exchange for political support in many developing democracies, this has almost never been investigated directly as a manifestation of clientelism. Finally, justice systems in developing countries are notorious for their failure to neutrally enforce contracts, but scholarship on these questions rarely moves beyond the relegation of these systems to the realm of dysfunction, irrationality, and anomaly. Yet all these provide powerful tools for clientelists occupying national office to manipulate the most basic goods provided by government.

24. Stokes (2007) provides the clearest statement of the dominant view of the voting problem surrounding clientelism. Poor voters care about asymmetry of excludability and will vote for the clientelist who can exclude because the clientelistic good is of high value to them. All other voters, who are essentially unaffected by whether they receive a material reward from the clientelist, *and who are the beneficiaries of the collective goods* that all elected politicians must provide in order to remain electorally viable, can ignore the exclusion the clientelist can impose. As I discuss more fully below in this section, this is an accurate characterization of the voting choice if structural conditions at the given level of aggregation yield collective goods provision as the equilibrium electoral strategy. If the clientelist can in fact exclude almost any voter from the vast majority of goods provided by government, this alters how we think about the problem of the voter's choice and electoral accountability. When structural conditions yield clientelism as the equilibrium strategy voters must take strategic considerations into account, because it is only if they vote for the winning clientelist that they will receive most government-provided goods.

If structural conditions make generalized clientelist offers viable at the national level, however, those who do not or cannot join the quid pro quo system are shut out of virtually all goods provided by the government. In other words, in this case voters face a prisoner's dilemma, in which their best choice is to vote clientelist (defect) regardless of the choices of other voters. It is only when structural conditions dictate that politicians must provide basic collective goods to win elections that the choice the voter makes becomes largely irrelevant to the political goods he or she receives. But these structural conditions are most certainly a special case, and it is only in this special case that a given individual voter can relatively costlessly focus on the types of collective goods that he or she would prefer politicians to supply. And it is only in this special case that electoral accountability can be accurately characterized as a coordination problem.

The differing collective choice problems that characterize electoral accountability, as well as the asymmetry of return on the same voting choice across the two equilibria is summarized in Table 2. The clientelistic equilibrium is depicted in column I, while the policy-based equilibrium is depicted in column II. As is clear from column II and as is well known, the voter's action has very little impact on his or her return in policy-based systems. Column I, however, summarizes what is less well recognized—the fact that in clientelistic systems the voter's return is very much dependent on his or her actions. The asymmetry in the return on the same type of vote across the two equilibria is seen in the fact that a vote for nonexcludable goods in a policy-based system has no effect on the voter's return, whereas in a clientelist system such a vote means the receipt of the costly sucker's payoff: exclusion from most government-provided goods.[25] Moreover, as is made clear in cell IB, the voter must vote for the winning clientelist in order to receive such government-provided goods.

At this juncture, it is useful to clearly delineate and summarize the interrelationships between the three different moving parts considered in this discussion of poverty-based theories of clientelism and my alternative. I have developed a strategic interaction theory of clientelism based on the notion that when structural conditions render clientelism viable on a national scale, voters in any institutional environment and at any level of income will have a strong incentive to vote clientelist unless they have alternatives that can be easily substituted for the clientelist offer. This theory

---

25. For a vivid description of the costs of being excluded in a clientelistic system, see "In Arab Hub, Poor Left to Their Fate," *New York Times*, March 1, 2007.

Table 2 Democratic accountability as collective choice

Voter's Party/ Candidate Wins?	I. Structural Conditions Render Clientelistic Offers Viable	II. Structural Conditions Render Clientelistic Offers not Viable
A. Yes	**Prisoner's Dilemma** with high cost to sucker's payoff—most voters defect and vote clientelist	Prisoner's Dilemma with low cost to sucker's payoff—voters treat electoral sanctioning as effectively a **coordination problem** and vote for nonexcludable goods
	Voter receives exclusionary government benefits	Voter receives his or her preferred nonexclusionary government benefits (collective goods)
B. No	**Prisoner's Dilemma** with high cost to sucker's payoff—most voters defect and vote clientelist	Prisoner's Dilemma with low cost to sucker's payoff—voters treat electoral sanctioning as effectively a **coordination problem** and vote for nonexcludable goods
	Voter is excluded from exclusionary political system and receives virtually no government benefits	Voter receives nonexclusionary government benefits (collective goods) that were not his or her first preference

of clientelism, however, is applicable at any level of aggregation at which the political authorities can manipulate sufficient resources to make an anticlientelist vote costly for most voters.

A theory of clientelism based on strategic interaction, along with greater analytic clarity about the differences between locally or sectorally targeted collective goods (pork barrel and rents) and clientelism (including direct exchange organized by territory and sector), would seem to provide a much more plausible explanation than a poverty-based theory for the kind of long-term local dominance of single parties seen in the American South and rural Japan.[26] The prevalence of clientelism at the local level driven by the voter's dilemma, and thus and the threat of exclusion from most locally

---

26. On the American South, see Key 1949; on Japan, see Scheiner 2005.

provided political goods, provides a powerful logic to explain why political entrepreneurs from the permanent minority party could not outflank the dominant party by offering *local* collective goods. Clientelism of the strictly poverty-driven variety exists as well, where isolated pockets of voters can be induced to sell their vote simply because their low standard of living leads them to value the clientelist good highly (Stokes 2007). It seems unlikely that appeal to such poverty-stricken voters would be sufficient to shut out local-level entrepreneurship aimed at providing local collective goods (efficient taxes, improved education, neutral justice) for long periods of time in nations as wealthy as the United States and Japan in the second half of the twentieth century. And the implausibility of the dominance of clientelism at the national level based simply on poverty was one of the reasons analysts failed to consider this possibility. But as will be shown in the remaining chapters of this book, a theory of voting that yields two distinct equilibrium electoral strategies, including a clientelist equilibrium strategy driven by strategic considerations rather than individual income, provides the best explanation for empirical patterns in our four cases that highlight the democracy-development paradox.

It should be noted that voting for politicians who promise collective goods is almost always "irrational" in the strict sense that the costs of voting will always outweigh the expected benefit, since that benefit is conditional on the likelihood that the individual voter's action will alter the outcome of the election. For the voter's dilemma to play out in full, then, we have to assume that voting is essentially "cost free" or has some positive, expressive value. An important body of literature, however, suggests that when the costs to cooperation are very low, individuals often will contribute, even in the absence of an institutional solution to the free-rider problem. (For discussions of this possibility from different points of view, see Barry 1970; Olson 1982; and Aldrich 1995.) And empirically, we know that in many democracies voters *do* vote for collective goods.

Ironically, this critique applies much more forcefully to the well-elaborated positive theory of voting and elections developed to study advanced democracies than to the systems that the voter's dilemma sheds most light upon. The question of why voters would vote for collective goods is no different from the standard question of why voters would ever vote in a policy-based system, which remains the Achilles' heel of the positive theory of voting and elections. In contrast, the voter's dilemma provides a very rational explanation for voting in clientelist systems—a voter's individual vote is linked directly to receiving political benefits in an exclusionary political system.

The individual-voter calculus developed in this section must be combined with a theory of supply and demand at the district level in order to say anything about the conditions under which clientelist or policy-based strategies will dominate. At any level of aggregation, whether local, state, or national, if politicians can find sufficient resources to provide clientelistic offers that voters find valuable, clientelistic politicians will dominate. Even as voters' ability to substitute clientelistic goods improves, if clientelistic politicians can find sufficient resources to increase offers commensurately, they will defeat politicians who are making policy-based appeals, and democratic accountability will be short-circuited. This implies a complex logic of supply and demand that determines whether clientelism or policy-based politics will actually prevail in any given election. In this chapter below, in the section "The Structural Conditions of Quid Pro Quo or Policy-Based Politics," I will sketch the supply-and-demand conditions favoring either clientelistic or policy-based politics and discuss how a shift from clientelism to policy-based politics can occur. Having established that both clientelism and policy-based politics spring from the same electoral mechanisms; that an analysis of strategic interaction reveals a heretofore unrecognized clientelistic equilibrium; and that structural conditions, rather than voluntaristic motivations, determine which will predominate, in the following section I explore how clientelistic or policy-based competition alters politicians' winning strategies.

Electoral Competition: Differentiating Winning Strategies Based on Delivering Quid Pro Quo Versus Delivering Policy Goods

As a result of the dominant view that all democracies are characterized by the same basic electoral dynamic, the implications of a clientelistic equilibrium have remained almost completely unexplored.[27] At the same time, area specialists have developed a rich literature documenting a large number of patterns that are difficult to reconcile with theories of electoral politics in the advanced industrial democracies. The lack of a theory to explain these anomalous patterns has led many to attribute them to voluntarist mecha-

---

27. The recent work on clientelism in the edited volume by Kitschelt and Wilkinson (2007) is an exception to this generalization.

nisms and in many cases to characterize them as dysfunctional or pathological. Yet if we consider how a clientelistic electoral dynamic alters what constitutes a winning electoral strategy, these patterns no longer appear anomalous or dysfunctional. They are rational responses to clientelistic electoral imperatives. Clientelistic competition profoundly alters the strategic relationships between members of the same party, between parties, and between government and opposition in comparison with policy-based competition. These differences in strategic relationships in turn alter what kinds of party behaviors, party internal design, and legislative organization will best serve politicians' individual goals of winning elections and controlling government.

Effective Voter Appeals Based on Quid Pro Quo: The Uneven Playing Field for Government and Opposition

"If this country turns communist, someday I'll be the biggest leader of the Brazilian left," claimed Antonio Carlos Magalhaes, prominent Brazilian rightist party leader and governor appointed during the military dictatorship, underscoring his ability to ally with those in power, regardless of their espoused political leanings.[28]

Scholars of developing democracies have long noted that incumbents and opposition do not compete on a level playing field. Incumbents are widely depicted as enjoying extraordinary competitive advantages, and this often makes it possible for them to easily "co-opt" the opposition. The descriptions of opposition parties' inability to stake out and maintain clear positions differentiating themselves from those in power are legion, as are the exhortations to opposition parties to grow a backbone and become a principled opponent to the government. An electoral theory of clientelism suggests a competition-based logic for these choices: these *apparently* dysfunctional opposition-party behaviors are driven by what is required to make credible claims to deliver clientelist goods.

Consider the position of the opposition when votes are won with policy-based appeals versus when they are won with quid pro quo exchange. When voters make policy-based choices, then neither government nor opposition has an inordinate advantage in developing a competitive profile for the next election. Neither incumbents nor opposition has a monopoly on the best

---

28. Larry Rohter, "Antonio Carlos Magalhaes, Brazil Politician, Dies at 79," *New York Times*, July 21, 2007.

ideas for turning government resources into programs that will effectively address the major social questions of the day. For the opposition to regain political office when voters exercise policy-based voting, they must develop a reputation for supporting an alternative mix of policies that can win a larger number of votes. This can be done through all the typical behaviors, such as speech-making and voting in the legislature, which is equally available to government and opposition parties (Cox and McCubbins 2005, 44). The opposition party's distinct position-taking and voting activity provide the basis for making credible claims to voters that they support different programs from those of the existing government and that they will implement them if the voters put the opposition in office.

When voters make their decision based on quid pro quo, however, credible claims require demonstration of access to resources. If resources for building networks of direct exchange are derived primarily from control of government offices (that is, the opposition does not have some comparable alternative resource base), then the opposition has little to gain by differentiating itself from governing parties. On the contrary, successful appeals to voters opting for quid pro quo requires some kind of accommodation with those controlling the resources. Under these conditions incumbents clearly have an inordinate advantage in competing in the next elections.[29] As I will discuss more fully in Chapter 3, the differing requirements for effective voter appeals in clientelist and policy-based systems allows us to provide a systematic explanation for differing patterns of inter- and intraparty voting behavior, government and opposition behavior, and cabinet formation across clientelist and policy-based democracies.

This potential incumbent advantage has many implications for political behavior and choice, and thus it is important to explore its consequences a bit further. If the incumbent in a given office controls resources that trump all others in that district, then he or she should be invincible in that district. The importance of this point for choices regarding government formation and legislative organization will become clearer in subsequent chapters; here I wish to underscore the definition: a *trumping resource* is one that would allow the actor who controls it to outbid any others in buying votes in the relevant district, which can be a subnational district or, in the case of

---

29. Maintenance of this incumbent advantage of course requires incumbent unity and agreement on how to distribute resources within the party (coalition, group of elites, etc.). Conflicts within incumbent parties and coalitions over resource distribution, and the alliance of some faction of the incumbents with the opposition, is one of the most likely ways that incumbent advantage can be undermined in clientelist systems.

competition for the national executive, the nation as a whole. Examples of such a trumping resource include ownership of the majority of the arable land in a district in an agricultural economy or control of revenues from the sale of a lucrative commodity, such as oil. In sum, when structural conditions drive voters to opt for quid pro quo, the fact that resources are captured through elective office, and that such resources are used to buy votes directly, makes it much more difficult for the opposition to compete with the incumbent.[30] An opposition that does not have an alternative resource base and that fails to gain access to government resources becomes the "outs"—excluded from public office *and* access to what is required to regain it: resources for quid pro quo exchange.

It should be emphasized that this incumbent advantage is only a potential advantage. A variety of factors may reduce that advantage, including the incumbent delivery record during the current term, the delivery record of the opposition during past episodes of government control (if any), and the expectations voters have regarding the reelection chances of the current incumbent. These factors are not independent but in fact are often interrelated—if incumbent performance in delivering during the current term was abysmal, then expectations of reelection will be reduced. In short, the size of the incumbency advantage may vary widely. The key difference between the two types of competition is that under some conditions incumbents are able to monopolize the electoral currency—resources—in clientelist systems. Since policy platforms are a key currency in policy-based systems, such monopoly control of electoral currencies is never possible in policy-based systems.

In our discussion of incumbent advantage in clientelist competition up to this point, we have considered just one political office. This needs to be qualified in two ways. First, even if the incumbent controls a trumping resource in the district, he or she is vulnerable to intervention from those who can bring in resources from outside the district. This is especially the case in lower-level offices in federal systems.[31] Second, the best insurance

---

30. Such resources may not always be controlled directly by incumbent politicians, as is often the case with land in primarily agricultural economies. On the one hand, this explains how actors who are not professional politicians associated with a political party can often compete effectively in clientelist systems. On the other hand, nonpoliticians controlling such a resource often form long-standing alliances with politicians or political parties. Politicians support the property rights and policies (no land redistribution, for example) that maintain the value of the trumping resource and those who control the resources deliver the votes to their political allies.

31. The machine politics literature in the United States suggests that FDR's New Deal trumped Republican machines at lower levels of government (Erie 1990). Prominent analyses of Vargas's semiauthoritarian rule in Brazil from 1930 to 1945 suggest that Vargas used federal resources to outbid state-level politicians in Brazil (Skidmore 1967).

against such incursion is control of the national policy-making machinery, which implies organizing to capture national office. This leads us to a discussion of when this incumbent advantage can be parlayed into true barriers to entry.

*Regaining Office When in Opposition Based on Quid Pro Quo:
Barriers to Entry*

Under certain conditions, incumbent advantage in a clientelist system can be fashioned into formidable barriers to entry. One of the central determinants of the degree to which a governing party or coalition can actually shut out the opposition depends on the degree to which such a party controls and effectively manages resources for providing clientelist benefits. If a group capable of organizing for collective action can monopolize a resource that trumps all others in all districts at all levels of government, then such a group can create barriers to entry in a clientelist system and effectively shut out the opposition or, more generally, any players it wishes to exclude. As I will discuss more fully in subsequent chapters, one party's (coalition's) ability to monopolize a trumping resource at all levels in the context of clientelist competition dramatically alters the implications of majoritarian rules.[32] In the context of a national trumping resource, rules that turn an electoral majority into a legislative majority create powerful barriers to entry that seriously diminish the electoral viability of the opposition. Any party or coalition able to gain control of a resource that trumps all others at all levels of government will be able to exercise monopoly control.[33] This of course presumes an ability to manage the trumping resource within the organization. This leads to the next major strategic fact of clientelist politics: members of the same party do not share any common component in their electoral appeal, as in the case of policy-based politics. When votes are won based on quid pro quo exchange, all constituent support, even among members of the same party, is mutually exclusive.

*Quid Pro Quo and the Mutual Exclusivity of Electoral Support
Within the Party*

A third key characteristic differentiating winning strategies in clientelist versus policy-based systems relates to the presence or absence of commonality

---

32. Lijphart (1990) provides a typology of the degree to which institutional rules allow a majority party or coalition to rule unconstrained by the preferences of the opposition.
33. The purest example is probably Mexico, with the Institutional Revolutionary Party's control of oil revenues. See Grayson 2000.

in the bases of electoral support among members of the same party. This is perhaps one of the most counterintuitive aspects of clientelistic politics, because the term *political party* has long been considered synonymous with a common electoral appeal based on a common policy reputation that is shared by all members of the same party. As a number of scholars have noted, when voters and politicians are linked through indirect exchange, the link between voter and politician is forged both through a party reputation for certain policy positions that all members share and, often, through the individual politician's personalist appeal based on delivering classic pork barrel, rents, or constituent service as well (Cox and McCubbins 1993; Kitschelt 2000; Lyne 2008). The party's position on issues is crucial to all politicians' electoral appeal even in systems in which electoral law leads politicians to focus heavily on their personal reputation, as in the United States (Cox and McCubbins 1993) and Brazil (Lyne 2005, 2008). When voters and politicians are linked through this type of indirect exchange, all party members can claim credit for a given policy program that was clearly advertised and promulgated by the party. If such a program is passed with the majority support of the party, and its results are not parceled out and distributed on a quid pro quo basis at the time of delivery, all members of the party can claim credit for these outcomes.

When politicians win by delivering quid pro quo goods, by contrast, there is no common basis of electoral support among members of the same political party. The result of quid pro quo politics is that one politician's support is necessarily another's lack of support, even when both are members of the same party. This is because an excludable good that is exchanged for political support can necessarily only be claimed by one politician, and only one politician can receive the support that is directly proffered in return. The job that one legislator delivers to his or her supporter in a quid pro quo exchange to build his or her network cannot be used to fortify any other copartisan's base of support. The result is that in the absence of some mechanism to adjudicate which voters belong to which politicians, clientelist competition means that one politician's pursuit of his legitimate individual interests in capturing votes is threatening to all other politicians. This implies either some mechanism for adjudicating which votes a given legislator should pursue, such as the construction of individual bailiwicks, or constant conflict and bidding wars over votes (Greenfield 1972).[34]

   34. Politicians who are not in direct competition for the same office can organize to deliver votes across offices and thus share credit for the delivery of a clientelist good. Thus, a mayor, a legislator, and a presidential candidate can coordinate the delivery at the local level in return for a set of choices for these offices. The single-*tarjeta* vote, in which voters cast one

Quid Pro Quo and Internal Party Organization: Efficient Vote Buying

Scholars have long recognized that voting unity sufficient to inform a party reputation for consistent issue positions does not emerge spontaneously. One of the key functions of party leaders is to manage the party's reputation by ensuring sufficient discipline in members' position taking and voting.[35] Recent scholarship has highlighted both why individual members often have an incentive to vote against the party, and how the party organizes to ensure that individualistic behavior does not excessively damage the party policy reputation.

The classic example of a conflict between individual legislators and their party is the case of trade policy. Whereas individual legislators would gain support from powerful members of their districts by protecting their industries from foreign competition, if such behavior becomes universal within the party, overall policy degenerates into rampant protectionism and the economic growth benefits of free trade policy is lost. At some point the collective costs of such a policy outweigh the sum of the individual benefits. Cox and McCubbins (1993, 123) use the example of party leaders distributing individual exemptions to a general tax reform bill to illustrate the same tension between the interests of the party and the interests of individual legislators. As these scholars argue, parties that fail to rein in rank-and-file behavior that may serve individual interests, but that will hurt the policy reputation of the party, will be vulnerable in the electoral arena (123). Those parties that act to balance personal and party reputations will prosper electorally in comparison with those who fail to do so. In the case of the United States, party leaders wield valuable perks, such as coveted committee assignments, to reward those who follow leaders' directives and to punish those who do not.[36] By manipulating rewards that have an indirect, yet important, impact on reelection prospects, party leaders are able to ensure rank-and-

---

vote for all offices across all levels of government, with the exception of president, as was used in pre-Chávez Venezuela for most of the democratic period, facilitates such coordination of delivery and receipt of the vote across offices. But candidates for the same office, as with individual legislators, for example, cannot share credit for the delivery of a clientelist good. In a case such as Venezuela, in which candidate's names did not appear on the ballot, and party leaders determined the order on the closed list, typically the electorate must be divided up into mutually exclusive bailiwicks in order to ensure efficient vote buying. See discussion below on internal party organization.

35. Scholars who discuss the importance of a public reputation include Kiewiet and McCubbins (1991), Cox and McCubbins (1993), Snyder and Ting (2002), and Strøm (1990).

36. On the leadership as the enforcer within the party, see Cooper and Brady 1981; Sinclair 1983, 1995; Rhode 1991; Binder 1997; Doring 2001; and Cox and McCubbins 1993.

file behavior does not excessively damage the public reputation of the party (Cox and McCubbins 1993).

This understanding of internal party organization, however, rests on an assumption that *voters exercise policy-based voting*. The problem of reconciling individualistic behavior with the party's policy reputation arises because voters' *policy* preferences and their evaluation of *policy* outcomes are important components of voter choice. If voters in fact *do* consider policy outcomes in determining their vote, a party that fails to manage individualistic behavior and organize to safeguard the party's policy reputation will be defeated by parties that do so.

The analogous conflict between party and individual electoral goals in clientelist systems in which proportional-representation systems are used revolves around how resources are employed to buy votes. Individual legislators are most concerned with their own reelection and thus want to use the resources under their control most effectively to ensure their own electoral success. The party, however, wants to ensure that each legislator's use of resources also maximizes the number of seats won for the party as a whole. In other words, individual legislators are most concerned with spending the resources under their control to ensure their own reelection, whereas the party prefers to spend as little as possible on each vote bought in order to maximize seats won by the party.

Two possible conflicts between the party and the rank-and-file member arise. First, if individual bailiwicks are not well defined and managed, individual legislators may engage in bidding wars with other members of their own party. This will bid up the price of votes and reduce the number of votes bought for a given quantity of resources. Second, individual legislators may not use the resources under their control efficiently to buy as many votes as possible, but simply use those resources to gain enough votes to secure their own (re)election. In other words, rather than attempt to buy as many votes as possible, legislators may simply confer as high a price as possible on the minimum number of voters they calculate are necessary to win a seat for themselves. Once again, this clearly means fewer overall votes for the party as a whole, which in PR systems means fewer seats won. The result is that parties must eliminate any kind of competition between their own individual members while at the same time providing incentives for each individual member to maximize votes through efficient use of resources. Failure to reconcile these conflicting collective and individual goals with appropriate party organization will give the result that the party as a collective will spend too much for each vote bought, and there will be a loss of seats to competitors who organize internally to align individual and collective goals.

A slight modification of institutionalists' insights regarding candidate-centered or party-centered electoral rules sheds considerable light on systematic variation in how parties organize to reconcile these conflicting goals in clientelist systems employing proportional representation. If we examine whether resources, rather than institutions, are candidate or party centered, we can develop systematic hypotheses about how parties will address these conflicting goals. In Table 3, I summarize the generic differences in the individual-collective conflict, depending on whether voters opt for quid pro quo or exercise policy-based voting, and also the variations in how the same internal organizational problems are addressed within the two equilibria.

Comparative institutionalists have developed the theory differentiating cells IIA and IIB (Cox and Rosenbluth 1995; Ramseyer and Rosenbluth 1993; Carey and Shugart 1995). The central findings of this literature are that parties build and maintain a policy reputation for providing collective policy goods both in systems with party-centered rules and in systems with

Table 3 Alignment of individual and collective goals within the party

	Equilibrium electoral strategy	
Candidate or Party-centered	I. Clientelism Reconcile Individual and Collective Goals in Vote Buying	II. Collective Goods Provision Reconcile Individual and Collective Goals in Policy Formulation
A. Candidate-centered resource control or electoral rules	**Leadership aligns** party and individual goals through **indirect influence**: perks distributed **to reward efficient vote buying**	**Leadership aligns** party and individual goals through **indirect influence**: perks distributed **to reward faithful party voting**
B. **Party-centered** resource control or electoral rules	Brazil 1945–64 **Leadership aligns** party and individual goals **directly**: bidding wars discouraged by limiting rank and file role in vote buying	U.S., Brazil 1989–present **Leadership aligns** party and individual goals **directly**: excessive personalist politicking discouraged through distribution of ballot positions
	Venezuela, 1958–93	Federal Republic of Germany, United Kingdom

candidate-centered rules, with the central difference being that in the latter systems alignment of individual and party goals is accomplished through more indirect means and that such systems produce fewer national collective goods and more locally targeted collective goods than party-centered systems.

When structural conditions drive voters to opt for a quid pro quo, it is the centralization or decentralization of resource control that determines how the collective-individual conflict will be resolved, as depicted in cells IA and IB, in Table 3.[37] When resources are concentrated in party leaders' hands, leaders can determine the behavior of rank and file directly. The safest way to ensure that resources are not squandered by legislators who are concerned about their own (re)election is to eliminate their role in vote buying altogether. Under these conditions party leaders strive to render legislators simple delegates who pass the legislation that allocates the resources necessary to maintaining the party's networks. The actual distribution of these resources will typically be taken out of the hands of legislators who must compete in elections and will be given to "nonpolitical" entities. Thus, in Venezuela, as I will discuss in Chapter 4, by the mid-1970s the decisions regarding the allocation of an astounding 75 percent of government revenues bypassed the congressional arena altogether and were allocated by a decentralized administration made up of unelected political appointees. In sum, the more centralized control party leaders enjoy, the more they will choose rules that make them all-powerful bosses who eliminate direct electoral competition between members of the party and that allow them to dictate rank-and-file behavior from the first attempt at elective office to the point of leaving public life.

When resource control is dispersed across different levels of government or across a range of leaders belonging to different parties, regions, or ascriptive groups, and such heterogeneous leaders become entrepreneurs who amass their own resource pools and build their own clientelist networks, party leaders become organizers and facilitators who can use their powers to indirectly influence rank-and-file behavior, rather than bosses who can completely dictate that behavior. Under these conditions, a variety of players

---

37. Undoubtedly there are other factors that influence how parties organize to ensure efficient vote buying. Yet the importance of control of resources for capturing votes in clientelist systems means that this dimension is crucial. Moreover, the decentralized/centralized dichotomy presented here is certainly too crude to capture empirical reality. I ignore nuance and focus on paradigmatic cases to illuminate the logic of reconciling party and individual goals.

will build up their own individual networks and will often have incentives to do so at the expense of co-partisans. Given the individualist structure of clientelist networks, under these decentralized conditions party leaders cannot completely eliminate the incentive for internal party competition. But they can create incentives that indirectly reward those who avoid bidding wars and spend as little as possible to gain each vote, thus rewarding those who maximize the collective's electoral return on the pool of resources under the party's aegis. The central goal in this case will be to determine some basis on which to evaluate individual legislators' efficiency in vote buying and then distribute any rewards under leadership control on that basis. As I will discuss in Chapter 4, by rewarding those with the highest vote totals with a seat, Brazil's open-list proportional representation rule (PR) encouraged efficient vote buying and discouraged bidding wars and other inefficient behaviors and thus was an effective tool for rewarding individual behavior that redounded to the benefit of the party.

Just as parties in policy-based systems will suffer electorally if they do not effectively manage personal politicking in order to safeguard the policy reputation, parties in clientelist systems that fail to ensure that their overall pool of resources is used as efficiently as possible in buying votes within the given system parameters will also suffer in comparison with their rivals who use their resources efficiently. This applies equally to highly centralized systems, such as that of Venezuela, and highly decentralized systems, such as in Brazil, as well as more mixed systems falling somewhere in between these two extremes. Spending too many resources per vote in clientelist systems is analogous to producing too much particularism in the policy-based case highlighted by Cox and McCubbins (1993).

The Short-Circuiting of Democratic Accountability: Clientelism and Policy Outcome

Clientelism severs the link between voter preferences and policy choice (Stokes 2007). When voters exchange their vote in a quid pro quo for a clientelist benefit, overall policy outcome no longer plays a role in voters' decisions. In our ordinary understanding of democracy as a delegation from voters (as principals) to representatives (as agents) to produce public policy, when voters opt for quid pro quo, they surrender their role as principal. The principals in clientelist systems are the actors who can deliver votes (Kitschelt 2000; Bueno de Mesquita et al. 2001). The electoral connection's ability to discipline policy decisions in clientelist systems is reduced to that of forcing politicians to maintain a resource stock sufficient to buy the requisite number of votes and to reconcile the conflicting clientelistic demands of those who deliver the votes. The critical result is that in clientelist systems, *the electoral connection fails to impose some minimal level of discipline on the overall welfare impact of policy choice.* Policy is designed to maximize resource streams that can be turned into excludable goods.

Volumes have been written on how special interests intervene and dilute the link between voter preferences and policy outcome in policy-based systems as well.[38] Yet despite the well-documented importance of money and other resources that special interests can provide, voters remain the principals when policy informs their choices (Gerber 1999). And as long as voters maintain the ability to include overall policy outcome as one component of their choice, the electoral connection does discipline the policy choices of politicians. In policy-based systems, the anticipation of political entrepreneurship aimed at exposing rent seeking, and the predictable voter wrath based on poor overall outcomes, create strong incentives for politicians to carefully monitor and manage the degree to which their policies serve the few at the expense of the majority (Joskow and Noll 1981; Verdier 1994; Baron 1994).

It is certainly true that considerable particularism and rent seeking can fly under the radar of rationally ignorant voters in policy-based systems. Recent research, however, indicates that voters have a variety of shortcuts to good information about how well politicians are serving their interests (Popkin 1991; Lupia and McCubbins 1998). The level of particularism and rent seeking that the electorate will tolerate when voters cast a policy-based vote is a complicated function of many political variables. Nevertheless, a clear and crucial distinction between policy-based and clientelist systems remains: when policy outcomes are a component of the voter's choice, the electoral connection serves to select out policies that create widespread social welfare losses, whereas in clientelist systems, the welfare-enhancing feature of the electoral connection is lost.

The Structural Conditions of Quid Pro Quo or Policy-Based Politics

As pinpointed in the logic of the voter's dilemma, developed above, the variable driving a given voter to opt for quid pro quo or policy-based voting

---

38. See, for example, Stigler 1971; Peltzman 1976; Becker 1983; and Magee, Brock, and Young 1989.

is the risk the voter faces in rejecting clientelism. To link this individual voting calculus to the strategy that will prevail in any given election, we must explore both sources of supply and determinants of demand, as well as how resource supply stacks up against aggregate demand in a given election.

Structural Conditions as Determinants of the Price of an Election

The logic of the voter's dilemma implies that voters have a strong incentive to opt for the quid pro quo instead of policy-based voting if the clientelist offer holds out the promise of valuable goods. Structural variables, such as social and economic structure and distribution of income, long emphasized by area and development specialists, alter voters' ability to substitute for clientelist benefits and thus alter the value of the clientelist benefit that they can forgo without undue risk.

I define the voter's *reservation price* as the lowest price that he or she will accept in a clientelist exchange. Although there are myriad factors involved, as a rough cut, we can say that a voter's reservation price will be set at the level of what he or she can easily procure through his or her own efforts in the private market. What is available to a given voter in the private market is in turn a complex function of individual characteristics, such as private asset ownership and skill endowment, as well as of systemic economic factors, such as level of economic development and labor endowment. Private assets can provide the voter with an income stream that would render negligible a variety of clientelist offers. Similarly, certain combinations of level of economic development and distribution of human capital will imply that voters with higher education will have little trouble finding employment with at least middle-class levels of remuneration. If economic differentiation proceeds rapidly, and human skill endowment does not keep pace, then technological and professional skills will be in high demand and those with these skills may be less dependent on quid pro quo exchange to maintain their standard of living. In short, these are highly complex interactions that cannot be specified in general but that ultimately play a role in determining what a given voter cannot easily substitute and thus what he or she will demand in a quid pro quo exchange.

Some examples help illustrate the argument. Middle-class voters typically will not trade their vote for the minimal reward offered to voters in the informal economy (shoes, building materials, food) or even for a working-class job, because they typically own sufficient assets or have skill levels that would allow them to maintain a considerably higher standard of living through employment in the private market. Thus, they face little risk in rejecting such clientelist offers. A middle-class voter may even refuse the relatively high remuneration and the very generous benefits associated with a white-collar position in the government bureaucracy if he or she owns assets or has secure employment with comparable pay that is beyond clientelist manipulation. In this case, once again, the voter would face little risk in refusing the clientelist offer. But a middle-class voter who does not own such wealth or have such opportunities immune to clientelist manipulation will find such a government position highly valuable. A similar logic explains why working-class voters typically will not sell their vote for the minimal reward offered to voters in the informal economy, such as shoes or food, but will sell it for steady income and retirement and other benefits typically associated with unionized industrial and service jobs.

In sum, the logic of the voter's dilemma shows that voters of all income levels will trade their vote for clientelist benefits if they can receive something they cannot easily procure themselves. If they are not offered a sufficiently valuable good, they have little to lose by rejecting clientelism and opting for policy-based voting. This holds true even if all other voters continue voting clientelist. By defining the reservation price as equivalent to goods that the voter could easily procure without joining a clientelist network, he or she has not lost anything of value by rejecting an offer below that price, even if the clientelist wins. To translate this individual calculus to the aggregate level, we can define the reservation price of a given election as the sum of the reservation prices of the voters who make up a given winning coalition.

Although the language of reservation prices is cumbersome, it is important to distinguish analytically between the lowest price the voter will accept (the reservation price) and the price that he or she actually receives in any given election. As discussed above, a party's ability to keep the cost of its votes as close to the reservation price as possible, by avoiding bidding wars, is key to its electoral success. Moreover, if above-reservation prices become institutionalized (through legislated salary increases, for example), there is a great deal of "slack" in the system—that is, voters would in fact sell their votes and elections could be bought, for considerably less than what is regularly spent on them under the given set of institutionalized practices for aggregating votes. As I will discuss in Chapters 2 and 6, this slack provides an opening for a new party or politician to undercut existing networks of exchange with a lower-cost clientelist strategy in the event of a resource crisis.

Structural Conditions as Determinants of Politicians' Supply

The reservation price of an election is one side of the coin determining whether clientelist or collective goods strategies will prevail in a given district.[39] The other side is the stock of resources available for buying votes. As with the determinants of voters' reservation price, there are numerous variables that affect the supply of resources available for clientelist exchange. Resource supply encompasses much more than simply fiscal or other government revenues. As a result of the control of production rights, import-export rights, and myriad other property rights, as well as control of the justice system, politicians have many tools beyond basic taxation through which to create benefits for quid pro quo exchange. A number of structural factors are critical determinants of the limits of resource supply at any given time, some of these factors being characteristic of the country itself, among them natural resource endowment, size of the economy, and borrowing potential. Parameters associated with the international economy also play a critical role, such as level of demand for different types of exports and international liquidity. A final highly intangible factor is politicians' ingenuity.

Once again, some examples can help give an indication of the available strategies, but also the complexity involved in assessing this variable. Politicians can augment resources and create benefits for clientelist exchange by increasing taxes and royalty payments on foreign direct investment in extractive industries, inflating the currency, nationalizing industries, distributing production opportunities and jobs in a closed economy, or distributing import and export opportunities in a purportedly "open" economy. While government intervention through nationalization of industry or other direct control of economic activity is an obvious means with which politicians can augment the resources available for building clientelist networks, there are many more subtle methods of augmenting supply that can be built on virtually any orientation toward the role of the state in the market.[40]

Ingenious politicians can turn an economic "liberalization" that entails reducing protectionism and a new emphasis on exports into production, trade, and job opportunities for clientelist distribution. Licensing or other

---

39. This could be either a local district for electing legislators or a national district for electing a president. The logic of supply and demand applies to any level of aggregation, although lower levels are always subject to incursion from higher levels of government.

40. For a more detailed discussion of how any development strategy can be fashioned to create clientelistic benefits for distribution in return for votes, see Lyne and Hawn 2007.

more subtle forms of control of who is able to import can be just as useful for clientelists as similar controls on who is able to supply a protected domestic market. Likewise, governments can distribute the right to exploit abundant cheap labor in order to produce light manufactures for export.[41] Apparent specialization based on comparative advantage and integration into the international economy through export of light manufactures can benefit clientelist politicians if they have implicit or explicit control of who is allowed access to the factors of production.

It is important to note that clientelists implementing such "liberalization" schemes are likely to benefit on the supply side in another way. At least since the debt crisis of the early 1980s, developing countries demonstrating progress in "liberalizing" their economies were likely to see a renewal of official aid and loans, as well as a return of private capital. Although such renewed access to international funds may have only a moderate impact in large economies, such as of Brazil or India, it can constitute a significant proportion of funds available to government leaders in smaller developing countries.

In sum, the means for expanding or modifying the types of resources available for clientelist exchange are legion and are compatible with virtually any development orientation.[42] Moreover, a variety of factors, such as economic crisis, rising reservation prices, vigorous competition coupled with failure to control bidding wars, or some combination of these, may motivate politicians to search for new resources. Myriad other variables determine which of these strategies will be most viable and most effective in creating new resources for maintaining clientelism in a given instance.

The Intersection of Demand and Supply: Quid Pro Quo or Policy Goods as Winning Strategy

The preceding discussion illustrates the fact that neither voters' demands nor resource supply are static, but rather, are both constantly evolving. The voting logic highlighted by the voter's dilemma implies that politicians have a strong incentive to search for new resources whenever changes threaten to exhaust supply. As the ability of voters to substitute higher-value clientel-

---

41. Indonesia under Suharto probably provides the most obvious examples of these strategies, in which import and export concessions were distributed directly to his family members and close allies.

42. Kitschelt (2000, 863–64) notes that privatization in Russia and liberalization in Latin America yielded many new clientelist opportunities.

ist offers increases, for example, politicians who can find the resources necessary to continue making nonnegligible clientelist offers will defeat contenders trying to compete by offering collective policy goods. Similarly, a politician who discovers a new fund of resources to address a crisis of supply will continue to defeat politicians who attempt a shift to a policy-based strategy in the face of a crisis.[43]

To more fully specify the conditions under which quid pro quo or policy-based strategies will predominate, we must delineate the relationships between politicians, producers, and voters in each equilibrium. Producers may be either client-producers or entrepreneurial producers. Client-producers exploit monopoly or oligopoly production rights conferred by the government in direct exchange for political support.[44] Entrepreneurial producers confront competitive markets and thus must innovate to survive. Producers have a reservation income (I), at or above which they prefer to be client-producers because the marginal return on their time investment is higher.[45] Below this threshold I, producers will trade leisure for effort, will become entrepreneurial producers, and will accept a move to more competitive markets in order to increase their income. Voters likewise may play one of two roles. They can sell their vote in a quid pro quo exchange for some excludable political good and become a *client*. Alternatively, they can exercise policy-based sanctioning, giving varying weights to national and locally targeted collective goods and become *citizens*. Voters have a reservation price at or above which they will trade their votes for a quid pro quo good and become a client. The election for any given office has a reservation price that is equal to the *lowest-priced possible winning coalition* of voters.[46] Finally, *politicians*

---

43. I will discuss how crisis affects voters' and politicians' strategies in detail in Chapter 6.

44. Governments may confer these rights directly through licensing (Bates 2001) or indirectly through different types of production assistance that renders only those so-favored viable producers. The classic example is the feudal or latifundista system in which the crown grants land ownership to feudal lords in return for political support, and the lord or the latifundista then trades access to land for subsistence agriculture in return for the political support of the serfs/peasants. In most developing countries initial conditions after independence were characterized by this type of system. As development and urbanization proceeded, typically led by an increasingly interventionist state, bureaucratic and industrial jobs also became an important source of buying political support in the cities (on this point, see Weingrod 1977 and Soares 2001).

45. When production opportunities are conferred by politicians producers employ resources to create output, whereas selling one's products in competitive markets typically requires the much more difficult task of using resources to create output *more efficiently* than under current practice.

46. The size of the winning coalition of voters depends on electoral law and may also be constrained by other institutional or organizational factors. As I will argue in the following chapter, in clientelist systems voters are typically organized into blocs that deliver their votes

may be the agents of either citizens and entrepreneurial producers or of vote brokers—those who control scarce valuable resources and can deliver votes.

No government, of course, ever adopts property rights that enforce completely competitive markets. But some governments do adopt property rights that ensure that most producers have to innovate most of the time in order to survive. Moreover, competitive markets are not the only form of property rights that reward innovation. As scholars such as Wade (2003) and Amsden (1989) have argued, governments can often mimic the innovation-rewarding features of competitive markets with well-managed intervention. And some state-led programs *were* run with relatively well-managed, efficiency-rewarding intervention, and the most prominent examples led to dramatic ascension in the international division of labor and impressive improvement in distribution of income.[47] Many state-led programs, however, were run using political criteria for distributing production rights to a specific economic agent through licenses, privileged access to crucial inputs, and so on, and infant industries were never forced to grow up. Such quid pro quo policies do not preclude economic growth, but they typically fail to produce consistent growth in income per capita over time.[48]

---

in toto. To the extent that brokers can control the members of these blocs, it will not be possible to bid away individual voters. Any deal that includes one voter of the bloc will have to include all voters in the bloc. Thus, winning coalitions may be constrained by the way voters are organized into blocs. Such blocs may, but do not necessarily, correspond to political parties or corporatist interest groups. A given election in a given district may cost more than the reservation price if there is limited control of bidding wars. The reservation price of the office is thus the price at which each voter in the winning coalition receives no more than his or her reservation price.

47. The obvious examples are South Korea and Taiwan. Some scholars have pointed to the Asian financial crisis to argue that policies in South Korea were not as beneficial as previously thought. But Taiwan did not suffer much in this crisis, and unlike the vast majority of developing countries hit by crises, South Korea recovered rapidly and maintained most of the gains made under the pre-crisis policies.

48. Economic growth under such quid pro quo policies typically stems from simply bringing more resources into production, rather than from increasing the efficiency with which such resources are used. Economists have labeled this *extensive* growth (Furtado 1970; North 1990). Rules that approximate competitive markets, in comparison, reward producers for innovation and typically lead to a steady rise in income per capita over time. Economists have labeled this type of economic growth *intensive* growth (North 1990). It should be emphasized that employment of new technology is not what differentiates quid pro quo systems from competitive markets. Producers favored by quid pro quo policies may employ existing domestic technology or the most advanced imported technology (whose cost is typically subsidized); the critical difference between quid pro quo and competitive markets is that political criteria determine who is a viable producer under the former, whereas innovation that consumers find valuable primarily determines who is a viable producer under the latter. Of course, sectorally targeted policies such as tariffs or regulatory interventions, commonly used in policy-based systems, do give some producers an edge over others. The difference with

With these definitions and the theory of the voter's dilemma, we can say that at any level of aggregation, whether local, regional, or national, quid pro quo politics will dominate as long as producers can obtain their threshold income and politicians can pay the reservation price of the election. As long as voters are offered their reservation price and producers are receiving at least their threshold income, both will opt for quid pro quo politics. *This is the root cause of the democracy-development paradox:* despite the fact that most voters would be much better off with a collectively oriented development policy rather than with the quid pro quo good they receive, under some structural conditions they face great individual risk in exercising policy-based voting.

Politicians championing collectively oriented development policies will defeat clientelists only when the process of "upping the ante" in vote buying is exhausted. Ultimately, it is how politicians' supply of resources for building clientelist networks stacks up against the reservation price of the election that determines whether quid pro quo or policy-based strategies will dominate. When the demands of making nonnegligible offers to voters outrun politicians' best efforts to find new resources, clientelism and short-circuited democratic accountability will be replaced by policy-based politics and much more effective electoral control. If strategies for adjusting supply and demand to resource constraints have been exhausted, and clientelism is no longer sufficient to maintain producers' threshold income and pay the reservation price of the election, the implication is that there is no longer any viable winning coalition of voters that faces significant risk in rejecting the available clientelist offers. Under these conditions, voters will find it possible to ignore the implications of the voter's dilemma and opt for policy-based voting. Politicians will respond by adopting a mix of national collective policy, pork, and rents, which forces sufficient entrepreneurial behavior to ensure gradual yet steadily rising standards of living over time.[49]

---

sectoral clientelism is that these rents do not directly designate who can produce and sell in the market and who cannot.

49. I have argued that politicians offering collective policy goods that reward innovation will begin winning when structural conditions shift such that voters can exercise policy-based sanctioning without undue risk. I emphasize policy that rewards innovation because empirically I am concerned primarily with cases where economic growth is a paramount policy concern. But policies rewarding innovation is only one type of national collective policy. In practice politicians opt for a mix of policy goods that they believe will meet with the greatest voter approval. The literature on the advanced industrial democracies has indicated that as per capita incomes rise, other policy goods such as environmental protection also become important to voters (Inglehart 1990).

The argument has some features in common with Cox's (1987) in *The Efficient Secret.* Cox argues that economic development and technological change rendered the buying of votes in

Policy-based strategies become more competitive once politicians can no longer pay the reservation price of the election because collective policy goods are not zero sum.[50] Whereas there is a limit to what can be extracted from a given endowment of resources, and what one client-producer receives from preferential production rights another client-producer loses, the profits available from innovation are technically unlimited. One entrepreneurial producer's gain from innovation does not preclude another entrepreneurial producer's gain based on distinct innovations. Similarly, when votes are bought with quid pro quo goods, what one client receives, another client necessarily loses. In comparison, when votes are won with the provision of collective policy goods such as economic growth based on innovation, this zero-sum problem is diminished. The job one citizen receives based on entrepreneurial success does not preclude the job another citizen receives based on some other investment that produces successful innovation. At the point at which the reservation price can no longer be met, a politician can adopt a policy-based strategy, campaigning on the promise to replace quid pro quo rules with rules that reward efficiency and innovation, which will create entrepreneurial opportunities for former client-producers now willing to trade leisure for income and will generate jobs for former clients who are no longer receiving at least their reservation price.

Once again, exploration of some illustrative examples is helpful in clarifying the interaction between demand and supply. On the supply side, any increase in resources will typically extend the life of clientelism. This provides a theory to back the frequent observation that oil is more of a curse than a benefit for many nations (Karl 1997). This also helps unravel the conundrum of why natural resource abundance is often coupled with poor policy outcomes, but in addition, it can explain why some natural resource–abundant countries, such as the United States, do well. Similarly, a decline in supply

---

England too expensive. Thus, broad socioeconomic change that rendered the existing practices unworkable drove members of Parliament to delegate legislative powers to the prime minister to be able to provide more general policy goods. The difference with the argument presented here is that Cox does not ask the question of why politicians who were controlling rotten boroughs were not vulnerable to political entrepreneurs who were offering better public policy at any point before the shift he examines takes place. Cox does not frame the study as concerned with general questions about political accountability but instead takes the historical transformation in England as given, and is focused on explaining the political changes that took place concomitant with the social and economic transformations. He thus does not argue for any explicit constraint on voters' ability to throw the rascals out, as the discussion of the voter's dilemma does here.

50. For the greater economic efficiency of collective policy goods in comparison with clientelism, see Stokes 2007.

will motivate politicians to search for new resources. One example of a successful search for new resources can be seen in the impressive efforts of politicians to radically reformulate development strategies and forge new coalitions around heavy government intervention after the collapse of commodity exporting across the developing world from the 1930s to the 1950s.

On the demand side, if the reservation price of the election increases, but politicians can pay that increased price and still maintain producers' threshold income, then clientelist politics will continue to dominate. Plausible examples of this phenomenon are the cases of Middle Eastern oil exporters, in which socioeconomic advance has led the population to demand more and more benefits. Abundant oil revenues have made it possible for ruling elites to steadily increase the benefits distributed to the population while also maintaining very high incomes for themselves. Finally, on the demand side, under some conditions political competition may lead politicians to systematically bid the price of an election far above the reservation price. In this case we would expect politicians to respond to resource constraints with attempts to drive voters' prices back down to their reservation levels. The frequent occurrences of populist governments being followed by military governments with strict constraints on political activity are a plausible example of this phenomenon.[51]

In conclusion, it is important to underscore the nature of the mechanism of transition. It is not that voters eventually discern that clientelism produces detrimental collective results, or decide to cooperate. Empirically, if these solutions were possible we would not see such a striking correlation between low levels of development and clientelism. Moreover, if any of these solutions were possible, we would need a theory to explain why demonstration effects fail and why all voters in all democracies have not come to see that policy-based voting produces superior results. In addition, when structural conditions favor the clientelist equilibrium, there is no simple income effect—higher-income voters can be equally vulnerable if their income stems from politically conferred investment or production opportunities. It is only when rising income reduces voters' risk in forgoing the

---

51. In Brazil, for example, the military that came to power in a coup in 1964 took steps that can be understood to eliminate bidding wars and ratchet down reservation prices. In comparison with the freewheeling nature of competition from 1945 to 1964 (to be discussed more fully in the succeeding chapters), the military introduced a number of constraints. First, the leaders of those groups who were forced to pay the costs of the ratcheting down, primarily organized labor, were killed, exiled, or excluded from politics. Second, although the legislature functioned for most of the period, only two political parties were allowed to compete, and the rank and file were required to vote with the leadership.

insurance policy provided by a clientelist vote that voters can opt out of clientelist politics. Finally, the transition does not occur simply as a result of crisis. The key to understanding the role of crisis is once again the fact that the voter's choice turns on the *risk* that he or she faces in rejecting clientelism. Crisis typically will imply a reduction in clientelist offers. Unless voters' prices are uniformly at reservation levels, however, a crisis-induced reduction in clientelist offers does not necessarily imply that voters no longer face risks in rejecting clientelism. I will treat the issue of crisis in depth in Chapter 6.

The transition occurs because some combination of changes in supply and demand result in the fact that voters' irreducible demands outrun the best efforts of politicians to find new resources for maintaining clientelism. When politicians can no longer pay voters' reservation price, it means that politicians cannot supply anything that voters cannot attain through their own efforts, and thus voters face little risk in rejecting clientelism. When this risk diminishes, clientelist exclusion no longer implies the loss of valuable goods. Under these conditions, voters *can* ignore the prisoner's dilemma driven by collective accountability without undue risk, and it becomes relatively costless for them to use elections to hold politicians accountable for policy outcomes.

Refining the Link Between Structural Conditions, Individual Choice, and Democratic Performance

In the previous section, there was an implication that neither economic growth alone nor economic growth that raises voters' reservation price will necessarily lead to a shift from quid pro quo to policy-based voting. In this section I provide a more general discussion of how the theory allows us to refine the links between structural conditions, voter choice, and electoral outcomes. It is helpful to explore the argument about structural changes by examining the specific structural change of economic growth. This type of structural change is invoked in a huge body of literature linking economic development and democracy.

Economic growth is consistent with the continued dominance of clientelism under any conditions in which it does not push the reservation price of the election beyond what politicians can pay. This could be true when economic growth does little to reduce voters' dependence on clientelism, despite rising standards of living. It could also occur when economic growth increases politicians' resources faster than the reservation price. Once again, examples help make the point. Economic growth would have a limited impact on voters' reliance on clientelism when the fruits of such growth are strictly controlled by elected officials. If there are limitations on private-asset ownership (as in socialist systems) or new employment is controlled directly or indirectly by elected officials, economic growth could have little impact on voters' dependence on clientelism. This is a plausible alternative explanation for why the most advanced developing countries of the postwar period, Brazil and Argentina, in O'Donnell's classic study, did not become prosperous democracies. As I will argue in Chapter 6, the substantial production opportunities and employment generated under the postwar import substitution industrialization (ISI) programs were carefully controlled and distributed by clientelist politicians.

It is also possible that although economic growth may reduce voters' dependence on clientelism, and thus raise their reservation price, it might also increase the stock of resources available to politicians to distribute. ISI provides a prominent example. The closing of the domestic market and the subsidizing and licensing of domestic production created vast new production and employment opportunities for distribution. A second plausible case of this type is one in which a valuable natural resource is discovered. The obvious example today is oil. If the production and sale of the resource can be monopolized by politicians, they may control resource streams that can cover steadily increasing reservation prices for long periods. In particular, the combination of abundant resources and small populations makes quid pro quo politics compatible with relatively high per capita incomes, as in some countries in the Middle East.

Finally, by demonstrating that collective accountability coupled with asymmetry of excludability between clientelist and collective goods is what drives clientelism, we can explain relatively low income countries that are not clientelist. Here we can illustrate the obverse situation of the high-income voter who opts for clientelist benefits. If it is the risk of rejecting clientelism, rather than simply income, that drives voters to opt for quid pro quo exchange, then just as high-income voters who have much to lose from rejecting clientelism will vote clientelist, we should also expect that when low-income voters have little to lose in rejecting clientelism, they will exercise policy-based voting. If supply of resources is modest, and assets and income opportunities are distributed in a relatively egalitarian fashion, we can imagine a situation in which clientelists cannot meet the reservation prices of elections despite the fact that most voters have only modest incomes. The absence of clientelism in the early Scandinavian democracies, in which agricultural production was based on family farms, plausibly fits this scenario.[52]

Economic growth *can*, of course, have the effect postulated by the original modernization theorists—it can provide sufficient new (nonclientelist) income opportunities to a sufficient number of voters such that the reservation price of national elections exceeds what politicians can marshal to buy votes. The critical implication of the argument about collective accountability highlighted by the voter's dilemma, however, is that there is not a one-to-one correspondence between structural change such as economic development and the emergence of effective democratic accountability. Moreover, given the competitive incentives of clientelist electoral politics, clientelist politicians will exercise as much control as possible over the distribution of new production opportunities and new employment. Thus, the real key to the demise of clientelism is, rather than simple economic growth, economic growth that enables the relatively widespread acquisition of private assets. I will turn to this and other indicators of clientelist and policy-based politics in the following chapter.

---

52. For a discussion of the lack of clientelism in Scandinavia, see Papakostas 2001.

Are Voters in Brazil and Venezuela Opting for Policy-Based or Quid Pro Quo Voting?

In this chapter I begin the empirical tests of the theory of the voter's dilemma and the alternatives by analyzing the independent variable. As with any theory in which structural factors play a significant causal role, assessing the independent variable presents challenges, since structural factors often cannot be specified or measured in any straightforward fashion. In the case of the voter's dilemma, the independent variable is driven by how the supply of resources available for distribution of clientelistic goods stacks up against the price of the election in a given district. Supply, in turn, is a complex function of domestic and international structural economic, social, and political factors. On the demand side, each individual reservation price is determined by how individual conditions interact with structural variables, and these individual reservation prices must be aggregated to determine the price of an election. Clearly it is not possible to specify any general treatment of these variables that would yield a valid cross-national measure of supply and demand.

Despite these difficulties, I follow King, Koehane, and Verba (1994, 10), who argue that the availability of straightforward direct measures of variables should not drive social science inquiry. As these authors argue, we must elaborate as many observable implications of our models as possible and develop more subtle, indirect tests of our theories.[1] When clientelistic links between voters and politicians predominate, the electoral connection is rendered null and void as a means for controlling the direction of government policy. A better understanding of the causes and effects of clientelism

---

1. Kitschelt (2000, 871) and Kitschelt and Wilkinson (2007) emphasize the centrality of clientelism to the comparative study of democracy and call for the development of more accurate and sophisticated measures of indirect and direct voter-politician links. In this chapter I present two new approaches to measuring concrete voter behavior that can be linked to direct and indirect exchange.

therefore is central to solving the puzzles of variation in democratic performance.

Fortunately, testing the theory does not require an exact measure of how many voters vote clientelist and how many exercise policy-based voting. Indeed, a simple search for clientelist voters as an indicator of the clientelist equilibrium can be highly misleading, since vestiges of clientelism may very well survive for long periods even after a shift to policy-based competition at the national level. Since the predictions about politician behavior developed in the previous chapter are driven by equilibrium conditions, testing requires more subtle indicators—markers that will only be present if a clientelist or a policy-based equilibrium obtains. Below, I elaborate on two such indicators based on voting patterns: first, partisan tides and, second, in PR systems, a high concentration of voter support by sub-district unit. Individually, each of these indicators only partially meets this ideal for accurate testing. I use them together, as well as in combination with three other indicators (public opinion, macro conditions, and systems of vote monitoring and benefit delivery) to reinforce the conclusions on the basis of voting patterns.[2]

An examination of public opinion data allows us to ensure that the lack of provision of basic collective goods does not stem from voter preferences for some alternative goods. Macrolevel data, although far from conclusive in terms of voters' choices, allows us to establish broad trends in resource supply and election prices. All clientelist systems require vote monitoring in order to make the threat of exclusion credible, and large scale, society-wide systems of monitoring provide strong evidence of a clientelist equilibrium. Finally, our best proxies for supply-and-demand conditions that yield a clientelist or a policy-based equilibrium are behavioral indicators of the predominant voter-politician linkage: partisan tides and the degree of dispersion of voting support.

Public Opinion

Although surveys themselves cannot serve as a reliable indicator of what voters are actually *choosing*, we have no reason to believe that voters would

---

2. The indicators necessary for testing the theory ideally would uniquely identify one or the other equilibrium. Combined with the fact that policy-based systems may well exhibit considerable vestigial clientelism, this means that two commonly cited measures of clientelism are in fact highly misleading. Surveys have several serious drawbacks. Aside from the many incentives for inaccurate self-reporting, as discussed in Kitschelt and Wilkinson 2007, surveys, at best, can only establish the presence of clientelism, but are highly unlikely to be accurate indicators of one equilibrium or the other. Similarly, attempts to characterize some aspect of policy as clientelistic as an indicator of the clientelistic equilibrium suffers from

not report their real *preferences* for policy goods. An examination of voters' preferences for policy as expressed in public opinion surveys is valuable for two reasons. First, it allows us to establish that voters have a preference for basic collective goods such as macroeconomic stability, jobs, an efficient bureaucracy, and so on and thus rule out a lack of voter preference as the explanation for politicians' failure to provide basic collective goods. Moreover, if voters express preferences for standard policy goods but do not punish the parties that fail to provide them, this is prima facie evidence that something intervenes between their individual preference and the collective outcome of who is elected. It is important to examine public opinion data in the two Brazilian cases for another reason. New institutionalists argue that outcomes are a function of preferences and institutional incentives, so if the latter did not change, then different outcomes could possibly be the result of changes in preferences. Thus, to thoroughly test institutional theories, we must rule out a change in preferences as the explanation for the dramatic change in outcomes across the two Brazilian cases.

A Change in Voters' Preferences or a Change in Voters' Strategy in Brazil?

Preferences often do not receive explicit treatment in new institutionalist and other positivist analyses, because the assumptions that politicians want to further their political careers (in democratic systems, typically through attaining electoral office) and that voters want government to provide basic collective goods are considered to be universally valid. The data presented in this section suggest that Brazilian and Venezuelan voters in both periods wanted basic collective goods.

As has been discussed, in the two cases of democracy in Brazil studied here, all the major institutional features are identical in Brazil from 1945 to 1964 and from 1989 to the present, including presidentialism, federalism, bicameralism, open-list proportional representation with the state as the district, and electoral coalitions with pooling among the coalition for legislative elections. It might nevertheless be possible to construct an argument that is consistent with the institutional framework based on a change in voters' preferences. Before discussing public opinion data, it is worth repeating that in Brazil, the major policy issues in the early 1960s and in the

---

similar pitfalls—policy as a guide to clientelism is likely to be highly inaccurate, and even accurate characterization will do no more than indicate the presence of clientelism, but not which equilibrium prevails. For a more in-depth discussion of the pitfalls of using policy outcome as an indicator of clientelism, see Kitschelt 2000.

early 1990s were remarkably similar. Inflation, international debt, uncompetitive industry, bloated and inefficient bureaucracy and a regressive and fiscally explosive social security system were the principal sources of crisis in both periods.[3]

Public opinion polling was in its infancy in Brazil just as the postwar democratic regime was eclipsed by a military coup. What little data is available, however, indicates what one might expect, given the acute policy crisis the country faced in the early 1960s: voters wanted low inflation, economic growth, and bureaucratic reform. Lavareda (1991, 161) reports that in 1965 the top four problems cited by voters were inflation, agriculture (including agrarian reform), economic development and social problems. Geddes (1994) also reports that the importance of administrative reform was consistently emphasized by voters in public opinion polls during this period.

Public opinion data, then, indicates that voters in the earlier period *wanted* just what they have *rewarded* in the later period: low inflation, economic growth, and basic reforms.[4] If we assume that voters' substantive concerns were similar across the two periods, it might also be argued that what differed were the types of goods preferred. But to assert that voters preferred clientelistic goods over policy goods returns us to the argument of the previous chapter. We return to a claim that voters for some reason prefer the clearly inferior quid pro quo goods to the benefits available from holding politicians accountable for policy goods. Even if we assume that this is true, perhaps based on voters' cognitive or informational limitations, the results of such a choice should have enlightened voters regarding its disadvantages fairly quickly.

Public Opinion in Venezuela

Public opinion data from both regimes in Venezuela indicate that voters desired basic public goods. Data from pre-Chávez Venezuela provide evi-

    3. For the earlier period: on inflation and debt one can consult virtually any good history, such as Skidmore 1967; on the lack of competitiveness in industry, Bergsman 1970 is an excellent source; on social security, Malloy 1977 provides the best analysis; on bureaucracy, see Graham 1968 and Geddes 1994. For the later period, any popular periodical examining political and economic trends in Latin America in the 1990s, such as the *Economist*, repeatedly made the case for these policy ills.
    4. After the success of the Real stabilization plan in the mid-1990s, Fernando Henrique Cardoso was reelected easily in 1998. Lula, the Workers' Party candidate, won in 2002 with a pledge to maintain the fiscal policies of the previous administration and to continue with basic reforms in social security and the judiciary as well as to expand antipoverty programs. On the basis of that record from 2002 to 2006, Lula was reelected to a second term in 2006.

dence that in the face of the most dramatic crisis of the democratic period, voters were demanding basic policy goods. In 1989, voters consistently listed reducing inflation and increasing jobs as the top two priorities the government should address. Moreover, when asked whether it was more important for government to improve the quality of public services or broaden political participation, 96 percent opted for the former, while only 4 percent chose the latter (Myers 1995, 118–19). In August 2004 and October 2006, Venezuelans consistently and by large margins listed unemployment (25 percent and 58 percent, respectively) and safety and security (31 percent and 22 percent, respectively) as the most important problems for government to address (Evans/McDonough 2006, 3).

Just as in Brazil, voters in Venezuela expressed preferences for basic policy goods: low inflation, jobs, and an efficient public bureaucracy. As in postwar Brazil, these expressed preferences and the known outcomes in pre-Chávez and contemporary Venezuela raise questions about the efficacy of electoral accountability: why did nearly two decades of economic decline fail to generate parties that could effectively challenge those that were being blamed for the crisis in Venezuela (or induce the dominant parties to adopt serious reform)?[5] And why was the discredited former system replaced by a figure such as Chávez, whose "reforms" are unlikely to produce sustainable results?[6]

Structural Variables

Structural variables are examined to provide rough indications of trends in resource availability and election prices in each case. It is illuminating to examine broad trends in structural variables that will have a large impact on the balance between supply of resources for distribution and demand for higher-value clientelistic goods. Rather than build a laundry list of the many variables that might influence supply, I examine variables that can pinpoint whether politicians have exhausted available resources. Thus, I examine inflation rates and levels of international debt in the context of the international credit market as indicators of exhaustion of available resources from

---

5. The crisis in Venezuela was initiated with the devaluation in 1983. The AD and COPEI remained the dominant parties until 1998, yet neither they nor any alternative party articulated a competent reform program.

6. I will discuss Chávez's institutional and policy reforms more fully in subsequent chapters.

domestic and international sources. On the demand side, I look at factors that would lead to a generalized increase in the election price, such as changes in levels of private-asset ownership over time or large-scale changes in the franchise.

Resource Supply in Brazil

The two periods of democracy in Brazil exhibit important differences in the availability of resources for striking clientelist bargains. Unlike in the contemporary period, which has been characterized by an international debt crisis, at the end of World War II, most Latin American countries enjoyed a positive balance-of-payments position. Thus, in postwar Brazil politicians began with a comfortable external position, which eroded over the period but even by the early 1960s was not anywhere near as dire as when democracy was reinstituted in the late 1980s. In the early 1960s Brazil's international debt was roughly $3.5 billion, but had ballooned to $135 billion by 1992 (Banco Central Brasil 2003). There was also a major difference in the ability to tap new external sources of funds. By the early 1960s, Brazil was no longer considered a good credit risk. The big difference with the contemporary period was that in the 1960s, international capital markets remained liquid.[7] In the 1980s, Brazil's huge international debt was a significant contributor to a *systemwide* international financial crisis. No amount of policy reform in Brazil in the 1980s was likely to lead to renewed lending until the international crisis was resolved.

Both periods were also characterized by an inflated currency. In the early 1960s inflation was running at close to 100 percent annually (Skidmore 1967). Inflation in contemporary Brazil increased rapidly in the early 1990s, topping out at a whopping 900 percent annually in 1994 (McQuerry 2001). In sum, economic indicators in the postwar period signaled unsustainable policies, but were not indicative of imminent collapse. By the early 1990s, however, trends indicated the very real possibility of hyperinflation and complete exclusion from any new international finance or investment.

Voter Demands and the Price of Elections in Brazil

I turn now to the demand side of the equation in Brazil: voter demands and the price of elections. There are two important mechanisms that raise the

---

7. Indeed, after the Brazilian military reined in inflation and improved the balance of payments by the late 1960s, international capital returned to Brazil in force.

reservation price of an election. First, structural change can reduce voters' dependence on clientelist exchange, which will lead them to raise their reservation price. Second, the size of the electorate in a given district can increase, thus requiring that more votes be bought in order to win in that district. I argue that both these factors have increased the price of elections in contemporary Brazil.

One implication of the voter's dilemma is that simple measures of standards of living are inaccurate as indicators of when voters will find it possible to reject clientelism. Similarly, indicators based on the size of the private economy can lead to serious overestimations of the availability of jobs beyond clientelist manipulation, because access to jobs in the private economy, just as with jobs in the government bureaucracy and in state-owned enterprise, can be linked to clientelist exchange.[8] All this implies that measures of macro variables such as economic development, as proxies for voters' ability to forgo clientelist goods, can be highly misleading. We need a measure of voters' sources of income that are immune from clientelist manipulation. As a lower threshold, we can measure the stock of private assets.[9] The stock of private assets in home ownership per capita as well as all private assets per capita rose 450 percent in Brazil between 1970 and 1994 (Instituto Brasileiro de Geografia e Estatístico [IBGE] 2003).[10]

Turning to the size of the electorate, two factors were at work across the two periods: population growth and expansion of the franchise. Brazil's population more than doubled over the period between the two democratic regimes, increasing from roughly 70 million in the early 1960s to the very high absolute figure of more than 160 million by the mid-1990s, to make Brazil the fifth-largest democracy in the world. In addition, universal adult suffrage was instituted in 1988, which led to a large, one-time jump in the

---

8. For more discussion and for evidence on this point, see Chapter 6.

9. As was discussed in the preceding chapter, politicians control property rights and can manipulate them to alter the value of private assets. Putin's takeover of the oil, gas, and banking industries in Russia following trumped-up charges of tax evasion, and Chávez's essentially state-sponsored land invasions, are important cases in point. But a key constraint on such manipulation is the basis of elites' income. When the income of elites is built upon private-property foundations, as in Latin America, this will place certain important limits on the ability of politicians to manipulate their value. This is just one more caution to underscore that structural conditions cannot be linked to voting choices and electoral outcomes in any straightforward systematic way to determine whether clientelist or policy-based voting will dominate.

10. Ideally, we would also want to compare the increase in GDP per capita and increase in stock of private assets from 1945 to 1964 to assess the two measures of voters' ability to reject clientelism at the end of the earlier period. Unfortunately, data on the stock of private assets was not collected before 1970.

size of the electorate in all districts, clearly raising reservation prices.[11] A onetime dramatic increase in the electorate is much more significant than would be several gradual extensions of the franchise over time, which would give politicians time to adjust resources to rising demands. A large, onetime increase means a sharp, almost instantaneous rise in election prices.

In sum, there were three very dramatic structural changes that took place between the mid-1960s and the mid-1990s in Brazil. First, internal and external government debt reached its limits, in the former case because hyperinflation was a serious threat and, in the latter, because Brazil's huge debt was tied to an international financial crisis. Second, the size of the electorate dramatically and instantaneously increased as a result of the enfranchisement of people who were illiterate. And finally, the value of privately held assets more than quadrupled. Each of these macrolevel changes suggests a decrease in supply and an increase in demand in Brazil. This may be the unnoticed (and unintended) success of import substitution industrialization (ISI) in Brazil and other large Latin American countries. Although ISI failed in terms of its economic development goals, the policies created enough private ownership immune from clientelist manipulation that voter demands outran available resources, and clientelist politics on a national scale collapsed.

Given that these changes took place under an authoritarian military regime in Brazil, and the importance of O'Donnell's arguments about the links between bureaucratic authoritarianism and development in Latin America, a word about how my argument relates to O'Donnell's is necessary. In some important ways, my argument dovetails with O'Donnell's: we both view structural constraints as critical independent variables that create a political dynamic that excludes certain policy choices and we agree on the policy choices excluded—policies that drive welfare-enhancing entrepreneurship.[12] We differ, however, in the source and nature of those structural constraints.

---

11. Some readers might object that enfranchising illiterate voters, who are also typically low-income voters, might reduce election prices by allowing politicians to substitute cheap votes for more expensive ones. As I will discuss more fully in Chapter 6, however, political mobilization in clientelistic regimes does not follow a simple race to the bottom to find the cheapest votes. A clientelistic equilibrium means that those who are not tied into clientelistic networks are excluded from government benefits, and no group that can resist such an exclusion, through force or otherwise, will allow themselves to be excluded. In the clientelist equilibrium, political mobilization follows a top-down logic, not a logic of buying the cheapest coalition available on the basis of vote prices.

12. O'Donnell often makes reference to the Argentine political authorities' inability to force Pampan producers to become more efficient. In particular, see O'Donnell 1988.

O'Donnell's early work on development is rooted in Marxism and dependency theory, and his understanding of the structural constraints in Latin America was driven by all the supposed limitations that accompany late dependent capitalist development. The logic linking policy to the detrimental or at least inefficient development policies was not always clearly elaborated in these arguments, and some lost credence as the East Asian newly industrializing countries of South Korea and Taiwan succeeded with rapid ascension in the international division of labor and made great strides in poverty reduction and more equitable distribution of income throughout the 1970s.

In my argument, the structural constraint is driven by a problem of collective choice. The structural conditions create a political dynamic that results in clientelism as the winning national electoral strategy. In comparison to what is set forth in O'Donnell's argument, the logic of the voter's dilemma has the advantage of linking politics directly to the *specific* policy choices that were made (see Chapter 6) and it can also explain why apparently disadvantageous bargains with multinational corporations (MNCs) redounded to politicians' advantage.[13] In addition, unlike O'Donnell's approach, my argument can explain cases such as India, which had all the characteristic distortions of the typical ISI program, but barred foreign direct investment. Unlike O'Donnell's arguments, and others based on dependency, my theory can explain how countries such as Brazil are now adopting effective structural reforms.

It is worth emphasizing that all this discussion applies to countries in which structural conditions favor the clientelistic equilibrium. Once structural conditions shift to favor the policy-based equilibrium, adjustment to a crisis does not involve exclusion, but rather a reduction in some of a range of universally available programs. Thus, for example, balancing the budget to reduce inflation in a policy-based system means reducing or even eliminating spending on some programs, but after the cuts, all citizens continue to have access to all the remaining programs. In a clientelistic system, in contrast, balancing the budget to reduce inflation means politicians must cut programs that were targeted directly on individuals as their source of government benefits. Traditionally in Latin America, organized union workers who lose their jobs and their signed documents from the union lose not only their jobs, but typically also access to subsidized housing, exclusionary

---

13. For more elaboration on this latter point, see Lyne and Hawn 2007.

clubs, health care, subsidized loans, subsidized food, and retirement benefits, among other advantages.[14]

Structural Variables in Venezuela

As a result of structural conditions in Venezuela, which has one of the largest oil deposits in the world and a relatively small population, politicians have had an unusually robust resource base for building clientelist networks. As a rough benchmark from which to evaluate the value of oil revenues in pre-Chávez Venezuela, from 1958 to 1988, Venezuela earned roughly $300 billion in oil revenues, some fifteen to twenty times the cost of the Marshall Plan. In other words, a country with a population roughly half the size of Spain's enjoyed revenues equivalent to fifteen times what it took to rebuild Europe after the war. Oil revenue per capita was an astounding $1,631 in 1981, and it remained consequential at $478 in 1991 (Kornblith 1995). Indeed, Crisp (1998) argues that the Venezuelan government had more money to invest than the economy could productively absorb, and his study of the decentralized public administration shows that each of the three peak associations of labor, business, and agriculture had a development bank, credit agencies, or both, designed specifically to serve its interests. The sheer volume of the resources available for distribution in pre-Chávez Venezuela and the relatively small and impoverished population strongly suggest that politicians could easily maintain clientelistic offers above reservation prices for a sufficient number of voters such that clientelistic strategies prevailed.

Since his first election in 1998, Chávez has been tireless in employing time-honored strategies to increase resources that are available for building clientelistic networks. At the international level, he has worked to return the Organization of Petroleum Exporting Countries (OPEC) to a policy of raising prices. Whether his efforts in OPEC have had any influence in a context of war in the Middle East is difficult to assess, but regardless of the cause, oil prices have increased eightfold since Chávez came to power ("The Rise of the 'Boligarchs'" 2007). Chávez has assiduously courted new markets in China and new partners in the Middle East and has developed ambitious plans for investment to increase output. Most immediately, he has altered ownership rules in the oil sector, and the government has asserted majority

---

14. For a more comprehensive development of the argument that the requirements of policy adjustment are very distinct in clientelistic and policy-based systems, see Lyne 2006.

control over oil exploration; he has made retroactive changes to tax laws that have resulted in a bill of more than $2 billion for foreign investors; and he has increased royalty payments, in the case of pumping heavy crude, from 1 to 16 percent of earnings (Forero 2007; Romero 2007). Changes to tax and royalty laws have netted Chávez an additional $6 billion since 2004 and Venezuela's income from oil has increased fourfold over Chávez's eight years in power (Forero 2007). Venezuela earned $60.4 billion from oil in 2006 and is projected to earn $45 billion in 2007, which puts yearly oil income per capita back up to stratospheric levels, at about twenty-five hundred dollars (Romero 2007).

Adding to the sheer value of the resources available from the sale of oil, the continued reserves of this commodity place calculations about resource supply on a different plane from that of non-oil-exporting countries. Venezuela possesses the largest conventional oil reserves in the Western hemisphere and has trillions of cubic feet of natural gas. The country's as yet untapped reserves in the Orinoco belt, by some estimates, are greater than those of Saudi Arabia (Lotta 2007). As long as the industrialized economies remain heavily dependent on oil, and Venezuelan supplies are abundant, this resource virtually guarantees a steady flow of foreign exchange. Venezuela certainly accumulated a substantial international debt, as did most developing countries in the 1970s. But that debt is evaluated in the context of continued revenue from oil sales by both international lenders and domestic players. In other words, the classic "foreign exchange bottleneck," which influences availability of imports and ability to repay loans (and thus international lending decisions) is considerably wider in a country such as Venezuela than in non–oil exporters. Venezuelan politicians attempting to augment foreign funds would certainly face more eager lenders, because of the consistent availability of a steady stream of foreign exchange from oil sales. In particular, politicians seeking to gain dominance, with the crumbling of the democratic system in Venezuela, faced a far less critical balance-of-payments problem than did most politicians hit with the debt crisis.

In the case of resources from the domestic economy, trends in inflation also indicate continuing sources of supply. Although Venezuela began to experience nonnegligible rates of inflation in the 1980s, its rates of between 10 and 20 percent annually remained quite moderate by Latin American standards. This is substantially below levels sustained for long periods in other Latin American countries, and far below levels at which hyperinflation becomes a serious threat. Inflation rates have continued between 10 and 20 percent under Chávez since 2000, and although sustained rates at this level create challenges in terms of maintaining the value of clientelistic benefits, such levels are nowhere near an exhaustion of internal resources or the threat of hyperinflation. This would suggest that ingenious politicians such as Chávez, seeking to reorganize clientelism to deal with a resource crisis, still have considerable leeway in further inflating the currency if necessary.

Election prices in Venezuela also did not face the kinds of shocks that buffeted Brazil's new democratic regime. Universal suffrage was instituted with the inauguration of the first, short-lived democratic regime of 1945 and has been a constant since 1958. Thus, the transition to the current Venezuelan regime was not characterized by the kind of demand shock that accompanied the transition in Brazil, with the popular election of a president for the first time in almost forty years and with all adults eligible to participate for the first time in Brazil's history. In contrast, in Venezuela, population pressures on election prices were the result of gradual population increases that winning clientelist politicians had to adjust to on a continual basis to maintain clientelism.

Systems of Vote Monitoring and Benefit Delivery

If clientelists are to make good on their threat to exclude from the political benefits those who do not turn in their vote, then systems of vote monitoring are required. In the previous chapter, a number of implications of clientelist competition for politicians' winning strategies were developed. To fully evaluate systems of vote monitoring, we must also develop a few implications of the clientelist equilibrium for voting behavior. As with politicians' strategies, the best strategies for voters in the clientelistic equilibrium are often counterintuitive and appear dysfunctional from the point of view of a voter in a policy-based system. Perhaps most counterintuitive, but clearly most important, when direct voter-politician links predominate, voters have a very strong positive incentive to join rather than avoid schemes that ensure that their vote will be monitored. Since in a clientelistic system the voter's choice is either to ensure that his or her vote is counted and receive a benefit, or receive nothing, clearly joining an organization that ensures monitoring and benefit delivery is greatly to the voter's advantage. Table 2 in Chapter 1 helps clarify this point. If structural conditions result in most voters facing high risks in rejecting clientelism and the clientelistic equilibrium prevails, then the voter's choice is whether that voter prefers cell IA or cell IB. It seems noncontroversial to assume that the vast majority will prefer cell IA. But to be sure of landing in cell IA, the voter must allow his or her vote to be monitored.[15]

This, in turn, has important implications for the organization of the polling itself. In clientelistic systems it is commonly asserted that the presence of *all* parties in the polling place is indicative of the fact that the voting is fair and free. This arrangement reflects a concern that the incentives for cheating come primarily from one party's stealing votes from another, rather than a concern that the party might use its presence or any information gleaned by its presence in a fashion harmful to its own supporters. In advanced industrial democracies, in contrast, fair and free elections require that parties are barred from the polling place.

This difference in polling procedures between clientelist and policy-based systems is consistent with the incentives of clientelist competition that are developed from the theory of the voter's dilemma. If voters have every incentive to ensure that their vote is monitored, and that their patron (party) wins the most offices, then this polling arrangement is indeed in the voters' interest. First, voters want their party present to monitor their vote, and moreover, they want safeguards ensuring that their party will not be cheated of votes, because this implies that their party receives fewer elected offices and fewer benefits to distribute. In other words, when structural conditions create a clientelistic equilibrium, both patrons (parties) and voters recognize that they mutually benefit from a well-organized and monitored exchange.

The uniformity and efficacy of monitoring schemes will differ depending on the degree of centralization and institutionalization of clientelistic networks. In systems with centralized and institutionalized control of a trumping resource, as in Venezuela, vote monitoring and benefit delivery is also typically highly institutionalized. In pre-Chávez Venezuela, two principal systems for vote monitoring were used nationwide, one more transparently sacrificing the secrecy of the ballot than the other. Since Chávez's ascendance, at least two different systems have been employed, one for highly urbanized and highly populated areas, and a second for rural areas. Chá-

---

15. The immediate response to this logic of monitoring and exchange is often to advocate for the secret ballot as a way to resolve the voter's dilemma. A little reflection reveals that the secret ballot itself is a collective good that is supplied by politicians, and thus its provision falls prey to the same prisoner's dilemma logic. As long as most voters face significant risks in rejecting clientelism, any politician or party that invested resources in providing this collective good would be quickly undercut by those providing clientelistic benefits. Moreover, if technical solutions were possible, we would expect effective democratic accountability to be far more prevalent than is the case.

vez's current program of building territorial community councils (*consejos comunales*) nationwide is a project designed to completely replace the monitoring infrastructure of the previously dominant parties. By eliminating municipalities and states and building clientelist networks that directly link communities of no more than four hundred families to the executive bureaucracy, Chávez aims to construct a single nationwide network of exchange.

Before we examine vote monitoring in pre-Chávez Venezuela, some discussion of party organization is necessary. The two dominant parties, the AD and the COPEI, were organized in a pyramidal structure, bottom to top, beginning with the smallest base committees in each polling circumscription. These base committees fed into larger municipal-level organizations, which in turn fed into district organizations, which in turn made up the regional and then national organizations. At each of these levels, but most important at the base committee level, there was a committee with responsibility for carrying out the party's work in the given area. Embedded in this vertical organization, there were also horizontal organizations of functional groups, such as women, youth, and labor. These parties had extremely high levels of registered members, and by that measure, the AD was the largest political party in the world (Combellas 1985; Coppedge 1994a).

From 1958 to 1968, a very transparent system of vote monitoring was in place. Venezuela used a closed-list proportional-representation rule for legislative elections, and voters cast two votes, one for president and one for all other offices (the single-*tarjeta* vote). Upon entering the polling place, voters were given a large and a small card, one set for each party that was fielding candidates. The large card represented the candidate for president and the small card represented the party slate for all other offices. Voters placed the card of the party they preferred for each office in the ballot box and returned the other cards to the polling monitors. Since all parties had representatives in the polling place, it was quite a simple matter to monitor the vote.

Beginning in 1973, a less transparent system replaced the card scheme. Upon presenting themselves at the polling place, voters were given a *tarjetona*, or a large card or ballot, with a large and a small rectangle with the symbols and colors of each party that was fielding candidates. Voters stamped the rectangles of the presidential candidate and the party slate they wished to support. This system had one other interesting feature, however, in that the ballot had a tab on the corner that was numbered. Upon receipt of the ballot, the tab was torn off, and the party representative at the polls wrote the number on the tab by the voter's name on the voting rolls. At first glance, this system does not appear to sacrifice secrecy, since the tab is torn off before the card is stamped in the polling booth and placed in the ballot box in the polling booth. If the tab was still on the *tarjetona* when the ballots were counted, the ballot was invalidated.[16]

Yet this reasoning holds only in a policy-based system, in which the voter has no direct benefit at stake in voting for one party or another. Under these conditions, effective monitoring would require knowing exactly which party or candidate the voter selected in order to effectively punish defections. But in a well-institutionalized clientelist system in which voters must demonstrate loyalty and adherence to their party or patron in order to receive their direct benefit, they have nothing to gain by switching parties in the polling booth after demonstrating loyalty to a given party. By 1973 in Venezuela, there were only two viable choices (AD and COPEI), and each party had organizations at every level and in every type of civil association, with the largest number of registered members of any party in the world. Under this type of system, it would never make sense for a voter registered with or affiliated with the AD, for example, to vote for the COPEI. If the given voter was not registered with the COPEI, or well known by the local organizers to be a supporter, why would COPEI believe his or her professions of voting support, and provide benefits in return? In other words, unless there was an expectation that one party or another was likely to monopolize resources, an outcome that was institutionally prohibited in the pacted Venezuelan democracy, there would be no reason for a voter to vote for any other party than that to which he or she had demonstrated loyalty through registering with the party, joining a functional group, or simply making his or her support known to local organizers through attendance at party events and other types of activities. In short, in well-institutionalized clientelist systems, direct exchange is not a matter of casually buying votes on a street corner, but is instead conducted by means of enduring relationships that increase the confidence that both sides can and will uphold their end of the bargain.

The requirement that the number on the tab be written by the voter's name on the rolls thus provides the parties' monitors with ample information necessary to exclude those who do not turn in their vote. Voters have nothing to gain by voting for a party other than the one they are registered

---

16. Dr. Ángel Álvarez, interview with the author, July 10, 2007, and Dr. Herbert Koeneke Ramirez, interview with the author, July 9, 2007, both in Caracas.

with, and thus the records of who had voted and who had not were equally as revealing as a system that verified the vote for the "right" party. By numbering the ballots the party could even determine who came in early, and then perhaps were out bringing in more voters, and who only showed up at the end of the day or not at all. Most important, these lists provided very clear evidence of which party members in the base community organizations were doing a good job of bringing in the vote and therefore provided good information about which party activists should be promoted and which areas should be rewarded with benefits.

This characterization of the monitoring system in pre-Chávez Venezuela is supported by other unusual facts about the system. In the pacted Venezuelan democracy, the two dominant parties did not try to win voters away from the other party, and it was extremely rare for voters to switch parties or even vote for any other than the party they initially joined.[17] When voters receive benefits by establishing their allegiance and voting loyally for their party, absent some great upset to the pacted distribution of resources, it would be highly counterproductive for voters to switch parties. It would take time and considerable effort to make their new loyalties credible enough for them to receive benefits from their new party. Again, short of some dramatic change in the rules for dividing offices and benefits, why would voters abandon the party with which they had spent time building their credibility as loyal supporters?

Interestingly, Chávez is now relying on a very similar mechanism to monitor the urban vote. In the most recent presidential elections, computerized voting was used in the urban areas, and voters were required to give their fingerprint in order to vote. International observers discouraged the use of the fingerprint, arguing that it was not necessary in order to prohibit fraud, yet Chávez insisted. As the European Union Election Observation Mission (2006) noted, "Validating and authorizing the citizens' right to vote and guaranteeing the principle of one vote per voter are *redundant functions* of the fingerprint reader system" (emphasis added). The Venezuelan government justified the use of the fingerprint system as a way to prohibit the fraud of voting in more than one jurisdiction, but in most democracies this is easily controlled through voter registration and voter rolls. When any anomaly arises in which a voter does not appear on the rolls, his or her ballot is counted separately and not added to the official total until the anomaly is resolved.

17. Dr. Naudy Suarez, interview with the author, July 5, 2007, and Dr. Ricardo Combellas, interview with the author, July 7, 2007, both in Caracas.

Proceeding from reasoning that is appropriate to policy-based voting, international observers completed extensive analyses of the computer programs to ensure that the fingerprint could not be matched to the specific vote. But when voters are trading their vote directly for a clientelistic good, and there is only one national party with goods to distribute, all the government needs to know is who voted and who did not. The government could match fingerprints to names and residency and, with knowledge of the geographic distribution of Chávez support, could distribute resources accordingly. As the European Union report noted, many voters were suspicious of the fingerprint requirement, and the theory developed here suggests that their suspicions were well founded. In rural areas, the military monitored the vote and, in a fashion akin to that of the old card system, voters did not place their ballots in ballot boxes after marking their choice, but turned them in directly to the military monitors (voters in the town of Carolinas, Venezuela, interviews with Mary Allison Joseph, December 14–17, 2006).

Finally, it has been amply documented that Chávez has used every opportunity to punish anti-Chávez political expression through exclusion from employment. Under the new constitution promulgated under Chávez in 1999, after half the term of a given public officer has elapsed, a recall referendum can be initiated through a petition containing the signatures of at least 20 percent of the registered voters in the district. If a larger number of voters than the total for the winning candidate vote for revocation, as long as at least 25 percent of registered voters participate, then the public officer is considered recalled. Voters were required to provide name, date of birth, signature, and fingerprint on the petitions and a list of those names was widely circulated and even available on the Internet, with government instructions to sack them from their jobs, bar them from any future employment, or both. A similar tactic has been used against employees of the crucial Venezuelan Oil Company (Petróleos de Venezuela [PDVSA]). White-collar workers of the company have been pivotal players in the opposition movement, and a strike at the company in April 2002 was a catalyst that led to a coup and a brief ousting of Chávez. A two-and-a-half-month strike that began in December 2002 led to the firing and blacklisting of twelve thousand white-collar workers who were considered anti-Chávez and who had participated in the strike. White-collar employees have alleged harassment and intimidation, including the monitoring of e-mail and phone calls, and at least in one recently nationalized foreign oil company, engineers deemed anti-Chávez were dismissed with the takeover (Romero 2007).

Currently, Chávez is attempting to completely supplant the clientelist networks and government administration that served the previously dominant parties by promulgating the law of *consejos communales* and mandating the dissolution of all former parties and the registration in only one new party, the PSUV. If Chávez succeeds with these plans, he will have eliminated all vestiges of the infrastructure of the previous regime's clientelist networks.[18]

In postwar Brazil, clientelistic networks and vote monitoring were far more decentralized and heterogeneous. There were many different schemes used by the numerous decentralized networks to monitor the vote, but as in Venezuela, the schemes typically differed depending on the level of urbanization and the occupation of the voter. In terms of monitoring support from industrialists and agroexporters, the available evidence suggests that this was carried out by the Commercial Policy Desk of the Bank of Brazil (CACEX). The director of CACEX had authority over two of the most potent sources of protection and subsidy, the foreign exchange–control system and the market reserve system (total exclusion of foreign goods through program known as similarity analysis). The director of CACEX had de facto ministerial status and was considered extremely powerful. CACEX maintained all the records of what each firm received and also maintained a blacklist that was widely reputed to be used for punishing uncooperative firms (Abranches 1978).

Employers associations for each branch of industry were governed by the same state-corporatist rules as were labor organizations. They were mandatory, hierarchical and mutually exclusive, and their leadership was appointed by the government. As Schmitter notes: "It is important to stress that *peleguismo* is not restricted to workers' associations.[19] It is in the interests of the authorities to have consistent, loyal, and conciliatory leadership in the employers' associations also, although the manipulatory devices used for selecting and keeping employers' leaders in line may be more subtle than those used on workers' representatives" (1971, 129; emphasis in the original). In other words, in clientelistic systems, it is important to organize all types of supporters, not just workers, in a fashion that diminishes incentives for bidding wars, hence the mutually exclusive organizations with government-appointed leadership for both capitalists and workers.

The literature on corporatist labor organization in Latin American has

18. I elaborate on the *consejos comunales* and the PSUV in subsequent chapters.
19. *Peleguismo* was the term used to describe the state-chosen labor leaders who served to bring labor to heel to serve government interests, rather than to provide independent representation of labor.

amply documented that these unions organized the exchange of a job and social security benefits in return for a vote (Malloy 1977, 1979; Erickson 1977; Schmitter 1971). Votes in these firms were delivered in blocks via ex officio voting lists that were prepared by employers.[20] In Brazil, 23 percent of the national vote was delivered through these block lists in 1945 (Souza n.d.). Given that the corporatist organizations that prepared these lists increased roughly threefold from 1940 to 1960, and membership in these organizations quadrupled between 1940 and 1964, this 23 percent figure is certainly the very low end of the percentage of votes that were delivered through this system during the postwar regime (Schmitter 1971, 152–56).

The monographic literature discussing developing countries is replete with descriptions of various schemes for delivering the rural or less affluent vote. In Brazil, there were a variety of schemes, each with a descriptive name. The "ant vote" took its name from the practice in which the ward boss would enter the polling booth first and bring out a blank ballot, and then mark that ballot and give it to the following voter. If the voter brought out another blank ballot (implying that he or she had deposited the ballot marked by the ward boss in the ballot box) that voter would receive his or her clientelistic benefit. The "carbon vote" was named for a scheme in which the voter is given a sheet of paper and a piece of carbon paper of the same size as the ballot. If the voter brings out the sheet of paper with the carbon marks at the appropriate points on the paper, the voter would receive his or her clientelistic benefit. The "stencil vote" was so called as a result of a scheme in which the voter was given a template to place over the ballot and trace the numbers of the appropriate candidates. If the template was returned with marks over the appropriate numbers, the voter would receive his or her direct-exchange benefit (this method was commonly used with illiterate voters). Many countries have used schemes in which the parties are allowed to print their own ballots, with voters picking up their ballot from party headquarters to demonstrate their vote for the given party. Another common scheme involved a system in which the ballot had to be sealed in an official envelope, which the ward boss provided for the voter, who must seal his or her ballot in that envelope and then place it in the

---

20. An example of a published notice communicating to the employers in the pension institute of retail businesspeople the requirement that they register their literate employees through the ex officio system and that they must include information about any employee who had been terminated, and the reason for the termination, can be found in the PSD archives of the Centro de Pesquisa e Documentacao de História (CPDOC) at the Fundacao Getúlio Vargas in Rio de Janeiro (Document PSD 45.06.20/1).

ballot box, returning with an empty official envelope, known in Chile as the "magic envelope," that the ward boss would supply to the following voter (Gil 1966, 224).

Schemes for delivering the vote are not limited to monitoring individual voters. There are also ways to monitor the vote that encourage collective action among the voters themselves to ensure that the vote is delivered to a particular politician. In slums in Brazil, politicians have distributed goods that either can be revoked or that require a second delivery after the election to be of any use. Thus, a politician would arrange to pave a road in a particular slum area, and if the politician did not win in that precinct, he or she would return and dig up the road. Politicians have also distributed pressure cookers, used for preparing the staple black beans, giving out the cookers without their lids; or a politician would give one shoe of a pair of shoes. If the politician won in the local precinct, the lids or the second shoe of the pair would be delivered.

Voting Patterns as Indicators of Clientelistic or Policy-Based Equilibrium

The schemes for monitoring the vote are colorful and ingenious, yet absent concrete data on general voting patterns, they indicate no more than the presence of clientelism in a given system. Positive evidence of some clientelism is not determinative of the equilibrium electoral strategy, and ideally we want unique indicators of one equilibrium strategy or the other. We can approximate such an ideal indicator by examining the mechanics of winning votes. These mechanics are quite distinct depending on whether the dominant strategy is the provision of policy goods or quid pro quo exchange, and should be evident in distinct voting patterns. When politicians win votes based on policy provision, they are winning votes based on something intangible but necessarily common to all members of the party—the party's policy reputation. When politicians win votes based on quid pro quo exchange, they are winning votes based on tangible direct transactions that must be organized and executed on a large scale, but that cannot be common to candidates for the same office. These differences in how votes are won should lead to distinct observable indicators in voting patterns.

Partisan Tides in Brazil

If parties develop national public reputations for procuring certain policy goods, and voters respond to these policy packages in making their voting choice, we should see national trends in voting patterns, a phenomenon that many scholars have labeled "partisan tides." Cox and McCubbins (1993) view partisan tides as forces that affect the electoral fate of all members of the same party, and they argue that the most plausible explanation for their existence is a party reputation of support for certain policy positions that all members of the party share. When voters take cues from parties' national issue positions and policy legislation, we would expect to see partisan tides as all members of the same party are helped by a reputation for good results, or hurt by a reputation for bad results.

This argument holds even in the case in which the ballot allows voters to choose between individual members of the same party. As Kitschelt puts it, "The personal vote is the effect of a candidate's personal initiatives on his or her electoral success, *net of aggregate partisan trends* that affect partisans as members of their parties" (2000, 852; emphasis added). If there is a systematic relationship between parties' policy reputation and voters' choices in Brazil, for example, the success of Getúlio Vargas's and Juscelino Kubitschek's import substitution industrialization programs in the 1950s, the abject failure of José Sarney's Cruzado stabilization program in 1986, and the success of Cardoso's Real stabilization program in 1994 are all policies likely to generate partisan tides.

The absence of partisan tides over more than a decade is a reliable indicator of clientelist politics. If voters are exercising policy-based voting, partisan tides should be in evidence over time. The same is not true, however, for the presence of partisan tides. Most generally, partisan tides should be present in any system in which the party is the vehicle for delivering across districts. But this could be delivery of national collective goods policies that were advertised in the platform and in elections, or it could be the delivery of quid pro quo goods. The party is the delivery vehicle by definition in policy-based systems, since the party is the carrier of the policy reputation. An electoral theory of clientelism, however, suggests that partisan tides would also be in evidence in systems in which parties are the primary vehicle for delivering clientelist goods.

The new institutionalists' distinction between candidate-centered and party-centered systems provides the key to sorting out our expectations for partisan tides in clientelist regimes. If control of a trumping resource is highly centralized, and parties are the key vehicles for competing to control the trumping resource (party-centered electoral law), then we should see partisan tides even in clientelist systems. The analogue to the success or failure of the party's policy program in the clientelist case is events that favor or disfavor a given party's ability to gain control of the trumping resource. National events that clearly enhance or diminish a given party's likelihood of winning the key offices should drive partisan tides, as voters across all districts surmise that the given party will win (lose) and opt for that (another) party. The damaging split in the AD in 1968, or the well-developed reputation for delivering enjoyed by the AD candidate Carlos Andrés Perez when he ran for his second term as president in Venezuela in 1989, provide good examples.[21]

Candidate-centered clientelist systems, by contrast, are unlikely to exhibit partisan tides. In these systems, the individual candidate is the agent responsible for and who takes credit for delivering.[22] The electoral fate of each member is driven by his or her individual ability to amass resources and deploy them efficiently in buying votes. While a deputy from party A in district X may have done a good job of gaining access to new subsidized loans distributed at the subnational level, for example, a deputy from the same party competing in district Y may not have done so well. Recalling that there is no common party policy reputation, voters' response to candidates from the same party running in different districts will vary according to factors that vary only with the individual deputy rather than with the party. These evidentiary points are outlined in Table 4.

In sum, the *absence* of partisan tides provides strong evidence that parties are not providing policy goods. The presence of partisan tides indicates either policy reputations or party-dominated centralized resource control. In clientelist systems, the more individualized the access to resources and the

Table 4 Clientelistic exchange and partisan tides

No Partisan Tides	Unambiguous evidence for clientelistic exchange
Partisan Tides	Observationally equivalent between (1) centrally coordinated clientelism and (2) policy-based politics

21. Carlos Andrés Perez was president during the oil-boom years from 1974 to 1979, and was by far the most prolific creator of new government programs of any president in Venezuela's democratic history.

22. In policy-based systems, individual politicians can claim credit for delivering classic pork. But as the literature has shown, individual politicians cannot credibly claim credit for providing collective policy goods; only a party can credibly claim the ability to pass policy legislation and build a legislative record that can inform a policy reputation (see Fiorina and Noll 1979; Arnold 1990; and Cox and McCubbins 1993).

more candidate-centered the electoral law, the less likely we are to see partisan tides.

To examine whether partisan tides were present in the two periods in Brazil, I investigated the determinants of party vote share.[23] For each party, I regressed vote share at time t-1 ($Vote_{t-1}$) and the vote swing between t-1 and t ($Vote\ Swing$) on the vote share at time t.[24] The vote swing variable is designed to capture the effect of partisan tides and is calculated on the basis of the change in the party's fortunes across the two elections as seen in all districts *except* the one in which the voter share is observed. Thus, the vote swing value for the given observation of vote share is a composite measure of the swing for that party *in all other districts*. It is constructed by calculating the difference in the percentage of the vote between the two elections for the given party in all other districts and averaging those differences across all districts. If the average of the vote swing between t-1 and t *for all the other districts* is a significant determinant of the vote in the given district at time t, this indicates that partisan tides are present. The equation is of the following form: $Vote_{t,d} = \beta + \beta\ Vote_{t-1,d} + \beta_2\ (Vote\ Swing)$.

The data included all districts in all elections for which the percentage of the party vote was available. In the earlier period, only the three largest parties, the Social Democratic Party (Partido Social Democrático [PSD]), National Democratic Union (Uniao Democrático Nacional [UDN]), and Brazilian Labor Party (Partido Trabalhista Brasileiro [PTB]), reported enough data for meaningful estimation. In the later period, I examined the three largest parties on the right and in the center, the Liberal Front Party (Partido do Frente Liberal [PFL]), Brazilian Social Democracy Party (Partido Social Democrático Brasiliero [PSDB]), and Brazilian Democratic Movement (Party Partido do Moviemento Democrático Brasileiro [PMDB]), and the two largest parties on the left, the PT and the Democratic Labor Party (Partido Democrático Trabalhista [PDT]). There were four elections in the postwar period (1946–50, 1950–54, 1954–58, 1958–62) and five in the current period (1986–90, 1990–94, 1994–98, 1998–2002). There were twenty-seven states (districts) in the later period. There were twenty-one districts in the earlier period, but data is not available for all parties in all districts for all

---

23. This procedure for measuring partisan tides follows Cox and McCubbins (1993, 112–17), with adjustments for multimember districts and pooling in Brazil.

24. Brazil uses proportional representation in multimember districts, with the federal state as the district. The use of electoral coalitions and the pooling of votes among parties within the coalition to determine seat allocation means that seats won by a given party are not necessarily proportional to votes won. I thus set up the regression to evaluate the determinants of party vote share rather than seat share.

elections, because of the type of data reporting used with electoral coalitions. In some districts in which a party participated in an electoral coalition, data on percentage of the vote for the individual parties participating in the coalition was not reported. This lack of data no doubt resulted in part from the fact that candidates running on a coalition were not required to declare a party affiliation until *after* the election. Thus, the data are seriously incomplete, but the use of this system is also prima facie evidence that a significant number of politicians did not feel the need of a party label to convey information to voters in the earlier period. The result is that nineteen of the twenty-one states are included in the PSD data, and fifteen of the twenty-one are included in the UDN and PTB data.

I estimated four different pooled models that included all observations across both periods. I added a control for the current period (1990–2006) (*Current Period*) and interacted this variable with vote swing (*Vote Swing X Current Period*) to separate out the vote swing effects from each period. I included controls for party and election, and I clustered by district to control for possible nonindependence of observations over time within the same district (Table 5).

The results confirm no partisan tide in the earlier period, and the presence of partisan tides in the current period: *Vote Swing* is not significant, and *Vote Swing x Current Period* is significant at the .05 level. Since a number of scholars argue that the PT is the only policy-based party in Brazil, and that voters pay attention to party policy positions only in the more developed states, I also estimated the pooled model controlling for the PT's influence on the vote swing (Model 2), and then with all parties but without Rio de

Table 5 Party vote share at time t, pooled model, Federal Chamber of Deputies, Brazil, 1945–1964, 1990–2006

	Model 1	Model 2	Model 3	Model 4
$Vote_{t-1}$	.5789***	.5786***	.5646***	.5651***
	(.0423)	(.0424)	(.0454)	(.0463)
Vote Swing	.0600	.0600	-.0224	-.0636
	(.1656)	(.1658)	(.1883)	(.2117)
Vote Swing x Current Period	.5178*	.5210*	.5778*	.6162*
	(.1903)	(.1952)	(.2147)	(.2387)
Current Period	7.547***	7.557***	7.836***	7.943***
	(1.192)	(1.194)	(1.253)	(1.287)
Constant	.1366	.1367	.1485	.1474
N	722	722	658	624
% Predicted Correctly	62.5	62.5	61.6	60.8

*p<.05, **p<.01, ***p<.001

Janeiro and Sao Paulo (Model 3), then without Rio de Janeiro, Sao Paulo, and Minas Gerais (Model 4). The results were robust to all these model specifications: *Vote Swing* remained insignificant, and *Vote Swing x Current Period* remained significant at the .05 level, indicating that the difference across periods is a national, cross-party phenomenon.

To what extent can we interpret these findings as indicators of the predominance of clientelist or policy-based voting? We can say unequivocally that in the earlier period, with two decades of competition, parties were not attracting voters by means of national party reputations for policy goods. We can also say that in the current period, parties exhibit partisan tides. Could this simply indicate a new reorganized and centralized clientelism? There are a number of reasons to doubt this conclusion. First, as discussed above, Brazil is a candidate-centered system and, second, considerable fiscal decentralization took place in 1988, with the federal percentage of revenue decreasing from 59.8 to 47.1 percent and state revenue increasing from 36.9 to 49.4 percent (Garman, Haggard, and Willis 2001). Thus, rank-and-file members have the potential to tap into quite substantial quantities of resources at the subnational level, hindering any effort to develop a coordinated set of quid pro quo offers across the party. The conclusion that these partisan tides stem from party-coordinated clientelism would imply that parties managed to control and coordinate resource distribution across two federal levels and twenty-seven districts. This seems highly unlikely. To further buttress these findings, I next develop an alternative indirect measure of the predominance of clientelist or policy-based voting.

Concentration or Dispersion in Voting Patterns in Brazil

The measure developed in the previous section relied on the fact that when politicians win votes through policy programs, partisan tides will be in evidence in voting. While the absence of partisan tides is a strong indicator of clientelism, the presence of partisan tides is not unique to policy-based systems. This section provides an additional indicator that will trend unambiguously downward if there is a general shift from clientelist to policy-based voting. It relies on the fact that in clientelist systems, the quid pro quo exchange must be organized and executed on a large scale.

Exchanges that require direct distribution of benefits and monitoring can be carried out most efficiently in multimember districts by carving up the district into smaller discrete units or blocs and delegating the delivery and monitoring to brokers. Organizing to win most of the votes in a few blocs within the district rather than a few votes across many blocs, will minimize the physical and knowledge resources required per vote delivered. In other words, the competitors most likely to prevail in clientelist systems using multimember districts will be those who discern the basis on which the district can be carved up in order to deliver votes efficiently as a unit.[25] The vote distributions of winning politicians, in turn, will be constructed of concentrated blocs of votes.

In contrast, when votes are won on the basis of policy programs, we should not expect such a "carving up" of the district and we should not expect candidates' vote distribution to reflect such bloc delivery. When votes are won on the basis of policy goods, leading candidates' votes will be more evenly distributed across the district's units or blocs. Here there is no requirement for monitoring and exchange, and all else being equal, we would expect that policy preferences will be evenly distributed across the units or blocs that make up the district. Thus, as voters shift from clientelist to policy voting, we should see a "deconcentration" of vote distribution across the district, as politicians use policy commitments to appeal to all those with similar policy preferences across the district. The analysis requires knowledge of the unit of delivery, and this may not always be territorial. It could also be an occupational or functional unit, such as a corporatist-interest organization. But all clientelist systems should exhibit this carving up of the district on some dimension that minimizes the costs to monitoring votes and delivering quid pro quo goods.

If a polity employs highly candidate-centered electoral rules, which encourage personal reputations, as in Brazil, some geographic concentration of votes will certainly remain, even after a shift to policy-based voting. But once the shift to policy voting takes place, voters' choices are made up of some *combination* of emphasis on national policy and locally targeted nonexcludable goods, and thus the policy-based component of the vote should lead to a "deconcentration" of the vote distribution. Moreover, we can supplement the data on deputies who are competing in territorial districts with data on presidential candidates. Deconcentration of presidential-vote distribution will not be contaminated by any need to build a geographically specific personal reputation after a shift to policy-based voting, as is the case with individual deputies in candidate-centered systems. Thus, if both congressional- and presidential-vote distributions show a deconcentration of vote distributions across the same elections, this provides stronger evidence

---

25. As I will discuss below, in Brazil this was the municipality.

for a shift from clientelist voting and helps control for the confounding factor of personalist voting based on locally targeted collective goods.

Considerable monographic work indicates that in Brazil the unit of delivery of the vote was the municipality (Nunes Leal 1977; Bezerra 1999; Ames 1994). Building on the pioneering work of Ames (2001), I use a measure of dominance across municipalities as an indicator of the kind of vote that is being cast in the two periods in Brazil. A candidate's dominance score in each municipality (the unit of delivery) is simply the percentage of the total *municipal* vote received by the given candidate. A *district-level* composite dominance score across all municipalities can be constructed by calculating a weighted average of these individual municipal dominance scores. The municipal dominance scores are weighted by the contribution of that municipality to the deputy's overall vote in the district (votes candidate received in that municipality divided by total votes candidate received across all municipalities in the district). Candidates for federal deputy compete across all municipalities within the district of the federal state. Presidential candidates compete across all municipalities nationwide. If a candidate receives 100 percent of the votes from each of the municipalities in which he or she gains votes, that candidate's dominance score would be 1. If he or she receives only one vote in each municipality in which he or she wins votes, then the candidate's dominance score is at minimum and approaches 0.

Ideally, one should control for socioeconomic factors that may render voters' policy preferences highly homogenous across the delivery unit (municipality in the case of Brazil). If the units are highly homogenous in preferences, then candidates whose policy positions are closest to the unit mode will exhibit high dominance despite the fact that the link between voters and their representative is indirect. But if we assume that such contamination of the data is random across time, candidates, and units, then a comparison of simple dominance scores across elections should give a reasonable, albeit crude, measure of any trends in clientelist or policy-based voting.[26]

26. Moreover, coding and interpreting such controls is so fraught with difficulty that an attempt to control for contamination would yield very little payoff at a very high cost in data collection and analysis. Consider only two of the most basic dimensions along which one might classify municipalities: industry concentration and income level. Is a municipality that is heavily dependent on a single industry, but with considerable variation in income levels, likely to exhibit homogenous preferences? Or is a municipality that is home to a wide variety of occupations, but primarily of the same class, more likely to exhibit homogenous preferences? What variables might qualify even this very simple attempt to draw the relationship? Would a municipality with only one industry but employment concentrated in the tertiary sector differ in its homogeneity of preferences from one with most employment in manufacturing? In other words, any codification of the relationship between demographic characteristics and homogeneity of preferences is likely to be highly dubious conceptually, and empirical

In general, we should see higher dominance scores for winning candidates when clientelist voting predominates in comparison with a system in which voters opt for policy-based voting. The two types of systems should also differ in how dominance scores of winning candidates compare with those of losing candidates. In a clientelist equilibrium, the factor that will differentiate winning and losing candidates will be overall vote totals, not level of dominance. Winning candidates will be those who are able to string together enough dominated municipalities such that their totals exceed the electoral threshold. Losing candidates will have similar dominance scores across individual municipalities, but will dominate fewer municipalities overall, giving them smaller overall vote totals.[27] If policy-based voting predominates, winning candidates will be those who enjoy widespread support and thus may take a large percentage of the vote in many municipalities, particularly if they take a large percentage of the overall vote. Losing candidates, however, do not enjoy widespread support, and thus we would expect that they would gain a few votes in each municipality, but dominate few municipalities.

The data on presidential candidates for both periods is displayed in Table 6. The number in parentheses is the percentage of vote won; the first smaller-type number gives the raw dominance score. Since there will be a systematic relationship between percentage of the vote won and dominance, the larger-type number, at the bottom of each cell gives the ratio of dominance to percentage of the vote won. This number thus gives a measure of dominance that controls for vote percentage. This is useful for comparing similarly placed candidates across elections.

As the raw dominance scores indicate, in the vast majority of cases, dominance scores are considerably higher in the earlier period than in the later period for similarly placed candidates. In the cases in which dominance scores are similar for the same-placed candidates across the two periods (first placed: Kubitschek and Quadros versus Cardoso 1 and 2; third placed: Fiuza and Barros versus Garotinho; fourth placed: Salgado versus Brizola

---

analysis would require enormous amounts of data and sophisticated analysis of the interaction of large numbers of variables.

27. The argument applies most forcefully to presidential candidates. In the case of legislative candidates, this trend is attenuated when votes are pooled across parties or coalitions and it is possible to nominate more candidates than seats available. In this case, if parties lack sufficient candidates with well-established quid pro quo networks, they have an incentive to nominate anyone who will win votes, regardless of whether they have efficient delivery networks in place. Since these attenuating characteristics are present in Brazil, I analyze dominance scores across candidates in the same election only for the presidential elections.

Table 6 Municipal dominance of presidential candidates in Brazil, by election year

	1st Placed	2nd Placed	3rd Placed	4th Placed
1945	(Dutra	Gomes (I)	Fiuza	Telles
(% of vote) →	(52%)	(42%)	(5.3%)	(1.4%)
Dominance →	0.59	0.50	0.24	0.21
Dom/(% of vote) →	1.13	1.19	6.86	15
1955	Kubtischek	Tavora	Barros	Salgado
	(36.2%)	(31.0%)	(24.5%)	(8.6%)
	0.47	0.38	0.38	0.18
	1.30	1.23	1.55	2.09
1960[a]	Quadros	Lott	Barros	
	(48.8%)	(33%)	(18.2%)	
	0.51	0.40	0.26	
	1.05	1.21	1.43	
1994	Cardoso I	Lula	Quercia	Brizola
	(61.1%)	(30.4%)	(4.9%)	(3.6%)
	0.47	0.25	0.06	0.1
	0.77	0.82	1.22	2.78
1998	Cardoso II	4Lula	Gomes (II)	Carneiro
	(55.3%)	(31.0%)	(11.7%)	(2.1%)
	0.47	0.29	0.13	0.02
	0.84	0.93	1.11	0.95
2002 (1st Round)	Lula	Serra	Garotinho	Gomes (II)
	(46.4%)	(23.2%)	(17.9%)	(12.0%)
	0.44	0.26	0.22	0.16
	0.94	1.12	1.23	1.33
2006 (1st Round)	Lula	Alckmin	Heloísa	Buarque
	(48.6%)	(41.6%)	(6.9%)	(2.6%)
	0.52	0.46	0.09	0.03
	1.08	1.10	1.28	1.14

Note: Data disaggregated by municipality was not available for the 1950 and 1989 elections.
[a] Only three candidates ran in 1960.

and Gomez), there is only one case in which the ratio of dominance-to-vote percent is significantly higher in the later period, which is that of Salgado versus Brizola. Brizola, of course, was a clientelist holdover from the previous democratic regime, and it is significant that he won only 3.6 percent of the vote.

Differences in dominance scores between winning and losing candidates in the same presidential elections are also consistent with a shift from clientelist to policy-based voting. In contemporary Brazil, the winner's dominance score is almost twice that of the second-placed candidate, whereas in the postwar period this difference is only about 20 percent, despite the fact that the winner in the current period took a higher percentage of the vote than in the earlier period. Differences between winners and third-placed candidates are even more dramatic, with the exception of Garotinho. In the postwar period the winner's dominance score was roughly double that of the third-placed candidate, whereas in the current period the winner's score is roughly five times that of the third-placed candidate. In the case of Garotinho, as with Brizola, his outlier high dominance score is a result of his well-recognized clientelist networks.

Data on federal deputies show similar trends. In Table 7 I report the very incomplete results from the earlier period. The most complete data came from the 1946 election, in which eleven out of twenty-one states reported data (Alagoas, Bahia, Ceará, Goiás, Mato Grosso, Minas Gerais, Pará, Pernambuco, Rio de Janeiro, Rio Grande do Sul, and Santa Catarina). For 1950, data exist for only three states: Bahia, Pernambuco, and Rio Grande do Sul. The same states reported data in 1954 as those who did in 1950, with the addition of Sergipe. For 1958, data is available from Acre, Bahia, Mato Grosso, Rio Grande do Sul, and Sergipe. Finally, for 1962, we have data from Espírito Santo, Goiás, Mato Grosso, Piauí, Rio Grande do Sul, and Sergipe.

The data from 1946 are by far the most complete and most representative of the country as a whole, with two or more states reporting from four out of the five most important regions of the country, and one state from the fifth, northern region. The levels of dominance in 1946 look very similar to those in 1986. On the basis of these limited data, there appears to be an upward trend in dominance in the postwar period, as average dominance

Table 7 Percentage of deputies with given level of dominance, Federal Chamber of Deputies, Brazil, 1946–1962

Level of Dominance	1946	1950	1954	1958	1962
> .1	80.0	68.0	74.3	72.6	85.7
> .2	45.2	29.3	28.6	42.1	44.0
> .3	25.2	5.3	6.7	11.6	8.8
> .4	10.5	2.6	0	1.1	0
> .5	4.3	0	0	0	2.2
Avg. Dominance	0.223	0.162	0.163	0.173	0.193

Source: Brazilian National Electoral Court Archives, individual state reports.
Note: These data were gathered by the author, with the help of able research assistants in Brazil, by searching the stacks of the Brazilian National Elections Archive for the individual reports sent to the National Election Commission. As discussed in the text, reports for many of the states was unavailable. To my knowledge, this is the only centralized and the most complete database of municipal-level vote distributions for legislative candidates for the period.

scores increase over the last three elections. This is precisely what we would expect with a clientelist equilibrium, as politicians expand and optimize their vote-delivery systems in order to compete more effectively.

Turning to the current period, the evidence presented in Table 8, in contrast, shows a declining trend of dominance in the current period up through 2006, with a small blip in 1998.[28] And although the dominance scores for 1998 show an increase over those of 1994 and 1990, the average level of dominance in 1998 remains lower than in 1986. Overall, there is a clear decline in dominance over time in the current period. In sum, both the cross-sectional data access periods and the longitudinal trends within each period are consistent with a clientelist equilibrium in the postwar regime, giving way to a policy-based equilibrium in the contemporary period.

Equilibrium Indicators in Venezuela

At the microlevel, straightforward yet indirect indicators of the two equilibria are not available in closed-list systems such as Venezuela's. From 1958 to 1993, Venezuelan voters were restricted to a vote only for the party, and thus there are no individual candidate vote distributions. Moreover, since this is clearly a system with centralized party control of a trumping resource,

Table 8 Percentage of deputies with given level of dominance, Federal Chamber of Deputies, Brazil, 1986–2006

Level of Dominance	1986	1990	1994	1998	2002	2006
> .1	63.4	58.2	51.1	69.2	61.8	63.5
> .2	46.4	38.6	16.8	44.2	34.3	27.8
> .3	29.2	23.9	2.9	17.7	9.2	6.2
> .4	15.2	10.5	0.39	4.7	2.3	0.5
> .5	4.7	2.2	0	1.2	0	0
Avg. Dominance	0.229	0.181	0.118	0.185	0.158	0.147

Sources: 1986–90 from Barry Ames; 1994–2006 from official Web site of the Brazilian Electoral Tribunal: http://www.tse.gov.br.
Note: In 1986 and 1990, some states are missing. The calculations of percentages are thus taken on the basis of the total number of deputies for which dominance scores are available, rather than the total number of deputies in the Chamber for that legislature.

28. The drop in 1994 may well reflect the fact that the sitting president was impeached in 1992. This may have pushed dominance scores below normal for the subsequent election. Alternatively, the blip may reflect an unusual increase in 1998 because that election was the first opportunity to reelect the chief executive. In other words, extreme discontinuity or unusual continuity of the chief executive (for this series) could well have introduced noise in the trend.

partisan tides are likely to be present, and thus the partisan tides indicator is ambiguous. Nevertheless, I examined the data and, as I expected, found that both parties exhibited strong partisan tides, as seen in Table 9.

These results suggest that in party-centered systems we need to develop other indicators that can distinguish between direct and indirect links between voters and politicians. In the absence of systematic measures, I argue that two prominent features of the Venezuelan system are strongly indicative of a clientelistic equilibrium. First, the system was governed by a pact that amounted to an a priori emasculation of the electoral connection. Second, the expected result of such a pact was confirmed in Crisp's (2000) study of the decentralized public administration. He finds that voters could not alter either the policies pursued or the relative influence of the groups empowered to distribute 75 percent of government resources by changing their partisan preference in voting.

The Pact of Punto Fijo, which reigned throughout most of the period from 1958 to 1989, was an agreement between the three major parties (AD, COPEI, and Republican Democratic Union [Unión Republicana Democrática (URD)]) to distribute all legislative and executive posts among the largest parties regardless of the electoral results (Coppedge 1994b, 325).[29] Although many would mark the end of power sharing by 1974, when executive cabinets were no longer coalition cabinets, but had reverted to being single-party cabinets (Amorim Neto 1998), this indicates less deviation from power-sharing politics than it might at first appear for a series of important reasons. First, the Venezuelan presidency has very weak legislative powers, with no legislative veto, and cabinet ministers can be censured by a two-thirds vote of the Chamber of Deputies (Shugart and Carey 1992). Second,

Table 9 Determinants of party vote share, Federal Chamber of Deputies, Venezuela, 1958–1988

	AD	COPEI
Vote t-1	.641**	.775**
	(.037)	(.035)
Vote Swing	.765**	.777**
	(.067)	(.052)
Constant	16.54	7.46
N	138	138
% Predicted Correctly	68.2	74.9

*p <.05, **p <.01

29. The URD dropped out in late 1960.

Coppedge (1994b) has argued that when the AD was forced to turn over the presidency it used its majority power in Congress to further restrict the already very weak powers of the president.[30] Third, the executive's power over the public administration had been drastically reduced by the mid-1970s. As Crisp states: "During the democratic era, the positions of the centralized and decentralized public administrations have virtually reversed themselves. In 1960, the central government accounted for 70 percent of government spending and the decentralized public administration for 30 percent, but by 1980 the figures had flip-flopped to 33 percent and 67 percent respectively.... Many of these entities have the ability to borrow money and to make and spend their own revenues" (1998, 13). These spending numbers, coupled with the fact that roughly half these bureaucracies were created by AD and half by COPEI, indicates that power and power sharing in the executive administration was simply shifted to the decentralized administration. For key posts that remained in the direct executive administration, Coppedge (1994b, 326) argues that these continued to be covered by power-sharing agreements. Finally, in Congress, power-sharing agreements continued to be used up through the early 1990s for the key positions controlling the legislative agenda, including president and vice president of both chambers and all committees (Coppedge 1994b, 326).

These facts indicate that changes in the executive cabinet represent milder changes in partisan power than might be inferred from conventional assumptions about budget control and more balanced executive and legislative powers. Thus, there are strong reasons to believe that even after 1974, when explicit power-sharing was abandoned, and up until the disintegration of the party system and convening of a constituent assembly by Chávez, a change in election results had little effect on the distribution of partisan power in government and on authority over resource distribution. This in turn suggests that voters' preferences had little influence on policy direction throughout the democratic period.

Crisp's examination of the decentralized public administration confirms this prediction. In a comprehensive analysis of commissions designed to formulate and implement policy, he found no relationship between the party in power and the policies pursued, nor in the relative position of the

---

30. Coppedge (1994b, 339) details how the AD restricted judicial appointment power and borrowing power, and adopted new rules ensuring more AD representation in the autonomous institutes. These measures both restrict a COPEI president's ability to amass new resources through borrowing as well as ensure AD's continued dominant role in distribution of current resources through the autonomous institutes (see below).

groups with government authority. As he states, "The fact that changes in party do not significantly influence access to government decision making for any particular sector on any type of policy clearly calls into question . . . the impact of elections on policy making" (2000, 116).

Why would voters consent to the vitiation of their most powerful sanctioning tool in this fashion? This is no minor modification of the democratic accountability mechanism—it is a repudiation of it. If voters understood that their best option was a clientelist vote, however, then rules that emasculated the electoral connection, but facilitated the distribution of oil revenue to the populace, were an unmitigated plus. This choice no longer appears counterintuitive if we recognize that voters do not use elections to alter policy direction in clientelist systems—they use them to demand a share of the distribution. Rules that eliminate policy influence do not shortchange voters when they opt for quid pro quo—when structural conditions result in high risks in rejecting clientelism, voters relinquish policy influence themselves. Rules that force elites to distribute resources more broadly across the citizenry, however, as Venezuela's power-sharing agreements did, are in fact a gain for voters in clientelist systems and serve voters' interests well.

At the elite level, one might ask, Why was an agreement to allow all major parties to participate in government seen as crucial to removing the issue of party survival from the electoral process?[31] Why would existing parties fear for their survival even in the context of free and fair elections? And how would simple participation in government that was guaranteed through power-sharing agreements alleviate this fear? Why was it not legitimate to link government participation to the ability to appeal to voters in elections?[32] If Venezuela in 1958 had a system in which structural conditions drove voters to choose clientelist goods, and in which elected officials stood to monopolize a trumping resource, then we can explain these unusual choices for determining which parties would have a hand in governing. The AD was overwhelmingly dominant electorally in 1958 and, as the governing party, would control phenomenal oil revenues. Other elite players understood that this would allow the AD to construct formidable barriers to entry. The result, as discussed in the previous chapter, is that free elections were no guarantee of an opposition party's ability to regain office. In the context

---

31. Levine (1978) explains the need for power-sharing agreements on this basis.
32. As discussed elsewhere, these questions become more crucial as democracy matures and the vulnerable early period has passed.

of clientelist voting and a trumping resource, guarantees of government participation were the only means for guaranteeing future electoral viability.

In conclusion, public opinion in all four cases demonstrated preferences for basic collective goods. Structural trends, vote-monitoring schemes, and two indirect micro measures of voter behavior, however, differentiate contemporary Brazil from the other three cases: while the data from postwar Brazil and both Venezuelan regimes are consistent with the dominance of clientelist voting, the data from contemporary Brazil, particularly in comparison with that of the earlier period, indicates a strong shift to policy-based voting. In the succeeding chapters, I investigate how clientelist versus policy-based voting alters what kinds of party behavior, party and legislative organization, and policy choices are most competitive, and thereby explain why politicians in contemporary Brazil alone have adopted collective goods reforms.

PARTY BEHAVIOR:
POLICY-BASED OR QUID PRO QUO APPEALS TO VOTERS?

When Sartori examined Brazilian party behavior he was so stunned by what he observed that he declared, "Compared to Brazilian parties, the German ones during the Weimar period were 'model parties'" (1994, 113). The literature is replete with scathing indictments of Brazilian party behavior, characterizing parties as undisciplined, feckless, lacking collective identity, and incapable of articulating national policy alternatives (Sartori 1994; Shugart and Carey 1992; Geddes 1994; Geddes and Ribeiro Neto 1992; Mainwaring 1992, 1995, 1999; Mainwaring and Perez-Linán 1997; Ames 1995a, 1995b, 2001; Hagopian 1996; Weyland 1996a). In contrast, the dominant scholarship long viewed Venezuelan parties as strikingly successful and virtually unrivaled in Latin America in terms of their ability to articulate and aggregate mass-based preferences and effectively structure electoral and legislative politics (Levine 1973, 1978; Levine and Kornblith 1995; Martz 1977).

Many features of Brazilian party behavior in the postwar period lend support to the received wisdom: the parties' long-standing low internal unity and inability to articulate clear alternative policy positions contributed to their failure to pass even the most modest reform in the face of the crisis of the early 1960s. Yet Brazilian and Venezuelan parties' distinct responses to the crisis of the 1980s have raised a strong challenge to the conventional view: Brazilian parties have proved capable of an effective policy response, whereas the traditional Venezuelan parties proved hapless. How do we explain these paradoxical results?

In this chapter I argue that we can explain these patterns by developing the differences between effective quid pro quo appeals and effective policy-based appeals. Parties employing policy-based appeals must provide voters with credible evidence of their support for certain policy positions, through published platforms, position taking, voting records, and other party activity. Parties appealing to voters based on quid pro quo, in contrast, must demonstrate access to resources and ability to deliver excludable goods. Very different behavioral imperatives follow from these distinct voter appeals.

The chapter proceeds as follows. First, I examine intraparty unity and interparty difference in legislative voting as well as government-opposition cleavage in cabinet formation to demonstrate that party behavior in postwar Brazil and pre-Chávez Venezuela was inconsistent with making a policy-based appeal. I then flesh out a more general set of expectations for intraparty unity and interparty divisiveness based on whether parties are implementing a quid pro quo or policy-based appeal and whether institutions are candidate or party centered. I show how this more general set of expectations for party behavior can explain the apparent accountability vacuum in the two historical cases. Next, I discuss how Chávez's isolation of the previously dominant political parties in the name of a more participatory democracy is a clever means for substituting his own clientelist networks for those of the AD and COPEI.

Finally, I examine party behavior in contemporary Brazil, and I find that intraparty unity, interparty divisiveness, and government-opposition cleavage have all changed in just the fashion we would expect if voters are now exercising policy-based voting. I also examine party switching in contemporary Brazil and show that the dominant pattern of switching does not diminish the governing coalition's ability to deliver the policy goods promised in the election or the opposition's ability to advertise an alternative. Additionally, I show that the data provide strong evidence that the shift in the type of party appeal in contemporary Brazil was demand driven.

The Party System in Postwar and Contemporary Brazil

A brief introduction to the party system in the two Brazilian cases will inform the more detailed data on behavior presented in the following sections. Brazil adopted a democratic regime in 1945 after fifteen years of authoritarian rule under Vargas. Six main parties emerged in Brazil from 1945 to 1964: three large parties, the UDN, the PSD, and the PTB; and three small parties, the Progressive Social Party (Partido Social Progresista [PSP]), the Christian Democratic Party (Partido Democrata Cristão [PDC]), and the PR.

The PSD was composed of a diverse set of interests that included both regional oligarchies, which were primarily agricultural, and elite urban groups such as industrialists. The PSD was strongest in the state of Minas Gerais and was the overwhelmingly dominant party of the period (Hippólito

1985; Soares, 1973, 67, 70). It held the greatest number of legislative seats; it dominated leadership positions in the legislature and also the cabinet ministries in most governments. Its candidate won the presidency in two out of the four races of the period (Eurico Dutra in 1945 and Kubitschek in 1955).

The UDN had its roots primarily in regional oligarchies in the northeastern states; it represented primarily rural, agricultural interests, but also some middle-class groups (Benevides 1981, 28–32; Soares 1973, 70). It was very strong in the states of Bahia and Minas Gerais. The UDN was the second-largest party, in legislative seats held, for the vast majority of the period, but it never captured the presidency, and it had a much smaller participation in cabinet ministries and in legislative leadership positions than did the PSD.[1] As will be seen below, a systematic analysis of the evidence demonstrates that there was little to differentiate the parties in their alliance patterns and voting behavior. But in its rhetoric, the UDN defended antistatist, pro-international capital positions. It was thus the party most likely to oppose nationalizations and state-led development programs.

The PTB grew out of the groups favored by Vargas's introduction of labor legislation under his authoritarian rule. This legislation applied only to organized urban workers, and thus the PTB's support was initially overwhelmingly urban and working class. The national PTB party was dominated by the faction from the state of Rio Grande do Sul. All its most important politicians were from the state, including Vargas, João Goulart, and Lionel Brizola (Soares 1973, 66). The PTB was the smallest of the big three in 1945, but it grew rapidly, increasing its legislative seats in every election and holding as many seats as the once-dominant PSD by the end of the period.

One of the characteristics of each of the three small parties was that they tended to derive most of their support from one state. The PSP's base of support came predominantly from the middle and working classes in São Paulo. The PR was a local party that had little expression outside the state of Minas Gerais. The PDC derived most of its support from the middle classes in São Paulo and tended to ally with the UDN. Thus, this period was characterized by a multiparty legislature, with the effective number of legislative parties shown in Table 10.

---

1. Some would argue that the UDN won the 1960 presidential elections with the candidate Jânio Quadros. But Quadros was never a UDN politician, and he accepted UDN endorsement with some reservation. He presented himself as an antiparty candidate. In addition, the UDN distanced itself from Quadros after his election.

Table 10 Effective number of parties, Federal Chamber of Deputies, Brazil, 1945–1962

Year	1945	1951	1955	1959	1963
Eff. no. of parties	2.8	4.1	4.6	4.5	4.6

Source: http://www.iuperj.br/Ingles/leex/Brasil/Compet/PARTEFEF.htm.

As can be seen from the table, the effective number of parties almost doubled from 1945 to 1950, and then hovered around 4.5 for the rest of the period. This initial jump reflects the rapid decline of the dominance of the PSD, as seen in Table 11. The parties are arrayed from Left to Right, as major analysts have placed them on the ideological spectrum.[2] In March 1964, this democratic regime was overturned by a military coup, and Brazil did not return to fully democratic rule until 1989, with the first popular election of the president in almost three decades. The party system that took shape in the late 1980s in Brazil had many similarities with the earlier period, as can be seen in Table 12.

It is once again a multiparty regime, with four large parties (the PMDB, PFL, PSDB, and PT) and two smaller parties (the PDT and the PDS/PPR/PPB [Democratic Social Party (Partido Democrático Social)/Republican Progressive Party (Partido Progresista Republicana)/Brazilian Progressive Party (Partido Progresista Brasileiro)]). As they did in the earlier period, many of these parties have their roots in the past. Under military rule, Brazil maintained limited political competition for legislative seats structured by two

Table 11 Seat shares per party, Federal Chamber of Deputies, Brazil, 1946–1963 (%)

Left -- Right					
Year	PTB	PSP	PR	PSD	PDC	UDN
1946	7.7	0.7	2.4	52.8	0.7	26.9
1951	16.8	7.9	5.8	36.8	0.6	26.6
1955	17.2	9.8	5.8	35.0	0.6	22.7
1959	20.2	7.7	5.2	35.3	2.1	21.5
1963	28.4	5.1	1.0	28.8	4.9	22.2

Source: Tribunal Superior Eleitoral 1945, 1950, 1955, 1963, 1966.

2. This placement follows Soares (1973) and Santos (1986). Some disagreement exists about the position of the PR. Mainwaring, for example, places it to the right of the UDN. Where this difference affects the analysis, as in section the section titled "Emergence of Ideological Consistency in Electoral Alliances in Federal Deputy Elections," below, I discuss its ramifications.

Table 12 Seat shares per party, Federal Chamber of Deputies, Brazil, 1991–2007 (%)

	Left					Right
Year	PT	PDT	PSDB	PMDB	PFL	PDS/PPR/PPB
1991	7.0	9.1	7.4	21.5	16.5	8.3
1995	9.5	6.6	12.1	20.8	17.3	10.1
1999	11.3	4.9	19.3	16.0	20.7	11.7
2003	17.7	4.1	13.8	14.4	16.3	9.6
2007	16.2	4.7	12.9	17.4	12.7	

Source: 1991, 1995 from Nicolau 1998, 78; 1999–2007 from www.tse.gov.br.

official parties. The National Renewal Alliance Party (Associação Renovadora Nacional [ARENA]) was the party of the ruling military, and the Brazilian Democratic Movement (Movimento Democrático Brasileiro [MDB]) was the official opposition party. The PMDB, a center-left party, grew out of the MDB, and the PDS and the PFL, both rightist parties, grew out of ARENA. The PSDB, a centrist social democratic party, was formed when a group of influential deputies defected from the PMDB in 1989. The PDT is a small leftist party that, until his death in 2004, was led by Leonel Brizola, a figure who gained prominence near the end of the 1945–64 period. The PT is the largest leftist party, with its roots in the new independent labor movement that arose in the closing decade of the dictatorship (Keck 1992). An important difference that has emerged between the two periods is the increase in the average fragmentation of the legislature from approximately four to about seven (Amorim Neto 1998).

Party Behavior in Postwar Brazil:
The Missing Policy Reputation

As a number of scholars have argued, individual legislators cannot make credible claims to voters to provide collective policy goods (Mayhew 1974; Fiorina and Noll 1979; Arnold 1990). Individual legislators organize with like-minded politicians into parties in order to harness sufficient voting power to pass policy legislation. This voting power, coupled with voting patterns that convey information to voters about preferred policies, allows parties to make credible policy-based appeals in elections. Consistent voting to support legislation consonant with the policy program, and to oppose legislation that would damage such a program, generates a party reputation that informs voters about party positions (Cox and McCubbins 1993; Snyder and Ting 2002). When two or more such parties compete for elective office, elections offer voters alternative visions for national policy.

In multiparty presidential regimes such as Brazil's, it is rare for a single party to win a majority of seats in the legislature. Parties thus often create coalitions to form a government and a legislative majority (Amorim Neto 2002; Figueiredo and Limongi 2000; Ames 2001). If parties built their policy reputation by passing legislation to deliver the policy goods they promised, and they needed to ally with other parties to pass such legislation, they would typically be expected to form governing alliances with other parties with relatively similar policy positions and avoid allying with parties espousing contrary positions. Similarly, if parties sought to differentiate themselves from others and claimed responsibility for adopting a clear set of policies, then cabinet composition would be expected to exhibit a clear governing-opposition cleavage.

The same logic applies to patterns of legislative voting. If governing coalitions were formed to implement a policy program, we should expect the members of the coalition to both demonstrate intracoalition unity in voting, as well as intercoalition difference in comparison to the opposition. In this way the parties in the governing and opposition coalitions can point to a clear legislative record that both demonstrates their position and differentiates them from the alternatives (Cooper, Brady, and Hurley 1977; Bartolini 2002).

Absence of Intraparty Unity and Interparty Divisiveness in Legislative Voting

Despite a wealth of important work on Brazilian parties, basic aspects of party behavior in the postwar period remain understudied. Although we have aggregate and yearly data on party unity in legislative voting, which demonstrate that individual parties exhibited low levels of voting unity (Amorim Neto and Santos 2001), we lack information on the unity of key agents presenting legislative programs in such a multiparty regime: government and opposition coalitions. Moreover, we lack systematic data on how well governing and opposition coalitions differentiated themselves from one another in order to present voters with clear alternatives.

Table 13 provides data on intracoalition unity (Rice index) and intercoalition divisiveness (number of party votes and index of likeness) for all roll call votes and for all party votes. I adapt Cooper, Brady, and Hurley (1977) and Cox and McCubbins's (1993) definition of a party vote to multiparty coalitions by defining a coalition vote as a vote in which at least 50 percent of the members of each of the parties in the governing coalition oppose at least 50 percent of the members of each of the parties in the opposition coalition. I define the government coalition as the parties holding cabinet positions, and the opposition coalition is defined as the largest contiguous coalition outside government; the opposition coalition may be to the left or the right of the government coalition.

The Rice index, the standard measure of voting unity, is calculated by taking the absolute value of the difference between percentage of no votes and percentage of yes votes (R = |% of yes votes–% of no votes|). If a party scores 70 on the Rice index, for example, it means that on a roll call, a party majority of 85 percent was pitted against a minority of 15 percent. If on a roll call a party splits exactly in two halves of 50 percent each, its Rice index will be 0. For each roll call, I calculated a weighted average Rice index, using the relative percentage of each party's participation in the coalition as the weight. Each of these individual weighted averages was averaged over all votes that took place during a given cabinet to generate an overall average Rice index.

Examining average Rice indices for both governing and opposition coalitions, it is clear that voting unity was quite low. The average Rice index for the governing coalition exceeded 70 on only 4 percent of all roll calls (cabinets 1, 3 and 11). This means that for 96 percent of roll calls, on average, more than 15 percent of the members of the parties in the governing coalition dissented from the majority. There is only slightly more unity within the opposition coalition, with Rice indices hovering around 65–70, indicating that on average, 15 to 17 percent dissent from the majority.

Turning to intercoalition divisiveness, a crude measure is given by the number of coalition votes as a percentage of all roll calls. As demonstrated in Table 13, lack of intercoalition divisiveness is even more dramatic than the lack of internal unity. The number of coalition votes is extremely low in every cabinet. With an average of 5.1 percent over the period, there was scarcely a coalition vote throughout the entire democratic period. A more fine-grained measure of divisiveness is given by the average index of likeness for all roll calls and for all coalition votes. The index of likeness is a measure of the degree to which members of two groups (in this case, government and opposition coalitions) vote the same way on a bill; the higher the index of likeness, the less difference between the voting records of gov-

Table 13 Roll call voting, Federal Chamber of Deputies, Brazil, 1946–1964

Admin. (Cabinet #)	Date	Gov. Coal.	Opp. Coal.	Tot. Roll Calls	Avg. W.Gov. Rice	Avg. W.Opp. Rice	Avg. Index of Likeness	Cln. Vts. (% of Roll Calls)	Avg. W.Gov Unity	Avg. W.Opp. Unity	Avg. Index of Likeness
Dutra I Gov. Cab. (1)	1/46–9/46	PSD-PTB	PDC-UDN	5	76.2	80.2	25.4	0	0	0	0
Dutra II Gov. Cab. (2)	10/46–4/50	PR-PSD-UDN	PTB-PSP	97	70.2	61.1	69.7	2 (2%)	82.0	65.0	26.5
Dutra III Gov. Cab. (3)	5/50–1/51	PSD-UDN	PTB-PSP-PR	21	82.0	83.9	73.6	0	0	0	0
Vargas I Gov. Cab. (4)	2/51–5/53	PTB-PSP-PSD-UDN	PR	127	66.5	57.4	85.5	2 (1.5%)	56.7	33.9	54.7
Vargas II Gov. Cab. (5)	6/53–8/54	PTB-PSD-UDN	PSP-PR	141	57.5	56.7	88.5	1 (0.7%)	53.2	50.0	48.4
Café Filho Gov. Cab. (6)	9/54–11/55	PTB-PR-PSD-UDN	PSP	132	60.8	64.3	78.3	2 (1.5%)	43.7	33.3	72.9
Ramos Gov. Cab. (7)	12/55–1/56	PTB-PSP-PR-PSD	PDC-UDN	8	56.1	61.4	58.9	3 (38%)	85.1	90.1	12.4
JK Gov. Cab. (8)	2/56–1/61	PTB-PSP-PR-PSD	PDC-UDN	306	71.2	64.3	66.7	26 (8.5%)	74.5	74.0	25.7
Quadros[a] Gov. Cab. (9)	2/61–8/61	PTB-PSP-PR-PSD-UDN	PDC	19	64.8	67.4	83.7	0	0	0	0
Goul. I Gov.Cab. (10)	1/63–6/63	PTB-PSP-PSD	PDC-UDN	5	66.9	63.6	59.3	0	0	0	0
Goul. II + III Gov.Cab. (11)	7/63–12/63	PTB-PSD-PDC	UDN	8	79.1	49.5	72.4	5	83.2	75.0	20.9
Goul. IV	1/64–3/64	PTB-PSD	PDC-UDN	0	0	0	0	0	0	0	0
Total				869	69.4	65.7	68.1	41 (5.1%)	82.1	64.4	30.0

Left -- Right[b]

PTB – PSP – PR – PSD – PDC – UDN

Source: Roll call data provided by Octavio Amorim Neto and Fabiano Santos.

[a] The gap in dates between Quadros and Goulart results from the institution of a parliamentary regime after the resignation of Quadros. I do not include this period in which fifty-six roll calls took place, since it was under a different institutional structure.

[b] This placement follows leading analysts of the period such as Santos (1986) and Soares (1973).

ernment and opposition coalitions.³ If 100 percent of the members of the governing coalition square off against 100 percent of the members of the opposition coalition, the index of likeness is 0. If the two coalitions are each split 50–50, the index of likeness is 100. As can be seen from the table, the average index of likeness over the period is 70. If we take the average Rice index for the governing coalition for the period at roughly 70, an average index of likeness of roughly 70 means that 85 percent of the government deputies were typically joined by 55 percent of opposition deputies on a roll call vote. And although the index of likeness is lower for coalition voting, these were a very small proportion of the total.⁴

If it is assumed that parties are synonymous with making policy-based appeals it is no surprise that Sartori did not see parties in these patterns. This record would have seriously hindered any party's attempt to develop a policy-based appeal anchored in its legislative record. Intraparty unity in voting is consistently low, and the relatively high index of likeness indicates that narrow governing coalitions were typically joined by a large number of opposition deputies on most votes. Any claim to have been responsible for passing a government program that relied on legislative voting records would confront the problem of low voting unity within the governing parties as well as considerable support from the "opposition" parties. In short, postwar legislative voting was not consistent with making policy-based appeals to voters in Brazil.

Grand Coalitions in Cabinets and Governing Alliances

Patterns of governing alliances and the composition of executive cabinets also reveal key information about the extent of parties' policy-based appeals. Table 14 shows the parties that participated in the cabinets of each administration from 1945 to 1964. All three major parties (PSD, UDN, and PTB) participated in the administrations of three of the four elected presidents (Dutra, Vargas, and Goulart) as well as in the unelected government of João Fernandes Campos Café Filho.⁵ Thus, the parties supporting each of these governments spanned the entire ideological spectrum. The only exceptions are the Kubitschek administration, the caretaker government of Nereu

---

3. The index of likeness is obtained by calculating the percentage of members from two separate parties or blocs that vote in the same direction and subtracting the difference from 100.
4. For more details on analysis of roll call votes, see Appendix 1.
5. Café Filho was vice president under Vargas and took office after Vargas's suicide in mid-1954.

Table 14 Party composition of Executive Cabinet, Brazil, 1946–1964

Admin.	Date	Parties in Gov.	Parties in Opp.	% Legis. Seats	Tot. Roll Calls
Dutra I	1/46–9/46	PTB-PSD	PSP, PR, PDC, UDN	60.5	5
Dutra II	10/46–4/50	PR-PSD-UDN	PTB, PSP, PDC	81.0	97
Dutra III	5/50–1/51	PSD-UDN	PTB, PSP, PR, PDC	77.7	21
Vargas I	2/51–5/53	PTB-PSP-PSD-UDN	PR, PDC	88.1	127
Vargas II	6/53–8/54	PTB-PSD-UDN	PSP, PR, PDC	80.2	141
Café Filho	9/54–11/55	PTB-PR-PSD-UDN	PSP, PDC	83.8	132
Ramos	12/55–1/56	PTB-PSP-PR-PSD	PDC, UDN	67.8	8
JK	2/56–1/61	PTB-PSP-PR-PSD	PDC, UDN	67.8	306
Quadros[a]	2/61–8/61	PTB-PSP-PR-PSD-UDN	PDC	89.9	19
Goul. I1	/63–6/63	PTB-PSP-PSD	PR, PDC, UDN	63.4	5
Goul. II + III	7/63–12/63	PTB-PSD-PDC	PSP, PR, UDN	57.8	8
Goul. IV	1/64–3/64	PTB-PSD	PSP, PR, PDC, UDN	57.2	0

Left -- Right
PTB – PSP – PR – PSD – PDC – UDN

Sources: Hippólito 1985, 58, 293–303; Amorim Neto 1998, 2006.
[a] The gap in dates between Quadros and Goulart results from the institution of a parliamentary regime after the resignation of Quadros, which I do not include here.

Ramos, and the Goulart administration. Neither Ramos nor Goulart was elected president.[6] Nereu Ramos's term was less than four months, and Goulart's term lasted only two and one-half years and accounts for only thirteen roll calls.

Thus, the Kubitschek administration was the only popularly elected government that served out a full term and passed significant legislation in which cabinet composition provided a consistent differentiation between governing parties and opposition parties. During Kubitschek's term the UDN did not participate in the cabinet, but this did not translate into systematic opposition on major legislation, as is demonstrated in Table 13, in which the average opposition Rice index is 64.3 and only 8.5 percent of the votes

---

6. Nereu Ramos, the Speaker of the Senate, was installed in the presidency for a short time by the Chamber of Deputies during a short-lived dispute over the inauguration of Juscelino Kubitschek, the winner of the presidential election in 1955. Goulart was vice president under Quadros and took office after the latter resigned after nine months in office in 1961.

are coalition votes. In all other elected presidents' governments, the only parties that did not participate in the cabinet at some point in time were the PSP and the PDC, which together controlled barely more than 10 percent of the seats in the legislature.

The near-universal character of these cabinets is reflected in the proportion of legislative seats they controlled. The average for the period of 72.9 percent of the seats considerably exceeded even the most qualified majorities required to pass special legislation. While ordinary laws could be passed with a simple majority of members present, complementary laws, which are designed to fill in constitutional mandates, required an absolute majority. Finally, constitutional amendments required a three-fifths majority (60 percent). Each president thus had a coalition far larger than even the largest supermajority required for the most specialized legislation.

These patterns imply that cabinet composition provided very little distinction between the parties in government and the parties in opposition.[7] With the entire ideological spectrum included in most cabinets, it was impossible for cabinet participation to provide any information that might differentiate parties' issue positions or support a claim to be uniquely responsible for certain legislation. And except in the case of the Kubitschek administration, no major party could credibly present an alternative to the existing government by consistently refusing to participate in the cabinet. When all parties are in the government and no parties are in the opposition, no party can offer a credible alternative to the current administration.

The Party System in Punto-Fijista and Chávez's Venezuela

To provide context for the analysis that follows, in this section I will briefly review the patterns of party politics in Venezuela since 1958. Venezuelan

---

7. Some observers might argue that the UDN strongly opposed Vargas, and thus an opposition did exist in the period from 1945 to 1964. There can certainly be no doubt that the UDN wanted desperately to remove *the person* of Vargas, as well as his protégé, Goulart, from the political scene. What is significant is that despite this stance, the UDN allied in elections with Vargas's two protégé parties, the PTB and the PSD (see analysis of electoral coalitions below); the UDN participated in Vargas's cabinet in one of the three most important ministries of the period, the Ministry of Agriculture; and most important, majorities of the party consistently voted to pass the most important statist legislation of Vargas's administration. Moreover, all this behavior had the approval of the UDN leadership (Benevides 1981; Hippólito 1985). Thus, although the UDN displayed a strong personalist antipathy to Vargas, what they did not display was any kind of consistent *party* opposition to his government or his policies. What I wish to highlight here is that the UDN's oppositionist behavior was not consistent with developing a policy reputation that would support a policy-based appeal to

democracy began with the short-lived *trienio*, the AD-dominated democratic government that was installed through elections that were initiated with the support of reformist military officers in 1945. Opposition to the AD's attempt to consolidate control during this period led to its overthrow in 1948, and democracy did not return to Venezuela until the overthrow of Perez Jimenez and the formulation of a power-sharing pact between the three major parties, AD, COPEI and URD, known as the Pact of Punto Fijo, in 1958. As discussed in the previous chapter, this pact eviscerated elections as a mechanism for driving government policy, since the pact determined the distribution of political power in the executive cabinet and the legislature irrespective of electoral outcomes. When the URD withdrew from the pact in the early 1960s, the AD and the COPEI came to dominate the presidency and electoral politics in general.

The AD was considered to be a center-leftist party, since it had been organizing rural and urban workers since the early 1940s and had powerful union support. The COPEI was a Christian Democratic party and was more tied to business interests and women's groups, and thus was considered a center-right party (Crisp 2000). As the AD consolidated control over organized unions, in part by forcing out many former leaders of the Communist Party, some unions and other political groups remained outside the pacted democracy and mounted a guerrilla challenge that was defeated by the regime by the mid-1960s. Other currents within AD rejected its decision to support centrist positions in government and split from the party to form several minor leftist parties. These and other groups that were excluded from the AD- and COPEI-dominated governments would later become important supporters of Hugo Chávez. These two dominant parties received the vast majority of votes in presidential and legislative elections until the currency crisis of 1983, at which point the pacted democracy began to unravel.

As the crisis deepened throughout the 1980s, Carlos Andres Perez, a former AD president who had presided over the first oil boom of the 1970s, won a second term with promises to return to the glory days of old. Economic conditions, of course, made this impossible, and when Perez began making headway in implementing a stabilization program in 1992, he was impeached by his own party.[8] Despite numerous official studies of the malaise and many attempts to forge a new pact that could provide a solution to

---

voters. Below I will examine the factional patterns in the UDN in more detail and argue that they were consistent with quid pro quo politics.

8. I will discuss Perez and his strategy in detail in Chapter 6.

Venezuela's crisis, from this point on, the two dominant parties never recovered their footing.

The Caracazo in 1989, with riots that left hundreds dead, and two coup attempts in the early 1990s, one led by Chávez, highlighted the growing crisis and the failure of existing institutions. Abstention rates increased rapidly over the decade of the 1980s, and Rafael Caldera, a founding member of the COPEI, won the presidency in 1993 on an antiparty platform. Caldera proved no more adept than Perez, however, and after several years of dithering, implemented his own stabilization plan, which he later abandoned, leaving Venezuela adrift in the stop-and-go pattern of policy making characteristic of the Southern Cone of the 1960s. In 1998, after a decade and a half of unanswered economic decline, Chávez was elected president with the support of his personalist party vehicle, the Fifth Republic Movement (Movimiento V [Quinta] República [MVR]). Chávez is now calling for the dissolution of all existing parties, including the MVR and others that supported him in his 2006 reelection bid, in order to form one national party, the PSUV.

Party Behavior in Punto-Fijista Venezuela, 1958–1998: The Missing Policy Reputation

Venezuela was long considered a consolidated, stable, mass-based democracy (Levine 1973, 1978; Martz 1966, 1977; Alexander 1964). Early assessments were based primarily on party success in mobilizing mass participation, in maintaining legislative voting unity, and on the regular alternation of the major parties in the presidency. New institutionalists, with some caveats, also evaluated Venezuelan democracy favorably, on the basis of the fact that Venezuela's electoral law was highly party centered (Shugart and Carey 1992). From these analyses, both process and outcome in Venezuela pointed to parties that were well organized and that operated under rules that facilitated their ability to aggregate and articulate interests and translate them into public policy. Yet if we employ the indicators discussed above, in the case of postwar Brazil, it becomes clear that parties in pre-Chávez Venezuela also exhibited patterns inconsistent with an effective policy-based appeal to voters.

Of the three requisites of an effective a policy-based appeal examined above—distinction between government and opposition in the executive cabinet, differentiation across parties in legislative voting, and unity within parties in legislative voting—Venezuelan parties exhibited regular patterns consistent with policy-based appeals only on this last measure. High intraparty unity in legislative voting, however, is consistent with both a clientelist and a policy-based strategy (Kitschelt 2000).

Turning first to the executive cabinet, the data on cabinet composition are provided in Table 15. As can be seen from the table, Venezuela was governed by coalition cabinets, which were a result of the Pact of Punto Fijo, for most of the period 1959–70. The table also shows that these coalition cabinets were supported by legislative majorities far greater than a minimum winning coalition. Clearly, coalition cabinets that span most of the party spectrum make it difficult for voters to discern issue positions and assign political responsibility. If all parties are in the cabinet, what differentiates their positions? If all parties are in the cabinet, who should voters turn to if they dislike government policy?[9]

Table 15 Party composition of Executive Cabinet, Venezuela, 1959–1998

Admin.	Date	Parties in Gov.	Parties in Opp.	% Legis. Seats
Betancourt I	2/59–11/60	AD-COPEI-URD	none	94.7
Betancourt II	11/60–3/64	AD-COPEI	URD	69.2
Leoni I	3/64–11/64	AD	COPEI, URD	37.1
Leoni II	11/64–4/68	AD-URD-FND[a]	COPEI	65.7
Leoni III	4/68–3/69	AD	COPEI, URD	37.1
Caldera 1st I	3/69–5/70	COPEI-MEP-URD[b]	AD	47.2
Caldera 1st II	5/70–3/74	COPEI	AD, URD, MEP	27.6
Perez 1st	3/74–3/79	AD	COPEI, MAS, MEP	51.0
Campíns	3/79–2/84	COPEI	AD, MAS, MEP, URD	42.2
Lusinchi	2/84–2/89	AD	COPEI, MAS	56.5
Perez 2nd I	2/89–3/89	AD	COPEI, MAS-MIR	48.2
Perez 2nd II	3/89–5/93	AD-COPEI	MAS-MIR	81.5
Velásquez	6/93–2/94	AD COPEI, MAS-MIR		48.2
Caldera 2nd I	2/94–2/98	Convergencia-MAS	AD, COPEI	25.0

Sources: Amorim Neto 1998, 2006; Kornblith and Levine 1995.
[a] The FND was largely a personalist vehicle of Arturo Uslar Pietri that joined the URD in 1968.
[b] The MEP party's electoral success declined dramatically after 1968, the year it was formed through a split from the AD.

9. Some readers might object that this discussion fails to recognize a long literature explaining the importance of consensus in Venezuelan politics, beginning with Levine 1978. This scholarship has proved invaluable in our understanding of Venezuelan politics. At the

The practice of forming coalition cabinets ended in 1970. But the degree to which this signaled a transition to a system in which executive cabinet composition provided good information about whom to hold responsible for public policy must be heavily qualified by the importance of the decentralized administration in Venezuela. Karl (1982) reports that by 1975, a whopping 71 percent of public expenditure was under the auspices of the decentralized administration.[10] As noted in Chapter 2, many of these agencies had complete discretion over their own finances, with the power to borrow, as well as to raise and spend their own revenues (Crisp 1998, 2000). Thus, although executive cabinets reverted to single-party cabinets after 1970, almost three-fourths of the budget was no longer under the executive cabinet's direct control. When three-fourths of government spending is not controlled by the executive administration, the party occupying the executive is not really the entity responsible for implementing policy.[11] In this context, attempts to push policy outcomes in a given direction based on a vote for a given party for executive office will miss the mark.

Turning to interparty difference, the nearly unanimous consensus is that Venezuelan parties did not differentiate themselves through their positions on the issues. According to Coppedge, "So far as the public record is concerned, politics has very little to do with Left vs. Right, labor vs. capital, East vs. West, or agriculture vs. industry. . . . They [parties] compete for credit for policies they both supported" (1994a, 43). And Coppedge's thorough analysis of internal party competition removes any doubt that internal party contests were driven by policy differences. Crisp (1998) also argues that there

---

same time, a number of key questions remain. These include why Venezuelan democracy is so dependent on consensus and could not sustain the typical competitive dynamic of electoral politics, which is essential to offering voters clear alternatives; why such consensus decision making, even if important in the founding moment, would be maintained throughout most of the life of the democratic regime rather than be discarded once democracy was firmly established; and why in the face of crisis in the 1980s the major parties attempted to create a new pact, rather than formulate a policy to address the crisis and then use such a policy to champion themselves to the electorate as the party of responsible government (on the repeated attempts to renew the pact, see Navarro 1995). I acknowledge the invaluable literature illuminating the importance of consensus and pacts. In this section I pose the question as one of offering a policy-based appeal in order to build an argument that can begin to address some of these open questions.

10. These numbers differ from Crisp 1998, discussed in Chapter 2, because the numbers from Crisp were for those decentralized agencies governed by public law, whereas Karl's numbers include all the decentralized administration.

11. Indeed, this was one of the principal problems with democratic accountability in Venezuela, highlighted by the government-commissioned study, COPRE, and emphasized by one of the foremost analysts of the country (see Crisp, Levine, and Rey 1995; Crisp 1998, 2000).

was no debate between AD and COPEI over state-led industrialization, one of the two or three most prominent government programs adopted during Venezuela's democratic regime.

This lack of differentiation is reflected in the absence of a public record of party positions on legislative votes. There is no concise public record of how the parties voted, and voting outcomes can be discovered only by reading through the actual debates in the *Diário de debates* of the Chamber of Deputies and examining the party identity of the person who proposes a bill. As will be discussed in detail in Chapter 4, the leadership exercised extreme control over speaking and voting in the legislature. If a deputy was allowed to rise and speak in favor of a bill, it can be assumed that this was approved by the party leadership and that all members of the party of the proposing deputy voted in favor of the bill (Coppedge 1994b, 328). For many bills, however, even this laborious method will not suffice to determine the parties' voting record. If for any reason there is no debate on a bill, there is no way to discern the parties' votes.[12] In sum, there is very little evidence to support the idea that Venezuelan parties have voting records that would allow them to build reputations for supporting any given policy positions.

Turning last to intraparty unity in legislative voting, it is well known that Venezuelan parties exhibited some of the highest levels of unity in the world. Legislative debate was restricted to the designated deputy from each party rising to state the party's position. A single vote against the leadership was punished with summary expulsion from the party (Coppedge 1994a). It is not surprising that this was one of the most important features of Venezuelan party behavior that analysts pointed to in supporting the view that Venezuelan parties fortified democracy and served the Venezuelan citizenry well. Moderately high unity in legislative voting is essential to passing a national policy program. Moreover, in the postwar period, high unity in legislative voting was the norm in most consolidated democracies and was the exception in Latin America. At the same time, more recent scholarship has cast doubt on excessive reliance on intraparty unity as an indicator of policy-based politics: as Kitschelt (2000) has argued, high unity in legislative voting is compatible with both quid pro quo and policy-based appeals to voters.

In conclusion, the evidence is mixed, yet most of it is incompatible with an effective policy-based appeal. Venezuelan parties displayed high internal

---

12. Coppedge states that "congressional votes are almost never counted or recorded" (1994b, 328).

unity in legislative voting, but without clear distinct positions on issues, such unity did little to inform voters about the parties' policy commitments. The lack of clear government-opposition cleavage in the executive in the early years of the regime, the removal of decisions about three-fourths of the government's expenditures from direct control of the cabinet after the demise of power sharing, and the absence of differentiation on issues in the legislature all would make it difficult for voters to know which policy programs they were choosing in opting for one party over the other.

The Missing Policy Reputation Explained as Quid Pro Quo Appeal

If we assume that electoral politics drives parties to offer voters alternative national policy programs, the patterns in Brazil appear unintelligible, and those in Venezuela are highly suspect, at best.[13] If voters include an evaluation of national collective goods policy, or simply overall results, as one component of their vote, then how did these parties compete electorally? Why would voters not flock to a Brazilian party that maintained more internal unity and more coherent alliance patterns, and a Venezuelan party that staked out clear, distinct issue positions and advertised them openly? To put it another way, would the parties that altered their behavior in a fashion that would facilitate voters' ability to hold them accountable for policy not have an important electoral advantage? If policy-based voting predominates, would fierce electoral competition over several decades not have selected for parties that adopted such a strategy in both democracies?

If we recognize a more general logic of voter choice that endogenizes clientelism, we can make sense of these patterns and resolve the conundrum of the missing policy reputation. If structural conditions render clientelism voters' best strategic option, the parties that adopt behaviors that allow them to make effective clientelist appeals will be the winners. And the behaviors supporting effective clientelist appeals are quite distinct from those sustaining effective policy-based appeals. Columns I and II in Table 16 highlight the different behavioral imperatives for intraparty unity and

---

13. It is worth emphasizing that the argument is not that parties provide exclusively national policy goods. Parties that make policy-based appeals typically couple national policy programs with varying levels of pork and rents. The argument is simply that given the record of party behavior in postwar Brazil and in Venezuela, it is difficult to see how they could appeal to voters on the basis of any type of national policy.

Table 16 Clientelistic versus policy-based appeals in legislative voting

	I. Clientelistic Appeal (Conduit to Resources)	II. Policy-Based Appeal (Public Record of Policy Position)
A. Candidate-Centered Institutions	**Decentralized Direct Exchange**	**Policy-Personal Indirect Exchange**
	Observable implications: Lack of intraparty unity and lack of interparty divisiveness	Observable implications: Moderate intraparty unity and moderate interparty divisiveness
	Brazil, 1945–64	United States, Brazil, 1989–2006
B. Party-Centered Institutions	**Centralized Direct Exchange**	**Policy Indirect Exchange**
	Observable implications: High intraparty unity but lack of interparty divisiveness	Observable implications: High intraparty unity and high interparty divisiveness
	Venezuela, 1958–88	United Kingdom, Federal Republic of Germany

interparty difference associated with making clientelistic or policy-based appeals.

The behavioral imperatives common to column II stem from the fact that by definition, national and locally targeted collective goods are not delivered directly to voters, but are available to all members of the relevant political unit. This exchange does not require any direct contact with voters. Thus, voters can be sure of whom to reward for general policies only if the party regularly takes positions in favor of, and votes for, such policies, while other parties regularly oppose them. Moderate intraparty unity in legislative voting is necessary for demonstrating issue position and for passing a legislative program, whereas interparty difference in voting is necessary for claiming responsibility for passing certain types of legislation.

Thus, both intraparty unity and interparty divisiveness are crucial to surmounting the credit-claiming problems associated with the indirect delivery of policy goods. This holds even when executive-legislative relations and electoral law promote candidate-centered voting. Candidate-centered voting will lead individual politicians to buck the party line more often and focus on providing locally targeted goods. This will certainly dilute the party's policy reputation, and this will be exhibited in less intraparty unity and interparty divisiveness. But if politicians are to claim credit for *any* national policy goods, a moderate degree of intraparty unity and interparty divisiveness is necessary, for voters to identify the responsible party. To the degree that executive-legislative relations and electoral law create incentives for voters to cast a party vote, intraparty unity and interparty divisiveness will rise. Under these institutions, party unity is not diluted by legislators seeking to compete with co-partisans by cultivating a personal link to voters.

When voters opt for clientelist goods, the tasks of demonstrating issue position and political responsibility are transformed into those of demonstrating access to political power and resources. Demonstrating this access and obtaining resources for delivering clientelist goods is what makes a quid pro quo appeal credible. This is the root of the absence of interparty difference common to systems falling into column I. There are myriad possible policy packages and ways to pursue them. Interparty difference in voting and position taking informs voters about which package a given party supports. In contrast, in reasonably institutionalized systems, there is only one way to control resources flowing from public authority: by occupying that public office. In the context of the legislature, if regular legislative votes govern decisions about the content of property rights and allocation of government resources, we should expect low interparty divisiveness because legislators or parties will be eager to join any legislative deals that can provide them with access to resources.[14] By the same token, when goods are exchanged directly for votes, there is no need for parties to differentiate themselves in terms of issue position in the legislative arena. When voters cast their vote on the basis of the receipt of a direct benefit, rather than on the basis of issue position, interparty difference becomes superfluous. In clientelist systems, voters are not looking to a party's public policy record to determine their vote, but instead are judging whether the party has the ability to deliver and whether it has done so. Under these conditions, any legislative vote that increases a party's access to resources and ability to deliver is pure electoral gain.

The differences on the intraparty dimension in clientelist systems (cells IA and IB) are driven by how institutional rules determine who "owns" the clientelist networks and maintains the reputation for delivering. With party-centered rules in which voters are allowed only a choice between different

---

14. Rules that take decisions about resource distribution out of elected representatives' hands will alter this prediction.

parties (cell IB), the party will "own" the clientelist networks and will be the agent with the reputation for delivering. Individual legislators become delegates assigned the task of voting in the legislature in order to maintain these networks in the name of the party. Party leaders jealously guard the ownership of the clientelist networks and must ensure that rank-and-file behavior maintains and enhances the party's reputation and ownership. Unpunished votes against the party might damage its reputation for having the ability to work the machinery of government in order to deliver quid pro quo goods. By punishing any transgression with a withdrawal of the party imprimatur, the party minimizes dissent, protects its reputation, and maintains the upper hand in reputation building.

In contrast, in systems in cell IA, institutions permit voters to choose from among politicians of the same party. In these systems, individual politicians "own" their own clientelist networks and maintain the reputation for delivering. Under these conditions, the party's most effective electoral strategy will be to free individual politicians to make their own decisions about legislative voting. An individual member who owns his own clientelist network will have both the incentive and the best information for correctly determining how a particular vote will affect his or her network. Paradoxically, then, the best electoral strategy for solidifying a clientelistic appeal when networks are decentralized results in a pattern of low internal unity that has led many scholars to suggest that these organizations are not parties at all.

The Missing Policy Reputation in Postwar Brazil: Quid Pro Quo Appeals with Decentralized Networks

The data presented in this chapter above, in the section "Party Behavior in Postwar Brazil," clearly demonstrated a lack of intraparty unity and lack of interparty divisiveness in postwar Brazil and place this system squarely in cell IB. In the previous section I developed the argument that with clientelist competition and candidate-centered electoral law, such behavior is in fact electorally competitive. In this section I further buttress the argument that party behavior was driven by what it takes to maintain an effective quid pro quo appeal through a brief examination of the strategic choices of the UDN leadership, as well with an analysis of legislative voting associated with promulgation of the most important program of the period: import substitution industrialization.

The vast majority of the monographic work of the period depicts the UDN as the party most tied to state-level agricultural elites that vehemently opposed the shift in development policy toward industrialization spearheaded by Vargas beginning in 1930 and continued under the new democratic regime instituted in 1945 (Skidmore 1967; Benevides 1981).[15] But rather than present a united front opposed to the dominant policies of the period, the UDN was divided into various rather formal factions. One of the most important of these was known as the Chapa Branca, or the "realist" faction, which was willing to accommodate itself to PSD presidents proceeding rapidly with the adoption of new import substitution programs. The Chapa Branca voted regularly to support Vargas's and Kubitschek's programs, even after the UDN's vigorous efforts to bar Vargas from elections and extreme opposition to both Vargas's and Kubitschek's inauguration. Two members of the UDN, José Américo de Almeida, from Paraíba, and Joao Cleofas, from Pernambuco, even joined Vargas's cabinet, perhaps the ultimate act of sanction of an administration's policies. These voting and governing decisions had the full approval of the party leadership (Benevides 1981).

These choices can be understood as driven by the competitive imperatives in a clientelist system with individualized networks. The UDN's clientelist networks were primarily associated with the exporting and latifundista oligarchies based at the state level that dominated before 1930. Presidents who manipulated exchange rates to transfer income from exporters to industrialists, and nationalized industries and therefore jeopardized relationships with international capital, presented a considerable threat to the continued smooth functioning of these networks. The UDN thus had strong incentives to oppose the inauguration of Vargas and Kubitschek, who made no secret of their plans to continue and expand import substitution industrialization. At the same time, once these presidents took power, the calculus changed. Most of the members of the Chapa Branca came from the Northeast—one of the poorest regions of the country, where most of the landed oligarchies depended on agricultural commodities (sugar and cotton) that were no longer highly competitive. As presidents proceeded to increase the quantity of resources being distributed at the national level, these northeastern legislators were probably among the most vulnerable in the party to being outbid by Vargas or Kubitschek. Thus, these legislators needed to ally

15. The Dutra government, elected in 1945, did not aggressively pursue ISI, but it also did not dismantle what Vargas had put in place under his previous dictatorship. Under Vargas (elected in 1950) and Kubitschek (elected in 1955), ISI was vigorously promoted.

themselves with the party's ostensible enemies and maintain a conduit to these nationally distributed resources to maintain credible claims to deliver. The party leadership, in turn, understood that their choice was either to allow these legislators to adopt behaviors that contradicted ostensible party positions, or run the very likely risk of both losing the legislative seat *and* the ability to contest it effectively in the future. If northeastern legislators from the UDN party did not tap into the large resource streams being created at the federal level, the party would be shut out of those seats.

A more specific analysis of legislative voting reveals a similar logic across the spectrum of parties when it came to legislation adopting import substitution industrialization programs. While the very high index of likeness shown in Table 13 indicated that there were no clear-cut distinctions between how government and opposition voted, Table 17 reveals that very few legislators were willing to vote against the legislation establishing the state-led industrialization program.

The first column indicates the content of bills and separates successful from unsuccessful bills. The succeeding columns separate the bills out according to level of support across parties. "Grand coalitions" are coalitions in which no party majority opposed the bill.[16] The "all four major parties" category designates bills in which majorities of all four of the largest parties (PSD, UDN, PTB, PSP), which controlled 86 percent of the seats in the legisla-

Table 17 Party voting on executive-initiated economic development legislation, Federal Chamber of Deputies, Brazil, 1946–1963

Content of Bill	Number of Bills	Grand Coalition	All Four Major Parties	All Three Major Parties	Bills w/ Rice Index > 70
Economic Develop. (All Bills)	35	19 (54%)	21 (60%)	21 (60%)	9 (26%)
Economic Develop. (Bills Passed)	16	10 (63%)	12 (75%)	12 (75%)	6 (38%)
Executive Credits (All Bills)	40	22 (55%)	26 (65%)	30 (75%)	15 (38%)
Executive Credits (Bills Passed)	32	22 (69%)	24 (75%)	27 (82%)	15 (47%)
Total Bills	75	40 (53%)	47 (63%)	51 (68%)	24 (32%)
Total Bills Passed	49	32 (65%)	36 (73%)	39 (80%)	21 (43%)

Source: Database on roll call voting provided by Octavio Amorim Neto and Fabiano Guilherme dos Santos.

16. On one of these bills, the PDC did not vote, which is the only case in this category in which *majorities of all of the six parties* listed in Table 17 did not vote the same way on a bill.

ture, on average over the period, voted the same way on a bill. The "all three major parties" category provides the same information for the three largest parties (PSD, UDN, PTB), which controlled 81 percent of the seats in the legislature. Finally, the last column indicates the number of bills on which all three of the major parties had a Rice index above 70.

As can be seen from the table, taking even the most conservative reading of the data, on 53 percent of all bills, there was no difference between *any* of the parties in how their majority voted. If we examine just those bills passed, important vehicles for credit claiming, we see that there was no difference between any of the parties on 65 percent of the bills. Finally, if we consider the bills which established the major economic development programs of the period, and thus with the highest profile in terms of credit-claiming, we see that there was no way to differentiate between any of the parties on 63 percent of these bills. If we employ a slightly less demanding criterion and look at the three major parties that controlled more than 80 percent of the legislature throughout the period, we see that there is no distinction in party voting in 68 percent of all bills considered, no distinction in party voting in 80 percent of all bills passed, and no distinction in party voting in 75 percent of the bills passed that were related to economic development programs. Finally, we see that on almost half of all the bills passed, not only did all three of the major parties vote the same way, but with a Rice index of at least 70, this means that more than 85 percent of all deputies in all three parties voted the same way.

These voting patterns obscure parties' policy responsibility and thus seriously undermine voters' ability to hold them accountable for *a mandate to provide policy goods*.[17] If structural conditions make it risky for voters to reject clientelism, the winning strategy will be to turn government resources into benefits that can be traded directly for votes. To compete, individual politicians and parties must demonstrate an ability to deliver. When major new resources are being distributed, and individual politicians build and maintain their own networks, opposition politicians cannot afford to vote against the government. Individual legislators who fail to secure their cut of the new distribution and who do not have sufficient resources under their own control to fend off an attempt to outbid them will find their electoral position very precarious. In sum, patterns of legislative voting that appear unusual or dysfunctional from the point of view of sustaining policy-based

---

17. In Chapter 6 I discuss import substitution industrialization policies in detail and show how a theory of electoral choice that endogenizes clientelism can explain some of the most important outstanding puzzles of the policy.

appeals can be understood as electoral survival strategies when clientelist exchange predominates.

The Missing Policy Reputation in Punto-Fijista Venezuela, 1958–1998: Quid Pro Quo Appeals with Centralized Resources

In this chapter above, in the section "Party Behavior in Punto-Fijista Venezuela, 1958–1998," I argued that the evidence for policy-based appeals in Venezuela was mixed at best. Venezuelan parties demonstrated high internal unity, but governing cabinets and interparty behavior provided little information to voters about issue position or political responsibility. A theory of clientelist competition, with party-controlled networks of exchange and a national trumping resource, reveals the consistency in the three patterns of behavior discussed above.

As was discussed in the section "The Missing Policy Reputation Explained as Quid Pro Quo Appeal," in this chapter above, if structural conditions render clientelism the best strategic choice for voters, parties must demonstrate access to resources and an ability to deliver clientelist goods in order to compete effectively in elections. In Brazil, a multiparty regime, combined with the lack of intraparty unity and resource control distributed across two federal levels, virtually ensured that election results would not confer the ability to dominate clientelist exchange networks on any one organization. Conditions in Venezuela were a near polar opposite. In both 1945 and 1958, one party, the AD, was both capable of winning the presidency and majorities in both houses of Congress and was quite unified and capable of effective collective action. Moreover, any party in Venezuela with such characteristics stood to gain control of an obviously trumping resource—oil. This combination meant that the AD could create formidable barriers to entry and shut out other contenders. Contenders were thus unwilling to agree to respect the outcome of elections without mechanisms allowing them to demonstrate access to power and resources independent of electoral outcomes. Thus, all the major parties demanded guarantees of cabinet participation. More generally, an a priori formula providing all major contenders with the ability to credibly claim access to government resources was necessary for the acceptance of democratic rules of the game.

In the absence of some compensatory mechanism, the reversion to single-party cabinets would be expected to be very destabilizing in such a regime. If a single party could gain control of the administration of oil revenues, it would have a formidable advantage in making credible appeals to voters. This helps explain the growth of the decentralized administration. One way to explain this unusual pattern of taking authority over public resources out of the hands of the elected government is that this was a means for the initially dominant parties to insulate their access to resources from reprogramming by future cabinet ministers. With roughly three-fourths of government revenue insulated in such a way by 1974, reversion to single-party cabinets did not threaten parties without cabinet representation with extinction.[18] In addition, transfer of power to a single-party opposition cabinet was far from conflict free. As Coppedge (1994b) notes, the AD acted to further restrict the powers of an already weak executive before turning it over to COPEI for the first time in 1970.

The pattern of grand coalitions voting to adopt import substitution industrialization in Brazil is mirrored by the lack of differentiation across parties on the same issue dimension in Venezuela. This lack of differentiation stems from the fact that demonstration of difference on issues is worse than superfluous in clientelist systems. It is a diversion from the more important task of demonstrating ability to capture government office and thus control resource distribution. The lack of differentiation on issues is not limited to the absence of distinction between AD and COPEI positions on development programs. Coppedge (1994a) also elaborates in great detail how internal competition in AD revolves around gaining the endorsement of state-party bosses who can deliver the vote, rather than around staking out distinct issue positions. The greater importance of such coalition building with state-party bosses in comparison with discussion of issues is not so puzzling if parties are not competing through policy appeals. When winning votes based on clientelist exchange, the more of these endorsements a potential presidential candidate has, the more his or her claims to deliver become credible. By guaranteeing votes, these endorsements increase the likelihood of election, and thus control of resources.

Finally, turning to intraparty unity, we can make sense of Venezuelan legislators' willingness to submit meekly to the leadership's demands for rigid discipline. A unified party capable of effective collective action controlling a trumping resource such as the AD or COPEI clearly owned the reputation for delivering quid pro quo goods. Without the party imprimatur, individual deputies had little chance of furthering their careers. In order to

---

18. Recall, as discussed in Chapter 2, that roughly half the organizations in the decentralized administration were created by AD and half by COPEI.

be credible contenders, the rank and file needed to convey that they were in the good graces of the party leadership.

In sum, only one of the patterns of party behavior in Venezuela—high intraparty unity—was consistent with making policy-based appeals. At the same time, high intraparty unity is also consistent with centralized, party-controlled quid pro quo exchange. A theory of electoral choice that endogenizes clientelism can make sense not only of high intraparty unity but also of low interparty divisiveness and grand coalitions. All three of these patterns are consistent with structural conditions that are conducive to clientelist voting and centralized party control of resources for clientelist exchange.

Chávez's System for Mediation Between Citizens and Government in Venezuela

Chávez has characterized his project as one of building a "participatory" and "protagonist" democracy. Opinions on this project are divided into roughly two camps. Some condemn it as a naked power play designed to install Chávez as a dictator, a tragedy that is unraveling the painstakingly constructed tradition of modern, representative liberal democracy in Venezuela. Others praise it as designed to include and empower the poor majority for the first time, remedying the abject failure of the previous regime to accomplish this essential democratic function (Canache 2007).

An electoral theory of clientelism provides a distinct perspective that suggests that Chávez's choices are more a result of structural constraints than they are of personal characteristics. From this point of view, Chávez is neither a demon nor a savior, but rather an adroit politician who is constrained by clientelistic politics. While he is certainly an extremely skilled politician, Chávez has not divined some new and superior form of democracy—the history of all the major stable democracies makes clear that a pluralist system of political parties is essential to, and the most efficient and effective means for, articulating voter preferences and aggregating them into competing visions *for national collective goods policy*. The first important point to make in order to rethink our understanding of Chávez's political project is that if structural conditions continue to favor the clientelistic equilibrium, as I have argued that they do in Chapter 2, then neither Chávez, nor any other politician, can win based on a collective goods program. And if structural conditions favored the clientelistic equilibrium under the Punto Fijista system, then Chávez is not destroying an effective liberal democracy—the previous system collapsed under the constraints that the voter's dilemma and clientelistic competition impose on all such systems.

If structural conditions continue to favor the clientelistic equilibrium, the politician who will emerge victorious from the wreckage of the previous regime will be the one who discerns how to most efficiently restructure clientelism. Chávez's genius has been to construct a narrative that paints his reorganization to reduce some of the inefficiencies that plague clientelistic systems as a project designed to remedy the democratic deficiencies of the previous regime. This shrewd presentation reinforces the conclusions about the failures of the previous purportedly unrepresentative and elitist regime, while simultaneously providing democratic legitimacy to his alternative organization of clientelistic politics.

In arguing that the new system be built upon more direct participation, Chávez's narrative picks up on the dominant critique of the previous system—that the reigning political parties were not sufficiently democratic, and that the previous system failed to serve the majority of the citizens. By arguing that representative democracy is a fraud that fails to generate a government responsible to the majority of citizens, Chávez is adroitly turning an inherent characteristic of clientelism into a unique failing of the previous regime. His alternative system will no more provide the majority with national collective goods than did the previous, but while flush with oil revenues, he can certainly create an appearance of majority inclusion, by directly distributing resources to those who were previously excluded. This, of course, is also one tenet of an efficient strategy for reorganizing clientelism—these are likely to be cheap votes that can be relatively easily bought. To put it differently, Chávez has painted organizational changes designed to achieve an efficient restructuring of clientelism as democratic virtues of his rule.

Initially elected in 1998, Chávez was at first constrained by limited resources, and his incipient efforts at circumventing previous intermediary associations were restricted to deploying the military to create joint military-civilian development projects in poor barrios and rural areas and diverting some resources that had previously served the wealthy to build a coalition around parties and organizations of the far Left that had refused to join or had split from the AD—the classic "outs" under the Punto Fijista democracy (Sustar 2007). As nationalizations and the increase in oil prices made more resources available in 2003–4, Chávez created cooperatives of worker-owned and run businesses and social missions (*misiones sociales*) that developed projects to provide food, basic health care, literacy programs, and other services to poorer communities. A large proportion of the funds for these social missions come from the budget of the Venezuelan National Oil Company, PDVSA. In 2004, $1.7 billion of the state oil company's $15 billion budget was spent on social programs; in 2005, PDVSA contributed $6.91 billion; and in 2006, a staggering $13.26 billion went from the state oil company to social missions. There is now a total of twenty-two social missions in Venezuela (U.S. Department of Energy 2004; Venezuela Information Office 2006).

With the assumption that this is simply a policy-based system with lots of clientelism thrown in, or even with the view that this is a clientelist system and the acceptance that the chief clientelist should try to run it as efficiently as possible, this choice for funding social programs appears unwise. Using the PDVSA budget to fund social programs seems whimsical and likely to introduce unneeded inefficiencies into what was previously a fairly efficiently run company. But such a conclusion would miss one of the most important functions Chávez has in mind for PDVSA in his clientelist system, and it would miss an important aspect of his genius. When oil was simply the cash cow that funded clientelistic networks, as in pre-Chávez Venezuela, it was in politicians' interests to run PDVSA with as much efficiency as possible.[19] But Chávez's plan is to present PDVSA as the model of the type of "socially responsible" corporation that increasingly is the only kind that will be allowed to operate in Venezuela. Thus, PDVSA will be the stick he will use to beat large foreign and domestic firms into submission in sponsoring social programs, in addition to the increased taxes and royalties they are already contributing to his clientelistic reorganization. This is an extremely clever means for obviating the criticisms that could easily be leveled at Chávez if he tried to gain these resources directly through taxation or other means. That approach would launch a hailstorm of critiques about his populism, his totalitarianism, his demagoguery, and his hostility to private enterprise. With this scheme, however, he is merely asking capitalist firms who do very well in Venezuela to do their share in meeting social needs!

Chávez's project, not yet fully realized, is to completely replace the previous federal system of administration with direct links between citizens and the state, with the central organizing structure that of the *consejos comunales* (Canache 2007). Chávez's first goal, as it must be for anyone forging a clientelist reorganization to respond to a crisis of the previous system, is to

---

19. It should be noted that providing jobs on the basis of direct exchange does not preclude competence. Unless there is a dearth of competence, politicians can reward jobs to the competent who also are willing to maintain political loyalty.

eliminate both the party organizations and the administrative bureaucracy that structured the previous system, in his case the pacted Venezuelan democracy. By replacing the municipal and state-level administration with *consejos comunales,* he not only eliminates the structure that supported the earlier regime, but also simultaneously creates a more efficient organization for determining where resources should be distributed. By his making the *consejos* self-initiated, resources are automatically channeled toward areas that have the capacity to organize, and thus the capacity to actively oppose Chávez if not well served by his regime. Similarly, by his organizing the links between citizens and government around a single-level territorial organization, this type of system also has the advantage of reducing incentives for members of competing levels of government to engage in bidding wars. Finally by restricting the *consejos* to no more than four hundred families, and requiring detailed information about each of the families that makes up a given *consejo,* he places the onus of providing the information necessary for monitoring support for his regime on the supporters.[20]

In sum, Chávez is devising a system that not only directly replaces the structures that sustained the previous elites, but also validates his new alternative, defining it as more "democratic," when in fact it is designed to reduce the inefficiencies that plague all clientelist systems. By denigrating the cumbersome and "corrupt" bureaucracy of the previous system, characterizing it as being removed from "the people" (*el pueblo*), Chávez is also attempting to legitimize his new delivery structure, one that will make him a formidable force in what is actually a clientelist system. If Chávez succeeds in creating a single centralized organization that can adjudicate the distribution of resources, he will avoid many of the crises that plague clientelistic systems in which resources must be adjudicated across distinct organizations.[21] Particularly if oil revenues remain high, this new structure new structure will pose a formidable challenge to any potential competitors.

Party Behavior in Brazil, 1989–2006: Building Policy Reputations

To what degree has party behavior changed in contemporary Brazil? If structural conditions have in fact shifted to now favor a policy-based equilibrium,

---

20. The law of *consejos communales* requires the completion of very detailed paperwork providing comprehensive data on each of the families in order to petition the government for benefits.

21. I will discuss these problems inherent to clientelistic systems more fully in Chapter 6. I also develop the ideas much more fully in Lyne 2006.

we should see changes in party behavior that facilitate policy-based appeals. Does the data support the view that Brazilian party behavior is now more consonant with offering voters alternative national policy programs? To answer this question, I examine the identical voting and governing behavior for the current period and also analyze additional data on electoral coalitions. The results from each of these measures suggests that parties have indeed changed their strategies in just the manner we would expect if voters were now demanding policy goods.

Emergence of Intraparty Unity and Interparty Divisiveness in Legislative Voting

Table 18 provides the data on intracoalition unity and intercoalition difference in contemporary Brazil.

As can be seen from Table 18, both intracoalition unity as well as intercoalition divisiveness has risen considerably in the current period.[22] The average Rice index on all roll calls for the government coalition has risen from 69.4 to 84.3 for the governing coalition, and from 65.7 to 89.4 for the opposition. We see a similar shift in unity on coalition votes for the opposition (from 64.4 to 90.9). And although intracoalition unity is roughly the same for the government on coalition votes between the two periods, it must be emphasized that the percentage of coalition votes has risen by a factor of nearly 10 (from 5.1 percent to 45 percent of all roll calls). Distinct government- and opposition-coalition voting behavior is seen in both the rise in the number of coalition votes as well as the decrease in the index of likeness across periods. The weighted average index of likeness on all roll calls and on party votes is more than 50 percent higher in the earlier period. Figure 1 provides a graphical comparison of the patterns of unity in the governing coalition across the two periods and Figure 2 provides the same for the opposition coalition. As these figures show, the difference in average unity on roll calls between the two periods is clear in all except a few minor cabinets, in terms of roll calls, in one or the other period (Cabinet 3: Dutra III and Collor III, both minor; Cabinet 8: Franco V and JK, the former a minor cabinet).[23] In Figure 3, the decrease in index of likeness on roll call

22. These calculations are identical to those in Table 13. For more details, see Appendix 1.
23. In two-party systems, it is customary to eliminate votes with some threshold of unanimity in calculations of Rice indices. I followed Carey's (2007) argument that in multi-party regimes such arbitrary elimination of votes is misleading. Rather than exclude any roll calls, I weighted roll calls based on Carey's (2007) closeness measure. This weighting en-

votes is manifest across the two periods, with a much lower index of likeness in the current regime.

In the current period, governing parties can point to consistent records of support for the coalition's legislative program, and more dramatically, opposition parties can point to a voting record that demonstrates consistent opposition to the government. In other words, although Brazilian parties' legislative voting records previously provided little information on issue position and political responsibility, they now perform that function, comparably, as well as in other presidential systems such as that of the United States.[24] This shift results from the fact that opposition parties can now vote against the government and remain competitive, even when major decisions about resource distribution are being made, because government resources are no longer exchanged directly for votes. Since government resources must now be used to create overall outcomes that voters evaluate favorably, opposition parties can, and must, in fact, maintain a consistent voting record that differentiates them from the government in order to be competitive.

Institutionalists have raised a range of concerns about the validity of roll call voting as an indicator of the national policy orientation of contemporary Brazilian parties. The argument and evidence presented here suggests that the Brazilian polity is in transition from a clientelist to a policy-based equilibrium. Even once actors have fully internalized the new incentives, vestiges of clientelism will remain. Moreover, Brazil's candidate-centered electoral law means that legislators will still be intensely interested in locally targeted collective goods, as institutionalists have ably argued. The question, therefore, is not whether some clientelism or considerable pork barreling can still be observed, but rather, whether overall party behavior indicates that politicians also find it necessary to develop a party reputation for the provision of national collective policy goods.

A number of newly documented trends cast doubt on the institutionalists' objections to a straightforward interpretation of the roll call data. Ames (2001) presents two arguments to discount the increase in voting unity in Brazilian parties in the current period as indicators that parties are now

---

hanced my conclusions (1) that parties failed to present a record that could create a policy reputation in the earlier period and (2) that there has been a marked increase in intracoalition unity in the current period. For more details, see Appendix 1; for unity measures based on Carey's closeness, see Lyne 2005.

24. For data on the U.S. House of Representatives from 1889 to 1969, see Cooper, Brady, and Hurley 1977. For data through the late 1980s, see Rhode 1990. For more recent data on all democracies with roll call data, see also Carey 2007.

Table 18 Roll call voting, Federal Chamber of Deputies, Brazil, 1990–2007

Admin. (Cabinet #)	Date	Gov. Coal.	Opp. Coal.	Tot. Rl Cls	Avg. W.Gov. RICE	Avg. W.Opp. RICE	Avg. Index of Likeness	Pty. Vts. (% of Rl Cls)	Avg. W.Gov. RICE	Avg. W.Opp. RICE	Avg. Index of Likeness
Collor I Gov. Cab. (1)	3/90–10/90	PMDB-PRN-PFL	PT-PDT-PSDB	25	74.0	82.4	46.5	9 (36%)	72.0	87.1	53.8
Collor II Gov. Cab. (2)	11/90–1/92	PRN-PFL-PDS	PT-PDT-PSDB-PMDB	74	75.8	78.9	48.2	11 (15%)	71.5	84.1	37.1
Collor III Gov. Cab. (3)	2/92–4/92	PFL-PDS	PT-PDT-PSDB-PMDB	15	84.0	85.4	53.8	6 (40%)	78.5	81.5	20.6
Collor IV Gov. Cab. (4)	5/92–9/92	PSDB-PTB-PFL-PDS	PT-PDT	11	87.4	88.5	37.1	2 (18%)	91.0	81.4	14.0
Franco I Gov. Cab. (5)	10/92–12/92	PDT-PSDB-PMDB-PTB-PFL	PT	2	81.7	1	16.3	1 (50%)	1	1	2.2
Franco II Gov. Cab. (6)	1/93–5/93	PT-PDT-PSDB-PMDB-PTB-PFL	PPB	28	72.0	68.7	62.2	5 (18%)	74.1	55.4	35.9
Franco III + IV[a] Gov. Cab. (7)	6/93–12/93	PSDB-PMDB-PTB-PFL	PT-PDT	24	78.6	90.1	41.2	8 (33%)	82.9	91.2	13.8
Franco V Gov. Cab. (8)	1/94–12/94	PSDB-PMDB-PFL	PT-PDT	9	75.1	89.2	54.8	2 (22%)	89.8	83.9	14.7
Cardoso I Gov. Cab. (9)	1/95–3/96	PSDB-PMDB-PTB-PFL	PT-PDT	126	79.1	90.1	43.9	89 (71%)	82.6	92.1	13.9

Cabinet	Period	Coalition									
Cardoso II Gov. Cab. (10)	4/96–3/99	PSDB-PMDB-PTE-PFL-PPB	PT-PDT	362	79.3	94.8	23.2	259 (72%)	80.3	96.8	12.5
Cardoso III Gov. Cab. (11)	4/99–2/02	PSDB-PMDB-PFL-PPB	PT-PDT	359	90.2	97.7	53.5	139 (39%)	86.5	97.7	8.1
Cardoso IV Gov. Cab. (12)	3/02–12/02	PSDB-PMDB-PPB	PT-PDT	31	87.6	97.5	63.9	9 (29%)	87.1	97.6	8.1
Lula I Gov. Cab. (13)	1/03–12/03	PT-PPS-PL-PCDOB-PDT-PSB-PTB	PSDB-PFL	150	93.2	68.9 (66.6)	58.8	59 (40.7%) 50 (34.4%)	93.1 92.9	62.9 (61.5) 62.6 (63.1)	21.7 30.4
Lula II Gov. Cab. (14)	1/04–6/04	PT-PPS-PL-PCDOB-PSB-PTB-PMDB	PSDB-PFL	69	90.0	78.7 (62.4)	66.2	46 (70.8) 11 (16.9%)	90.0 77.1	77.8 (55.3) 76.5 (77.3)	23.9 59.6
Lula III-V Gov. Cab. (15)	6/05–4/06	PT-PL-PCDOB-PSB-PTB-PMDB	PSDB-PFL	140	85.1	91.0 (82.5)	63.2	62 (44.2%) 23 (16.4%)	88.8 86.4	86.9 36.8	58.6 15.5
Lula VI Gov. Cab. (16)	5/06–12/06	PT-PCDOB-PSB-PTB-PMDB	PSDB-PFL	35	89.5	95.9 (87.4)	78.6	9 (25.7%) 7 (20%)	85.2 82.9	88.8 (62.1) 88.9 (79.1)	34.4 15.8
Lula VII Gov. Cab. (17)	1/07–4/07	PT-PCDOB-PSB-PTB-PMDB-PP-PV	PSDB-DEM	55	94.9	88.3 (58.8)	55.7	26 (47.2%)	94.1	86.7 50.9	38.0
Total				1515	89.2	87.5	44.8	742 (50.0%)	86.9	90.9	17.9

[a] Collor II and Collor III and Franco III and Franco IV are combined because the major parties in the governing coalition do not differ. Cardoso III and IV are combined because there was only one change of cabinet which does not affect the presence of a legislative cartel.

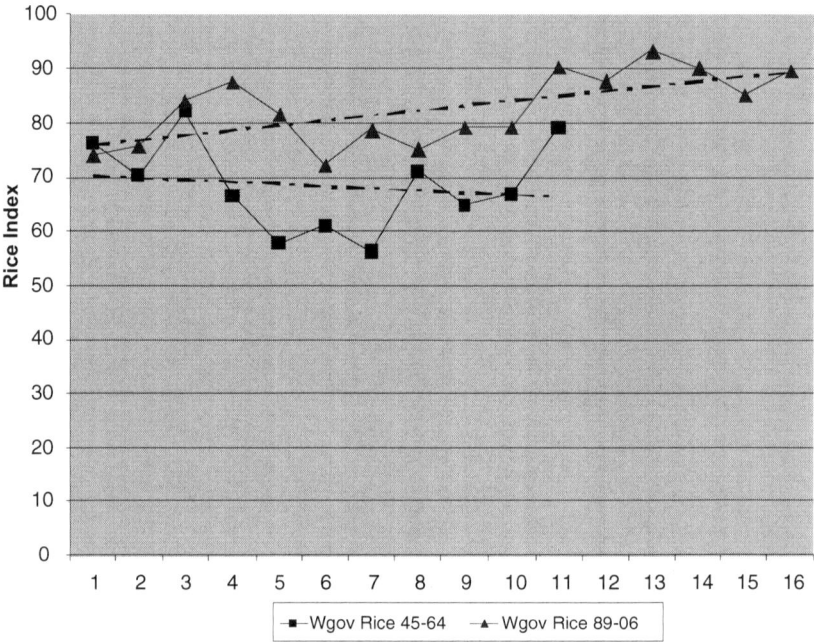

Fig. 1 Roll call voting unity (Rice indices), government coalition, Federal Chamber of Deputies, Brazil, 1945–1964 and 1989–2006

providing national policy programs. First, he argues that the president's ability to achieve his legislative agenda must also be considered when assessing parties as collective actors. While this factor is certainly an important variable to consider when assessing outcomes, Ames's construct holds Brazilian parties to a standard that is not widely employed in the literature. The classic and current works on whether parties are coherent collective actors capable of implementing a policy program examine Rice indices, indices of likeness, and party votes.[25] Second, Ames provides a multivariate analysis of the determinants of rank-and-file voting and argues that his analysis shows that leadership recommendations do not drive rank-and-file voting. Yet he fails to take into account coalition dynamics when coding votes, and he codes as contested votes, votes in which the major parties *in the governing coalition* give opposite recommendations. In the original defini-

25. See, for example, the traditional work of Cooper, Brady, and Hurley (1977), as well as more recent work, such as Cox and McCubbins 1993; Groseclose and Snyder 2000; Cox and Poole 2002; and Carey 2002.

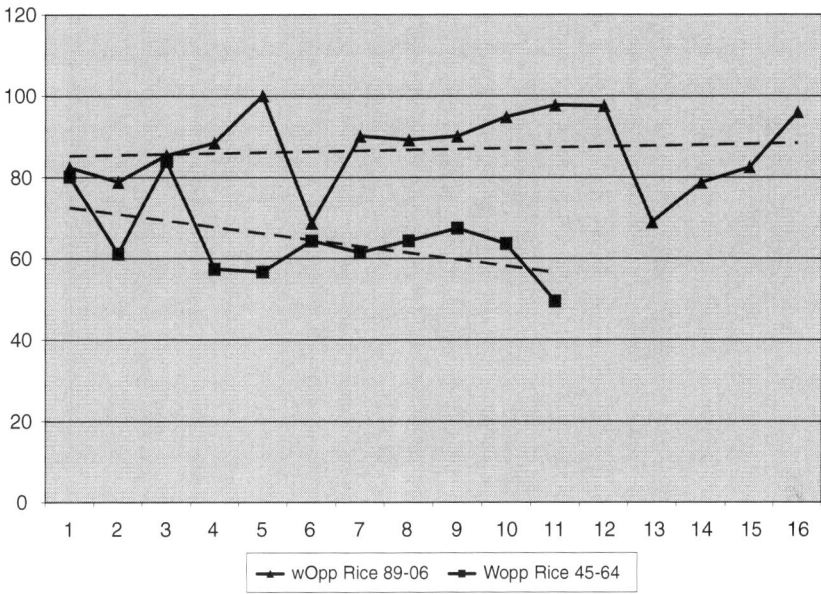

Fig. 2 Roll call voting unity (Rice indices), opposition coalition, Federal Chamber of Deputies, Brazil, 1945–1964 and 1989–2006

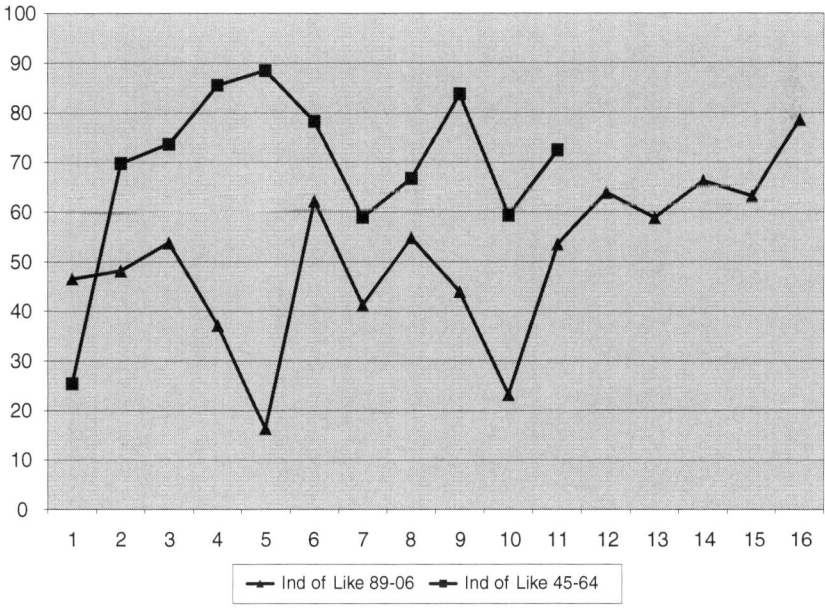

Fig. 3 Index of likeness, Federal Chamber of Deputies, Brazil, 1945–1964 and 1989–2006

tion, contested votes are those in which government and opposition are opposed.[26]

Others have argued that the low reelection rates in the Brazilian legislature weaken parties, but Leoni, Pereira, and Rennó (2004) and Pereira and Rennó (2001) show that Brazilian legislators' reelection attempts and success rates are not unusually low. Analysts have also asserted that parties exhibit gubernatorial as opposed to presidential coattails (Samuels 2000), and yet Brambor, Clark, and Golder (2006) find that the author's methodology was flawed and that, when corrected, gubernatorial coattails disappear and a short presidential coattail is in evidence. Carey and Reinhardt (2004) also tested the purported strong influence of governors on national legislators and found that governors have no influence on national legislators' voting behavior. Many of the institutionalists' conclusions rest on evidence from the early years of the new democracy, and the limited observation period, combined with the inevitable settling that occurs with a shift to a new equilibrium, may well be the basis for many of their conclusions. More data, and more recent analysis, however, suggest that few of these objections stand and that there is little reason not to accept the roll call data results at face value. One other common objection relates to party switching, which I will analyze in detail below.

Emergence of Government-Opposition Cleavage in Governing Alliances and the Executive Cabinet

Table 19 shows the party composition of the executive cabinet from 1990 to 2007. The participation of all major parties in most administrations seen in the earlier period is no longer evident in the current period. The only administration that exhibits the kind of shifting coalitions that encompass the entire ideological spectrum is that of Itamar Franco, an unelected president who served out the last two years of Fernando Collor's term after Collor's impeachment. In every other administration, governing alliances unmistakably separate parties into government and opposition camps and provide clear indications of political responsibility. Collor relied on rightist cabinets, the two Cardoso administrations were made up of center-right coalitions, and the Lula cabinets are leftist. Moreover, the government controls fewer seats in the legislature, on average, than in the earlier period: the average proportion of legislative seats controlled by a governing coalition is

---

26. For a fuller discussion of these issues, see Lyne 2005.

Table 19 Party composition of Executive Cabinet, Brazil, 1990–2007

Admin.	Date	Gov. Coal.	Opp. Coal.	% Legis. Seats	Tot. Roll Calls
Collor I	3/90–10/90	PMDB-PRN-PFL	PT-PDT-PSDB	77.6	24
Collor II	11/90–1/92	PRN-PFL-PDS	PT-PDT-PSDB-PMDB	32.8	74
Collor III	2/92–4/92	PFL-PDS	PT-PDT-PSDB-PMDB	24.8	15
Collor IV	5/92–9/92	PSDB-PTB-PFL-PDS	PT-PDT	40.0	11
Franco I	10/92–12/92	PDT-PSDB-PMDB-PTB-PFL	PT	62.3	2
Franco II	1/93–5/93	PT-PDT-PSDB-PMDB-PTB-PFL	PPB	69.3	28
Franco III + IV[a]	6/93–12/93	PSDB-PMDB-PTB-PFL	PT-PDT	53.2	24
Franco V	1/94–12/94	PSDB-PMDB-PFL	PT-PDT	45.6	9
Cardoso I	1/95–3/96	PSDB-PMDB-PTB-PFL	PT-PDT	56.3	126
Cardoso II	4/96–3/99	PSDB-PMDB-PTB-PFL-PPB	PT-PDT	66.4	362
Cardoso III	4/99–3/02	PSLB-PMDB-PFL-PPB	PT-PDT	67.7	359
Cardoso IV	4/02–12/02	PSL-B-PMDB-PPB	PT-PDT	45.1	31
Lula I	1/03–12/03	PT-PL-PPS-PCDOB-PDT-PSB-PTB	PSDB-PFL	49.3	145
Lula II-V	1/04–4/06	PT-?L-PCDOB-PSB-PTB-PMDB	PSDB-PFL	64.9	197
Lula VI	5/06–12/06	PT-?CDOB-PSB-PTB-PMDB	PSDB-PFL	58.4	35
Lula VII	1/07–4/07	PT-?CDOB-PSB-PTB-PMDB-PP-PV	PSDB-DEM	56.5	55
Lula VIII	5/07–12/07	PT-PCDOB-PSB-PTB-PMDB-PP-PR-PV-PDT	PSDB-DEM	66.1	149

Source: Amorim Neto 2007.

[a] There are some small discrepancies in the number of roll calls in Tables 18 and 19 because in Table 18 I excluded roll calls in which the government did not make a recommendation for rank and file voting from the Rice index calculations whereas Table 19 includes all roll calls.

53.9 percent. Given that in contemporary Brazil constitutional amendments that require two rounds of voting and a three-fifths (60 percent) majority for approval in both houses were unusually prevalent, this reduction in the proportion of seats controlled gains even more significance. Although the incentive for the executive to form larger coalitions has increased with the supermajority required to pass much major legislation, the average number of seats controlled has decreased.

These patterns of cabinet formation clearly distinguish which parties should be held responsible for the policies and legislation of a particular administration. A party's membership in the governing coalition or its place in the opposition provides information regarding the party's support for particular policies. Once again, we can explain the willingness of parties to remain out of the cabinet in the current period with a theory of the differences in credible appeals based on quid pro quo versus national collective goods policy. Cabinet positions typically confer control over resources, and thus, in clientelist systems, it is imperative for parties to participate in order to make credible claims to deliver. With a shift to policy-based voting, however, direct control over resources is no longer necessary to maintain electoral competitiveness. Cabinet participation is not necessary to make an effective policy-based appeal. Indeed, remaining outside the cabinet enhances the opposition's credibility, showing it to be committed to policies that are distinct from those of the government.

Emergence of Ideological Consistency in Electoral Alliances in Federal Deputy Elections

Figueiredo and Limongi (1998, 2000) have advanced an institutional explanation for the greater internal party unity seen in contemporary Brazil, arguing that the executive's increased agenda-setting powers explain the increase in discipline in legislative voting. But if the changes in Brazilian politics are broader than those that might plausibly be affected by altered executive agenda-setting powers, the authors' explanation remains only partial. Evidence on the ideological consistency of electoral coalitions provides such a demonstration of broader changes.

Electoral law in Brazil allows parties to make alliances in proportional-representation elections for federal deputy, and votes are pooled across all parties in the alliance. Parties face constraints in forming these alliances if they wish to maintain a reputation for supporting certain policy positions. Parties should ally with their nearest neighbors along the policy spectrum more frequently than with parties further away if they are concerned about making a policy-based appeal. Preponderance of noncontiguous alliances and patterns of strange bedfellows, namely, alliances with parties of contrary policy positions, render policy-based appeals more difficult. If parties are attempting to win votes by means of a policy reputation, then we should expect to see parties align with their ideological neighbors most frequently. Table 20 displays the frequency with which different parties formed electoral coalitions in elections for federal deputy between 1950 and 1962.[27] Parties are placed along the top row from Left to Right according to how leading scholars of the period evaluated their relative stances on major issues.

The data for a given party is read across the row corresponding to that party. The first entry in each cell indicates the number of alliances made between the two parties throughout the period. The number in parentheses provides a relative measure of the degree to which the party favors or disfavors its nearest ideological neighbor over other parties in making alliances. It is the ratio of the number of alliances with the given party and number of alliances with the nearest ideological neighbor with which it allies most frequently. Thus, for example, the PTB, reading across the row, makes alliances with the PR 0.7 times as often as with the PSP, its nearest ideological neighbor. The shaded square in each row identifies the most frequent alliance partner for that party.

Table 20 Electoral alliances, federal legislative elections, Federal Chamber of Deputies, Brazil, 1950–1962

	PTB	PSP	PR	PSD	PDC	UDN
PTB		10	7 (0.7)	14 (1.4)	3 (0.3)	9 (0.9)
PSP	10 (0.8)		13	11 (0.8)	8 (0.6)	17 (1.3)
PR	7 (0.5)	13		8 (0.6)	7 (0.9)	12 (1.5)
PSD	14 (1.8)	11 (1.4)	8 (0.9)		9	9 (1)
PDC	3 (0.3)	8 (0.9)	7 (0.8)	9 (0.8)		11
UDN	9 (0.8)	17 (1.5)	12 (1.0)	9 (0.8)	11	

Source: Tribunal Superior Eleitoral, Dados estatísticos, vols. 2–5.

27. Electoral coalitions were not allowed in the 1945 elections. Tables 19 and 20 include all registered electoral alliances for all legislative elections for the respective period.

If electoral-alliance behavior were to provide coherent information about issue position, parties should be aligned most often with their nearest neighbors along the issue spectrum. In this case, the shaded cells would be adjacent to the blacked-out diagonal. In addition, if policy consistency were important, we would expect that the numbers in parentheses would decrease as one read along the row on each side of the blacked-out cell toward the ends of the table. This would indicate that alliances decrease monotonically as distance along the ideological spectrum increases. As can be seen from the table, however, the first criterion holds only for the PDC and the PR, two small parties that together never attained more than 7.3 percent of the seats in the legislature. No party meets the second criterion—in all cases parties ally with greater frequency with those further away than with their nearest neighbor. In one case, that of the PSD, the largest party throughout the period, we see a monotonic trend of increasing alliances as ideological distance increases! Finally, we can see that there is no important difference in the number of alliances each party forms with its nearest neighbors and with those on its furthest extremes—the ratio of alliances with the given party and the nearest ideological neighbor, once again with the exception of the PDC and the PR, are all close to 1.[28]

In the earlier period, all parties allied with all other parties with roughly the same frequency, and thus parties' electoral-alliance behavior failed to provide any information that could indicate support for distinct policy programs. The importance of alliances in informing the party's policy reputation is demonstrated by the fact that alliances increased in each successive election, forming 40 percent of all tickets in 1950 and rising to 60 percent of all tickets in 1962 (Lima 1980, 73).

Alliance behavior in the current period is depicted in Table 21. The parties are aligned from Left to Right, as leading scholars characterize their major positions on issues, and the entries are calculated on the same basis.

The shift in electoral-alliance behavior is quite striking. Whereas in the earlier period only the two smallest parties allied most often with their nearest neighbor, in the current period, all parties adopt this strategy, as seen by the fact that the shaded squares are all adjacent to the blacked-out diagonal. This clearly shows the pattern that would be expected if parties were con-

---

28. Mainwaring (1995) uses an alternative placement along the spectrum from Left to Right of PTB-PSP-PSD-PDC-UDN-PR. This placement does not change the findings. In fact, with this placement, only the PDC allies most often with its nearest ideological neighbor, whereas with the placement used here, both the PDC and the PR, two of the smaller parties, make the largest number of alliances with their closest ideological neighbor.

Table 21 Electoral alliances, federal legislative elections, Federal Chamber of Deputies, Brazil, 1986–2006

	PT	PDT	PMDB	PSDB	PFL	PDS/PPR/PPB
PT		21	6 (0.29)	7 (0.33)	0	0
PDT	21 (0.9)		27	23 (0.85)	13 (0.48)	12 (0.44)
PMDB	6 (0.29)	27 (0.6)		45	36 (0.8)	24 (0.53)
PSDB	7 (0.33)	23 (0.51)	45		43 (0.96)	26 (0.57)
PFL	0	13 (0.23)	36 (0.64)	43 (0.77)		56
PDS/PPR/PPB	0	12 (0.21)	26 (0.46)	24 (0.43)	56	

Sources: Schmitt 1999; http://www.tse.gov.br.

cerned about creating a public record of support for a distinct policy program. Moreover, with the exception of the PFL, which allies with essentially the same frequency with the PMDB and the PSDB, the number of alliances now decreases monotonically with distance between the parties along the spectrum. Distance between parties along the ideological spectrum is now a good predictor of whether two parties will form an electoral alliance.[29] The pattern of strange-bedfellow alliances that characterized the earlier period has been replaced by a consistent pattern of coherent alliances in the current period. Thus, electoral-alliance behavior in contemporary Brazil does provide information that distinguishes between the parties' issue positions. We can conclude that the increased agenda-setting powers of the executive emphasized by Figueiredo and Limongi (2000) have certainly facilitated the

---

29. Samuels (2000) has argued that state-level conflicts determine who will form electoral alliances, without regard to national partisan platforms. Ames (2001, 68, 76) also suggests that state-level deals and conflicts are central to determining party alliance behavior. Yet, while *specific* alliances across states differ in any given election, the data presented here indicate that the vast majority of those differences represent alliances with one of the two available ideological neighbors (there are two for most parties), rather than with strange bedfellows. This pattern holds across elections, indicating that even if local conflicts determine specific alliance partners in a given state and election, ideological considerations constrain the range of permissible partners across states and elections. Parties need not form alliances with exactly the same partners in each election or in each state to provide consistent information about their positions. Rather, they need only consistently ally with the parties with the most similar stances on the issues.

formation of legislative majorities, but they cannot explain the changes in electoral alliance behavior, which are quite striking.

Party Switching: Limited Threat to Building Policy Reputations

Some have argued that the changes in party behavior in contemporary Brazil are less important than one might assume because of party switching (Ames 2001; Mainwaring 1999). It is well known that Brazilian legislators do switch parties with a frequency that is unusual. There are several reasons to discount the view that party switching nullifies the behavior more consistent with policy-based appeals discussed here. First, Desposato (2006b) found that switchers change their voting behavior to conform to the leadership dictates of their new party. In other words, switchers vote with the leadership of their new party with the same relatively high frequency with which they voted with the leadership of their old party. If the party is the main vehicle informing voters of policy positions, then as long as the switcher votes with his or her party, such switching does not dilute the party's ability to sustain an effective policy-based appeal. If individual legislators vote with their party, regardless of whether they have switched or not, switching does little damage to parties as unitary actors.

Some might object that if a legislator switches parties after an election, and a voter had chosen the legislator both for his or her party's policy positions as well as his or her personal reputation, the given voter's policy preferences have been subverted. This would only necessarily be the case, however, in a two-party system, in which a switch between parties also implies a switch between legislative agents—the agent capable of advertising and promulgating a policy program. In a multiparty system, switches between parties within the governing or opposition coalition does not imply a switch across legislative agents. An analysis of switching within versus across coalitions shows that the vast majority of switches take place within the governing or opposition coalition. Table 22 shows the number of switches between parties within the governing or opposition coalition, and the number of switches from a party in the government coalition to a party in the opposition coalition, and vice versa. I counted switches for the six largest parties in the governing and opposition coalitions.[30]

---

30. I excluded the PDS/PPR/PPB because the mergers and changes of party name vastly complicated the determination of what was an actual party switch, and because this is only the fifth-most-important party among the seven major parties of PFL, PMDB, PSDB, PT, PDT, PTB, PPB (PDS/PPR).

Table 22 Party switching within and across coalitions, within and between legislative sessions, Federal Chamber of Deputies, Brazil, 1989–2007

	Within Coalition	Across Coalition	Within-Across
48.4	10	12	−2
Between 48.4 and 49.1	2	1	1
49.1	7	2	5
Between 49.1 and 49.2	9	4	5
49.2	7	2	5
Between 49.2 and 49.3	5	3	2
49.3	11	9	2
Between 49.3 and 49.4	2	3	−1
49.4	0	1	−1
Between 49.4 and 50.1	2	1	1
50.1	17	6	11
Between 50.1 and 50.2	9	5	4
50.2	16	2	14
Between 50.2 and 50.3	25	3	22
50.3	40	3	37
Between 50.3 and 50.4	17	1	16
50.4	1	0	1
Between 50.4 and 51.1	28	1	27
51.1	0	0	0
Between 51.1 and 51.2	6	1	5
51.2	11	1	10
Between 51.2 and 51.3	16	0	16
51.3	19	1	18
Between 51.3 and 51.4	7	0	7
51.4	0	0	0
Between 51.4 and 52.1	1	0	1
52.1	3	19	−16
Between 52.1 and 52.2	1	2	−1
52.2	0	02	−2
Between 52.2 and 52.3	2	1	1
52.3	22	17	5
Between 52.3 and 52.4	3	0	3
52.4	0	2	−2
Between 52.4 and 53.1	1	2	−1
53.1 (through 6/2007)	1	2	−1

Source: Calculated from Camara dos Deputados official records of party ID for individual legislators for each roll call vote.

As the table indicates, with the one exception of the legislative session of 52.1, the vast majority of switches were within the governing or opposition coalitions. Thus, most switches occur within the legislative agent. If the parties in the governing coalition adopt a common policy program, this means that most switches in fact do not sever the link between the voter and his or her preferred policies as expressed in that person's voting choice.

Just as with party recommendations in legislative voting discussed above, we have to modify our analysis of party switching in multiparty regimes if the outcome of interest is the preservation of the mandate expressed in elections. And if the analytic variable of concern is whether party switching compromises the voters' mandate, the conclusion has to be that the vast majority of party switches in contemporary Brazil are innocuous. These switches do not diminish the ability of the legislative agent (the governing coalition that won the election) to deliver the policy program that was triumphant at the polls.

Did Available Political-Party Options Limit Voters' Choices in Postwar Brazil?

One objection to the voter-driven electoral explanation for these changes in Brazilian party behavior might be that the changes are primarily supply, or party, driven, as opposed to demand, or voter, driven. According to the supply-driven argument, voters did not opt for policy goods in the earlier period because the existing parties did not organize to provide them. Theoretically, twenty years of vigorous electoral competition should have been sufficient to foster considerable experimentation on the part of competing parties. And given that Latin American parties have been criticized as excessively personalistic, and lacking ideological or policy commitments at least since the early 1900s, we would expect such strategies to be attempted, and to have led to electoral success, if they had had electoral appeal. Thus, such a supply-driven argument would have to posit some unusual impediment to such experimentation.

The logic of the voter's dilemma and the deductions about what constitutes an effective clientelist appeal suggest that policy-based strategies did not fail to emerge in the earlier period because of lack of imagination, experimentation, or enlightenment. Parties failed to adopt policy-based strategies because they were not an electoral winner when structural conditions favored the clientelist equilibrium. Empirically, this view is borne out. Parties exhibiting high internal unity and coherent alliance behavior existed in both periods. In the earlier period, the PDC was widely considered to be more policy oriented than were the other major parties. As we saw above, the PDC had consistent alliance patterns in legislative elections and never joined the governing cabinet, except for a short time before the coup. Moreover, the party had by far the highest average unity in legislative voting over the period, with an average Rice index of 87.6. In the later period, both the PT and the PSDB began as small parties with high internal unity and consistent alliance patterns. The PT began competing in elections in the early 1980s, and the PSDB was formed in 1988 as a breakaway from the PMDB during the Constitutional Convention. What is striking is the difference in success rates for these small policy-based parties in the two periods. In the earlier period the PDC managed to elect no more than a dozen deputies per legislature. In the later period, these parties have had some of the fastest-growing trajectories, as demonstrated in Figure 4.

The PT has increased its seat share rapidly throughout the period and then leveled off in 2006. Its rapid upward trajectory from 1999 to 2003 reflects the fact that the party also won the presidency for the first time in 2002. And although the PSDB lost some ground in 2002, certainly in part because of having lost the presidential elections, it held steady in 2006 and is now the same size as the previously much larger PFL. Moreover, subsequent contests of the period point to the continued centrality of these two parties. The PT and the PSDB were the only real contenders for the presidency in the four most recent presidential elections, out of the five that have been held in the current period. In addition, the results from municipal elections in 2004 reaffirmed the PT and the PSDB as the dominant parties contending for executive posts. An additional sign of other parties imitating

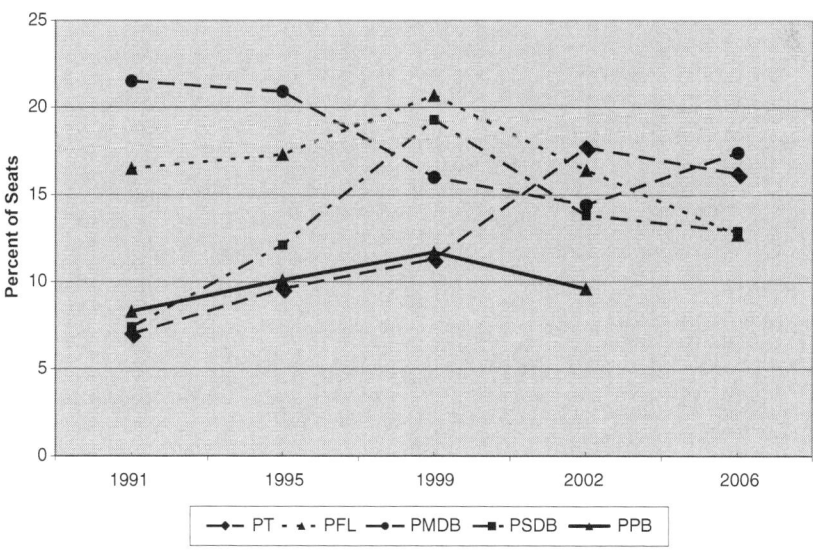

Fig. 4 Party seat shares, Federal Chamber of Deputies, Brazil, 1991–2006 (%)

the more successful contenders is the fact that for the first time since its founding, the PFL opted to remain out of the cabinet in 2002, thus maintaining a consistent opposition stance to government policy. It will be interesting to watch the evolution of the PFL with the recent death of Antônio Carlos Magalhães, one of the last of the old clientelists with roots in the earlier regime.[31]

Conclusion

In this chapter I demonstrated that party behavior in pre-Chávez Venezuela and postwar Brazil was inconsistent with making policy-based appeals to voters. I argued that we could explain the lack of any successful challenge to the parties responsible for the resulting accountability vacuum by considering a structurally driven clientelist equilibrium. I further argued that we could make sense of the apparently dysfunctional patterns by investigating the systematic differences in the requisites for making quid pro quo or policy-based appeals to voters. I refined these predictions by exploring how party- or candidate-centered rules would affect behavior in clientelistic regimes and showed that they could explain the accountability vacuum and other aspects of party behavior in these two systems. These predictions are fully amenable to further comparative tests. A theory of clientelistic competition also shed considerable light on Chávez's championing a "participatory" and "protagonist" democracy and on his choices for reorganizing interest intermediation in Venezuela. Finally, I demonstrated that contemporary Brazilian parties have altered their behavior in precisely the manner necessary to improve their ability to make policy-based appeals to voters.

The logic of the voter's dilemma provided a basis for broadening our understanding of the types of party behaviors that are electorally competitive, depending on whether structural conditions favor the clientelistic or policy-based equilibrium. This more general understanding of party behavior provides new insight into the current debate surrounding party behavior in Brazil. Some scholars have argued that Brazilian parties are not nearly as unorganized and undisciplined as the received wisdom suggests (Fi-

---

31. The PFL delegation was often split in the legislature during the first Lula government. A minority faction led by Antônio Carlos Magalhärses (ACM) often voted with the Lula government, despite the fact that the PFL remained formally out of the cabinet. Currently a fierce struggle is being waged for control of the PFL, between those who are maintaining more policy-based appeal, led by Jorge Bornhausen, and a more clientelist faction led by ACM. For more discussion of these internal dynamics, see Chapter 4.

gueiredo and Limongi 2000; Limongi and Figueiredo 1995; Lyne 2005, 2008). Those favoring institutional explanations continue to emphasize how Brazilian institutions weaken parties' ability to offer policy alternatives and encourage personalism, while at the same time conceding that some aspects of party behavior appear to be changing (Ames 2001).

The data presented in this chapter strongly suggest that Brazilian parties are responding to a shift to policy-based voting in the electorate. The pursuit of personal reputations unquestionably remains important, given Brazil's electoral institutions. But in the ongoing debate, institutionalists often point to the continued emphasis on personalism as evidence that not much has changed. An analytic approach that fails to distinguish between direct and indirect exchange, and thus that conflates clientelism with "ordinary" pork, reinforces this view.[32] From this theoretical perspective, the voters' shift from quid pro quo to national programs, from direct to indirect exchange, from relinquishing policy-based voting to favoring it, is a nonevent. But from the perspective of effective democratic accountability and improved policy outcomes, it is a blockbuster.

---

32. For further discussion on this point, and for an integrated typology of pork, rents, and clientelism, see Carroll and Lyne 2006.

4

INTERNAL PARTY ORGANIZATION:
ALIGN INDIVIDUAL AND COLLECTIVE GOALS TO BUILD A POLICY
REPUTATION OR TO ENSURE EFFICIENT VOTE BUYING?

Just as Brazilian parties have been pilloried, so Brazilian electoral law has come in for heavy criticism. Institutionalists, in particular, have argued that open-list PR electoral rules employed in Brazil seriously hinder party leaders' ability to manage the behavior of the rank and file in order to maintain a coherent policy record and offer voters clear national policy alternatives (Ames 2001; Mainwaring 1999; Geddes 1994; Carey and Shugart 1995; Nielson 2003). In contrast, the closed list used in Venezuela was traditionally considered a valuable tool providing party leaders with the necessary leverage to enforce discipline and ensure that parties could function as unified collective actors.[1]

Despite these divergent leadership powers, however, parties in both countries failed to promulgate policies that could produce steady, sustained economic growth, and neither was able to respond effectively to the crisis resulting from the exhaustion of import substitution industrialization in the 1980s. As the crisis in Venezuela wore on, many scholars concluded that the country's extreme rules, such as rigid internal discipline and absolutely closed lists, resulted in parties that were *too* strong, rendering them unresponsive to the policy preferences of voters (Crisp 2000; Shugart and Haggard 2001; Coppedge 1994a).

These analyses provided astute insight into how internal party organization in these historical cases weakened democratic accountability. At the

---

1. Many analysts became more critical of Venezuela's institutions as the decade of the 1980s wore on. Coppedge (1994a), for example, labeled Venezuela a partyarchy, to emphasize that political parties were too rigid and hierarchical to provide effective representation. New institutionalists also began to qualify their views of the positive link between party-centered institutions and effective representation in the early 1990s. See, for example, Shugart and Carey 1992 (198); Shugart and Haggard 2001 (88); and Crisp 2000 (11).

same time, they raise another important puzzle: how can we explain the fact that neither the existing parties nor any new contenders attempted to organize (or reorganize) to provide an effective policy response and therefore fill the accountability vacuum that clearly plagued both democracies? What explains the continued dominance of parties responsible for this accountability vacuum and why was there an absence of successful challengers acting to fill it?

With a theory of voting that generates two equilibria, we can gain a new perspective on the choices for highly decentralized parties in postwar Brazil and highly centralized parties in pre-Chávez Venezuela. Organizational choices that appear to create an accountability vacuum, and thus that would be expected to generate electoral losses under the assumption of policy-based competition, can in fact enhance parties' electoral success when structural conditions favor the clientelist equilibrium. If clientelist competition predominates, then the leadership's traditional role of managing rank-and-file behavior to build a policy reputation is superfluous, since voters are not evaluating parties on the basis of policy positions. When clientelist competition prevails, the key collective-individual conflict is not one of relative emphasis on the party reputation versus personal reputations, but instead a conflict over how to employ resources in buying votes.

Open-list PR in Brazil and extremely closed lists in Venezuela served to resolve the collective-individual conflict and ensure efficient vote buying in a system with decentralized and centralized resource control, respectively. Additional data in each case is marshaled to support this interpretation of the apparently dysfunctional institutional choices. For Brazil, I show that the leadership's criteria for distributing the most valuable committee assignments of the period created the same incentives: efficient individual vote-buying was a significant determinant of receiving a valuable committee assignment, but loyal party voting had only a marginal effect on receiving such a committee assignment. For Venezuela, I show that what succeeded and what failed in the electoral reforms of 1993 ensured that party leaders maintained control of centralized clientelistic networks and thus ensured their electoral viability. Finally, I discuss how Chávez's ongoing reorganization of the Venezuelan party system is designed to achieve what all victorious leaders in clientelist systems must accomplish: asserting control of clientelistic networks and organizing them to ensure efficient vote-buying.

If it is true that the kind of behavior that generated an accountability vacuum in postwar Brazil would be selected out if voters exercised policy-based voting, and if voters in Brazil have indeed shifted to policy-based voting as argued in Chapter 2, then we should see changes in party behavior that eliminates the accountability vacuum. We should see party leaders acting to counteract the extreme individualist incentives generated by open-list PR in order to develop a policy reputation and facilitate voters' ability to hold them accountable. In the section "Circumventing the Obstacles to Policy Reputations in Contemporary Brazil," below in this chapter, an analysis of the determinants of receipt of locally targeted resources shows that the leadership now provides perks to members of the rank and file who act to maintain the party's policy reputation, by voting loyally with the party.

Open-List PR and the Accountability Vacuum in Postwar Brazil

A political party is a national collective actor made up of individual legislators, each elected in subnational districts.[2] The interests of individual legislators who serve their district and the interests of the party as a collective often diverge (Cain, Ferejohn, and Fiorina 1987; Mayhew 1974). Parties as embodiments of a national program must develop a reputation for supporting a given set of policies, and this requires consistent voting as a collective. At the same time, any given piece of legislation designed to fortify the party's reputation may not be in the electoral interest of some individual legislators.

Rules such as Brazil's open-list PR are argued to exacerbate this conflict. New institutionalists draw a key distinction between rules that encourage a candidate-centered versus a party-centered vote. Candidate-centered rules encourage voters to focus on an individual candidate, as is the case with primaries and rules that promote intraparty competition in multimember districts. These rules require that individual candidates differentiate themselves from co-partisans in order to win nomination or election (Cain, Ferejohn, and Fiorina 1987; Ramseyer and Rosenbluth 1993; Cox and Rosenbluth 1995; Carey and Shugart 1995). Thus, electoral laws that create strong incentives for intraparty competition, such as open-list PR and the single nontransferable vote, should increase individualistic behavior that can often damage the party's reputation for providing national policy goods.

Party-centered rules, in contrast, are those that encourage voters to make choices based on their party preference rather than their preference for individual candidates. These include rules such as closed-list PR, in which voters can only choose between party lists, and party leaders determine the order

---

2. There are a few exceptions of single nationwide districts.

on the list and thus the order of election of individual candidates. Other rules that vest control over candidate selection in party leaders' hands also tend to create a party-centered vote. Under these rules politicians do not have to differentiate themselves from fellow partisans to gain nomination or election; instead, they must adopt behaviors that allow them to maintain the favor of party leaders in order to get a high place on the list. This set of rules was originally theorized to lead to greater emphasis on national-level policy goods because party leaders have direct control over the electoral fate of the rank and file, and thus can use their power to curtail any excessively personalistic behavior that might damage the party's policy reputation.

In sum, rules such as open-list PR weaken the ability of party leaders to align individual legislators' incentives with party goals such as presenting voters with alternative visions for national policy. Absent some countervailing action, strong candidate-centered rules should exacerbate the collective-individual conflict and diminish the level of collective goods that parties are able to provide. Brazil is often exhibit number one to illustrate this logic, and it has been employed widely to explain the personalist behavior of Brazilian legislators and parties' ostensible absence of policy reputations and national programs (Ames 2001; Mainwaring 1999; Geddes 1994). As demonstrated in the previous chapter, there is considerable evidence to support the view of weak parties and negligible policy reputations in postwar Brazil, including strange-bedfellow alliances and grand coalition governments, and low internal unity and negligible interparty difference in legislative voting.

New institutionalists have powerfully highlighted the links between internal party organization and effective democratic accountability. At the same time, new institutionalist arguments raise key questions about how elections drive the resolution of lapses of accountability in democratic regimes. If elections are the mechanism that drives parties to remain attuned to the voters, how can parties that persist with an internal organization that actively hinders their ability to articulate voters' policy preferences survive electorally? Such parties should be quickly replaced by parties organizing to articulate the electorates' policy preferences through greater internal unity and external differentiation. The record in postwar Brazil (and in pre-Chávez Venezuela, to be discussed below) raises quite a conundrum: why did electoral competition fail to call forth challengers that organized internally to ensure better articulation of policy preferences and fill the accountability vacuum created by excessively candidate-centered rules?[3]

---

3. One potential answer to these questions has been developed by Shugart and Carey (1992), who argue that the combination of candidate-centered electoral law and presidents with strong legislative powers has the advantage of delegating national policy to the president, while freeing legislators to serve their local constituents. Calling this combination "the

Absolutely Closed List PR and the
Accountability Vacuum in Venezuela

The collapse of Venezuela's party system in the 1990s was one of the most unexpected failures of long-standing democratic rule in the region, if not the world. Until the crisis of the 1980s, most analysts viewed Venezuela as possessing effective democratic institutions that were unique in Latin America. Scholars of Venezuelan politics emphasized Venezuela's mass-based elections; stable two-party rule with low electoral volatility (Mainwaring and Scully 1995); parties' extraordinary unity in legislative voting; and finally, alternation in the presidency as indicators of a healthy democracy (Levine 1973; Martz 1977). Yet in the 1990s, Venezuela's legendary party system disintegrated.[4] In that decade the two parties that were considered

---

inefficient secret," the authors argue that this institutional choice is attractive when a system is created by strong regional bosses, who want neither the responsibility for nor the intrusion of national policy in their local organizations. The authors do not make explicit whether such local bosses are providing locally targeted collective goods (pork) or clientelistic goods. In this model, local constituencies choose their legislator entirely on the basis of service to their local district, and national policy considerations are irrelevant.

Theoretically, the argument raises questions about how presidents sustain credible policy-based appeals and how they get a national policy program through the legislature. How do presidential candidates credibly promise to deliver certain types of policy goods if not through their endorsing party's legislative record? If individual politicians cannot credibly claim to provide policy goods, as the literature has argued (Arnold 1990; Fiorina and Noll 1979; Cox and McCubbins 1993), how can policy reputations be developed without parties that build public records of support for specific policy programs?

In a related question, how are the inevitable conflicts between the president's goal to deliver national policy goods and individual legislators' desire to serve their local supporters resolved in such a system? If the legislative party has no need for a national policy reputation, what incentive do individual legislators have to ever forgo the needs of their local district in the interest of national policy? In short, it seems highly implausible that presidents could produce and claim credit for national policy goods without legislative parties that do the same. Empirically, there is considerable evidence to support the view that voters *do* take party reputation into account in choosing which legislator to support, even in highly candidate-centered systems such as that of the United States (Cox and McCubbins 1993) and Brazil (Lyne 2008). Amorim Neto and Santos (2003) also provide evidence that Brazilian legislators propose substantial national policy legislation. It should be noted that the inefficient secret model proposed by Shugart and Carey is a hybrid *across branches* (executive and legislature) at the national level and is distinct from a system in which clientelism dominates in specific areas at the local level, as in the American South or rural Japan. In these latter cases, I argue that clientelism is driven by structural conditions at the *local level,* as discussed in Chapter 1, whereas in Shugart and Carey's inefficient secret model, clientelism is dominant at the national level for only one branch.

4. Venezuela implemented an electoral reform in 1993, but its historically stable two-party system had already begun to disintegrate before this reform took effect. In addition, the changes brought about by the reform, which were to change some PR districts to single-member districts, cannot explain the increased fragmentation of the Venezuelan system or why the traditional parties have failed to maintain the loyalty of the electorate in presidential races. Barring many strong regionally concentrated parties, altering the system from one of pure PR to a mixed one of PR and single-member districts, if anything, would be predicted to

the enduring anchors of the system lost their dominance in the legislature, lost control of the presidency, and were outmaneuvered by Chávez's personal party vehicle in the election of a Constituent Assembly to draw up a new constitution. The patterns of party control in the legislature can be seen in Table 23.

If the seats lost by AD and COPEI were won by new stable parties, it might be argued that no accountability vacuum existed and that electoral competition was merely serving to select out bad performers and reward good ones. If the dominant parties became sclerotic and unable to address voters' concerns, we would expect others to arise to fill the void. As can be seen from Table 23, however, this was not the case. With the partial exception of the Movement for Socialism (Movimiento al Socialismo [MAS]), the seats lost by the previously dominant parties were won by different parties in each election. In addition to this high electoral volatility in legislative elections, the major parties also lost control of the presidency in the 1990s. Caldera, a founding leader of COPEI, left the party and won the presidency on an explicitly antiparty platform in 1993. In 1998, the results were even more ominous: the presidential winner was none other than the perpetrator of one of the failed coups in 1992. Since taking office, Hugo Chávez has

Table 23 Seat shares per party, Federal Chamber of Deputies, Venezuela, 1958–1998 (%)

Party	1958	1963	1968	1973	1978	1983	1988	1993	1998
AD	54.9	37.1	30.8	51.0	44.2	56.5	48.3	27.6	29.1
COPEI	14.3	21.3	27.6	32.0	42.2	30.0	33.3	27.1	12.1
URD	25.5	16.3	7.9	2.5	1.5	1.5	1.0		
FND (IPFN)		12.3	1.9						
FDP		9.0	5.1						
MEP			11.7	4.0	2.0	1.5	1.0		
CCN			9.8	3.5					
MAS				4.5	5.5	5.0		12.6	12.1
MAS-MIR							9.0		
Convergencia								12.6	
Causa R								20.1	
MVR									19.8
Proyecto Venezuela									10.1
Others	5.3	4.0	3.2	2.5	4.6	5.5	7.4	0.0	16.8

Sources: Kornblith and Levine 1995; Amorim Neto 1998.

---

reduce fragmentation. I will discuss these reforms in greater detail below in this chapter, in the section "The Failure of Decentralizing Electoral Reform in Venezuela."

rewritten the Venezuelan constitution, rebuffed a coup, prevailed in a referendum on his rule, and won reelection under the new rules in 2006. In short, the two traditional Venezuelan parties have declined in a startlingly rapid fashion, losing control of the legislature, the presidency, and the process of drawing up a new set of institutional rules that will govern Venezuelan politics for the foreseeable future.

In light of these developments, new institutionalists and other scholars have argued that on closer scrutiny, Venezuela's party leaders were in fact *too* strong. In the words of Shugart and Haggard: "The highly party-centered Venezuelan system did not produce legislators attentive to providing broad collective goods." They introduce a caveat into the theory by arguing that "even in extremely party-centered formulas, there is still the possibility that voters' preferences over policy issues might be unimportant to individual legislators. Under such formulas . . . legislators have the incentive to curry favor with party leaders and lobby for higher list positions rather than cultivate ties with voters. Therefore, while legislators are likely to exhibit greater policy responsiveness when they are elected under highly party-centered rules rather than highly candidate-centered rules, it is possible for parties to be *too* strong in the sense that they provide incentives to ignore constituent interests" (2001, 88; emphasis in the original). Crisp has also argued that "the closed-list, proportional-representation electoral system meant that voters could only choose among parties rather than individual deputies or senators. As a result, legislators were accountable to the leaders of their parties rather than to constituents" (2000, 11).

Coppedge (1994a) has provided the most detailed analysis of how Venezuelan party leaders' extreme powers hindered effective democratic accountability. Coppedge labeled Venezuela a "partyarchy" to highlight the degree to which parties interfere with meeting Dahl's criteria for a polyarchy. Among other features, the draconian measures that the unelected party leadership employed to control the behavior of the rank and file hindered effective representation. The party leadership in Venezuela, the National Executive Committee of the AD (CEN) and the National Committee of COPEI (CN), was not popularly elected, nor was it selected by those who had a popular mandate, as, for example, the rank and file of the party.[5] This leadership retained control of the nominations for all national congressional depu-

---

5. The CEN was chosen by the delegates to the National Convention, which consisted of state-level party bosses and leaders of the sectoral groups of labor, youth, women, peasants and professionals. None of these delegates were popularly elected, but instead were chosen in internal party elections. The CN of COPEI was selected in a similar fashion.

ties, state assemblymembers, and municipal councilors and thus determined who was elected based on the single-*tarjeta* vote. On this type of ballot, Venezuelans had one choice for president and one choice between parties for every other elected office. Venezuela used an "absolutely closed list" proportional representation system for federal legislators, in which candidates' names did not appear on the ballot. The leadership allocated electoral votes to all candidates at all levels of government (Coppedge, 1994a, 21–26; 1995).[6]

The leadership also rigidly controlled rank-and-file position taking and voting in the legislature through adherence to "democratic centralism," which resulted in near-perfect party unity in the Venezuelan Congress. In the words of Coppedge, "Discipline is so tight that congressional votes are almost never counted or recorded. Debate consists of one spokesman designated by his party standing to state . . . the party position on the legislation at hand" (1994b, 327–28). Any attempt to flout this control resulted in summary dismissal from the party.

More important, the party line that the rank and file must toe exactly was determined by the CEN. As Coppedge (1994a, 39–44, 177) points out, this rigid control by an unelected leadership, in combination with other features of Venezuelan parties, severed the link between voter policy preferences and policy choice. If the leadership that sets policy is not subject to some ultimate sanction based on popular vote, either directly or through the mediation of the party caucus, the ability of elections to translate voter preferences into policies is severely curtailed.[7]

If postwar Brazil was a case of extreme laxity of party leader stewardship, Venezuela was a case of extreme rigidity of leadership control. If in Brazil it seems that party leaders failed to act to insulate the rank and file from excessively individualistic constituent demands in order to present a coherent policy program, in Venezuela, party leaders failed to provide any conduit through which constituent policy preferences could be transmitted to the

---

6. In 1988 Venezuela adopted reforms through which governors became elected (they had previously been appointed by the president) and that created an elected post of mayor (previously there had been no mayoral post). In 1989, a reform was passed requiring that half of the national deputies be elected in single-member districts beginning in 1993 (Coppedge 1995, 179). Here I treat the period of 1958–93; I discuss the reforms in greater detail below.

7. As Coppedge (1994a) is careful to point out, if the internal party elections and factional competition within the AD were driven by policy disputes, this could create a link between voter preferences and the policy decisions of the internally chosen CEN. Yet the author provides a wealth of data to demonstrate that there is no relation between policy position and factional conflict in internal party competition.

hermetically sealed leadership. Just as in Brazil, these rules in Venezuela severed the link between voter policy preferences and party decisions and raise the issue of an unanswered accountability vacuum. How did these parties, whose organizational features inhibited linking party behavior to voter policy preferences, remain viable electoral players? Would they not be vulnerable to challenge from parties that organized to forge stronger links between voters' preferences and the policies adopted? Would such alternative parties not stand to reap substantial electoral gains?

One simple reform that would have gone a considerable way toward achieving such a goal in Venezuela would have been to allow the rank and file to select party leaders, delegating the leadership power to organize the party internally such that it could maintain a policy reputation, and punishing this leadership with no reelection if they failed to organize the party effectively.[8] In Brazil, party leaders could have used indirect means to counteract the incentives of open-list PR, using any perks at their disposal to reward those who voted with the party and who maintained their personal electioneering within bounds that did not excessively damage the party's policy reputation. If voters' choices are in fact determined at least in part by overall policy, the absence of party movement in a direction that could respond to this policy component of the vote remains quite puzzling. As I will show in the following two sections, a theory of voting that yields two equilibria can explain why neither dominant parties nor challengers adopted these changes.

Open-List PR in Postwar Brazil: Aligning Individual Legislators' Incentives with the Party Goal of Efficient Vote Buying

Many analysts have noted the choice of Brazilian politicians to organize parties as loose federations with the return to democratic rule in 1945. One aspect of this choice was the decision to use open-list PR, which denied leaders the ability to determine the order of election. Another was to give

---

8. In the United States, for example, it is customary for the majority leader in the House of Representatives to lose his or her job as ultimate leader of the party in the legislature if the party does not retain majority status in an election.

As I will discuss below, it is interesting that in choosing reforms in the 1990s, Venezuelan party leaders studiously avoided any that would submit party leadership positions to either direct or indirect popular sanction. In fact, in the 1980s, such a reform was proposed and explicitly rejected. See Coppedge 1994a, 112–16.

leaders only limited powers over access to the ballot.[9] The result of these choices was that postwar parties were unable to effectively aggregate or articulate policy preferences to present national policy alternatives (Souza 1976, Cardoso 1973, Furtado 1965, Jaguaribe 1958). Yet with a better understanding of how clientelistic competition alters the organizational strategies that will best serve the party's electoral interests we can explain this apparent accountability vacuum. Rules that would have weakened the leadership in the case of policy-based competition were in fact well chosen to ensure efficient vote buying and minimize bidding wars when national parties were made up of loose federations of individually owned and operated clientelist networks.

To demonstrate how these rules actually strengthened parties and their ability to win votes and elections in postwar Brazil, a brief digression on resource control in the two regimes that preceded the postwar democracy is necessary. In Brazil's Old Republic (1889–1930), a semidemocratic regime with limited suffrage, state-level government resources obtained through taxes on exports far outweighed those available at the federal level. States had exclusive authority to tax both interstate and international commerce, including the booming export trade (Soares 1973). This period corresponded to the heyday of commodity exporting across Latin America, and Brazil was no exception. Political parties were organized at the state level, and the presidency alternated between the two most prosperous and populous states, Sao Paulo and Minas Gerais (Skidmore 1967; Soares 1973).

The Old Republic was followed by fifteen years of semidemocratic and authoritarian rule under Getúlio Vargas, from 1930 to 1945. During this period, the existing state-level distribution system was overlaid with a vast new range of resources for distribution at the federal level. These included a program of coffee price supports, the initiation of import substitution industrialization programs for subsidizing a rapid industrialization drive, and the organization of state-corporatist labor unions and the creation of a range of new worker benefits (Skidmore 1967, 33–35). The key point is that by 1945, a clearly state-level system of distributing resources was overlaid with a national system for subsidizing agriculture and industry and providing jobs and benefits to newly organized labor.

---

9. There were several aspects to this feature of party law. As discussed in Chapter 2, candidates joining a given coalition were not required to name their party affiliation until after the election. Brazil also uses what is known as the *candidato nato* rule, which allows anyone who has been elected on a given party label automatic access to that label in future elections.

If structural conditions favor the clientelistic equilibrium, the collective-individual conflict that plagues party organization in policy-based systems does not disappear, but the substance of the conflict differs. In a policy-based system, the conflict revolves around the balance between building a party reputation versus building personal reputations. In clientelist systems, however, the conflict revolves around how to use resources in buying votes: while the rank and file prefer to employ resources in a fashion that will maximize the chance of their own (re)election, the party's preference is to ensure that each individual member expends resources in a fashion that maximizes overall seats won by the party. As discussed in Chapter 1, legislators have incentives to engage in two possible types of inefficient vote buying. They may attempt to "lock up" their clients by spending all their resources on just enough voters to get them elected or they may engage in bidding wars in order to win votes from co-partisans.

When the legislator's own seat is dependent on his or her individual vote total, however, as with open lists, then that legislator will be motivated to use the resources under his or her control efficiently in order to buy as many votes as possible *in order to ensure his or her own (re)election*. All else being equal, such efficient vote buying will maximize an individual legislator's chances for reelection in comparison with his or her co-partisans who spend more than the minimum necessary to buy each vote. At the same time, this incentive structure is also efficient for the party as a whole because it also maximizes the party's overall vote return on the resources under its label, which consist of the sum of all the resources controlled by individual networks under the party label. With multimember districts and pooling of votes, this individual behavior maximizes seats for the party.

Paradoxically, then, open-list PR was a tool that served *the party's* interest, by aligning the goal of individual legislators of winning a seat with the party goal of maximizing the number of seats won overall. The incentives created by the fact that individual vote totals determined the individual candidate's election encouraged efficient vote buying and discouraged bidding wars within the party. We can further test this interpretation of open-list PR by examining how party leaders distributed valuable perks under their control. If other rewards were also distributed on the basis of efficiency in buying votes, and loyalty to the party line in legislative voting was *not* important to how valuable plums were distributed, this would provide further evidence to support the clientelist model and the implications for the choice of open-list PR deduced from it.

One of the most prized positions during this period in Brazil was a seat on the powerful Budget Committee in the Chamber of Deputies. Legislators obtained resources for their local districts by submitting individual amendments to the annual budget. A seat on the Budget Committee was coveted because individual members with authority over specific portions of the budget had ultimate authority over whether a given deputy's individual amendment would be accepted or rejected (Rocha 1995, 30).[10] I completed an analysis of all appointments to the Budget Committee throughout the period.[11] Party leaders had the exclusive power to appoint individual deputies to the Budget Committee. Appointments were for one year, with unlimited reappointments. Thus, the criteria used to allocate these plums provide important insight into what kind of behavior party leaders wished to reward.[12] The independent variables used to predict budget committee appointments include party loyalty in legislative voting, electoral performance in the most recent election, seniority, and dominance. Each of these variables requires some discussion.

From 1945 to 1964, we have no indication of the voting recommendations of party leaders. I measure party loyalty as the percentage of the time the deputy votes with the majority.[13] The electoral performance is the number of votes the deputy receives divided by the number of votes it takes to win a seat in that district (the electoral quotient). This variable provides a measure of electoral performance that is standardized across states (districts). Seniority is a count of how many terms the given deputy has served.[14]

---

10. The budget was subdivided according to executive ministry, and individual members of the budget committee were assigned as rapporteurs for each of these subdivisions. The budget committee members drew up written reports for each individual budget amendment submitted in their area, in which they also recommended acceptance or rejection. The budget committee member's recommendation was routinely followed in the final floor vote on the budget (Rocha 1995).

11. The committee with authority over the budget was originally called the Finance Committee. In 1955 a new committee, the Budget and Financial Oversight Committee, was created, and authority over the budget was transferred from the Finance Committee to this new committee. I analyze distribution of seats on the appropriate committee with authority over the budget throughout the period.

12. More precise data on actual receipt of funds based on submission of individual amendments is not available for the postwar period. Nevertheless, the Budget Committee remained the key gatekeeping entity in the legislature, and many budget amendments were rejected at this stage.

13. For a more detailed discussion of measurements of party loyalty, see Appendix 2.

14. In Brazil, a set of *suplentes*, or substitutes, are elected with each slate of deputies in the district. If a deputy leaves his or her seat for any reason before his or her term is up, the first *suplente* (the member of his party with the next-highest vote total) takes the seat. If another deputy from the same party leaves, the second *suplente* takes the seat, and so on. I estimated the models with four different versions of seniority, including counting all terms both as deputy and substitute as a term, and counting only contiguous terms as deputy and

Dominance, as discussed in Chapter 2, is a measure of the degree to which the deputy's vote total is constructed from concentrated municipal chunks.[15] I also included control variables for the state of the deputy. State-level influences were very important during this period, and it is likely that party leaders attempted to maintain some balance in terms of state representation on this powerful committee.[16] I analyzed each party separately to determine the best predictors of gaining a Budget Committee seat.[17] The coefficients, with robust standard errors in parentheses, are reported in Table 24.

Table 24 Determinants of seat assignments, Finance and Budget Committee, Federal Chamber of Deputies, Brazil, 1945–1964

	PSD	UDN	PTB	PSP	PR
Ployl	2.15*	−3.26*	.027	−.396	−.595
	(1.10)	(1.29)	(.761)	(1.70)	(2.06)
Eperf	1.68**	5.14***	.417*	2.64***	4.25***
	(.556)	(1.21)	(.179)	(.791)	(.967)
Sen	.527**	.331	.270	-.930*	.407*
	(.180)	(.297)	(.147)	(.396)	(.168)
Dom	−8.59***	9.25***	—	—	—
	(1.72)	(2.52)			
Constant	−3.48	−4.78	−1.54	−19.9	−2.81
Log-likelihood	−191	−86.2	−292	−83.9	−54.1
N	622	281	908	307	185
% Predicted Correctly	12.0	25.1	6.6	21.5	27.9

*$p < .05$, **$p < .01$, ***$p < .001$

---

suplente, and the same for terms only served as deputy. None of these variations changed any of the results.

15. I was able to obtain dominance data for only a limited number of deputies during this period. For all parties except the PSD and the UDN, the inclusion of dominance in the model cut the sample down so drastically that I had to drop the dominance variable. By including dominance, the number of observations for the PSD was reduced from 1,993 to 649, and for the UDN from 1,237 to 365 (using state controls led to a few additional observations being dropped because no deputy from the given state gained a seat on the Budget Committee). I opted to include dominance for these parties when I estimated the models, because of the importance of dominance to our understanding of clientelist politics and because the variation explained is higher with the inclusion of dominance. With the inclusion of dominance, R^2 increased from .06 to .25 for the UDN and remained essentially unchanged for the PSD.

16. I do not report the results for the state dummies. Inclusion of state dummies almost doubles the percentage of variation explained. Full results are available from the author upon request.

17. The PDC, the sixth-largest party of this period, had very few assignments to the Budget Committee, and none of the variables were significant, so I did not report these results.

The results reported in Table 24 demonstrate that electoral variables were the most important determinants of when a deputy would gain a seat on the powerful Budget Committee. Electoral performance is positive and statistically significant for all five parties: at the .001 level for the UDN, PSP, and PR; at the .01 level for the PSD; and at the .05 level for the PTB. This provides strong evidence that party leaders were intent on encouraging the rank and file to bring in as many votes as possible. One might argue that party leaders would reward high vote totals even when organizing to provide policy goods if votes were pooled across the party. Encouraging candidates to maximize vote totals is not inconsistent with providing collective policy goods. To investigate whether this emphasis on electoral performance is designed to reward pure vote-buying or is a strategy used in combination with providing policy goods, we must examine whether party loyalty in legislative voting has any bearing on gaining a seat on the budget committee.

Party loyalty is positive and significant for only one party, the PSD, and in this case it is a weak association—the coefficient just barely misses the conventional cutoff for statistical significance at the .05 level. It is not significant for three of the other four parties (and negatively associated with gaining a Budget Committee seat for two of those three) and was *negatively* associated with appointments to the budget committee for the UDN. These results are very difficult to reconcile with providing any level of collective policy goods. If electoral politics drives politicians to provide policy goods, and party leaders have no direct means to ensure that the rank and file vote with the party, we would expect loyalty in voting to play a key role in how valuable indirect rewards are distributed. The fact that there is very limited evidence, at best, for only one party supports the explanation of the choice for open-list PR deduced from the theory of clientelist competition. The significance of electoral performance combined with the lack of significance for party loyalty buttresses the argument that party leaders were using the tools at their disposal to encourage efficient use of resources in buying votes and to discourage bidding wars in a clientelist competition.

Dominance, which is also a measure of electoral behavior, is significant for the two parties for which I was able to estimate with this variable included. Rather than a standardized measure of how many votes the deputy gained, it is a measure of the degree to which he or she was able to lock up large percentages of the vote in each municipality in which he or she garnered votes. In other words, as discussed in Chapter 2, this is a measure of how efficient a clientelist the deputy was, in organizing the delivery of the vote into municipal blocs. For the UDN, dominance is positively associated with gaining a seat, along with electoral performance. For the PSD, dominance has a negative sign, indicating that a standardized measure of electoral performance is more important than efficient clientelist vote buying *by municipality*.

This finding, while appearing at first glance to be contradictory, may very well reflect the differences in PSD and UDN constituencies and corresponding clientelist networks. The vast majority of UDN support came from rural areas, where vote delivery had long been organized in hierarchical networks based on the municipality (Nunes Leal 1977). The rural oligarchies that delivered the local vote in rural areas continued to dominate local politics throughout the postwar period. The PSD's support, by contrast, came from a combination of rural agricultural municipally based networks, as well as from the urban bureaucracies created to administer the new industrialization programs. As was discussed in Chapter 2, these votes were organized and delivered by the government bureaucracies through the ex officio voting system (Souza n.d.). Dominance in this type of delivery system will show up not as geographically concentrated by municipality, but instead as concentrated on the basis of the officially sanctioned corporatist interest groups created to represent each of the different government occupations. Such organizations proliferated from 1930 to 1964 as Vargas and later presidents organized not only labor, but also white-collar bureaucrats into officially sanctioned, hierarchical, corporatist-interest organizations with exclusive authority to represent each professional and labor group (Schmitter 1971). What remains a key finding, however, is that the less ambiguous measure of electoral performance is positive and significant for all parties.

In sum, these data provide strong evidence to support the argument that in fact there was no accountability vacuum in postwar Brazil, but rather a distinct electoral connection driven by structural conditions. If structural conditions favor the clientelistic equilibrium, then parties must align individual legislator incentives with efficient vote buying. This logic accounted both for the open-list PR rule that rewards those with the highest vote totals with reelection, and the distribution of valuable committee assignments based on electoral performance but with minimal regard for upholding the party's policy reputation by loyally voting with the party. In other words, internal party organization did not result in an unanswered accountability vacuum in a policy-based system; rather, parties were well tuned to winning a clientelist competition.

Absolutely Closed Lists and Decentralized Administration in Venezuela: Eliminating Competition in Vote Buying

Unlike in Brazil, where political leaders inherited well-entrenched patterns with the return to democracy in 1945, in Venezuela, the new leaders gained control of the reins of government after a violent change of regime in the mid-1940s. If the victorious powers expected that structural conditions would favor clientelistic competition and that government leaders would have centralized control of a trumping resource, it is not surprising that they opted for rigid hierarchical rules for organizing parties. Apparently dysfunctional rules that severed the link between voters and policy outcome in Venezuela were well chosen to eliminate incentives for members of the rank and file to bid against one another at all stages of the electoral and legislative process and thus avoid wasteful dissipation of the party's resources in buying votes. These rules were also chosen to demonstrate the party's ability to work the institutional machinery of government and thus fortify the party's reputation for turning control of centralized resources into goods that could be exchanged directly for votes.

With closed-list PR rules, in which the party leadership determined who got on the ballot and in what order, Venezuelan party leaders chose rules that eliminated rank-and-file incentives to compete with one another for voter support in order to gain nomination. Further extreme rules can be interpreted as designed to eliminate incentives for competitive bidding in order to gain election. If voters have virtually no influence over the electoral fate of individual party members, and electoral outcomes within the party are determined by party leaders alone, this eliminates any incentive for rank and file members to bid against one another in an attempt to improve their electoral fortunes. In Venezuela, the absolutely closed nature of the list, in which individual names do not appear on the ballot, once again reduces incentives for rank and file to attempt to woo voters. The absence of names on the ballot reflects the fact that rank-and-file members are simply delegates given the task of maintaining clientelist networks in the name of the party.

Potential incentives to engage in bidding wars to improve one's position vis-à-vis fellow party members are not confined to gaining nomination or election. If reelection is a goal, the legislature also becomes an arena for potential competition between individual members. In Venezuela, the incentive to compete with one's fellow partisans in the legislature for the resources needed to build clientelist networks was eliminated through "democratic centralism," the rule that stipulates that the rank and file must slavishly follow the marching orders of the leadership in the legislature. Any attempt to gain access to resources or build one's own reputation by voting against the party line is summarily punished with expulsion from the party. Thus, party leaders eliminate attempts by individual legislators to outmaneuver and outbid one another on the floor of the legislature in order to enhance their electoral chances by dictating legislative behavior.

Such draconian control of legislative behavior might seem unnecessary with the absolutely closed list. But if a legislative career is a stepping-stone to a position as a state party leader, or to the presidency, legislative competition could arise in pursuit of these offices.[18] The other side of this coin is that any apparent weakness in the party's ability to control legislative outcomes would be seen as weakening its ability to deliver in comparison with its competitors. The party that can reliably deliver the entire caucus vote will be better able to work the institutional machinery and deliver excludable goods to voters and thus will be able to make more credible claims to be able to deliver than will the party that cannot ensure the vote of the rank and file.

An understanding of the competitive imperatives of clientelistic politics provides an answer to the puzzle of the accountability vacuum by explaining these choices as designed to minimize bidding wars and ensure the most efficient use of the party's resources in buying votes. Venezuelan leaders chose rules that severed the link between voter preferences and rank-and-file behavior because this also eliminated the incentive for the rank and file to bid against one anther and thus waste precious resources needed for maximizing votes won through direct exchange. By the same token, rules that severed the link between voters' policy preferences and legislative outcomes were not detrimental to electoral success, because when structural conditions favor the clientelistic equilibrium, overall outcomes do not inform voters' choices.

Finally, rigid hierarchical control of leadership positions within the party by the CEN and CN meant that they maintained control over how resources were distributed and thus maintained their electoral dominance. When resources buy votes directly, relinquishing positions with authority over resources to the uncertainty of elections is vulnerable to the same problems outlined in Chapter 1 with regard to the position of the government and the

---

18. As Coppedge (1994a) discusses, there is considerable evidence that Venezuelan presidential candidates from the same party do in fact compete to build clientelist followings.

opposition. The extreme advantage of incumbency and the weakness of the opposition apply to positions of leadership within the party just as they apply to competition between parties. When resources buy votes directly, those who control resources and who can organize collectively can control outcomes. When policy is an important component of voting choice, in contrast, control of resources (through leadership positions, for example) does not confer the same ability to determine outcomes. Venezuelan party leaders chose these rules that insulated the leadership from any popular control because ceding control of leadership positions to the vagaries of elections would risk ceding the tremendous power conferred by the control of resources in clientelistic systems.

In sum, internal organizational choices that should have led to punishment at the polls if parties were competing to provide the collective policy goods most preferred by voters in fact served parties' electoral goals very well in a clientelistic competition. The Venezuelan parties that dominated the electoral arena in pre-Chávez Venezuela chose apparently dysfunctional internal rules that severed the link between voters' policy preferences and party behavior because providing policy goods was not an electoral winner. These "dysfunctional" rules were chosen because they ensured control and efficient deployment of centralized resources, the key to electoral success in clientelistic pre-Chávez Venezuela.

The Failure of Decentralizing Electoral Reform in Venezuela

The growing economic crisis in Venezuela, as well as the increasing levels of voter rejection of the Venezuelan political establishment, including the dominant political parties, led to a national debate on needed reforms. A widely praised study, Presidential Commission for the Reform of the State (Comisión Presidencial para la Reforma des Estado [COPRE]), made a number of recommendations for party and electoral reform. In 1993, Venezuela adopted an important set of electoral reforms. Curiously, however, the recommended reforms that would have forged a stronger link between voters' policy preferences and politicians' policy choices were precisely those that were ignored.

Although the COPRE recommended major changes to the role of the party leadership, such as reducing their absolute grip over nominations and the procedures for choosing the leadership, the major parties repeatedly blocked implementation of these reforms. The reform that was adopted consisted primarily of introducing single-member districts into what was previously exclusively a closed-list PR system. This new mixed system allowed voters to cast votes for individual candidates, but it did not alter rank-and-file party members' incentives to respond to voters' policy preferences. As Shugart (1992) notes, these reforms did not do much to increase voters' *intra*party choice. This would be one route to empowering the rank and file to be more responsive to voters' policy preferences. If voters' choices had some influence on who gained a seat *within* the party, this would provide an electoral reward to those within the party who were more attuned to voters. But as the reform was implemented, the best the voter could do was vote for one party's nominee in the single-member district and the list of another party. This would have little effect on the rank and file's position vis-à-vis the leadership within a given party.

Party leaders also maintained total control of nominations, and thus the rank and file remained absolutely beholden to the leadership in order to gain access to the ballot. As Crisp (2000, 56) puts it, "The highly centralized nomination process renders the whole effect [of the reforms] somewhat moot. Each party's national executive committee still controls the nomination of deputies." Finally, these reforms did not alter the lack of popular accountability of the CEN. Thus, although the reforms allowed voters to vote for individual candidates in the single-member districts, it is not clear how this change would actually empower these deputies to better represent constituent preferences. As long as nominations and election are strictly dictated by a leadership that is not held accountable to some entity with a popular mandate, it is not clear where and how popular preferences could actually be channeled through these parties. If the leadership retains strict control of nominations and order on the list, and cannot be dismissed by the party caucus, this reform does not in fact provide an avenue by which backbenchers chafing under party dictates could better represent voters and simultaneously advance their careers.

The fact that party leaders refused to adopt the changes necessary for creating increased responsiveness to constituents' policy preferences again raises questions about a policy accountability vacuum. If voters were disenchanted with parties because of their lack of responsiveness to their *policy* preferences, why would existing parties or new challengers not alter their internal rules to fill the policy accountability vacuum and reap electoral rewards? If we consider a theory of voting that yields both a clientelist and a policy-based equilibrium we can make sense of the refusal to address the purported accountability vacuum.

How does a theory of clientelist competition account for the decisions for what to discard and what to adopt in the proposed reforms? If policy informed some portion of voters' choices, it is hard to explain why all the choices for creating a link between voters and policy decisions within the party were rejected: primaries or some other decentralized candidate selection, intraparty choice on the list, or making the leadership accountable to the party caucus. But if structural conditions render clientelism voters' best strategic choice, we can explain why party leaders avoided any such reforms like the plague: any such choice would diminish the party's ability to efficiently deliver the vote based on direct exchange and thus would diminish the party's reputation for delivering.[19]

Primaries or intraparty choice on the ballot would allow individual deputies to build their own clientelist following, allowing them to insert themselves between the party and the voters as agents capable of delivering. The other alternative of making the leadership accountable to a popular mandate within the caucus would similarly mean the CEN's ceding control of resources and thus the reputation for delivering. As has been discussed, legislators were extremely weak in this system—the rank and file were selected by the leadership who assigned the votes, were excluded from any legislative leadership positions, and dutifully followed the leaderships' voting directives. Party leadership posts were thus the real source of power in this system, and those who occupied them determined how resources, and thus votes and seats, were allocated. When voters and politicians are linked through direct exchange, surrendering any positions with exclusive control over resources to electoral uncertainty is extremely risky, because it can be tantamount to surrendering electoral viability itself. Surrendering the leadership posts to some kind of electoral process would possibly mean that the all-crucial control over resources could fall into the hands of someone other than the CEN. In sum, the initial choices for highly hierarchical and insulated parties and the decisions for which aspects of recommended reforms to adopt and reject are of a piece and reflect the imperatives of competition in a clientelistic system with a centralized trumping resource.

Party Organization in Venezuela Under Chávez

Chávez has built consistent support among parties on the left, including his own personalist vehicle, the MVR, as well as the MAS, the Venezuelan

---

19. As Ellner (1996) reports, COPEI's experiment with primaries to select the presidential candidate was seen as having weakened the party and was short lived.

Communist Party (Partido Comunista de Venezuela [PCV]), the Homeland for All Party (Patria para Todos [PPT]), and Podemos. Moreover, the AD and the COPEI have all but collapsed. Yet in December 2006, Chávez called for the dissolution of all previous political parties and the formation of a single national party, the PSUV. Why would Chávez find it necessary to dissolve all political parties in order to form a single party if he had received the loyal support of most of the currently viable political parties in recent elections?

Chávez and his supporters justify the change as a way to definitively sweep away all the vestiges of the previous internal party bureaucracies, one of the central obstacles to realizing the "revolution" and building a participatory and protagonist democracy. As Chávez has stated, the votes won by the various parties in past elections "belong to Chávez, that is, they belong to the people" (Ciccariello-Maher 2007, 2). Accordingto advocates, the PSUV will sweep away internal bureaucracy such that everyone enjoys equal conditions. In Chávez's words, "For this new era we need a new political structure that is placed not at the service of parties and their distinct colors, but rather at the service of the people and the Revolution" (Ciccariello-Maher 2007, 3). Chávez's critics, however, see these moves as worrying signs that the goal is not a true empowerment of the poor, but simply government control and cooptation by other means (Canache 2007; Roberts 2003). The penchant for organizing one political party that is loyal to his leadership alone is seen by many as the fateful mark of a power-hungry populist. A theory of clientelist competition suggests that these moves are neither those of a true defender of the people nor those of an incorrigible populist, but rather those of an astute politician who understands that the new leader will be the one who achieves an efficient reorganization of clientelism under his control. An understanding of clientelist competition highlights four reasons why these choices will facilitate an efficient reorganization.

First, by forming a single political party and eliminating all others, Chávez will consolidate all intermediation between citizens and government under his own personal control. Despite the claim that the PSUV will purportedly do away with bureaucracy, Chávez has exercised personal control over appointing a bureau to guide the creation of the party. Thus, he has personally named the members of the technical committee that will formulate the basic structure of the PSUV and accelerate its consolidation. Under the technical committee's guidance, eleven thousand activists have been chosen, purportedly based on their exemplary ethical values. These activists have begun canvassing the country to activate "socialist battalions," and both groups will help complete a census and registry of the new party in preparation for elections. Chávez has also appointed all members to the PSUV's "promotional commission," charged with the party's ideological development (Ciccariello-Maher 2007).

While it may seem obvious why Chávez would want to organize interest intermediation under his personal control, one of the payoffs of an understanding of clientelist competition is that we gain more insight into how this type of organization is advantageous. The second benefit of this strategy is that it allows Chávez to undercut any potential challengers who may have built up their own network of clientelistic support through one of the currently viable political parties. Manuel Rosales's position as governor of the major oil-producing state of Zulia, for example, was central to his ability to challenge Chávez in the 2006 presidential elections.[20] Although Chávez has concentrated vast resources, including oil revenues, in his own hands, state and local governments still have control over considerable government resources. If Chávez can eliminate all power bases rooted in the old system and place his own supporters in control of organizations that report directly to him, these competitors will find it virtually impossible to challenge him through elections. Leaders in clientelistic systems, particularly those with a trumping resource, must be especially vigilant in eliminating competitors. As discussed in Chapter 1, any player that can consolidate control over a national trumping resource gains extreme power to determine the outcome of elections. Venezuela's oil revenue, especially since the increase in prices after 2004, certainly meets the criteria of a national trumping resource. Clearly gaining control of those resources was key to Chávez's meteoric rise, but could equally well lead to his demise if they fell under a competitor's control.

The third benefit is that this single political party will help eliminate bidding wars and conflicts over resource distribution. In this chapter I have emphasized the bidding wars that can erupt *within* clientelistic political parties and how parties can organize to limit their occurrence. Competition between parties, however, is another powerful source of incentives for interparty bidding wars that are often more difficult to control. Power-sharing agreements, as discussed in Chapter 2, are one means for decreasing incentives for costly competition (in resource terms) between parties. Ultimately,

---

20. As many analysts have noted, his ability to unite the opposition, which had been extremely divided in several previous elections, was also important.

however, conflicts over resource distribution between distinct political parties prove to be some of the most difficult to solve in clientelistic systems.

As I will discuss in Chapter 6, a single hierarchical organization greatly facilitates adjustment to a resource crisis and is more likely to avoid regime-threatening conflicts over how to adjudicate a change in resource distribution. A single hierarchical organization facilitates institutionalization of solutions to mutual exclusivity of support and the bidding wars that can result. In Venezuela, the conflict between the two dominant parties about how to share the burdens of the needed clientelistic adjustment in the 1980s was an essential cause of the collapse of the previous system.

Finally, by organizing all his supporters under a single political party, Chávez can more easily reduce conflicts over access to elective office within his support coalition. One of the most contested issues in the Punto Fijista system was the position on the ballot within the AD and COPEI, since higher positions on the ballot vastly increased chances of election.[21] One of the reasons that Chávez's supporters swept the 2005 elections for the legislative chamber was that his coalition nominated only as many candidates as seats were available, and thus they did not divide their vote between too many candidates. The opposition, however, which was extremely atomized, nominated far more candidates than there were seats in each district. While Chávez was able to exert sufficient control over his support coalition to ensure they did not split the vote in this first election, it is easy to envision that mutual exclusivity and the one-to-one correspondence between control of resources and power would create conflicts over how many candidates each party would field in future elections. By Chávez's unifying his support under a single political party, the ability of distinct parties to simply ignore his directives and run as many candidates as each party is allowed under electoral law is avoided. Under the single-party scenario, it becomes more difficult to slip Chávez's control over nominations and damage the overall electoral strategy.

In sum, Chávez's ongoing program to reorganize clientelism in Venezuela within a single political party under his personal control can be seen less as a result of his leadership vices or virtues, and more as being driven by an attempt to reorganize clientelism while avoiding some of the inefficiencies of the previous regime.

21. Author's interviews with Paciano Padron, July 9, 2007; Naudy Suarez, July 4, 2007; Marco Bruni Telli, July 11, 2007; Canache Mata, July 11, 2007; and Nelson Chitty, July 10, 2007, all in Caracas.

Circumventing the Obstacles to Policy Reputations in Contemporary Brazil: Counteracting the Effects of Open-List PR

If policy-based voting predominates, unmodified open-list PR will in fact create an accountability vacuum. As new institutionalists have ably argued, parties will likely find this rule to be a hindrance to providing the level of policy goods desired by the electorate. By creating strong incentives for individualist behavior, and limiting party leaders' ability to reconcile personal politicking and the party's policy reputation, open-list PR would mean that parties fail to provide the level of policy goods that voters prefer. Once again, if voters include overall policy in their voting choice, this accountability vacuum should be vulnerable to challenge, and those parties that move to fill it should reap electoral gains. If Brazilian voters are now choosing based at least in part on collective goods policy, then we should expect parties to develop ways to modify the incentives created by open-list PR.

I test this hypothesis by examining how party leaders distribute valuable perks in the current period. The process by which individual legislators obtain locally targeted resources is highly institutionalized and centralized in contemporary Brazil. The annual budget process includes individual legislators' formal submission of requests for locally targeted funds. Resources distributed through the budget by means of individual legislators' amendments continue to be very important to their ability to build personal reputations in the current regime (Ames 2001).[22] Legislators typically submit amendments totaling the maximum allowed sum of 2 million reais, and they constantly agitate for the release of amendment funds, especially in election years. As in the earlier period, the Budget Committee approves budget amendments. The difference in the current period, however, is that Budget Committee decisions have become largely a formality—the vast majority of requests up to the maximum individual limit are approved. The gatekeeping role in the current period is now held by party leaders in conjunction with the executive, who determine which amendments will actually be funded. In other words, the key decision in the current regime is the

---

22. Samuels (2003) has argued that receipt of funds requested through individual budget amendments does not help legislators get reelected to the legislature. He concludes, however, that these funds are important to politicians' overall career goals. The analysis presented here only requires that receipt of budget-amendment funds affect legislators' individual goals, which is consistent with Samuels's analysis. Moreover, reelection rates have risen considerably since the completion of Samuels's study, and thus this conclusion may warrant revisiting.

decision by the relevant ministry to release the funds, as approved by the president and party leaders. This has become a powerful tool that party leaders can employ to counteract the effects of open-list PR and reduce the accountability vacuum its incentives create.

Interviews with staff and party leaders from the PMDB and the PSDB confirmed that the executive, in conjunction with party leaders, keep careful account of how rank-and-file members vote and distribute budget amendment funds on the basis of whether party members vote as recommended by the leadership.[23] This interview data is supported by a regression analysis of receipt of budget funds.

Receipt of Budget Funds

Since 1996, the Brazilian Chamber of Deputies has maintained public data on the release of funds requested through individual budget amendments. An analysis of the receipt of budget funds indicates that party loyalty in legislative voting is now a key determinant who receives resources for their local district. Independent variables used to predict receipt of budget funds are the same as those used to predict who got a seat on the Budget Committee in the earlier period: party loyalty, electoral performance, seniority, and dominance. In the current period, however, party leaders make their voting recommendations public, and so loyalty to the leadership is measured directly as the percentage of the time the legislator votes as recommended by the leadership.[24] I also included control variables for the state of the deputy.[25]

As the data in Table 25 demonstrate, party loyalty is positive and statistically significant at the .001 level for four out of the six major parties. For the PDT, there are only ninety observations, so including twenty-six control variables for the states in addition to the four substantive predictors results in a very small ratio of observations to predictors. I thus ran the PDT model controlling for the five regions rather than the twenty-six states, and in this

23. Author's interviews with Dr. Eugenio Greggianin, director of the Office of Budget Affairs, Camara dos Deputados, June 12, 2002; Lincoln Cardoso, staff to PMDB leadership, June 8, 2002; Diogo Álves de Abreu Junior, chief of staff for the PSDB party leadership, June 10, 2002; Ana Márcia Petriz, chief of staff for government leadership in the Camara dos Deputados, June 15, 2002, all in Brasilia, Brazil.
24. For details about measurement of these variables, see Appendix 2.
25. Brazil has twenty-six states, and I do not report these results; they are available from the author upon request.

Table 25 Receipt of budget amendment funds, Federal Chamber of Deputies, Brazil, 1996–2001

	PSDB	PFL	PMDB	PPB	PT	PDT
Ployl	.687***	.062	.478***	.586***	1.51***	.540
	(.121)	(.161)	(.071)	(.094)	(.297)	(.377)
Eperf	.067	.028	-.049	-.018	.122	.035
	(.069)	(.068)	(.066)	(.077)	(.091)	(.108)
Sen	.023	.055***	−.003	.041*	.004	.015
	(.015)	(.014)	(.017)	(.019)	(.026)	(.056)
Dom	.411***	−.022	.296*	.562**	−.128	.040
	(.128)	(.147)	(.143)	(.213)	(.218)	(.325)
Constant	.041	.321	.051	.099	−.827	−.063
N	378	405	361	282	189	90

$*p < .05$, $**p < .01$, $***p < .001$

Note: Standard diagnostic tests revealed unusual or influential data and heteroskedasiticity initial regression results for the PMDB, PFL, and the PSDB. To correct for these problems, I ran the regressions with the rreg command.

case party loyalty is significant at the .05 level (with a coefficient of .668 and a standard error of .325) while none of the other variables, including region, were significant. If we note also that electoral performance is not significant for any party, these results are almost *the exact mirror image* of the earlier period on these two variables. Party loyalty was irrelevant in the earlier period, but electoral performance was crucial, whereas in the current period party loyalty is critical whereas electoral performance is irrelevant. Clearly, party leaders are now concerned with how the rank and file vote in the legislature and are much less interested in racking up high vote totals. This constitutes strong evidence that party leaders are responding to a shift to policy-based voting. If voters are now examining the credibility of parties' policy-based appeals, voting records are critical to electoral success. To ensure a party voting record that can inform a policy reputation, the leadership must act to mitigate the effects of open-list PR such that personal electioneering does not excessively damage the party's policy reputation. The data indicate that in five out of the six major parties in contemporary Brazil, this is precisely what party leaders have done.

Finally, the absence of party loyalty as a predictor of which PFL deputies receive locally targeted resources deserves some comment. Until his death in mid-2007, this party was dominated to a significant degree by a powerful figure from the earlier period, Antônio Carlos Magalhães (ACM), a senator from the state of Bahia. It is well known that ACM exercised considerable control over PFL deputies, especially in the Northeast. It may be that adaptation to new rules requires a change in long-standing leadership and the passing of the leadership to a new generation may result in changes in the PFL's internal organization.

Examining the other variables, seniority is significant for the PPB and the PFL, and dominance is significant for the PSDB, the PMDB, and the PPB. The importance of dominance may well reflect problems of credit claiming in multimember districts when deputies are delivering nonexcludable goods at the local level (namely, classic pork as discussed in Chapter 1). As Samuels (2003,121–24) has argued, claiming credit in multimember districts is problematic—who will receive credit for locally targeted public works in a multimember district? How can voters discern which of the many representatives in the district was responsible for bringing home the bacon? Ames (2001) provides an answer. Dominance of a given municipality within the larger multimember district makes it easier for a deputy to claim credit for the resources delivered to that municipality. Thus, parties may concentrate more locally targeted resources on deputies who are able to dominate some municipalities, because this scenario facilitates credit claiming, in contrast to the case when a number of deputies receive significant votes in the same municipality.

Conclusion

The theory developed here can explain the longevity of institutional choices that appeared to create an accountability vacuum in pre-Chávez Venezuela and postwar Brazil. Analysts of these democracies have provided crucial insight into how both Brazil's highly decentralized parties and Venezuela's exceedingly centralized parties inhibited the translation of voters' policy preferences into national collective goods platforms. At the same time, these analysts' conclusions suggest that the dominant parties' choices created an accountability vacuum that remained unanswered despite decades of fierce electoral competition. Moreover, these analyses are of little help in understanding why Chávez appears to be taking Venezuela down an even less representative path, and they shed little light on why parties in contemporary Brazil, in contrast, have reorganized to provide policy goods and reduce the accountability vacuum.

With a theory of voter choice that yields both a clientelistic and a policy-based equilibrium, we can explain these puzzles. Variation in the electoral equilibrium will lead to variation in the collective-individual conflict that plagues party organization. With clientelist competition, party leaders must align rank-and-file incentives with efficient vote buying for the party as a whole. I argued that decentralized rules that rewarded the rank and file on the basis of vote totals (namely, open-list PR) were in fact highly effective in promoting efficient vote buying and thus in maximizing the party's electoral success in a system with decentralized clientelistic networks, as in postwar Brazil. This explanation for open-list PR was also supported by an analysis of the way in which valuable Budget Committee assignments were distributed—on the basis of electoral performance alone, rather than some combination of loyal party voting and electoral performance. I also argued that leadership control of nominations, the single-*tarjeta* vote, closed lists, and "democratic centralism" in Venezuela served to ensure that the rank and file never had any occasion to waste resources in costly internal competition to buy votes. I also showed that the same theory of clientelist competition could explain the failed 1993 electoral reform, as well as Chávez's choices for reorganizing parties in Venezuela. Finally, I argued that a shift in voters' strategy to policy-based voting provides an explanation for why parties have reorganized to develop a policy reputation in contemporary Brazil, despite a lack of change in key institutional rules. There is no doubt that institutional rules in Brazil continue to encumber the formation of governing majorities and continue to create incentives for personalist politicking, but there is also strong evidence that elections now select for those parties that organize internally such that they can balance personal electioneering with credible policy-based appeals.

Legislative Organization: Governing Majority Agenda Control or Mutual Veto?

In the previous two chapters I discussed the link between voters and parties and between rank-and-file party members and party leaders. These relationships precede and undergird the central work of government—the promulgation of laws. In this chapter I turn to the legislature, the prime locus of policy deliberation in democracies. As they have with other aspects of behavior and choice, analysts have noted unusual features of legislative organization in developing democracies. Curiously, legislatures are often organized in a fashion that would appear to thwart legislative production, and many scholars have concluded that this certainly was the practical result in many developing countries. As will be shown in this chapter, we can understand these purportedly dysfunctional choices, apparent in postwar Brazil and both Venezuelan regimes, as designed to serve the interests of politicians competing in clientelistic systems. A theory that yields both a clientelistic and a policy-based equilibrium can also explain why politicians sometimes alter legislative organization to eliminate such obstacles to the promulgation of effective collective goods policy, as has been the case in contemporary Brazil.

In the first section I review the scholarship documenting that legislative power was not turned over to a winning majority party or coalition in many developing democracies, but instead was parceled out in a way that gave many players veto power, but that placed extreme constraints on proactive power to change policy. In the second and third sections, I examine legislative organization in postwar Brazil and pre-Chávez Venezuela, documenting how mutual vetoes evolved as a result of freewheeling competition and decentralized decision making in the former, but were fashioned through highly centralized a priori agreements in the latter. In the fourth section, I develop the implications of clientelistic competition for legislative organization and show both why mutual vetoes are essential and why governing majorities are anathema in clientelistic systems.

In the fifth and sixth sections I revisit legislative organization in the two historical cases and discuss how their respective legislative organization served politicians competing in a decentralized and centralized clientelistic system. In the seventh section I discuss Chávez's gutting of the legislature with adoption of a new constitution in 1999, as well as the legislature's granting of sweeping decree powers in 2006. In the last section, I argue that legislative organization that is characteristic of clientelist politics seen in postwar Brazil has given way to new rules that we would expect politicians to adopt if they now must respond to voters exercising policy-based voting: in contemporary Brazil, the legislature has been reorganized such that a governing coalition can assert control over the legislative agenda in order to deliver the collective policy goods that it promised in elections. Key measures of legislative output indicate that the three most recent governments, of the five elected in contemporary Brazil, have in fact seized control of the legislative agenda to implement their program. Thus, in the legislative arena as well as in electoral behavior and in internal party organization, we see politicians reorganizing in exactly the fashion we would expect if there has been a shift from a clientelistic to a policy-based equilibrium.

Legislative Organization as Impediment to Governing Majorities in Developing Democracies

Early scholars who turned their attention to the actual political decision-making machinery of developing democracies were puzzled by the patterns they observed. Although legislatures were superficially organized in ways similar to those in the advanced industrial democracies, with executive boards (speakers), committees, and voting rules, they found that decision-making authority was either removed from the legislative arena or was constrained by the construction of mutual vetoes across the range of major parties represented in the legislature. To put it differently, no party or coalition, even while demonstrating the ability to mobilize the consent of a majority in an election, was able to control the legislative agenda to implement its advertised policies. The distribution of authority over the legislative agenda essentially meant that any bill that became law had to have the support of all major parties.

In the words of Eldon Kenworthy, such institutional arrangements meant that governments could reign, by blocking change, but they could not rule: they could not "implement major contested changes in the pattern of allocation" (Kenworthy 1970, 116). If the legislature was not organized to deliver policymaking power to a party or coalition commanding an electoral majority, then what was it designed to do? Many scholars noted a widespread pattern in which policymaking authority is compartmentalized and parceled out to those interests with the greatest stake in a given issue area (Scott 1966; Kenworthy 1970; Menges 1966; Kaufman 1967; Crisp 1998, 2000).

The effect of this decision-making structure on public policy was not lost on these observers. Not only were governments unable to "give binding and realistic decisions on controversial questions" (Kenworthy 1970, 115), such as how to implement much-needed macroeconomic stabilization, or how to restructure bloated and inefficient bureaucracies in order to spearhead state-led development; more generally, these governments were prone to "immobilism in the face of redistributive issues, [and] incoherent when viewed *in toto*" (Kenworthy 1970, 124). According to many prominent analysts of the postwar democracies, the development policy failures were the natural result of this decision-making structure.[1] As with the features of party organization and behavior discussed in the previous two chapters, these choices for legislative organization once again raise the question of an accountability vacuum. Why wouldn't a majority party or coalition that mobilizes consent in an election pursue ways to restructure the legislative agenda in order to implement the policies it advocated in the election and claim credit with its constituency?

Decentralized Prohibition of Governing Majorities in Postwar Brazil

Given Brazil's electoral rules, a governing majority would need to control the legislative agenda in order to control legislative output. Rules that limited party leaders' ability to control floor voting meant that managing legislative output would require careful management of what came to the floor for a vote. Control of the legislative agenda in postwar Brazil was divided be-

---

1. Kenworthy (1970) and Scott (1966) both forcefully make this point. Anderson (1967) develops a more elaborate model of politics that includes other variables in addition to legislative organizational design, but comes to the same conclusions about the debilitating effects on development policy.

tween the president of the Mesa Diretora (roughly equivalent to the Speaker of the House in the United States) and committee presidents. The Mesa president had ultimate gatekeeping authority in that he or she made decisions about the introduction of bills. All bills were initially remanded to the Constitution and Justice Committee in the Chamber of Deputies (Comisão de Constituição e Justica da Câmara dos Deputados [CCJ]), which determined their constitutionality. Bills then passed through a more specialized committee appropriate to the subject matter of the bill.

Party leaders named committee members on an annual basis at the opening of the legislative session, and committees so constituted had significant agenda-setting powers. Formally, committee presidents were elected by the committee members, but typically a choice was arranged in advance among party leaders, and was a condition of committee appointments. There were no provisions for overruling committee jurisdiction—in other words, party leaders could not circumvent a committee or force a bill out of committee, and thus committees had the power to place bills on or remove them from the legislative agenda (Santos and Rennó 2004). Although in theory party leaders could replace committee members at any time, there was a strong norm of noninterference in committee appointments during a given legislature. Finally, although the president had authority to introduce a budget, if he did not do so by a given deadline, the Budget Committee had authority to submit legislation to the floor. The annual budget was always reviewed and considerably amended by the Budget Committee in the Chamber of Deputies.

With this distribution of agenda-setting powers, a governing coalition could still control the legislative agenda through monopolization of the Mesa presidency and the presidencies of all committees and with a judicious distribution of those presidencies among its members (Cox and McCubbins 1993, 2005; Carroll, Cox, and Pachón 2004). In other words, given committee presidents' considerable power to determine what made it to the floor, a governing coalition attempting to deliver a policy program would need to carefully control the delegation to committee presidents.[2] The Mesa president was always occupied by the PSD, the largest party and a party in government throughout the period, and thus the government did always

---

2. Consider, for example, delivering on the policy commitment of macroeconomic stability. To actually deliver this policy outcome, a governing coalition must have the ability to block any bill that might bust the budget. In the absence of either agenda control or high discipline in legislative voting, the governing coalition cannot exercise this level of control over legislative output.

control this powerful position. Committee presidencies, however, were not monopolized by the governing coalition. Instead, as the data in Table 26 indicate, there is a pattern in which individual parties tended to monopolize the presidencies of certain committees regardless of governing or opposition status.

The PSD was in every cabinet during the period, and the PTB was in every cabinet beginning in 1951, while the UDN was in opposition from 1956 to 1960, and in 1963. The UDN held the presidency of the Committees of International Relations (five years); Education and Culture (one year); Transportation, Communication, and Public Works (one year); and Civil Service (one year), all *while in the opposition*. The PR also controlled the presidency of the National Security Committee for two years while in the opposition. The data also indicate that certain parties preferred control over certain committees. The PSD controlled the presidency of the Budget Committee throughout the period and of the presidencies of the Constitution and Justice and the Economics Committees for the vast majority of the period.[3] The PTB controlled the presidency of the Social Legislation Committee for most of the period and the presidencies of the Civil Service, Transportation, Communication, and Public Works Committees for half the life of the democratic regime. The only committee the UDN controlled for more than half the period was the Foreign Relations Committee.[4]

Table 26 Party distribution of committee presidents, Federal Chamber of Deputies, Brazil, 1948–1963 (%)

Committee	PSD	UDN	PTB	PR
Constitution and Justice	75	6	19	0
Budget	100			
Economics	71	29	0	0
Education and Culture	56	6	0	0
Foreign Relations	31	69	0	0
Social Legislation	19	0	81	0
Public Health	50	38	19	0
National Security[a]	13	0	0	80
Civil Service	19	6	63	0
Transportation, Communication and Public Works	19	25	57	0
Financial Oversight	19	25	50	0

Source: Diário do Congresso, various years.
[a] For this committee no data was available for 1963.

3. As discussed in the preceding chapter, the committee with authority over the budget changed in 1955 and data collection was adjusted accordingly.
4. For a similar discussion of how parties concentrated control over specific committees from 1951 to 1963, see Santos and Rennó 2004.

This distribution of committee presidencies fits the pattern of mutual vetoes and parceling out of agenda control emphasized by early scholars of legislative organization in Latin America. A closer look at how the full membership of three of the most important committees evolved provides evidence of adjustment to maintain these mutual vetoes over time. The two most important committees in the Chamber of Deputies were the CCJ and the Budget Committee, which functioned throughout the period (Hippólito 1985; Santos 2002). All bills went first to the CCJ, and thus, after the president of the Chamber, this was the key gatekeeping entity of the lower legislative body. A refusal to consider the bill by the president of the CCJ essentially killed a bill. The Budget Committee was at least as important as the CCJ—this is where decisions about distribution of resources were made. These two committees had high externalities—their decisions had broad impact across the electorate. The distribution of seats on these committees is seen in Tables 27–28. The tables are split for a given committee because each was split into teams A and B or A, B, and C, in the case of the Budget Committee in the early 1950s.

A third committee with high externalities, the Economics Committee, was created in 1950. With jurisdiction over import substitution industrialization policy, this committee made decisions regarding major resource allocations, especially during the industrialization drive of the decade of the 1950s spearheaded by Vargas and Kubitschek. The party distribution of seats for this committee is shown in Table 29.

The key feature that readily strikes the observer is that each of these committees grows significantly in membership over the period. At the same time, the most important change in the electoral expression of the major parties over the period is the decline of the PSD and the rise of the PTB. Whereas the PSD held 51.8 percent of the seats in the Chamber in 1947, by 1963 its share had declined to 28.8 percent. In the case of the PTB, its seat share rose from 7.9 percent to 28.4, virtually equal to that of the PSD in 1963. Both parties served in every cabinet beginning in 1951.

If legislative power was distributed to reflect the ability to mobilize support in elections, this would lead to two expectations: PTB membership should have equaled PSD membership in the committees with major externalities by 1963, given that both were in government and their legislative seats were virtually identical. Moreover, by 1963, both parties should have had more seats in each of these committees than the UDN, given its opposition status and the fact that it held only 22.2 percent of the seats at this time. As the tables indicate, however, this is only partially approximated in

Table 27 Party membership on the Finance and Budget Committee, Federal Chamber of Deputies, Brazil, 1948–1963

Year	Members	Presidency	PSD	UDN	PTB
1948	24	PSD	13	7	1
1949	24	PSD	14	7	1
1950	24	PSD	13	8	1
1951	24	PSD	10	7	4

			PSD		UDN		PTB	
Year	Members	Presidency	A	B	A	B	A	B
1952	A:19, B:19	PSD	8	7	5	5	3	4
1953	A:19, B:19	PSD	8	7	5	5	3	5
1954	A:19, B:19	PSD	7	7	5	4	3	4
1955	25	PSD	9		6		5	
1956	A:19, B:19	PSD	7	9	4	4	3	4
1957	A:19, B:19	PSD	8	8	4	4	3	4
1958	A:19, B:19	PSD	8	8	4	4	3	4
1959	A:19, B:19	PSD	7	8	4	4	4	4

			PSD			UDN			PTB		
Year	Members	Presidency	A	B	C	A	B	C	A	B	C
1960	15 each	PSD	6	6	6	3	2	4	3	3	2
1961	15 each	PSD	6	6	6	3	3	4	3	3	2
1962	15 each	PSD	6	6	7	3	3	4	3	3	3
1963	15 each	PSD	6	5	4	3	4	4	3	4	4

Source: *Diário do Congresso*, various years.

the less important Economics Committee. PTB membership was equal to PSD membership on the Economics Committee, but not on the CCJ or the Budget Committee. And the PTB did have three more seats on the Economics Committee than the UDN, but only slightly higher participation than the UDN in the CCJ and the same number of seats as the UDN in the all-important Budget Committee. Thus, in addition to committee presidencies, committee membership on the most important high-externality committees was distributed among the major parties represented in the legislature, without regard to governing status or changes in electoral support.

We can gain additional perspective on what factors shaped distribution of legislative agenda control in Brazil during this period by investigating the determinants of appointment to committee presidencies. Using the same independent variables as in the previous chapter, party loyalty in roll call voting, electoral performance, and seniority, I investigated what factors best

Table 28 Party membership on the Constitution and Justice Committee, Federal Chamber of Deputies, Brazil, 1948–1963

Year	Members	Presidency	PSD	UDN	PTB
1948	23	PSD	14	7	0
1949	24	PSD	15	7	1
1950	24	PSD	14	8	1
1951	25	PSD	9	7	4
1952	25	PTB	9	7	5
1953	25	PTB	9	7	5
1954	25	PTB	9	6	5

			PSD		UDN		PTB	
Year	Members	Presidency	A	B	A	B	A	B
1955	A:13, B:12	UDN	5	4	4	2	2	3
1956	A:13, B:13	PSD	5	5	3	3	2	3
1957	A:13, B:13	PSD	5	5	3	3	2	3
1958	A:13, B:13	PSD	5	5	2	3	2	3
1959	A:13, B:13	PSD	5	5	3	3	3	2
1960	A:14, B:13	PSD	6	5	3	3	2	2
1961	A:14, B:14	PSD	6	6	3	4	3	2
1962	A:14, B:14	PSD	6	5	3	4	2	3
1963	A:14, B:14	PSD	5	4	3	3	3	4

Source: Diário do Congresso, various years.

Table 29 Party membership on the Economics Committee, Federal Chamber of Deputies, Brazil, 1950–1963

Year	Members	Presidency	PSD	UDN	PTB
1950	24	PSD	13	7	0
1951	24	UDN	10	7	4
1952	25	UDN	9	7	5
1953	25	UDN	9	7	5
1954	25	UDN	9	6	5

			PSD		UDN		PTB	
Year	Members	Presidency	A	B	A	B	A	B
1955	A: 14, B: 13	PSD	5	5	3	3	3	2
1956	A: 13, B: 13	PSD	5	5	3	3	2	3
1957	A:13, B: 13	PSD	5	5	3	3	2	3
1958	A:13, B: 13	PSD	6	5	3	3	3	2
1959	A:13, B:13	PSD	5	5	3	3	2	3
1960	A:14, B:14	PSD	6	5	3	4	2	3
1961	A:14, B:14	PSD	6	5	3	5	2	3
1962	A:14, B:14	PSD	6	6	3	3	2	3
1963	A:14, B:14	PTB	4	4	3	2	4	4

Source: Diário do Congresso, various years.

predicted whether a deputy would be awarded a committee presidency.⁵ The dependent variable was whether the deputy held a presidency in any of the permanent committees of the Chamber of Deputies throughout the period. As demonstrated in Table 30, the only factor that was significant was seniority for both the PSD and the UDN. Notably, party loyalty in roll call voting was not important in receiving committee presidencies for any of the three

Table 30 The determinants of committee presidents, Federal Chamber of Deputies, Brazil, 1948–1963

	PSD	UDN	PTB
Party Loyalty	.370	1.12	−.727
	(.838)	(1.41)	(.658)
Electoral Performance	.104	−1.17*	−.294
	(.417)	(.693)	(.193)
Seniority	.450	.496*	.328
	(.124)	(.235)	(.276)
Constant	−4.65	−3.40	−2.13
Log pseudo-likelihood	−325	−118	−164
N	1670	784	787
% Predicted Correctly	7.4	7.1	3.2

*p < .05, **p < .01, ***p < .001

Note: I ran logit regressions in STATA 8.0 with the robust option. Santos and Rennó (2004) present distinct findings. Their model, which is similar to the one presented here, employs independent variables of electoral results, seniority, party loyalty (as does the model presented here), expertise, and whether the deputy was a member of the Mesa Diretora, as well as several controls. They find party loyalty to be a significant predictor of receipt of a committee presidency. These authors measure the first three variables quite differently, however, by using exclusion and weighting rules for roll calls (I did not exclude any votes that reached a quorum and did not weight them), years in the Chamber rather than legislative terms for seniority, and nominal votes rather than a standardized measure of electoral performance across districts. They include only the years 1951–63, do not indicate how they address missing values for party loyalty for freshman deputies or party switchers, and do not include state controls. The choice of whether and how to exclude and weight roll calls is not straightforward (Carey 2007). In the current period we have party leadership recommendations for 95 percent of all roll calls, on average (a high of 98.5 percent for the PT, and a low of 93 percent for the PTB). Since we have such precise information about party leaders' wishes in the current period, I chose not to exclude any votes. I thus chose not to exclude or weight in the earlier period in order for it to be comparable with the current period. In the case of electoral results, their choice reflects the distinct logic of their argument. They are working with a modified collective goods theory of electoral competition, in which leaders and deputies are concerned with whether the deputy's seat is "safe." With this logic, one's main concern is competitors within one's own district. I am working with a clientelist theory of electoral competition in which the party is concerned with efficient distribution of resources in order to gain seats, and thus they will want a standardized cross-district measure of such efficiency.

5. I did not include dominance as an independent variable here because this would cut the number of presidencies down too drastically. I included state controls in each of these models. Inclusion of these controls did not change the significance or direction of any of the coefficients; they merely increased the variation explained.

largest parties. Thus, party leaders did not use their appointment power to ensure that legislators occupying key positions of agenda control had voting records that indicated positions similar to those of the median legislator of the party.

One might argue that with a tight grip on the presidency of the three high-externality committees (Constitution and Justice, Budget, and Economics), a party or coalition could exercise considerable control over legislative output by killing any bill it opposed in these committees. At the extreme, since the CCJ was the gatekeeping committee (Santos and Rennó 2004), the governing majority could control legislative output at this point by carefully choosing its president, although this would place severe constraints on positive legislative production. I investigated the determinants of who was awarded the presidency for the three high-externality committees and for the Constitution and Justice Committee alone. The PSD was the only party with enough presidencies on these universal committees for a meaningful estimation; the results are reported in Table 31.

In the high-externality committees, electoral performance and seniority are important determinants of who is appointed president. When we narrow the analysis to the central gatekeeping committee, we see that the signifi-

Table 31 The determinants of high-externality committee presidents, Social Democratic Party (PSD), Federal Chamber of Deputies, Brazil, 1948–1963

	PSD, All High Externality	PSD, CCJ
Party Loyalty	−.920	−1.32
	(1.13)	(2.74)
Electoral Performance	1.48*	5.75**
	(.587)	(1.48)
Seniority	.948**	.990*
	(.165)	(.400)
Constant	−5.07	−8.35
Log-likelihood	−137	−53.2
N	965	851
% Predicted Correctly	14.2	25.8

*$p < .05$, **$p < .01$

Note: Once again, I ran logit regressions in STATA 8.0 with the robust option and included state controls. Santos (2002), using a model substantially similar to the one discussed above (Santos and Rennó 2004), with the exception that he measures electoral performance with a standardized interdistrict measure, as I did, confirms the findings for the CCJ: party loyalty is not significant, whereas electoral performance is significant at the .01 level and seniority is significant at the .05 level.

cance of electoral performance increases, while party loyalty remains insignificant. In terms of the high-externality committees, then, the data support the conclusions from the previous chapter—efficient vote buying, as demonstrated through electoral performance, was far more important in receiving powerful positions in the lower chamber than was loyal party voting.

The clear implication of this data is that the governing coalition did not have control of the legislative agenda: they did not monopolize control of committee presidencies, which were positions with considerable agenda-setting power. Yet even if a governing coalition was not able to control the agenda, we might expect that individual parties would reserve positions of agenda control under their purview for members who exhibit voting records consistent with the median legislator of the party. Yet the data indicate that loyalty to majority party positions in voting was not a determinant of who received the committee presidencies controlled by a given party. Governing coalitions and individual parties did not use these positions as tools for controlling committee legislative output such that it conformed to a policy program. Committee presidencies often went preferentially to a given party, whether in government or not. Moreover, the individual members who were chosen to occupy the powerful committee presidencies did not necessarily vote with the majority of their party. Finally, even if we narrowed agenda control to the three universal committees or only the Constitution and Justice Committee, key positions were not reserved for those whose voting record demonstrated adherence to positions representative of the party, but instead went to those with exceptional electoral performance and seniority. Early observers' conclusions that developing democracies lacked legislative machinery for translating a policy mandate from voters into law is supported by this data from Brazil from 1948 to 1963.

Centralized Prohibition of Governing Majorities in Pre-Chávez Venezuela

As in Brazil, rules that structured the legislature in pre-Chávez Venezuela prohibited the formation of a governing majority. Before considering internal legislative organization, however, it is important to examine the role of the Venezuelan legislature more generally as the institution designed to turn government resources into public policy. Venezuela exhibited a surprising characteristic seen in other developing democracies: much of decision making regarding allocation of public funds was removed from legislative control. In Venezuela, by 1974, an astounding 71 percent of public expenditures did not come under legislative jurisdiction through the normal budgeting process. The vast majority of public funds in Venezuela thus were not allocated through the legislative process, but were administered through decentralized state bureaucracies (Crisp 2000). The fact that almost three-fourths of public funds were removed from the purview of what is typically considered the locus of public decision making is in itself a major anomaly for a theory of government as the set of institutions that turn public resources into public policy.[6]

Turning to internal legislative organization, the Venezuelan legislature was organized around mutual vetoes rather than majority control, as was the case in postwar Brazil. The Pact of Punto Fijo, which distributed all government positions through a priori agreement among the parties, included agreements to split the key positions of control in Congress between the two major parties (president and vice president of both chambers and all committees). And although the more general Punto Fijo agreement lapsed after 1974 when executive cabinets were no longer coalition cabinets, but had reverted to single-party cabinets, power-sharing agreements continued in force up through the early 1990s for the legislature and key executive posts (Coppedge 1994b, 326).[7] If we couple this legislative organization with the fact that the Venezuelan president had extremely weak legislative powers, it becomes clear that, as in Brazil, Venezuela's rules did not turn policymaking power over to a party or coalition legitimized through mobilizing majority consent in elections. Positions of agenda control such as committee presidencies were shared by both major parties, regardless of which won a majority in the elections. Moreover, the decisions about how agenda control positions were distributed within the party were highly centralized. Only members of the leadership body (CEN or CN) could chair congressional committees (Coppedge 1994a, 26).

This choice to preclude majority control of the legislative agenda is perhaps more puzzling in pre-Chávez Venezuela than in postwar Brazil. Unlike in Brazil, in Venezuela a party with clear majority support emerged in early

---

6. Indeed, in reform proposals such as those presented through COPRE were references to how such structures inhibited efficient use of public funds and adaptation of public policy to changing circumstances. Noted analysts of Venezuela also highlight how such institutional arrangements led to rigidity and a weakened Venezuelan democracy (Crisp, Levine, and Rey 1995; Crisp 1997, 2000).

7. For a more detailed discussion of why the demise of coalition cabinets does not signal the end of power sharing in Venezuela, see Chapters 2 and 3.

elections.[8] AD's early electoral strength in 1945 would lead one to expect that it would have had a very legitimate claim to control of the legislative agenda in order to implement its policy vision. The AD won 75 percent of the seats in Congress and 70 percent of the presidential vote (Coppedge 1994b, 345n9). But when majority control of the legislature was attempted during AD's first foray into government, in 1945, it was soon overturned by a coup. As Coppedge points out, this is curious from the perspective of government provision of collective policy goods: "AD's majoritarian governing style was clearly an obstacle to the consolidation of this first Venezuelan democratic regime. There is nothing undemocratic about majority rule in a consolidated democracy; indeed, democracy is often *defined* as majority rule" (1994b, 352). When Venezuela returned to democratic rule in 1958, the AD once again emerged as the clear majority party. But other major parties were willing to allow AD to assume power only on the condition that they accepted a set of rules that restricted the AD to reigning.

In this examination of legislative organization in Brazil and Venezuela, we note a pattern seen earlier. Both countries reach the same end result, but one through decentralized bargaining and the other through highly centralized a priori agreements. In both Brazil and Venezuela, legislative rules prohibited turning power over to a unified legislative agent, even when a party or coalition clearly demonstrated its ability to mobilize majority support in elections. Instead, in both countries the legislature was organized to confer mutual vetoes on the major parties. Brazil achieved this through decentralized and ongoing negotiations throughout the period, whereas in Venezuela, this was achieved through an a priori power-sharing agreement. I argue that the common pattern of mutual vetoes is driven by the imperatives of clientelistic politics.

The Prohibition of Governing Majorities Explained as Maintenance of Resource Conduits Through Mutual Veto

The implication in the previous sections was that control of legislative output is necessary for implementing a collective goods policy program. As Cox and McCubbins expressed it: "Parties compete in mass elections, just like business firms compete in mass markets, by developing brand names. These brand names are public goods to the members of the party and *the*

---

8. The PSD did gain a majority in Congress in the first elections of 1945 in Brazil, but its control of seats declined rapidly thereafter.

value of the brand depends on the party's legislative record of accomplishment. Thus, a key problem for legislative parties is to manage the legislative process, securing the best possible record, hence the best possible brand reputation" (2005, 31; emphasis added).

Early scholarship emphasized one route to control of legislative output, and thus to implementation of the winning party's (coalition's) program: internal unity in legislative voting. Parties that routinely displayed high unity in voting were considered effective collective actors capable of delivering on their policy promises. Recent scholarship, however, has highlighted another route to controlling legislative output: control of the legislative agenda—that is, control of what comes up for a vote (Cox and McCubbins 2005). When party leaders lack the ability to tightly control the outcome of votes on the floor, as in cases where they lack direct control over the electoral fate of the rank and file, they can rely on the alternative of controlling what comes to a vote in order to manage legislative output. Party leaders who control the agenda are trusted to never bring any bill to the floor that would divide the governing majority *and pass*. In other words, party leaders control the agenda such that the opposition cannot ally with a minority of the majority party and pass bills against the will of the majority of the majority party. In this way the governing party (coalition) can ensure that any changes to the status quo will be in the direction preferred by a majority of the governing party or coalition.

These two distinct strategies for controlling legislative output have implications for the degree of change from the status quo. When party leaders must rely on controlling the legislative agenda, there will be a status quo bias, since the party cannot control voting as tightly as it controls what comes to the floor. When the party is seriously split, the leadership cannot ensure passage of controversial bills, but only block them. When leaders can use the more well-recognized means of controlling legislative output, through control of voting on the floor, the governing party will be able to implement more of its policy agenda (Cox and McCubbins 2005).

This articulation of the link between electoral imperatives and control of the legislative agenda is consistent with the early analysts' conclusions that legislative organization in developing democracies was a key hindrance to responsive governments. When voters opt for policy-based voting, governing parties must control the legislative agenda, or exhibit very high unity in voting to deliver on their policies. The point can be best illustrated with an example. Consider a party that wins elections based on a macroeconomic stabilization platform. Absent monopoly control over the legislative agenda to shut out any bills that might bust the budget or voting unity sufficient to defeat such bills, the party will not be able to deliver on its campaign promise.

Yet if voters opt for quid pro quo rather than policy-based voting, a party or coalition does not need to monopolize control of the legislative agenda to deliver to voters. There is no need to control the overall impact of what comes out of the legislature, to control the factors that determine voting choices. Maintaining one's ability to deliver in a clientelistic system requires the ability to block any legislative action that might interfere with one's own resources streams, as well as the ability to insulate one's own conduit of resources from interference by others. In clientelistic systems, then, parties burnish their reputation with voters in the legislature by insulating their resources from legislative interference and thus ensuring their ability to deliver reliably over time. This implies that parties will demand a veto over decisions with universal impact and that party-specific resource conduits will be insulated from legislative interference. Thus, just as with other aspects of political behavior and choice that from a policy-based perspective appear counterproductive, organizing the legislature around mutual vetoes and the parceling out and compartmentalizing of agenda control actually serves politicians' electoral goals well when structural conditions favor the clientelistic equilibrium.

This logic can also explain why parties in these systems apparently have an aversion to ceding agenda control to any one party or coalition agent. A governing majority exercising agenda control implies that these parties have exclusive control over what can come to a vote in the legislature. Such a governing majority could simply exclude any bill from the agenda that distributes resources to opposition parties. Recalling the discussion in Chapter 1 of the uneven playing field that characterizes clientelistic competition, exclusion from allocative decisions not only means that you are shut out of current distributions in an exclusionary system; in a system in which political support is built upon quid pro quos, it also means that you will be highly disadvantaged in the next round of competition for control of distribution. In other words, legislative agenda control would allow those parties in the governing majority to shut all other parties out of what it takes to compete electorally (resources derived from government office that are traded for votes).

Thus, when clientelistic politics prevails, exclusion from the legislative agenda is anathema. Any contender with the power to block such an outcome will do so. The result is that the legislative agenda is organized in a fashion akin to the United Nations Security Council.⁹ For the key contenders to accept a democratic legislature at all, they must each be afforded the kind of veto that would allow them to vet any decisions that affect their access to resources. This signal difference in legislative organization in clientelistic and policy-based systems is depicted in the difference across columns I and II in Table 32.

The table makes use of Cox and McCubbins's (2005) measure of the degree to which a governing coalition controls legislative output. These authors argue that if a governing party or coalition controls the legislative agenda, they should never see bills that they oppose pass in the legislature. In other words, parties in government should never vote against a bill that passes. By measuring the percentage of the bills that pass but were opposed by a majority of a governing party, we can measure the degree to which governing parties are able to keep bills they oppose off the floor.

When a governing party votes against a bill that passes, this is labeled a "roll" of the party. If a governing party or coalition exercises effective control over the legislative agenda, then parties in the coalition essential to the government's legislative majority should never be rolled. Each party that is critical to the government's majority should be able to use this leverage to ensure that no bill that it opposes ever makes it onto the legislative agenda (Cox and McCubbins 2005; Amorim Neto, Cox, and McCubbins 2003).

Examining the difference across the two columns first, it is worth repeating here, as discussed in Chapter 1, that the more level playing field of policy-based politics means that parties shut out of the legislative agenda are neither shut out of the policy benefits nor inordinately disadvantaged in the next round of competition. Control over allocative decisions in policy-based systems means control over which policy goods will be produced, not who will be cut in and who will be cut out of exclusionary politics. The policy goods that are produced are enjoyed by all who meet the general criteria.¹⁰ Moreover, to compete with an incumbent in the next round, one needs only a more compelling argument about what policies are needed,

---

9. Kenworthy (1970) also characterizes developing-country legislative organization as akin to that of the Security Council.

10. It is certainly true that politicians and parties competing to provide policy goods choose a set of policy goods that will disproportionately favor their constituents. For example, President George W. Bush adopted tax cuts that disproportionately favored those in higher income brackets, while President Bill Clinton's earned-income tax credit was designed to help those at the lowest income levels. Nevertheless, because they must win some large percentage of the vote as a result of voters' evaluation of overall policy, politicians competing in policy-based systems must ensure that such favoring of their core constituencies is consistent with providing broad policy goods, such as national security and economic growth.

Table 32 Legislative organization in clientelistic and policy-based systems

	Equilibrium Electoral Strategy	
	I. Clientelism (Mutual Vetoes)	II. Collective Goods Provision (Control of Legislative Output)
A. Candidate-Centered Institutions	**Postelection distribution of agenda control offices** among parties in the legislature.	**Control of legislative output through control of the agenda.**
	Observable implications: No clear pattern of roll rates across "ideological" spectrum. Parties in government with very high roll rates	Observable implications: Status quo biased, low roll rates for governing part(ies) controlling the agenda. U-shaped curve moving outward from median party if no governing party control
	Brazil, 1945–64	Brazil, 1995–present U.S., 1889–present
B. Party-Centered Institutions	**A priori, proportional distribution of agenda control** among parties. Party leadership maintains control of positions of agenda control.	**Control of legislative output through control of floor voting.**
	Observable implications: Long-term power-sharing agreements that create mutual vetoes and insulate resource conduits from legislative decisions.	Observable implications: Governing-party biased, low roll rates for governing part(ies) controlling the agenda, roll rates form a U-shaped curve moving outward from median party if no governing party control of agenda.
	Venezuela, 1959–1993	United Kingdom Federal Republic of Germany

or how best to produce them, and a legislative record that demonstrates commitment to provision of these alternative policies. Since neither government nor opposition parties have a monopoly on good ideas for how to address collective goals, and both can generate legislative records to support their preferred positions, being excluded from allocative decisions does not imply being shut out of the necessary means to compete in the next round.

Just as the candidate or party centeredness of electoral law leads to variation in how legislative control is achieved in policy-based systems, this same institutional variation, combined with resource availability, determines how mutual vetoes and the insulation of resource conduits are constructed and maintained in clientelistic systems. When rules are candidate centered, and no centralized trumping resource exists, agenda control will be distributed among and within the parties on an ongoing and ad hoc basis. A norm of proportional distribution of agenda control assures parties that their current ability to deliver will not be undercut. With a proportional distribution of agenda powers, parties that make effective use of their control of resource streams should be able to continue as viable players. Distribution of positions of agenda control within the party to individual members demonstrating prowess in building clientelist networks, as shown in the previous sections and chapters, helps align individual members' incentives with party goals.

When rules are party centered and a trumping resource exists, parties once again have an incentive to construct mutual vetoes. But in this case, the distribution of positions of agenda control will not be left to post hoc negotiation, either between or within parties. If an agent capable of unified collective action can mobilize majority support and stands to gain control of trumping resource, distribution of legislative powers based on electoral results would mean that such a party could construct barriers to entry. All other contenders will thus refuse to play by "normal" democratic rules and will demand rules that ensure access to resources independent of electoral outcomes. A priori agreements on how to distribute positions of agenda control both across and within parties also helps ensure that existing players maintain a lock on the trumping resource and its distribution. Such agreements help dampen bidding wars between parties, just as preassigned votes and seats dampen bidding wars within parties.

Decentralized, Ad Hoc Mutual Veto in Postwar Brazil

Brazil's decentralized system, combined with open-list PR rules, meant that it was rare for any individual party to win a majority of seats in the legislature. Although the PSD did win a majority in the first election in 1945, the party did not have the capacity for unified collective action, as was demonstrated in the previous two chapters. Parties were far from monolithic units, and moving legislation through the Chamber would have certainly necessitated alliances with other parties. Moreover, the decentralization of control over government resources across federal units meant that even with the presidency and a majority in both houses of Congress, no party would gain control of a trumping resource. The potential outcome of elections did not present any party with the possibility of being shut out, and thus the distribution of positions of legislative control could be safely left until after the election. Nevertheless, the decentralized and freewheeling decision making in Brazil led to the same outcome we will see in Venezuela: the construction of mutual vetoes and the insulation of resource streams.

The proportional distribution of seats on high-externality committees and the dominance of the presidencies of particular committees by certain parties can clearly be seen as constituting a legislative organization that allows parties to protect their own resource streams. The proportional seats on high-externality committees ensured that no party could indirectly attack the conduits of another party, for example, through control of the budget or through agenda control in the CCJ. As can be seen from the data in Tables 27–29, after 1951, no single party had the votes to pass anything out of the three high-externality committees. The parceling out of the presidencies of the more specific committees allowed each party to insulate its own resource streams from interference by other parties. The clearest case here is that of the PTB, which dominated the committee with jurisdiction over social security, which most analysts considered the primary source of its clientelist benefits (Malloy 1979; D'Araujo 1996). The PTB held the presidency of the Social Legislation Committee for every year from 1951 on. As the overwhelmingly dominant party throughout most of the period, the PSD maintained monopoly control over the presidency of the Budget Committee.

The UDN's choice to control the Foreign Relations Committee might at first appear unusual. But this committee had jurisdiction over policy toward foreign investment, and this was a very critical issue for a long-standing rural-based party such as the UDN. The UDN's base was the commodity-exporting oligarchies in the Northeast. Good relations with foreign investors were important in maintaining good relations with agroexporters' foreign commercial partners, who were essential to the marketing of Brazilian exports. Good relations with foreign investors in turn were essential for remaining in the good graces of foreign powers such as the United States, also key to maintaining good relations with foreign capital. Indeed, policy toward foreign investment became one of a few extremely polemical issues in the early 1960s before the regime was overthrown.

The expansion of the universal committees over time also reflects maintaining mutual vetoes in a decentralized clientelist system. Primary responsibility for forging and expanding clientelistic networks lay with individual members within the parties. As the period wore on, and the electorate grew, more clients were incorporated into the system. Legislators delivering to these voters required positions on the key committees distributing resources to maintain their credible commitments to deliver. As demonstrated in Chapter 4, those selected to serve on the Budget Committee and those occupying the presidency of high-externality committees were those who most effectively bought votes, as demonstrated by their exceptional electoral performance.

Centralized, A Priori Mutual Veto in Venezuela

Scholars of Venezuela's rather exceptional stable democracy emphasized the skill and willingness of elites to compromise in governing as central to the country's success (Levine 1973; Martz 1977). Venezuelan elites were certainly skilled and conciliatory. But it is difficult to explain the specifics of many of their decisions unless we recognize that they were also constrained by structural conditions that favored the clientelistic equilibrium. Supplementing the narrative of elite conciliation with an analysis of clientelist competition allows us to explain a number of specific characteristics of this democracy, as well as why this exceptional leadership was unwilling to move to a more competitive electoral system over time.

The unusual limitations these leaders imposed on translating electoral results into legislative power certainly partly reflect the precariousness of the new democracy. Yet if voters are opting for policy-based voting, it becomes more difficult to explain why Venezuelan leaders clung to rules that a created rigid, unresponsive legislature, even after the early vulnerable period had passed.[11] Despite the emergence of a clear majority party in many elections, Venezuelan politicians continued to be wary of majoritarian rules, as Coppedge (1994b) and others discuss. With an understanding of the strategic context of clientelist competition, we can better understand the

---

11. These are the descriptive terms used by the COPRE study as well as prominent analysts such as Levine and Crisp.

motivation behind the fear of majority rule, especially in the case of the AD in 1948 and 1958.

As discussed above, in clientelist competition, no party or major contending group can allow itself to be excluded from allocation decisions, lest it be rendered incapable of competing in the next election. If an electorally dominant party can also organize effectively for collective action and stands to gain control of a trumping resource, majority control of the legislative agenda confers clear power to construct barriers to entry in the system. Clearly, the conditions for AD to erect barriers to entry were met in both 1945 and 1958. AD was the overwhelmingly dominant electoral force in both years, was very well organized for unified collective action, and was poised to seize control of a resource that would have trumped all others in this relatively poor and underdeveloped country: oil revenues. COPEI's internal organization mirrored that of AD (Coppedge 1994a), and thus AD would face the same threat if COPEI was allowed to control the legislative agenda. With the legislature organized around mutual vetoes, regardless of electoral results, both parties were assured that they could credibly claim ability to deliver clientelistic goods. By forging an a priori pact that distributed all legislative authority proportionally and maintaining this pact throughout the life of the regime, elites' well-justified wariness of majority rule was managed within the framework of democratic rules.

The legislature in Venezuela was not only organized around mutual vetoes. As was discussed in Chapter 2 and above, over time, approximately three-fourths of the budget in Venezuela was insulated from congressional interference. This presents a major anomaly for a theory of policy provision through legislation. But it is also an effective means for those controlling the decentralized administration to insulate their access to resources from future legislative meddling and thus to enhance their credibility in delivering clientelist goods over time. In comparison with other players that do not enjoy such insulated resource streams, such parties will enjoy a major competitive advantage in winning votes. As was discussed in Chapter 1, the fact that roughly half the organizations that characterized the decentralized public administration were created by AD and the other half by COPEI reinforces the point—these were the two parties that cut a deal to divide up the resources and manage clientelist competition. And Crisp's finding that voters could not alter either the policies pursued or the relative influence of the groups empowered to formulate policy by changing their partisan preference in voting is very strong evidence to support an insulation of resource streams and delivery networks across time. In sum, the logic of clientelistic competition and the imperatives for electoral survival deduced from it provide a positive, electorally based explanation for the major dysfunctions in legislative organization so aptly described by Kenworthy, including "immobilism in the face of redistributive issues" and politicians' inability to "implement major contested changes in the pattern of allocation."

Legislative Organization Under Chávez in Venezuela

The changes to Venezuela's legislative institutions under Chávez are nothing short of breathtaking. As part of a larger radical restructuring of Venezuelan political institutions, the new constitution promulgated in 1999 eliminated the previous bicameral structure and instituted a unicameral system. Cleverly adapting to the new electoral rules for electing legislators by running only as many coalition candidates as seats available in each district, Chávez's supporters swept the 2005 elections to the new unicameral body. This control of the new legislature facilitated his plan to obtain sweeping decree powers. And in 2006, after his reelection, Chávez requested and received powers that allow him to rule in almost all policy areas, including the very important one of property rights, by decree. The legislature thus plays a very minimal role in contemporary Venezuela, but it is highly likely that it still constrains Chávez in the interests of important players in his restructured clientelistic system. The fashion in which the current legislature might provide powerful interests with mechanisms for influencing and constraining Chávez is a fascinating subject that would no doubt greatly add to our understanding of clientelistic regimes but it is beyond the scope of this work.

Legislative Organization in Contemporary Brazil: Governing Majority Agenda Control Replaces Mutual Vetoes

If voters are now opting for policy-based voting in Brazil, we would predict that politicians would reorganize the legislature to allow governing coalitions to assert control over the legislative agenda in order to deliver the policy goods that the electorate demands. Is such a shift reflected in the current organization of the legislature? A superficial examination of the same leadership posts would suggest that it is not: committee presidencies and seats are still distributed on a proportional basis among all parties, regardless of government or opposition status, and opposition parties often occupy the presidencies of all but the most important committees, such as the CCJ and the Budget Committee. This looks very similar to what prevailed in the postwar period, yet the conclusion that agenda control remains dispersed would be valid only if the allocation of agenda-setting powers across different leadership positions had remained constant across the two periods, but this is not the case.

Party leaders, who were quite weak in the postwar period, now have the authority to vote with the force of their respective caucuses and pass considerable legislation on the basis of symbolic votes (Figueiredo and Limongi 2000). Moreover, party leaders, as well as the president, now have the power to override committee jurisdiction through urgency requests (Santos and Rennó 2004). Two types of urgency requests exist. Simple urgency allows two-thirds of the Mesa membership, one-third of Chamber membership (or party leaders representing this number), or two-thirds of a committee membership to ensure that a bill is considered within the given legislative session.[12] Superurgency can be invoked by an absolute majority of Chamber membership or party leaders representing that number and requires that a bill be discharged from committee and immediately placed at the top of the floor's agenda. Finally, the president can request urgency for his or her bills, and this request requires that both houses of Congress deliberate on the bill within forty-five days. Failure to do so results in the bill moving to the top of the legislative agenda.[13]

A second important change from the previous period is the relative power of party leaders vis-à-vis committee members. Party leaders can, and regularly do, alter committee assignments within a legislative session. Committee members threatening to return a committee report unfavorable to, or vote against, the government's position are regularly replaced by one or more other members willing to accede to the government's legislative will. These changes do not provoke any general outcry or protest, but are seen as expected and routine (Pereira and Mueller 2000, 48–50). Moreover, any bill that falls under the jurisdiction of at least three committees automatically is referred to a special committee that is formed on an ad hoc basis at the

12. Recall that the Mesa Diretora (Governing Board) is similar to the Speakership of the U.S. House. Although the Governing Board is a collective body, its president has agenda-control powers similar to those of the Speaker—he or she can kill any bill by simply not placing it on the agenda and, conversely, can accelerate consideration of bills by placing them at the top.

13. This discussion is taken primarily from Amorim Neto, Cox, and McCubbins 2003.

discretion of party leaders. These rules provide powerful tools for overriding standing committee preferences (Santos and Rennó 2004; Pereira and Mueller 2000). In short, party leaders have strong levers for circumventing committees and ensuring their preferred outcomes on committee votes.

Finally, it is important to discuss the president's enhanced agenda-setting powers in comparison with those of the previous period. Presidents can rule by decree, through what are called *provisional measures*. These measures have immediate force of law, and the Congress has thirty days to deliberate on the decree. If no action is taken, the decree is nullified. This nullification power was rendered moot, however, by the fact that presidents had unlimited power to reissue decrees. In 2001 the Congress modified these powers by requiring that provisional measures had to be considered within sixty days, and the president could reissue a decree only once. These powers give the president extraordinary control over setting the legislative agenda and led Shugart and Carey to characterize the Brazilian president as endowed with some of the most comprehensive legislative powers among all presidential regimes (1992). It is worth noting as well that despite strenuous opposition to these presidential powers by the perennial PT opposition party, when the PT took the reins of government in 2002, the demands to rescind these powers disappeared. This supports the view that powers of agenda control are necessary for delivering policy and burnishing one's record of achievement when voters opt for policy-based voting.

Some might object to the characterization of agenda-control powers as emanating from a new electoral imperative to provide policy goods because many of the executive's new agenda-setting powers were a legacy of authoritarian rule. Indeed, most of the president's agenda-setting powers were inherited from the military regime. Yet the Congress has acted to amend the legislative powers of the president since the return to democracy on several occasions. In some cases this has meant a restriction of presidential power, as in the case of decree powers, mentioned above, and in other cases this has meant an expansion of executive power, as in the case of the Social Emergency Fund (Fundo Social de Emergencia [SEF]). The SEF allowed the executive to reprogram roughly 20 percent of federal expenditures that were formally committed to certain budget items by law.[14] This expansion of executive power was essential to loosening the straitjacket of myriad specific rules for public expenditures that hamstrung any attempt to rationalize the

---

14. The Social Emergency Fund (Fundo Social de Emergência [SEF]) was later renamed the Fiscal Stabilization Fund (Fundo de Estabilização Fiscal [FEF]).

budget and implement macroeconomic stabilization. Thus there is considerable evidence that when the institutional inheritance did not provide the executive powers that were needed to deliver on policy promises, the legislature delegated such power to the executive. By the same token, when the institutional legacy gave the executive more power than the Congress deemed necessary, it acted to rescind those powers. In other words, in at least two important instances the legislature acted to modify existing institutional rules to better serve their interests. Moreover, if the agenda-setting powers that in theory allow the governing coalition to implement its policy program are merely a holdover from the previous regime and are not necessary to electoral success, then we would expect that in practice they would not be used. As the discussion and data below make clear, more than three-fourths of the procedural and final-passage bills in the contemporary period have been passed by governments exercising effective agenda control.

These centralizing rules now make possible a ruling government (in Kenworthy's [1970] terminology) with control over the legislative agenda, whereas in the postwar period a ruling government was precluded by the rules. How can we discern whether governments actually use these powers to rule rather than simply reign? Cox and McCubbins (2005) have developed a direct measure of the degree to which a governing coalition controls legislative output: the degree to which governing parties essential to maintaining a legislative majority see bills that they oppose passed in the legislature. They dub such an event a "roll" of the party. If a governing coalition controls the legislative agenda, then parties in the coalition essential to the government's legislative majority should never be rolled. Each party that is critical to the government's majority in the legislature should be able to use the threat of leaving the coalition to ensure that no bill that it opposes ever makes it onto the legislative agenda (Cox and McCubbins 2005; Amorim Neto, Cox, and McCubbins 2003). Given that information is never perfect, and based on data from parliamentary regimes, these authors argue that a roll rate below 5 percent for all governing parties indicates that the governing coalition is exercising control over the legislative agenda, what they call a *legislative cartel*. They further argue that in the absence of agenda control, we should expect to see a U-shaped roll rate curve as we move out from the center to the extremes of the ideological spectrum. If no governing majority forms a cartel, and legislation from all parties has an equal chance of making it to the floor, parties in the center should be able to see more of their preferred legislation pass. Centrist parties can form alliances with parties on either side of the ideological spectrum, whereas parties at the extremes have a much more limited set of allies.

Table 33 shows the roll rates for all the major parties in contemporary Brazil. The data include final-passage bills, as well as procedural votes related to final-passage bills; these are the roll calls that are considered important to parties' legislative record and public reputation, and thus votes on which they will not want to be rolled. If competitors can publicize the fact that a party was defeated on an important procedural vote or final-passage bill related to its policy program, this could be very damaging to the party reputation. Governments that form a legislative cartel are italicized.

As the data demonstrate, the governing majority has effectively controlled the legislative agenda since 1995, with the exception of Lula's second cabinet (Cardoso 1 + 2 cabinets, Cardoso 3 + 4 cabinets, and Lula 1 cabinet). In each of these governments, all governing parties exhibit roll rates below 5 percent. Moreover, there is a U-shaped pattern to the roll rates when there is no agenda control, which also provides strong evidence that parties are campaigning and winning votes on the basis of distinct national programs. This is one more indication that parties are presenting distinct policy programs and allying primarily with parties with similar programs in legislative voting. The fact that three-fourths of the legislation of the period was passed with government agenda control, combined with the U-shaped curve when control is absent, once again is consistent with a shift from quid pro quo to policy-based voting.

Amorim Neto, Cox, and McCubbins (2003), examining data up through Cardoso 1 + 2, draw the conclusion that Brazilian presidents use mixed strategies, sometimes building shifting coalitions, and sometimes using government agenda control to pass their legislation. But as a characterization of the current Brazilian system, this conclusion may be misleading for several reasons. First, they include data from the Sarney government, which was unelected and came to office through highly unusual means. Sarney was the vice president on a ticket chosen by Congress and became president only after the designated president died before taking office. It seems highly unlikely that this selection process would have transmitted new electoral incentives to the winner.

Collor was the first elected president after more than twenty-five years of authoritarian rule. If political actors glean the implications of new incentives only through trial and error (Carroll, Cox, and Pachón 2004), it is not surprising that the first elected government did not assert agenda control. Col-

Table 33 Roll rates on project and agenda-setting votes, by cabinet period and party, Federal Chamber of Deputies, Brazil, 1990–2007 (%)

Admin. (Cabinet #)	No. of Roll Calls	PT	PCDOB	PPS	PSB	PDT	PL	PSDB	PMDB	PTB	PFL	PPB
Collor I 3/90–10/90	10	100	NA	NA	NA	100	NA	30	20	0	0	0
Collor II + III[a] 11/90–4/92	32	75	NA	NA	NA	53	NA	41	6.3	12.5	18.8	28.1
Collor IV 5/92–9/92	7	77	NA	NA	NA	57	NA	28.5	0	0	0	0
Franco I + II 10/92–5/93	8	50	NA	NA	NA	50	na	0	12.5	37.5	37.5	37.5
Franco III + IV 6/93–12/93	11	90	NA	NA	NA	54.5	NA	9	0	0	0	9
Franco V 1/94–12/94	6	66	NA	NA	NA	50	NA	16.6	0	16.6	16.6	16.6
Cardoso I 1/95–3/96	56	85.4	NA	NA	NA	74.5	NA	1.8	5.3	5.3	0	8.9
Cardoso II 4/96–3/99	105	89.5	NA	NA	NA	81.7	NA	1.9	1.9	3.8	2.8	4.8
Cardoso III + IV 4/99–12/02	131	41.5	NA	NA	NA	46.5	NA	0	2.1	4.9	1.4	0

Table 33 (Continued)

Admin. (Cabinet #)	No. of Roll Calls	PT	PCDOB	PPS	PSB	PDT	PL	PSDB	PMDB	PTB	PFL	PPB
Lula I 1/03–12/03	72	1.4	2.8	2.8	1.4	9.7	1.4	27.8	2.8	1.4	33.3	90.3
Lula II 1/04–6/04	51	2.0	13.3	13.0	0	27.5	4.0	45.5	6.1	0	37.1	6.1 (now PP)

Left -- Right[b]
PT – PDT – PSDB – PMDB – PTB – PFL – PDS/PPR/PPB/PP

[a] Collor II and Collor III and Franco III and Franco IV are combined because the major parties in the governing coalition do not differ. Cardoso III and IV are combined because there was only one change of cabinet which does not affect the presence of a legislative cartel.
[b] This placement follows leading analysts such as Mainwaring (1995) and Figueiredo and Limongi (1995).

lor came from a small northeastern state renowned for clientelist practices, so if the new president simply decided to try what he knew best, we would not expect him to control the agenda. Moreover, Collor's party was created as a personalist vehicle to support his candidacy and disappeared soon after his impeachment in 1992. Thus there was minimal impetus for his party to organize the coalition to control the legislative agenda. It is also not surprising that this government was not characterized by any significant legislative achievements—the first elected government did not fully comprehend the new incentives, but its failures provided information about the new rules of the game for subsequent actors. The Itamar Franco government also failed to exercise agenda control, but this was once again a nonelected government—Franco was Collor's vice president and took office after Collor's impeachment.

Agenda control was not in evidence until 1995, but it is highly significant that this was the overwhelmingly most successful government of the four whom these authors analyze, and that Cardoso's second term and Lula's first cabinet, not analyzed in their study, are both also characterized by a legislative cartel. Moreover, the vast majority of legislation throughout the current period was passed by governments that controlled the legislative agenda. Lula's second cabinet is not characterized by a legislative cartel, and this, combined with the early absences of a cartel, may be inherent in Brazil's institutions, which as many observers have noted, certainly would not be characterized as smoothing the way to the formation of legislative majorities. This may also be an isolated artifact of the scandals that plagued the administration at this time, of the ongoing transition from clientelistic to policy-based politics, or of the ineptness of Lula or his advisors. More data will help resolve the question. What is key to emphasize, however, are the dramatic changes in legislative organization that a theory based on a single equilibrium, like the new institutionalism, misses entirely—that the generic legislative structure now makes legislative cartels possible, while the postwar structure prohibited them almost entirely.

It is interesting to examine the data from the earlier period for comparative purposes. As discussed above, however, legislative organization that allows a majority party or coalition to monopolize the legislative agenda is anathema in clientelist systems. And as was demonstrated, no majority party or coalition controlled the legislative agenda in postwar Brazil or in pre-Chávez Venezuela. In Brazil, the significant agenda-setting powers of committees, combined with the proportional distribution of seats and presidencies of those committees among major parties in the legislature, meant that no majority party or coalition could effectively control the agenda. In Venezuela all agenda-setting positions were split between the leaders of the two major parties, as stipulated in power-sharing agreements.

Although legislative organization that would allow a majority party or coalition to control the legislative agenda is unlikely in clientelist systems, roll rates below 5 percent, and thus consistent with such control, are certainly possible in clientelist regimes. A majority logroll within the governing coalition, in which the governing coalition's bills dole out resources for clientelist exchange to a majority of coalition members, would lead to roll rates that are consistent with policy-based agenda control. In this case each individual legislator in the logroll votes for bills that provide the resources for other legislators in return for their support of the bill(s) creating his or her own resource streams. In other words, in terms of roll rates, there is an observational equivalence between an effective cartel controlling legislative output to deliver policy goods and a majority coalition logroll designed to deliver resources for direct exchange to those in the coalition. In short, parties in government may exhibit low roll rates whether they are supplying policy or clientelist goods.

A crucial difference is that a low roll rate—indicating that the party is able to block legislation its constituents oppose—is not central to burnishing one's record with constituents when delivering clientelistic goods, as is the case with delivering policy goods. Moreover, the distinct requirements for making credible appeals to voters in the two types of systems suggest that governing status must be associated with low roll rates in policy-based systems, but may not necessarily go hand in hand with low roll rates in clientelistic systems. The indirect nature of the goods delivered in policy-based systems means that a party's legislative record provides important information about how well the party is serving its constituents. If a party frequently voted against bills that pass, this would indicate that it was fairly ineffectual in blocking legislation that its constituents oppose and in shaping legislation that passes to conform to its voters preferences. Such a party would have difficulty claiming credit with voters and maintaining their support.

In clientelistic systems, in comparison, participation in government alone, without control of legislative output, *can* fortify parties' ability to compete. Ministerial status typically provides a party with access to resources, and in clientelist systems this sends signals of ability to deliver independent of legislative outcomes. In other words, control of overall legislative output is not intimately linked to either credit claiming or ability to deliver in clientelistic systems, as is the case in policy-based systems. These differences lead us to expect that roll rates characteristic of agenda control will be less prevalent in clientelistic systems and that parties in government will often exhibit roll rates above the 5 percent level characteristic of effective agenda control.

Table 34 shows the roll rates for the earlier period. As was discussed in Chapter 3, cabinets in this period were typically oversized, and thus all parties in the governing coalition were not essential to maintaining a legislative majority. To facilitate the discussion below, all parties that were in the governing coalition in the given administration are underlined. Next it is important to examine the roll rates of the parties in government. If there are parties in government exhibiting roll rates below 5 percent that also control a majority of legislative seats, the roll rates for these parties are italicized. These governments exhibit roll rates consistent with a legislative cartel, and the name of these administrations at the left of the table are italicized.

The first notable result is that two governments that passed significant legislation (Vargas II and Café Filho) do not display roll rates consistent with agenda control. Moreover, for the governments that were not characterized by roll rates consistent with agenda control, the pattern of roll rates from the center to the ideological extremes does not display the characteristic U-shaped curve, as was the case in contemporary Brazil. The second very

Table 34 Roll rates on project and agenda-setting votes, by cabinet period and party, Federal Chamber of Deputies, Brazil, 1947–1963 (%)

Legislative-Presidential Period	N of Roll Calls	PTB	PSP	PR	PSD	PDC	UDN
Dutra II (10/46–4/50)	49/41	28.57	10.20	10.20	4.08	9.52	8.16
Dutra III (5/50–1/51)	15/8	6.67	0.00	6.67	*0.00*	*0.00*	*0.00*
Vargas I (2/51–5/53)	31/28	0.00	6.45	6.45	3.23	14.29	22.58
Vargas II (6/53–8/54)	32/26	21.88	15.63	12.50	15.63	15.38	9.38
Café Filho (9/54–11/55)	28/27	17.86	21.43	7.14	7.14	11.11	17.86
Ramos (12/55–1/56)	1/1	0.00	0.00	0.00	0.00	100.00	100.00
JK (2/56–1/61)	97/84	2.06	6.19	7.22	4.12	15.48	28.87
Quadros (2/61–8/61)	8/8	0.00	0.00	0.00	*12.50*	12.50	25.00
Goul. I + II + III + IV (1/63–3/64)	4/4	25.00	0.00	0.00	*0.00*	0.00	0.00

Source: Roll call data provided by Amorim Neto and Santos. Roll rates from author's calculations.

Note: Splits calculated as wins. Roll call counts for PDC are listed second.
The PDC was such a small party that for many roll calls they did not register any votes. The second number after the slash in the "N of Roll Calls" column indicates the subset of bills on which the PDC registered at least one vote.

interesting finding is that in every government with roll rates consistent with agenda control, there are additional parties in government with roll rates higher than 5 percent, with the exception of Dutra III. This is most dramatic in the case of Vargas I, but it is also clearly evident in Dutra II and JK.

The pattern of governments with no agenda control, as well as governments with governing parties with roll rates above 5 percent, are inconsistent with burnishing the party record with constituents by providing policy goods. If the governing parties in the Vargas II and Café Filho governments were providing policy goods, what evidence did they present to voters to demonstrate that they were responsible for legislative outcomes? In both these administrations, parties in government had among the highest roll rates of all the six major parties. It seems highly unlikely that with such a legislative record a claim to have provided policy goods would have been credible.

Turning to the second pattern, parties in government with roll rates above 5 percent likewise raise questions about public reputations and credit claiming. When voters exercise policy-based choice, we would expect that governing parties would expel any party that did not do its share in maintaining the coalition's public reputation, as was the case when the PDT was ousted from the Lula government as soon as its roll rate crept above 5 percent. If the governing coalition does not require that all parties enjoying cabinet posts do their part in passing the coalition's legislative program, the coalition's ability to enforce discipline and pass its program will fall apart. Moreover, participation in the cabinet makes it impossible for parties with high roll rates to represent a clear alternative to government at election time.[15] If mere participation in government, however, burnishes a party's

15. Alternatively, Amorim Neto and Santos (2001) ask why presidential hopefuls who are members of opposition parties in postwar Brazil did not work to burnish their record with voters by attempting to outlegislate incumbent presidents, as Mayhew (1991) predicts. They argue that such entrepreneurship was limited by legislative fragmentation which prohibited an opposition majority. But Cox and McCubbins's (2005) work on agenda control allows us to amend this conclusion. According to Cox and McCubbins, governing parties monopolize control of the legislative agenda precisely because if they do not, opposition parties will seize every opportunity to introduce legislation that could be passed with the opposition part(ies) and a minority of the governing party (coalition). Thus, with no governing coalition controlling the legislative agenda in postwar Brazil, if politicians were in fact competing in the provision of policy goods, we should have seen continual attempts by the opposition to outlegislate the incumbents. In particular, we should have expected the UDN to seize this strategy, as it was the largest party that was most frequently in the opposition and one that espoused vehement hostility to Vargas, Kubitschek (JK) and Goulart. But, as Amorim Neto and Santos note, the most prominent UDN leader, Carlos Lacerda, adopted a strategy of obstruction rather than outlegislating the incumbent. Although we do not yet

reputation for having access to resources, and politicians are competing in the provision of clientelist goods, then governing status despite high roll rates is perfectly consistent with credible claims to deliver.

Conclusion

In this chapter I have argued that the legislative organization necessary for parties to burnish their reputation with constituents differs depending on whether most voters are choosing quid pro quo or collective policy goods. I also argued that this generalization of our understanding of legislative organization provides an explanation for the absence of legislative machinery for turning policy-making power over to a governing coalition in postwar Brazil and pre-Chávez Venezuela. Parties competing to provide clientelistic goods confront the problem of maintaining access to resources when not in government, and thus they strive to *avoid* a structure that would allow a governing majority to monopolize control of the legislative agenda. Instead, to address the problem of maintaining credible claims to deliver, they organize the legislature around mutual vetoes.

In postwar Brazil and in pre-Chávez Venezuela, mutual vetoes were created by distributing legislative agenda power proportionally among the parties. In addition, Brazilian parties insulated their resource streams from legislative reprogramming by monopolizing the control of certain committees that were important for delivering to their constituencies. In Venezuela, the AD and COPEI insulated their access to resources by taking most of the authority over resource distribution out of the legislature's hands and placing it in the decentralized public administration, which was not subject to reorganization based on electoral outcomes. Chávez has likewise taken most legislative decision making out of the legislature's purview through decree powers that allow him to essentially legislate unfettered by a congressional check.

In contemporary Brazil, the former constraints on legislative production have been removed: legislative rules now allow a governing majority to assert control over the agenda, and three-fourths of the key legislation in the contemporary period has been passed by governments that controlled the agenda. These changes in legislative organization and behavior are exactly

---

have an articulated theory for why parties attempt to obstruct incumbent presidents in some regimes, we can safely say that such a strategy is inconsistent with claiming credit with voters for a legislative record of policy goods provision.

what we would expect if politicians now win elections based on providing policy goods. While assembling governing majorities remains a daunting task in contemporary Brazil, the difference is that unlike in the previous period, those parties that build enduring majorities and adopt important collective goods legislation are likely to be rewarded at the polls.

Policy Choice:
Generate Sustained Growth or Maximize Quid Pro Quo?

In this chapter I turn to the outcome that all the political machinery examined in previous chapters is designed to produce: government policy. In the historical cases, I examine both key choices for how to implement the most important development program of the second half of the twentieth century, import substitution industrialization (ISI), in postwar Brazil and pre-Chávez Venezuela, as well as the failed policy responses to the crisis of ISI in both countries. I also examine the divergent paths of contemporary Brazil and Venezuela, demonstrating that Chávez's choices reflect the continued dominance of clientelistic strategies, while a shift to competition favoring policy-based politics is the impetus behind the reforms adopted in Brazil since the mid-1990s.

As with behavioral and institutional choices in postwar Brazil and both Venezuelan systems, a close examination of development policy choices raises questions about the role of elections in fostering accountability in democracies. The typical ISI policy package, which included extremely high and variable levels of protection, an emphasis on capital intensive production, and no incentives for infant-industry maturation, exacerbated traditional balance-of-payments problems, limited job creation, and were ultimately self-defeating in terms of creating sustained growth. This set of alternatives, however, was not inherent in an ISI program; the inward-oriented strategy was perfectly compatible with more carefully managed protection, labor-intensive manufacturing, and incentives for infant maturation. Why did politicians in Brazil and Venezuela, and indeed, in most developing countries, choose to implement ISI in a fashion that undermined the policy's stated goals of balance in external accounts, sustained growth, and ascension in the international division of labor?

In this chapter I argue that both the maintenance of flawed ISI implementation choices and the inability to address the ensuing crisis are of a piece and reflect the constraints of clientelist competition. The choices for implementing ISI were among the more economically inefficient alternatives available within an inward-oriented program. But policies that are economically inefficient can be highly politically advantageous in a system in which structural conditions favor the clientelistic equilibrium. As I will show in this chapter, the economic inefficiencies that characterized the modal ISI policies were not random—they were precisely those that would result from implementing the program to maximize benefits that could be directly exchanged with supporters. Despite the unfavorable economic consequences, permanent subsidies, capital intensity, and high and variable protection turn out to be the more competitive *political* choice when structural conditions favor the clientelistic equilibrium.

A theory of voting that yields two equilibria can also enhance our theory of how politicians respond to crisis. In any polity, as an economic crisis unfolds, politicians will adopt strategies that protect their reputation for delivering as they await the inevitable policy adjustment. Yet the best strategy for maintaining that reputation will differ depending on two crucial variables. The first is whether structural conditions continue to render clientelism voters' best strategic choice, or whether as a result of the crisis most voters no longer face significant risk in rejecting clientelism and thus collective good policies become electorally viable. If the new, crisis-driven clientelist offers are below most voters' reservation price, politicians who can discern how to reorganize to provide collective goods will prevail. If the crisis-driven price still exceeds most voters' reservation price, however, voters will continue to vote clientelist even in the face of the most dire collective calamity.

If reservation prices can still be paid despite crisis, the politicians who can restructure clientelist networks to adjust to resource constraints will be the new winners, and "reform" will entail such an adjustment. Under these conditions the strategies for maintaining one's reputation for delivering vary, depending on whether individual politicians, or parties, "own" the clientelist networks and the reputation for delivering. These differences in how to guard a reputation for delivering in a clientelist system in crisis explains the varying, yet commonly failed, response to the crisis of ISI in postwar Brazil and pre-Chávez Venezuela. An investigation of the different strategies chosen by Carlos Andres Perez and Chávez will help highlight why Chávez has succeeded with reorganizing clientelism in the midst of crisis, while Perez failed.

Finally, I will argue that each successive government in contemporary

Brazil has opted for gradual reform, despite widely varying policy preferences of the governing coalitions' support base, because all these governments must now provide basic collective goods for the majority of voters now opting for policy-based voting. I distinguish between these collective goods reforms, which politicians will adopt if crisis conditions create an electoral imperative to provide policy goods, and a clientelist adjustment, which politicians will adopt when the electoral equilibrium continues to reward the most efficient organization of clientelism. Although the last policy is often dubbed "reform" and may mitigate the immediate budget or debt crisis, it rarely produces the steady increase in per capita income and improved distribution of income now emerging in contemporary Brazil.

I conclude the chapter with some of the implications of the argument for the relationship between development orientation (inward or outward, state or market-led) and the effectiveness of development policy. If structural conditions drive voters' strategic choices, which in turn create a clientelistic or policy-based equilibrium, then development orientation becomes less critical to understanding the democracy-development paradox. If the voter's dilemma is key to the dramatic failures of democratic accountability that are often observed in developing democracies, the inward or outward, state-led or market-friendly characteristics of development orientation are not critical to success in providing sustained growth and other basic policy goods. The key to whether governments provide basic policy goods is whether or not structural conditions make it risky for most voters to opt for policy-based voting.

The Flaws of Import Substitution Industrialization Policies: Overgrown Infants

Despite a wealth of work on import substitution industrialization policy, the near ubiquitous choice for the more inefficient trade-offs within the rubric of an inward-oriented program remain poorly understood. Many analysts have accepted the view that it was the simple fact of inward orientation, which led to extraordinary rent-seeking, that doomed the postwar development policies in most developing countries.

A great deal of empirical evidence, both on campaigning in advanced industrial democracies, as well as on policy choice across a range of cases suggest that a simple rent-seeking argument based on state intervention in the economy is seriously incomplete. First, it cannot explain how governments can ever extricate themselves from welfare-reducing intervention if all intervention leads to rent seeking and all rent seeking is a net plus for politicians. It thus can tell us little about the major deregulation of critical industries such as airlines, oil, and telecommunications across the developed world in the later part of the twentieth century. Moreover, in the case of development policy, many countries, both early and late industrializers, including Britain, the United States, Germany, Japan, South Korea, and Taiwan, used milder versions of an infant-industry strategy and did not get stuck in the trap of endlessly multiplying and permanent subsidies (Wade 2003, XV; Hirschman 1971, 116). In other words, the simple inward-oriented explanation for the failure of ISI cannot explain the crucial comparative question in the political economy of development: why are some countries able to follow the actual prescriptions of an infant-industry policy and, after the specified learning period, gradually withdraw subsidies and move to a competition-based policy, while other countries fail to do so?

The successful use of infant-industry strategies in some countries suggests that rather than inward orientation explaining the failures of ISI, it was the particular choices regarding how to implement ISI that doomed the policy to failure in many developing countries. Most developing countries, including postwar Brazil and pre-Chávez Venezuela, opted for an extreme version of ISI. This version entailed high and variable protection in which, paradoxically, firms with the greatest comparative advantage received the highest protection, an emphasis on capital-intensive rather than labor-intensive production, and no program for encouraging infant industries to mature. These policies fostered industrialization, but virtually ensured that the industrialization drive would fail to meet its larger goals: sustained growth, manufactured exports, and freedom from recurring balance-of-payments crises.

The single most important flaw of the implementation choices in most developing countries was the failure to follow the prescriptions of their chosen infant-industry policy and, after a specified learning period, force nascent industries to mature (Chang 2002; Sheahan 2002). Various options were available for gradually introducing more discipline into producers' investment decisions. Lower and more carefully managed levels of protection would have reduced some import substitution, but it would have been a clear gain in terms of static allocative efficiency.[1] Such a choice would not

---

1. I use North and Thomas's definition of *welfare enhancing*. In their words, policy must "create an incentive to channel individual economic effort into activities that bring the private rate of return close to the social rate of return. . . . The private rate of return is the sum of the net receipts which the economic unit receives from undertaking an activity. The

have jeopardized the industrialization goal, but rather would merely have reduced some of the excessively high costs to the rest of the economy.

The costs of the excessively high and highly variable protection in Brazil were assessed by Bergsman, through an estimate of its effects on static allocative efficiency. "One conclusion . . . is that removing all instances of very high protection could have cost Brazil very little of its industrialization and import substitution, and also could have produced great benefits by forcing older firms to improve their efficiency" (1970, 173). He estimated that the cost of excessively high protection to Brazil was approximately 8–10 percent of GNP over the postwar period, and he called for an optimization of the infant-industry policy: "Better policies would have included a real devaluation towards the free exchange rate . . . and reductions in most or all of the highest tariffs, especially for 'daddy' industries.[2] The results of these differences would have been the elimination or reduction of inefficiency in the 'daddy' industries, [and] elimination or delay in the establishment of some of the most costly new import substituting industries" (177–78). It is worth emphasizing that these recommendations were also being made by the United Nations Economic Commission for Latin America (ECLA) by the late 1950s and were fully realizable within the import substitution program itself.[3]

Even in the context of very high levels of protection, there remained two ways to discipline investment decisions—either the East Asian choice of export performance, or what was on paper in Brazil—domestic substitutes that in fact would really represent a similar to the imported alternative in terms of price and quality. Political leaders in South Korea and Taiwan tied the receipt of scarce subsidized foreign exchange to export performance

---

social rate of return is the total net benefit (positive or negative) that society gains from the same activity. It is the private rate of return plus the net effect of the activity upon everyone else in the society" (1973, 1). The most obvious, but certainly not the only, example of a welfare-enhancing policy is a policy that supports a competitive market. In such a market, entrepreneurs make profits by producing better, cheaper products. This same process raises aggregate welfare. Competitive markets are not the only way to achieve such alignment of individual and social rates of return. A well-managed infant-industry policy can have similar effects (Amsden 1989; Wade 2003).

2. Bergsman (1970) identifies "daddy" industries as the less sophisticated manufacturers of goods such as textiles, clothing, and furniture, which were promoted in the initial phase of import substitution. These were firms that had much greater comparative advantage than did industries producing more sophisticated goods, *and* that had had the most time to mature. He notes with surprise that although these were the firms with the greatest comparative advantage and the greatest potential to become efficient exporters, they had the highest levels of protection.

3. For an ECLA analysis critical of excessive protectionism within ISI programs in Latin America, see Macario 1964.

(Amsden 1989; Wade 2003; Chang 2003).[4] Yet even if it is argued that such a heavy emphasis on exports would not have made sense for an economy as large as Brazil's, one must ask why the alternative of requiring a true domestic similar (quantity *as well as* price and quality) was not chosen. The Brazilian government distributed a vast range of incentives, including subsidized foreign exchange, high effective levels of protection, long-term credit at negative real interest rates, and fiscal incentives. Yet none of these inducements were tied to any performance requirements in order to encourage industrial infants to grow up. If they had chosen to reward maturation, government officials would not only have improved the social welfare effects of the policy; by encouraging infants to grow up, political leaders would have improved the possibilities for manufactured exports, thus addressing the balance-of-payments problem, and they would have fostered a dynamic process with at least the potential for fueling sustained growth. Why were any of the available mechanisms, including targeted protection, performance requirements, or requirements to develop a domestic similar in terms of quality and price, not used to alter entrepreneurial behavior in the interest of improved aggregate welfare and to stimulate a dynamic process of growth?

An emphasis on capital-intensive production had the same effects: it ignored the fact that only some manufacturers had the potential to become competitive exporters and, instead, plowed more and larger subsidies into industries with no real possibility of becoming efficient producers. The basic criteria governing policies that promoted import substitution in both Brazil and Venezuela, which favored substitution of anything not yet produced domestically, continuously shifted incentives away from improving efficiency in already established industries, and maturation through movement down the learning curve, and toward new domestic production in more capital-intensive goods. In Brazil, the specific benefits provided to favored firms, including exchange subsidies and tariff reductions on imports, reduced the costs of investment in these increasingly capital intensive processes by approximately 40 percent (Gudin 1956). In addition, industrial wages were roughly twice as high as the opportunity cost of labor. Bergsman estimates that policy changes to reduce the cost of labor relative to capital

---

4. Kang (2002) argues that South Korea did not tie access to subsidies to performance, but he does not provide any systematic evidence to support this position, which contradicts the vast majority of the literature on postwar South Korean development. For one of the most recent reviews affirming the use of performance requirements in South Korea, see Chang 2003.

would have increased the number of workers employed in manufacturing by 130 percent (1970, 162). The absence of any type of discipline in the form of performance requirements or more careful use of protection reinforced the effect. Huge subsidies made capital appear artificially cheap, and protected markets and the absence of performance requirements eliminated any incentive to increase productivity once the onetime subsidy on investment had been given.

Finally, the decisions about how to manage protection in most developing countries employing ISI were perhaps the most astounding. One of the features of the policy that has surprised many analysts is the fact that protection was typically cascaded in a direction that was in *direct contradiction* to what an infant-industry policy would prescribe.[5] In Brazil, consumer durables and nondurables received very high protection, averaging 190 percent over the period. Intermediate goods that had also already undergone considerable import substitution received low to moderate protection, with an average of approximately 50 percent. Finally, capital goods, in which import substitution was lowest and ongoing, received roughly 15 percent, on average. These average levels mask the very high intrasectoral variation that characterized the Brazilian structure of protection. Once again, broad estimates indicate that for capital goods, levels varied from negative to 75 percent; for intermediate goods, from negative to 100 percent; and for finished consumer goods, from 100 to 500 percent (Bergsman 1970, 48–52). In short, the choices for levels of protection ran directly counter to what would be prescribed by an infant-industry policy. The system provided the highest levels of protection for "daddy" sectors in which Brazil enjoyed a comparative advantage and that had long been fully substituted and lower levels for sectors in which Brazilian producers could legitimately claim to need assistance in moving from infants to mature competitive industries. Why would policy makers opt for a structure of protection that ran directly counter to the prescriptions of their chosen policy?

The case of Venezuela is even more astonishing because the country did

---

5. The following figures on levels of protection represent Bergsman's estimates in Brazil as of June 1966. Although military rule was established in 1964, no major changes to the system of protection were undertaken until 1967. Given that the figures are broad estimates and are intended to provide only a sense of the general structure and approximate levels, they are appropriate for our purposes here. As Bergsman states, "The structure in 1966 was typical of the 1957–66 period, and in a rough way of the 1947–57 period as well" (1970, 102). The figures represent levels of effective protection resulting from estimating the composite effect of the various instruments used simultaneously that affected the level of protection, including the tariff rate, surcharges and auction premiums (foreign-exchange control), quantitative restrictions (similarity), and exemptions.

not embark on large-scale import substitution until the early 1960s, and it enjoyed a major advantage in its abundant supplies of foreign exchange from oil exports. It might be argued that some of the more subtle advantages of a milder ISI policy could only be grasped in hindsight, but such information was readily available when Venezuela embarked on its industrialization program.[6] By the early 1960s, both the most obvious as well as the most subtle flaws of the earlier programs in the Southern Cone and Brazil had been clearly identified and critiqued even by those most sympathetic to the inward- oriented approach. Moreover, Venezuela enjoyed abundant foreign exchange from oil exports, and thus the argument that the balance-of-payments bottleneck and need to "save" foreign exchange made it imperative to continue the substitution of imports is not credible.[7] Finally, Venezuela embarked on industrialization during a period of undisputed growth in international trade. Thus, lack of information about the likely effects of policy, foreign exchange bottleneck, or inelasticities of demand are not plausible explanations for what drove policy choice in the case of Venezuela.

Nevertheless, Venezuela's ISI program had all the flaws of the earlier programs. Moisés Naim, finance minister in the second Perez government, described the policy thus:

> Venezuela was the last of Latin America's large economies to initiate comprehensive, state-led efforts to industrialize. The government protected infant industries and provided easy financing terms to private investors. . . . Rising tariffs and import quotas, increased state intervention, price controls, [and] massive undirected subsidies . . . [meant that] entire industries lacking any possibility of a self-sustained long-term contribution to the country's economic well-being were encouraged to grow. Ever-increasing subsidies and trade barriers assured their profitability while buffering them from international and even domestic competition. (1993b, 20–22)

The trade regime imposed mandatory licensing for 80 percent of all imports and import duties as high as 940 percent on some goods (Naim 1993a, 51).

---

6. Such an argument about hindsight, however, is simply not plausible in the most egregious failing of the policy: the failure to force infants to mature. It was not lost on even the most sympathetic supporters of the policy that this failing doomed the overall development plan to failure. See Prebisch 1963.

7. For a discussion of why this argument is also not credible for the cases of Brazil, Chile, Colombia, and India, see Lyne 1999. A close examination of policy choice demonstrates that there was no real attempt to use foreign exchange efficiently, which seriously undermines the "foreign-exchange scarcity" argument for the flaws of ISI.

The results were that real income per capita in 1985 was almost 15 percent lower than in 1973, and from 1982 to 1989, the number of Venezuelans living in poverty increased by 21 percent (1993a, 43–44). Naim concluded that "Venezuela's experience with import-substitution industrialization was not that different from that of many other developing countries" (43).

In sum, in comparison with the case of Brazil, the prevailing choices in Venezuela for how to manage the overwhelmingly most important public policy program of the period did not exhibit any significant variation in the degree to which the policy aimed to limit inefficiencies or promote sustained growth.[8] Venezuela's party-centered institutions did no better than Brazil's candidate-centered rules in aligning politicians' incentives with those of the general public. Venezuelan policy, like many others across the developing world, degenerated into the self-defeating permanent and ubiquitous subsidy, with any and all products that could possibly be produced domestically receiving generous support. As in Brazil, these subsidies were never tied to any incentives for infant maturation. The "create as many domestic industries as possible regardless of the cost" approach was so dominant in Venezuela that even with its abundant oil revenues its ISI program also led to a balance-of-payments and foreign debt crisis.[9]

It is worth emphasizing that if the causal impact of institutions are likely to be seen anywhere in policy outcome, their effect should certainly be in evidence in the case of the overwhelmingly most important public policy programs of the second half of the twentieth century. Yet the data from Venezuela do not show any important difference from postwar Brazil. On all three dimensions of ISI policy choice, Venezuela's policy package looks virtually identical: high and variable levels of protection, capital-intensive industrialization, and no incentives for infant-industry maturation.

In sum, inherent in the choices for how to implement import substitu-

---

8. Crisp (2000) presents an argument that capital had greater participation in consultative commissions that formulated policy and in the decentralized public administration charged with implementing policy as an explanation for policy skewed to favor capital. While this is certainly a strong proximate cause, those same government organizations were created by elected politicians. Crisp's analysis provides excellent and much needed insight into policy making in Venezuela, but it also raises further questions: Why do all democratically elected governments not opt to line their own and their campaign contributors' pockets in such a manner? Why didn't smart political entrepreneurs challenge this arrangement and propose to reform to a milder ISI program that had been well proved to be more effective in promoting sustained growth by the early 1980s?

9. Venezuela's foreign debt ballooned from $2 billion in 1973 to more than $35 billion in 1982. Moreover, once a foreign-exchange shortage did emerge in Venezuela, a pattern that was more the norm than the exception in most of Latin America also emerged in Venezuela: the resort to foreign-exchange controls (Naim 1993a, 44).

tion in both Brazil and Venezuela were numerous missed opportunities to improve the results of the program that were perfectly compatible with the inward-oriented nature of the policy. A more judicious use of protection and subsidies based on potential for efficiency and competitiveness would have improved aggregate welfare and could have laid the basis for industrial exports. Incentives for infant maturation such as performance requirements could have sealed the deal. Continual, yet gradual, pressure on infants to become more efficient could have fueled a dynamic process of sustained growth, as better, cheaper products raised standards of living and forced a redirection of capital from industries with no chance of becoming competitive to those that did have such potential.

Despite the availability of these options within the rubric of ISI, policy makers chose incentives aimed at maintaining the pace of industrial investment regardless of the real resource costs involved. This choice virtually ensured the program's exhaustion. By pushing industrialization into ever more sophisticated and capital-intensive goods, continually increasing subsidies were provided to firms producing goods that were more and more distant from developing countries' comparative advantage. The result was that subsidies multiplied rather than diminished over time, and each increment of growth became more costly in real domestic resource terms.

This discussion can be summed up by the conclusions of an ECLA study of the early 1960s:

> While it is true that import substitution necessarily brings about a rise in prices, and that protectionism conduces, by definition, to the inefficient allocation of resources, those higher costs and this inefficiency, as well as the bottlenecks and distortions in the structure of prices and production, might on the other hand be reduced to reasonable levels and temporary status by virtue of a far-sighted and properly programmed substitution policy, and protection on rational lines. Moreover, industrialization would not then militate against the export trade, but on the contrary, would stimulate it, since the development of efficient industries would be promoted. (Macario 1964, 83)

To understand the failures of postwar ISI policy, then, we must ask why policy makers opted for an extreme version that virtually ensured continuing balance-of-payments crises and was self-defeating in terms of creating sustained growth, when less counterproductive options were available within the ISI program. And why could these flawed choices not be reformed toward a milder version of ISI once the costs of the chosen implementation became manifest?[10]

Crisis of ISI in Postwar Brazil and Pre-Chávez Venezuela: Paralysis Versus Aborted Reform

In postwar Brazil, neither the president nor individual leaders or parties in Congress succeeded in any serious effort to address the growing economic crisis. Indeed, a close examination of elected officials' response would seem to indicate that these officials were in fact determined to accelerate rather than mitigate the impending calamity. While many bills may have entered the lower chamber with the intent of implementing reform, by the time they were passed into law they exacerbated the problems they were designed to solve.

In Venezuela, party elites studiously avoided any of the reforms that would have reduced their grip on nominations and elections, despite these being widely viewed as indispensable to adjusting the system to new social and economic realities. Instead, there were repeated efforts to renegotiate a pact on the model of those that had been in place at varying times since 1958, a model that was widely held to have created the rigidity and lack of

---

10. Many analysts have relied on ostensible price inelasticities of demand and supply to explain these choices that unequivocally exacerbated the foreign-exchange shortage. Yet an examination of trends in domestic production and international trade cast doubt on the view that export earnings were weak because of demand-and-supply inelasticities. With regard to inelasticity of demand, the data on growth in world trade does not suggest weak demand. Although prices of Brazil's noncoffee exports dropped by about 8 percent from 1947 to 1962, world trade in these products over the same period grew at an annual rate of approximately 3.1 percent. And while the quantum of Brazil's noncoffee exports rose only 7 percent from 1947 to 1962, world trade rose approximately 49 percent (Leff 1967, 286–87). Similarly, some general figures on total and agricultural production in Brazil tend to discount the thesis of inelasticity of supply, pointing to policy choice as leading to a decline in exports. Of course, there is no way to definitively establish the counterfactual that policies reducing discrimination against exports would have improved Brazil's export earnings. But the response to changes in domestic demand indicates an ability and willingness to increase supply. Agricultural output expanded at an average rate of 5 percent a year, and the production of agricultural raw materials for domestic processing rose from a base of 100 in 1947 to 170 in 1962 (Leff 1967, 287). Finally, the rising price of coffee from 1949 to 1953 was met with rapid increases in supply, such that the market was glutted once again by the mid-1950s. It is hard to imagine that Brazilian policy makers lacked knowledge of these figures on production and exports, and they cast doubt on the importance of structural rigidities as an explanation for poor export performance. I present only suggestive data here. For a comprehensive refutation of the thesis of inelasticity of supply in Brazil, see Kahil 1973.

responsiveness of the system that led to crisis.[11] When repeated attempts at a new pact failed, and Carlos Andrés Perez began a serious reform effort without institutionalized party support in 1990, the major parties quashed the effort by impeaching Perez on corruption charges (Corrales 2002).

Paralysis in Postwar Brazil

The crisis that Brazilian politicians faced in the early 1960s had three key components: high and accelerating inflation; a bloated and inefficient government bureaucracy; and a regressive, exclusionary, and fiscally disastrous social security system. The legislative response to this crisis was the passage of laws that actually exacerbated the existing problems.

Six attempts at stabilization were made in Brazil in the 1945–64 period: under presidents Dutra (1947–48), Vargas (1953–54), Café Filho (1954–55), Kubitschek (1958–59), Quadros (1961), and Goulart (1963). But each of these programs was ultimately undermined by executive and legislative choices that made stabilization impossible (Thorp and Whitehead 1979; Skidmore 1977; Dornbush and Edwards 1991). Labor ministers routinely opposed restraints on the minimum wage (Vianna 1987; Kahil 1973; Skidmore 1967).[12] Despite the fact that presidents appointed labor ministers, Vargas, Kubitschek, and Goulart responded to this pressure by decreeing large minimum-wage increases that implied considerable real gains in income and that contributed to the downfall of their stabilization plans (Skidmore 1967, 133–34, 169, 242–43; Vianna 1987).[13] The military and the Congress also routinely fought for and won policies that undermined stabilization plans in the Dutra, Vargas, Kubitschek, and Goulart governments (Vianna 1987, 26–27; Skidmore 1967, 127, 178, 242–43).

Wage increases, along with the inflation they engendered, led to demands for increased credit from producers (Vianna 1987; Skidmore 1977).

---

11. The most important of these was the Pact of Punto Fijo, which set the ground rules for power sharing throughout the system. This pact was important in cabinet formation until the early 1970s and in dividing up positions of power in the legislature through the 1980s (Coppedge 1994b). There was also the Common Minimum Program, an agreement on which policy alternatives would be on and off the table. Although formal pacts became less important over time, analysts are virtually unanimous in the view that both formal and informal rules of the game favored consensus decision making. As the crisis unfolded throughout the 1980s, there were a number of attempts to return to a formal pact.

12. The adverse impact on government accounts resulted primarily from all retirement benefits being provided by the state and the level of those benefits being tied to the minimum wage.

13. In the Vargas government this constituted roughly a 54 percent increase in real wages (Skidmore 1967, 134).

Brazil lacked a central bank during this period, and many executive agencies had authority to disburse credit to private agents. Despite the president's statutory authority to appoint and dismiss directors of these agencies, however, they routinely failed to adhere to monetary targets set by the Finance Ministry with each stabilization program (Abranches 1978; Benevides 1976; Vianna 1987). The executive's lack of commitment to stabilization is seen in the fact that in the Dutra, Vargas, Kubitschek, and Goulart administrations, the conflict between the practice of government departments to exceed credit limits and the attempts by the finance minister to administer the stabilization plan routinely ended with either the resignation or the dismissal of the finance minister (Skidmore 1967).[14]

Policy responses that exacerbated the existing problem were not confined to macroeconomic stabilization. Social security is a second area of policy that became an increasingly chronic problem over the period 1945–64, in no small measure because of legislation that was supposed to provide solutions. Bills to reform the major shortcomings of the system, which included administrative redundancy, limited and uneven coverage (roughly 20 percent of workers, with some among this 20 percent receiving much more lavish benefits than others), and regressive and actuarially unsound financing, were introduced throughout the period. Benefits were not tied to contributions, and social security benefits were paid out of the general tax fund. The result was that the system was funded by regressive general taxes and, as time wore on, increasingly by the most regressive tax of all, inflation. Despite this, the only legislation that passed during the entire period simply equalized the benefits between the more and less privileged within the 20 percent covered by raising all to the top level, without any provisions for new financing of what was already a chronically underfinanced system (Malloy 1979). This legislation was widely regarded as the key cause of the fiscal crisis that emerged in the early 1960s and as one of the sources of resurgent inflation.

In addition to this legislation equalizing benefits for the few by bringing everyone within the covered 20 percent up to the highest levels, the last president of the period, Goulart, in his final days in office vastly increased the benefits received by those already in the system. The new benefits included eliminating the minimum-age requirement for retirement, an annual bonus of one month's salary for all beneficiaries, increases in family

---

14. The Café Filho and Quadros administrations were so short that the end of their terms in office were essentially coincident with the failure of their stabilization plans.

allowances, a new separate institute for members of the legislature with lavish benefits, and loans and subsidized housing for covered workers (Malloy 1979, 119). Thus, a system already in crisis, and one that was a major source of inflation, was not reformed; rather, its most problematic features were maintained or enhanced (regressivity, exclusivity, and deficit financing).

The structure and staffing of the administrative bureaucracy also began to place severe constraints on economic development possibilities from 1945 to 1964. Both the lack of a professional public service and the extreme burden salaries and other generous perks placed on the fiscal budget were an impediment to sustained growth (Geddes 1994). Yet as the fiscal deficit and the need for a professionalized bureau grew, Congress and the president took action that undermined the possibility of creating a competent and efficient bureaucracy. Presidents used their appointment power lavishly. Graham states, "In these years each government made its contribution to the expansion of public employment—no one government is more responsible for political patronage than another" (1968, 135). This can be seen in the growth of the bureaucracy overall and in the figures comparing the number of new civil servants who entered following competitive examination versus those who entered as political appointees. In 1938, the size of the federal civil service was 131,628 employees, whereas in 1960, the number of bureaucrats, including direct administration and autarchies, was 421,212, a more than threefold increase in roughly twenty years (Graham 1968, 132). More important, however, is that that only 15 to 18 percent of all federal employees entered the bureaucracy by way of competitive examinations (Graham 1968, 129), according to available data.

While presidents appointed new civil servants rapidly and without any general criteria, the Congress was busy providing permanent status and full benefits to all. Throughout the period Congress passed legislation that eliminated any status or pay differential between those who entered via a civil service exam and those who were appointed to nontenured temporary positions. Thus, the changes to civil service policy that were adopted from 1945 to 1964 looked very similar to changes in social security policy. Rather than addressing any of the key problems, new government policy exacerbated them.

In sum, in Brazil the legislative response to runaway inflation was to act favorably on a series of political demands that piled more obligations onto the federal budget, without any concomitant measures to increase revenues. The legislative response to a bloated, inefficient, budget-busting bureaucracy was to add more jobs, raise salaries, and eliminate criteria for rewarding competence. The legislative response to a regressive, exclusionary, fiscally explosive social security system was more unfunded benefits for the few.

Aborted Reform in Venezuela

Although the crisis in Venezuela began in the early 1980s, the country's leaders have not achieved any serious economic reform to this day. In the face of economic policy paralysis, the view became widespread that the political institutions that had previously functioned reasonably well had become an impediment to needed reform, and thus the need for economic reform was transformed into a call for political reform (Ellner 1996). From the onset of the crisis in the early 1980s until Perez's impeachment in 1993, there were repeated attempts to formulate a new pact and renegotiate the rules of political engagement. As the reforms that would have reduced parties' centralized control stalled in Congress, however, it became clear that the only way in which needed policy reform could be achieved would be to act outside of institutionalized party channels. Yet the first serious and comprehensive attempt at reform of the policies that had driven a massive devaluation, declining standards of living, and a debt crisis, begun by Carlos Andrés Perez in 1990, was cut short by his impeachment on charges that could have been leveled at any Venezuelan president.[15]

The first attempt at a more encompassing pact was articulated during the presidential campaign of 1983, when the Social Pact was proposed by AD candidate Jaime Lusinchi. An aim of this proposal was to move the axis of decision making from the exclusive domain of the political parties and create a more inclusive, centralized, permanent, corporatist structure of consultation made up of representatives of labor, business, and government. Although an ephemeral National Commission on Costs, Prices, and Salaries was created after Lusinchi's election, it never had any real power to alter party control of decision making (Navarro 1995). The second attempt was the most comprehensive and produced the clearest and most coherent set of proposals. The Pact for Reform, which was based on a highly regarded government report (COPRE), was officially signed by a majority of political parties represented in Congress in December 1990. But the key political

---

15. For a discussion of how the purportedly unprecedented corruption under Perez's second administration was no different from previous administrations, see Coppedge 1995.

provisions, which would have reduced party control over nominations, the judiciary, and the electoral process and would have required internal democratization of the political parties, were never implemented (Navarro 1995; Ellner 1994).

Two further attempts at a renewed pact were fueled more by the immediate signs of crisis seen in the riots of 1989 and the failed coup of February 1992. The first was initiated by Perez in early 1992 and dubbed the Advisory Council of the Presidency of the Republic. This body was composed of a small group of prestigious individuals who consulted with major social groups regarding their reform priorities. The results were singularly unproductive. The report was no more than a laundry list of petitions ranging from those so general and ill defined as to provide little actual guidance for policy, to those so specific that they were completely irrelevant to addressing a crisis of such proportions. A final attempt at a new pact was seen in the National Accord, attempted first between just the major protagonists of AD and COPEI in May of 1992, and then later including MAS and other minor parties. The accord was first formulated around economic policy proposals, but was later formally articulated as Guidelines for a National Accord, which included the economic policy proposals as well as most of the key political proposals from the earlier failed Pact for Reform. The major parties, and in particular, MAS, rather than take the document as a point of departure for negotiation, quickly publicized nonnegotiable positions, and the accord had no more success than had earlier attempts to reach consensus on new rules and policies (Navarro 1995).

Shortly after his election in 1989, Perez adopted a neoliberal economic reform package that was very similar to what had been adopted in many countries of Latin America in the 1980s and to what would be adopted in Brazil in the mid-1990s. The standard measures of liberalization and privatization were coupled with proposals for tax reform and new social service programs. Yet although by 1989 there could be no denying deep economic malaise in Venezuela, and Perez was the first politician to provide a serious response, Perez's own party, and all the other major parties, failed to work with him or with other leaders to achieve reform.

Many argue that Perez made key mistakes not so much in the content of policy, but in his implementation strategy. Given the paralysis of the preceding decade, it is not surprising that he opted to implement as much of the program as possible through executive decree. He forged ahead despite opposition both from traditional political leaders and from civil society. Perez's reforms provoked protest on a scale that was unprecedented. The first phase of his reform, which included eliminating price controls on basic goods, led to days of rioting, to government intervention, and to more than three hundred dead in February 1989. In May the same year, the normally deferential Confederation of Venezuelan Workers (Confederación de Trabajadores de Venezuela [CTV]) organized a national strike. Two coup attempts were made in February and November 1992 (Crisp 2000, 178–82).

There is no denying that Perez's reforms created upheaval. Yet this is not surprising, given the level of adjustment that was necessary; what is surprising is how little debate there was within the political elite about the necessity of reform, the inevitable opposition from vested interests, and the possible strategies for bridging the gap. By the early 1990s Perez had weathered a great deal of opposition and his policies had produced considerable results in macroeconomic terms (Naim 1993a; Crisp 2000). Nevertheless, the political elite chose to ignore the problems Perez was trying to address and focus on his person as the most severe problem facing Venezuela.

Party elites failed to renew a pact or carry through with any other strategies such as a proposed constitutional reform. Instead, all energies became focused on removing Perez. The Congress voted to suspend Perez from office in May 1993, while he was being investigated on corruption charges. He was eventually convicted of minor abuse of power related to sending support to Violeta Chamorro in Nicaragua (Crisp 2000). In addition to removing the only serious reformer from office and studiously avoiding any alternative solutions, political elites' indifference to economic crisis is seen in the fact that Caldera, Perez's successor, achieved little more than stop-and-go policies that exacerbated the existing problems. Caldera was then succeeded by Chávez, who defeated the traditional parties and remade Venezuelan political institutions in his favor but has done little in the way of structural economic reform.[16]

The discussion of these cases makes two points clear. First, crisis in and of itself does not create incentives to adopt collective policy reform: we need a better theory of *when* crisis will lead to effective policy reform. Second, there does not seem to be any clear relationship between institutions and incentives for reform. The two democracies in Brazil were governed by the same weak institutions, yet politicians succeeded with effective reform only in the later period. In Venezuela, by contrast, the institutional rules that

---

16. Some observers might point to Chávez's political success as confirmation of an effective economic policy. Yet the bulk of the evidence suggests that this is little more than the effect of high oil prices. If anything, Chávez's economic policy has further reduced incentives for economic efficiency in Venezuela.

were credited with fostering effective governance for the first three decades increasingly became viewed as part of the problem. Why would Brazilian politicians acting under the same institutional rules fiddle while Rome burned in one period and adopt effective reform in another? And why would the major parties in Venezuela defeat the reforms that were clearly necessary to modernize the Venezuelan polity and impeach the only member of their ranks who presented a serious attempt to deal with a decade-old economic crisis that was escalating dangerously? In the following three sections I will argue that these choices were a direct result of clientelist electoral incentives coupled with how institutional variation alters the best strategies for defending a reputation for delivering in a clientelist system in crisis.

Policy "Flaws" and Crisis Response Explained as Maximization of Quid Pro Quo Benefits

Two of the most puzzling aspects of the democracy-development paradox are, first, how can policies with disastrous collective consequences be politically successful in a democracy over long periods? And second, if a crisis creates widespread social welfare losses, why would electoral competition in all democracies not drive politicians to compete in building a coalition for collective goods reform that could reduce the detrimental effects of such a crisis? In this section I develop the policy implications of the voter's dilemma—how winning policy choices differ depending on whether structural conditions favor the clientelistic or the policy-based equilibrium. I also discuss the most competitive strategies for maintaining a reputation for delivering in the midst of a crisis depending on the degree of centralization of clientelistic networks.

Policy Implementation Designed to Provide Collective Goods or Quid Pro Quo

Clientelistic and policy-based competition will produce very different incentives for policy choice. Most generally, in clientelistic systems, elections reward politicians who are adept at extracting and efficiently distributing resources, and in policy-based systems, elections reward politicians who are adept at integrating the service of their specific support constituencies with welfare-enhancing policies. When clientelistic exchange predominates, electoral imperatives dictate that winning politicians must focus on maximizing benefits that can be exchanged directly for votes. Under such conditions a politician who neglects to maximize the creation of clientelistic goods will be defeated by those that do. Moreover, because overall outcomes do not inform any portion of voters' choices in these systems, winning politicians will be those who maximize quid pro quo regardless of the aggregate welfare consequences.[17] Unlike in the case when voters make policy-based choices, the de facto democratic principals in clientelist systems are no longer the voters, but instead those who deliver the votes (Bueno de Mesquita et al. 2001, 64; Lyne 2007).

When structural conditions make policy-based voting possible, however, voters *are* the democratic principal, and overall outcomes do inform their choices.[18] At the very least, politicians competing in these systems must keep a close eye on the welfare effects of their policies in anticipation of political entrepreneurs' competitive campaigning and voters' judgment at the polls. If overall outcomes inform voters' choices, welfare-reducing policies should be punished at the polls (Lewis-Beck 1988).[19] Vigorous electoral competition should create strong incentives for welfare-enhancing entrepreneurship (Joskow and Noll 1981). Columns I and II in Table 35 depict these differences in policy choice.

As with each of the other aspects of party behavior, party internal design, and legislative organization examined in previous chapters, institutional rules are key to sorting out variation within the two equilibria. In policy-based systems, institutional rules determine the degree to which welfare-enhancing policies are diluted by powerful veto players that can extract individual deals in return for support for national policy goods (Cox and McCubbins 2001; Evans 2004; Tsebelis 1995). In clientelistic systems, institutions

---

17. There may be other constraints on policy choice such that politicians cannot completely disregard the macro consequences of their clientelistic policies. One important constraint is, of course, the degree to which deterioration in macro conditions destroys the value of clientelist benefits or reduces the flow of resources such as foreign capital and aid. The point is simply that deterioration in aggregate outcomes is not directly reflected in voters' choices, as it is in policy-based systems.

18. I assume that myriad factors, including economic welfare, in some cases postmaterial values, and local concerns, are weighed in voters' decisions when they opt for policy goods. I also assume that economic welfare is almost always one component, and that the lower the average standard of living, the more heavily this component is weighted.

19. Myriad factors determine whether a particular party or politician will seek and champion welfare improvements. In general, however, with the right conditions and strategy, the political marketplace in these systems rewards improved aggregate welfare. This is not to deny that politically successful welfare-enhancing reform often also requires side payments to losers, as with trade liberalization policies, for example. But welfare-enhancing policies by the Kaldor-Hicks criteria create enough new wealth such that there is a net improvement in aggregate welfare even after losers are compensated.

Table 35 *Policy choice and response to crisis in clientelistic and policy-based systems*

	Equilibrium Electoral Strategy	
	I. Clientelism (Extract and Distribute Resources)	II. Collective Goods Provision (National Policy Goods Qualified by Number of Veto Players)
A. Candidate-Centered Institutions	**Policy:** Pulverized to create resource streams for many individual clientelistic networks.	**Policy:** Designed to balance particularism with provision of national collective policy goods. Pork and rent seeking at low levels of aggregation: many veto players extract side payments in return for supporting collective goods policy.
	Crisis Response: Each individual clientelistic network owner clings to existing resource streams and seizes as many new ones as possible to protect reputation for delivering clientelistic goods.	**Crisis response:** Parties build coalition for collective goods reform to maintain reputation for delivering policy goods.
B. Party-Centered Institutions	**Policy:** Centralized hierarchical organizations monopolize the distribution of scarce valuable resources.	**Policy:** Designed to balance rents and pork with national policy provision. Pork and rent seeking at high levels of aggregation: few veto players extract side payments in return for supporting collective goods policy.
	Crisis Response: Central agent (party) retains monopoly control over any crisis-induced restructuring of clientelistic networks to protect reputation for delivering clientelistic goods.	**Crisis Response:** Parties build coalition for collective goods reform to maintain reputation for delivering policy goods.

play a powerful role in determining the degree to which policy is designed to provide many different individual clientelists with control over scarce valuable resources, or whether a few overarching organizations manage the distribution of scarce valuable resources.

Crisis Response Designed to Maintain Resource Streams

The logic of the voter's dilemma illuminates the fallacy in the assumption of a direct causal link between crisis and effective collective goods policy reform. Since it is the *risk* of rejecting clientelism that determines voters' choices, a simple reduction in the quid pro quo offer is not necessarily sufficient to alter the choice for clientelism. Crisis may require a reduction in the clientelist offer, which will certainly be viewed negatively by the voter, but collective accountability means that a reduced offer does not necessarily mean the voter no longer faces significant risk in rejecting clientelism. It is only once the clientelist offer sinks below the voter's reservation price that she can ignore the implications of the voter's dilemma and vote for collective goods.[20] As numerous cases of cyclical crises attest, economic decline and downright calamity are not necessarily sufficient to produce collective goods reform. While all crises tend to focus the mind, electoral incentives driven by structural conditions and the voter's dilemma determine whether politicians will focus their minds on a clientelist adjustment or collective goods reform.

To see this more clearly, consider the scenario in which an economic crisis has rendered existing clientelistic exchange bargains untenable. Now consider a politician who convinces voter A to relinquish her clientelistic benefit purportedly to implement collective goods policy reform, which will ostensibly leave all better off. Yet instead of implementing collective goods reform, the politician divides voter A's benefit into two, offering voters B and C each a benefit of half the value of what voter A was receiving. If the benefits created by halving what A was receiving still exceed voter B and C's reservation price, voter B and C will accept the clientelist offer and the politician has begun to build a cheaper clientelist network at voter A's expense. The outcome is that voter A has relinquished her excludable benefit, and the politician has begun adjusting his clientelist network to the new resource

---

20. Recall that the voter's reservation price, as a rough cut, is defined as equivalent to what he can easily procure through his own efforts. The reservation price of an election is the lowest-priced winning coalition of voters. For the full development of these points, see Chapter 2.

constraint.[21] Understanding this dynamic, voter A will not reject a reduced clientelist offer that remains above her reservation price. In the aggregate, the result is that as long as resources for delivering clientelist goods are sufficient to maintain patrons' threshold income and pay the reservation price of the election, crisis will not lead to collective goods policy reform.[22]

This does not rule out *policy change* in response to crisis, often dubbed "reform." But adjusting a clientelist system to new resource constraints will not lead to the improved outcomes often expected from policies labeled "reformist." Rather than improve collective outcomes, such "reforms" will simply adjust clientelist networks to the new resource constraints. Given the common connotation of reform, this kind of policy change is better labeled "clientelist adjustment." Reform that will actually produce improved collective outcomes requires a shift to collective goods policies, which will only happen when a sufficient number of voters can reject clientelism with minimal risk.

It is important to underscore here that there is no one-to-one correspondence between policy adjustment to restructure clientelist networks and

---

21. For a very insightful discussion of just this kind of clientelist adjustment carried out by Fujimori in Peru, see Roberts 1995.

22. Some may conclude from this discussion that clientelist competition at the national level would result in a "race to the bottom" in which all patrons with resources to distribute attempt to buy the cheapest majority of votes. With a full understanding of the strategic context of national-level clientelism, and how it shapes political actors' strategies, it becomes clear why this race to the bottom does not occur and why in fact what we see is top-down mobilization strategies. When structural conditions favor the clientelist equilibrium, even national-level policy is parceled up into quid pro quo, and those who do not demonstrate their support are excluded. Under these conditions, powerful groups will not simply sit by while politicians mobilize a sufficient number of the cheapest votes to win the election. Recognizing the effect of the clientelistic equilibrium and the excludable politics it engenders, those who have the ability to mobilize violent opposition to the regime will do so unless they are cut into the clientelist distribution. The result is that "cheap" votes are included to the extent they are valuable to powerful patrons or to the degree that such voters can organize sufficiently to disrupt the existing distribution. Early scholars of Latin American politics have noted this dynamic—groups receive a slice of the pie when they have power resources sufficient to disrupt existing clientelist bargains, even if they no longer mobilize much support in elections, as with large landowners in the postwar (see Anderson 1967 and Kenworthy 1970). The incentives are for inclusion managed from the top down, based on ability to disrupt existing exchange networks, not a race to the bottom to mobilize the cheapest votes. This means, of course, that restructuring clientelist networks in the face of a resource constraint is no simple proposition. As scholars such as Anderson have long pointed out, politicians must assess not only vote prices but also collective action and the potential for violence of different groups. We can say that one of the first likely targets for reduction of benefits will be those voters whose prices have been artificially bid up through bidding wars. These voters are receiving a price above their reservation price not because they can employ force to keep their prices up, but because politicians competing among themselves have bid up the price of votes.

state intervention, as classically understood. Clientelist adjustment can be done under the rubric of "market-oriented" reform, just as it can with heavy state intervention. Governments can control access to economic opportunities that are available in the international market just as they can control access to economic opportunities that are driven by the domestic market. In an ostensibly open economy, the right to import can be distributed by the government. When comparative advantage in exporting is driven primarily by exploiting an abundant resource (including abundant labor), the government can control and distribute the opportunity to exploit this resource as a means for building clientelistic networks. Governments can provide subsidized inputs, cheap credit, tax breaks, or other special favors to exporting industries in a fashion that makes it possible only for those so favored to remain in business. Particularly in a context in which the adoption of more "market friendly" policies is necessary to renew international financial flows, as in the 1980s in most developing countries, political leaders can be extremely ingenious in controlling and distributing the economic opportunities that are associated with an "open" economy.

Turning to the differences between cells IA and IB in Table 35, once again institutional insights are valuable in understanding variation in politicians' response to crisis in a clientelistic system. In all systems politicians will act to protect their reputation for delivering. The best strategy for protecting that reputation in a crisis-ridden clientelistic system depends on the structure of ownership of the clientelistic networks. In centralized systems the hierarchical institutions such as parties that "own" the clientelist networks and the reputation for delivering will seek to maintain their reputation by retaining monopoly control over any clientelist adjustment. These centralized organizations may find it possible to use the institutional machinery that allowed them to adjudicate mutually exclusive support in times of abundance to adjudicate mutually exclusive support in times of scarcity.

When resources are abundant in clientelist systems, institutions must ensure that all players (both individual and collective actors) get a "fair" share. The discussion of COPEI's refusal to allow the AD to rule as a majority party in Chapter 3 provides an example of how the problem arises even in times of resource abundance. COPEI demanded rules that ensured that they received roughly half of available resources at a time when Venezuela was flush with oil revenues. When resources are scarce, institutions must ensure that all players relinquish their "fair" share in order to adjust clientelist politics to resource constraints. If all players can be given credible guarantees that all other players are relinquishing their fair share to adjust to the imperatives of reduced resources, it may be possible to construct an agreement for reductions in resource streams. With these credible guarantees, network owners can be assured that their relinquished resources will not simply be used against them to construct an alternative clientelistic network. In other words, client-producers must be assured that their subsidies and regulatory favors will not simply be given to a competitor, rather than used to balance the budget (and thus typically renew international credit and other financial flows). Systems that enjoy hierarchical, institutionalized means for adjudicating these conflicts may find it possible to use them to adjust to resource constraints.[23] But far worse than existing network owners' failure to successfully implement clientelist adjustment would be some other actor's success. These central agents (often parties) will block any clientelist adjustment that is not carried out under their auspices, because such a successful clientelist adjustment would confer the reputation for delivering on the actor's carrying out the adjustment.

When individual politicians "own" the clientelistic networks and the reputation for delivering, each of these individual network owners will also seek to maintain his reputation for delivering. Yet the absence of a central agent with authority to adjudicate mutually exclusive support creates very different incentives for maintaining one's reputation for delivering in comparison to centralized systems. In the absence of a trusted central agent (for example, a party such as AD or COPEI), each network owner will fear that relinquishing some portion of his or her resources in the common interest of adjusting to resource constraints will in fact simply be used to fortify another clientelist network at his or her expense. In these decentralized systems, there is no overarching entity with a vested interest in maintaining a reputation for efficient management of clientelism. Individual and collective actors will lack credible means for committing themselves to a "fair" reduction for all players, and to using the resources to actually adjust, as through balancing the budget. Absent these credible guarantees, as a crisis unfolds, all players have a very strong incentive to tighten their grip on their existing resource streams and seize control of as many new resources as possible. In decentralized clientelist systems in crisis, individuals who relinquish control of resources without credible guarantees that others will do so

---

23. Once again, Mexico during the reign of the Institutional Revolutionary Party (PRI) probably provides the best example. The PRI's ability to weather economic ups and downs without significant challenge to its rule no doubt at least in part results from its ability to restructure the party's network from the top down to adjust to changes in availability of resources.

as well will be consigning themselves to political oblivion. What ensues then is a free-for-all in which individual clientelists tighten their grip on existing resources and seize as many new ones as possible. This is the best way to ensure that they will be able to weather the inevitable adjustment and maintain an ability to deliver when it comes.

Although I have argued that systems with hierarchical, institutionalized means for adjudicating mutually exclusive support and dampening bidding wars will be better equipped to adjust clientelistic politics to resource constraints, this does not guarantee success. The point is simply that political leaders in systems in cell IB (Table 35) begin with a major advantage: an overarching institution which has a reputation to defend and machinery that has proved effective in adjudicating mutually exclusive support. Political leaders in systems in cell IA, in contrast, do not enjoy system-level institutional machinery that is tested and trusted in adjudicating mutually exclusive support. In these systems, mutual exclusivity has been resolved through ongoing negotiation and bargaining and through continual ad hoc compromises among individual and collective actors. In the absence of an overarching set of institutions that stand above individual clientelists and ad hoc compromises, no central agent can credibly commit to actually providing the collective good of a clientelist adjustment. In short, while systems in cell IB may succeed in achieving a clientelist adjustment, systems in cell IA are almost certainly doomed to failure.

Turning to the possibility of a shift from column I to column II, if crisis results in the fact that resources are no longer sufficient for maintaining client-producers' threshold income and paying the reservation price of the election, a crisis will make it possible for politicians to build a coalition to support collective goods reform. When voters are no longer receiving their reservation price, they can join a coalition for reform without undue risk. If a voter turns out to be one of only a few who make this choice to support collective goods reform, he or she has not lost anything of significant value by failing to select the clientelist insurance policy. As structural conditions make it possible for a sufficient number of voters to reject clientelism without undue risk, a politician offering collective goods reform will be able to build a viable coalition.[24] As discussed above, within the set of possible col-

24. As discussed in Chapter 2, the theory says nothing about the content of such collective goods. It may be a realignment of property rights to make them more efficient in the case of a dire economic crisis, but it may well also include collective goods such as social safety nets. The crucial point is that these programs will be provided to all who meet the criteria, regardless of how they voted and that overall social welfare considerations will govern policy design (see the section "Policy Reform in Brazil, 1989–2004," this chapter, below).

lective goods reforms, institutions will influence the outcome. In systems with candidate-centered electoral law, more pork and rents will have to be doled out to make the collective goods policy wheels turn. In systems with party-centered electoral law, fewer pork and rents will be necessary to achieve collective goods reform.

In sum, crisis neither makes collective goods reform possible nor precludes clientelist politics. Voters will not reject reduced clientelist offers that are designed to adjust clientelist networks to an economic crisis as long as the offer remains above their reservation price. In the aggregate, this means that as long as the reservation price of the election can be met, crisis will mean either stalemate or a restructuring of clientelist networks to accommodate the new resource constraint.[25] Only when crisis means that the clientelist offer drops below the voter's reservation price will the voter join a coalition for reform.

Import Substitution Industrialization Policy: Oversized Infants, Capital Intensity, and Excessive Protection as Maximization of Quid Pro Quo Benefits

Import substitution industrialization was a policy that political leaders in Latin America stumbled upon almost by accident. As politicians crafted an ad hoc response to trade disruptions emanating from World War I and from the Great Depression, they inadvertently fostered domestic industrialization (Hirschman 1971). The protection of the domestic market afforded by exchange controls that were designed to restore international payments balance stimulated domestic production of what were now prohibitively costly imports. As the effects of the policy were better understood, and as economists from the United Nations Economic Commission on Latin America (ECLA) began championing infant-industry strategies, what was initially a

---

As has been amply documented, although social safety nets such as social security existed in Latin America in the postwar, these benefits were tied to votes, and were fiscally disastrous (Cruz-Saco and Mesa-Lago 1999).

The argument about changing voter choices, on the basis of the risks of rejecting clientelism, as the key to successful collective policy goods reform is not meant to discount the importance of politicians' skill and ingenuity. Both are required to make this momentous transition. Nevertheless, the point remains that in the absence of a reduction in such risks for a sufficient number of voters, no amount of political skill and ingenuity will be sufficient to achieve collective goods reform.

25. As has been alluded to above, stalemate as was seen in Brazil in the early 1960s is often ultimately resolved by some central agent. In the case of Brazil it was the military.

stopgap measure became a component of a set of policy initiatives aimed purposefully at industrialization and renewed economic growth. Thus, the question of the flaws of the postwar import substitution industrialization (ISI) development strategies does not revolve around why an inward-oriented strategy was chosen or why a strong government role was preferred. The key question is why policy makers did so little to optimize the policy within the chosen rubric of state-sponsored industrialization for the domestic market.[26]

Why did policy makers consistently fail to adopt reforms that could have increased job creation; increased foreign exchange earnings; and avoided, or at least staved off, the early exhaustion of growth under ISI? And how can we explain policy makers' choice for a steady march toward crisis and exhaustion, despite the clear signals they received, and the options for alternatives that were repeatedly discussed in public policy circles?[27]

The choice for permanent subsidies rather than infant maturation, for capital rather than labor intensive production, and protection cascaded in contradiction to infant-industry prescriptions are of a piece and reflect the constraints of clientelist competition. Politicians who implemented ISI created industrial jobs through permanent and multiplying subsidies because such a policy allowed them to maximize benefits that could be exchanged directly for votes and other support. In contrast, an infant-maturation policy rewarding efficiency and competitiveness creates diffuse benefits that cannot be predicted or controlled a priori. A policy that rewarded efficiency and

---

26. A number of other arguments have been advanced to explain policy failure in developing countries, including position in the international division of labor (dependency theory), the nature of the state (statism), and some form of rent-seeking or interest group theory. Haggard (1990) makes a very strong case for the preeminence of policy choice and highlights some of the weaknesses of an explanation based on the influence of multinational corporations (MNCs). The most sophisticated version of dependency theory employed to study postwar development policy is provided by Evans (1979). Haggard (1990) makes a statist argument. For the argument that a statist explanation begs the question of a general theory of what drives politicians' choices for policy and institutional design, see Ranis 1990 and Lyne 1999. Finally, as discussed in the section "The Flaws of Import Substitution Industrialization Policies," in this chapter, above, rent-seeking theories provide no general argument to explain the vast differences in levels of "rent-seeking" across all democracies. Nor can these theories explain why some governments succeed in reducing rents, while others fail.

27. Ideological constraints are also not a plausible explanation. As Kaufman (1990) notes, even the most staunchly nationalist politicians such as Peron were willing to modify their stances when it became necessary in order to maintain the pace of import substitution. After substitution of less sophisticated consumer durables was completed, governments had to provide generous terms for MNC investment in order to attract the capital and technology needed for more sophisticated domestic manufacturing. These policies were certainly in conflict with earlier claims about a second, economic independence for Argentina based on domestic production and nationalization of foreign-owned enterprise.

competitiveness would have produced better, cheaper products and more efficient investment. The diffuse benefits in the form of rising standards of living derived from such policies cannot be targeted, but accrue to all consumers. The increased social welfare that would accrue to an infant-maturation policy is not targetable in a quid pro quo exchange.

Simple job creation through subsidy of industrial investment, however, creates both production and job opportunities that can be exchanged in quid pro quo. Brokers who can provide such scarce valuable jobs typically become very powerful players. There is considerable evidence that leaders of state-corporatist interest groups assumed precisely this function.[28] Politicians disregarded the prescriptions of their own chosen policy because the alternative permanent subsidy was the clear political winner in the context of clientelist competition. When structural conditions cash out to a clientelist equilibrium, allowing an infant-industry policy to degenerate into permanent subsidies—despite the ruinous collective consequences—is a winning political strategy.

Once it is understood that the permanent-subsidy strategy was not a mistake, but the most politically competitive policy, the choice to push ISI into ever more capital-intensive industrialization also falls into place. The strategy designed to successively replace more and more sophisticated imports with domestically produced goods is what led to increasingly capital-intensive production. As domestic demand for simpler goods was satisfied, production of these goods no longer provided a source of new clientelistic benefits. A policy of continuing import substitution into ever more sophisticated goods, however, although economically disastrous, was a means for continuing to create new production opportunities and jobs that could be traded for votes.

A policy designed to maintain growth based on something other than the

---

28. The role these state corporatist interest groups played in distributing jobs in return for votes has not been the major emphasis in the study of these organizations. Yet such an understanding of these organizations unifies and makes sense of many of their features. First, it helps explain why their leadership became extremely powerful players in a very short period of time, despite the fact that labor unions incorporated only a minority of workers in most developing countries employing ISI. It also helps explain why labor unions remained parochial rather than categorical, and thus why they were never able to effectively mobilize the majority of workers on the basis of a national program favoring labor interests. Finally, the requirement for monopoly representation of a given sector by one corporatist organization can be seen as a mechanism for dampening bidding wars. In Brazil there is a great deal of documentary evidence of the ex officio voting system, dubbed a typical tool of urban clientelism (Souza n.d.), in which the organization's leaders were held legally responsible for registering their voters and who turned in the vote as a bloc.

strategy of continual replacement of imports would have required disciplining investment decisions by allowing the market to determine the winners. The obvious alternative to capital-intensive investment suggested by Bergsman (1970) and other analysts discussed above is of this type. Any attempt to force "daddy" industries to become competitive would have led to a shakeout of firms and jobs that would have improved aggregate welfare but reduced the number of production opportunities that could be traded directly for support. The capital-intensive strategy, in contrast, had just this virtue of maintaining the creation of production opportunities that could be traded in quid pro quo. It was clearly a counterproductive choice from a sustained-growth perspective, but it was a winner in a political marketplace driven by clientelist competition.

Finally, the unusual pattern of protection, which directly contradicted the prescriptions of the chosen policy, can also be understood as driven by clientelist politics. The structure of protection, in which those firms with the greatest comparative advantage received the highest level of protection, evolved as a result of the effects of the progressive substitution strategy on early upstream producers. The first import substituting firms imported most of their machinery and inputs. As the program wore on, however, more and more of the inputs and equipment used by these initially established firms were produced domestically. And given the lack of any price discipline on the producers of inputs and equipment, the costs to the early substituting firms went up as they were forced to replace cheaper (and typically subsidized) imports with more expensive domestically produced inputs. As the costs of the early substituting firms went up, their own protection had to be increased so that their incomes could be maintained. Thus, we get the unusual pattern of protection that provides the highest rates to those sectors with the greatest comparative advantage. Because these sectors were the first to be substituted, and they then had to incorporate more and more costly domestic inputs as the program progressed, higher and higher levels of protection were necessary to protect their incomes.

The explanation for ISI developed here has rested heavily on a logical argument about the kinds of policies that clientelist competition would reward. There are several ubiquitous features of the policy milieu in Brazil and Venezuela that reinforce the argument. A theory of clientelistic competition would suggest that it is no accident that three features occur together in both countries, and indeed in virtually all developing countries that had disappointing results with ISI: a lack of both international *and* domestic competition, lack of any transparent criteria governing the distribution of incentives, and state-corporatist interest intermediation not only for blue- but also for white-collar workers.

Advocates of infant-industry policies often make the point that the intention of protection is not to completely eliminate price discipline on investors' decisions, but simply to shield them from the most ferocious competition during a learning period. Competition within the domestic economy is often cited as one way to achieve the twin goals of providing nascent industries with breathing room while at the same time maintaining some more manageable pressure on domestic producers. What is striking about the results in most developing countries is that policies eliminated both international *and* domestic competition, even in the largest economies, such as those of Brazil and India.[29] The failure to enforce domestic competition is consistent with a policy designed to turn industrialization policy into targeted quid pro quo benefits. It is also consistent with the absence of any transparent criteria for distributing incentives. Government-conferred production rights based on criteria that no policy maker is able to articulate reeks of a clientelist exchange bargain.[30]

The other ubiquitous feature of these programs was a pattern of state-corporatist interest intermediation, in which the government-approved class association had exclusive authority to represent the interests of a given sector. These were hierarchical, monopolistic interest-intermediation institutions, and their leadership was appointed by the government. Moreover, these institutions were not restricted only to the working class, but applied to white- and blue-collar workers alike. Why representation based on occupation rather than some other characteristic, why mutual exclusivity and

---

29. See Bergsman 1970 and Bates 2001.

30. As Kitschelt (2000) has emphasized, it is easy to both articulate and defend rents delivered to a given sector on the basis of generalized policy criteria. This is obviously much more difficult in the case of a direct exchange of production rights to individual producers in return for political support. See the excellent series sponsored by the National Bureau of Economic Research and synthesized in the volume by Bhagwati (1978) for discussions of the lack of transparent criteria in every developing country studied. Bergsman (1970) discusses this lack of criteria in the case of Brazil. In addition, in Brazil there is some anecdotal evidence of the quid pro quo with industrialists. The director of the administrative agency responsible for distributing incentives had de facto ministerial status and was considered to be extremely powerful. This agency, known as CACEX, maintained all the records of what each firm received, and also maintained a black list that was widely reputed to be a list that was used for punishing uncooperative firms (Abranches 1978). Naim notes that in Venezuela, subsidized foreign exchange was distributed to different lists of sectors and even to individual firms "according to criteria that were often changed and seldom very transparent" (1993a, 45).

monopolization of representation, and why mandatory for all categories of workers? All these features of interest intermediation fall into place as the organizational machinery designed to enforce the clientelistic bargain exchanging production rights, and industrial and bureaucratic jobs for votes, and designed to reduce incentives for bidding wars. A single hierarchical organization for each category of workers meant that competing organizations would not bid against one another for worker support. Mandatory organizations for all workers once again eliminated the possibility for rival organizations and provided efficient technologies of exchange for urban clients.[31]

Response to Crisis: Maintaining the Reputation for Delivering in Decentralized and Centralized Clientelist Systems in Crisis

Despite the common failure to enact reform, politicians in postwar Brazil and pre-Chávez Venezuela reacted differently to the crisis brought on by the exhaustion of ISI. I argue that these distinct yet similarly failed responses were driven by a logic of how politicians protect their reputation for delivering in centralized and decentralized clientelist systems facing economic crisis.

As has been discussed in preceding chapters, postwar Brazil was characterized by a decentralized clientelistic system in which individual politicians owned their own clientelist networks. Although parties did organize these individual networks collectively and managed them to minimize bidding wars, as was discussed in Chapter 4, the rank and file themselves clearly were the carriers of the reputation for delivering clientelistic goods. The response to crisis in postwar Brazil discussed in the section "Crisis of ISI in Postwar Brazil and Pre-Chávez Venezuela," in this chapter above, were driven by the sin qua non of survival in clientelist systems: maintaining access to resources. Bills and programs introduced ostensibly to correct growing problems such as inflation, bureaucratic inefficiency, and a pension debacle were disfigured to such a degree as they made their way through the legislative process that rather than decelerating the onset of crisis they actually accelerated it. With an assumption that voters opt for policy goods, it is difficult to makes sense of these choices. If overall outcomes informed voters' choices, the expectation would be that politicians

---

31. See Hawkins 2003.

who used their leadership to negotiate a reform program with their supporters, and then used this program as a basis for bargaining over the final shape of the reform policy would be the ones who fortified their reputation for delivering. The party or coalition that is able to build a general reform program based on a compromise coalition of such politicians should be the new electoral winners.

Yet in a context of crisis in which electoral competition continues to reward clientelist strategies, and there is no agreed-upon mechanism for adjudicating the necessary ratcheting down of benefits to adjust to new resource constraints, the strategy of grabbing all one can get in the short term is quite rational. Without any kind of agreement or focal point that could signal who will have the authority, and on what terms the inevitable adjustment will be achieved, individual clientelist network owners have a very strong incentive to maximize resources under their control, regardless of the collective consequences. Ceding resources, the action necessary for a clientelist adjustment, is clearly political suicide in a decentralized clientelistic system. Given the lack of any central authority with the ability to ensure that everyone pays his or her fair share, any relinquished resources will be quickly seized by other individual clientelist entrepreneurs. And any failure to grab one's share of the resources available from any new policies will certainly be seen as a sign of weakness that will undermine the network owner's ability to come out of the adjustment with his or her resource streams intact. From this point of view, the response to crisis in postwar Brazil is not driven by wildly corrupt or irrational politicians or a mass of ignorant voters who fail to understand the effects of such practices. What these patterns reflect is a completely unbridled bidding war that emerged as each network owner strove to fortify his or her position and hunker down to weather the inevitable adjustment to come.

Turning to the failed response to crisis in Venezuela, several explanations have been advanced to explain the debacle. One is based on errors of implementation. A number of analysts argue that Perez failed to adequately prepare the public and build a case for the necessity of the reforms and that it was his inept strategy that led to his defeat (Naim 1993b; Crisp 2000). These authors argue that the unprecedented opposition created by Perez's missteps led party leaders to remove him because they believed democracy in Venezuela would not survive his administration. A second explanation holds that the crisis was not "deep enough" to convince key actors of the need for such draconian measures (Weyland 1996b).

These arguments certainly capture part of the story. In support of this position, however, analysts point to the several high-profile events that took place from 1989 to 1992, discussed above. The riots, strikes, and coup attempts were certainly disruptive and traumatic events, but they were typically carried out by concentrated minorities. Public opinion data, however, which gives a more general view of how Perez was viewed, cast some doubt on the notion that he was overwhelmingly rejected by the populace. When voters were asked how well off they predicted they would be at the end of Perez's term, their outlook improved considerably from May to November 1992. Whereas in May, 28 percent said they predicted they would be better off, in November, 34 percent predicted this outcome. And while 43 percent predicted they would be worse off in May, only 30 percent gave this response by November. In addition, the number of voters who predicted they would be better off or the same dropped to 40 percent in May but was up to 50 percent by November (Myers 1995, 110).

These response patterns raise important doubts about overwhelming public opposition being the reason for Perez's impeachment. The number of voters who believed they would be better off and of those who believed they would be the same increased significantly throughout 1992. These results certainly do not corroborate the view that Perez was increasingly rejected by the public over time, nor are they consistent with the argument that he was overwhelmingly rejected by the public at the time of his impeachment. Indeed, these numbers appear to be more consistent with the idea that the difficult period of the adjustment had passed by late 1992 and that the beneficial results of the reform were beginning to be reflected in improved public opinion numbers.

More important, the two main arguments explaining Perez's failure and downfall are difficult to reconcile with the aftermath. Considering the argument about errors of implementation first, if collective policy reform was in fact politically viable, yet Perez simply botched the execution, why have there been no other serious attempts at reform? COPEI, in particular, was ostensibly the more rightist party of the two and was the representative of business interests. Why would a party with these policy commitments not capitalize on the failure of the ostensibly more left-leaning party? The same criticism can be leveled at the second explanation based on the severity of the proposed reforms. It is highly implausible that both the public and political elites did not believe that some type of reform was necessary by 1990. If Perez's medicine was simply too bitter, why were other alternatives not formulated? Why would the voters not reward the parties that came up with milder and therefore, according to this argument, more appropriate measures for halting a decade-long economic decline? In short, why did electoral competition not spur more well-designed reform attempts?

These explanations also rest on a characterization of Perez's political acumen that runs directly counter to how he was viewed before the crisis. Until his ill-fated reforms, most observers viewed him as an extremely skilled politician who was exquisitely attuned to the voters.[32] Moreover, Perez was instrumental in spearheading political reforms that had been resisted by the major parties for almost a decade (Ellner 1994). Can this politician be the same one who failed to grasp the possibility of major social opposition to a wrenching neoliberal policy adjustment and thus the need to tailor its implementation accordingly?

If we consider the differing requisites to successfully competing in clientelistic and policy-based systems, we can develop an explanation that takes Perez's extraordinary political skills as a given yet can explain his policy's failure as well as the absence of any other serious attempts at reform after his impeachment. If structural conditions favored the clientelistic equilibrium despite crisis, the new winner in Venezuela would be the politician who could adjust clientelist politics to the resource constraints. A politician as skilled as Perez most likely understood this dynamic and was in fact attempting to enact a clientelist adjustment under his aegis and thus supplant the dominant parties as the actors with the reputation for delivering.

Although it is impossible to know Perez's full strategy, as his experiment was cut short, Perez clearly not only implemented rapid economic policy adjustments, but also aimed directly at the bases of power of the traditional party elites'. He was instrumental in achieving key changes, such as the direct election of governors (Ellner 1996). Previously, presidents had appointed governors and had retained complete control over how federal resources were distributed within the states. One of Perez's key moves, after he achieved the direct election of governors, was to give them complete patronage rights over regional offices of the national ministries. These changes can be seen as a move to undercut the long-standing state-based networks of the AD and COPEI. By having governors be elected, Perez was creating an alternative path to state-based leadership that could circumvent the party networks. And by giving them control over resources, he was providing his protégés with the means to build their own clientelistic networks. It is highly revealing in this regard that this state-level resource control was one of the initiatives immediately reversed by his successor, with the explicit

---

32. See Coppedge 1994a, 111 and Karl 1982.

statement that decentralization could not be used to extend clientelist practices to the state level (Ellner 1996, 91).

Perez also attacked the traditional bases of party elites' power by advocating internal democratization of the political parties—reforms steadfastly opposed by the party elders. This attempted reform follows the same logic as that of instituting elected governors. By making internal party leadership positions elective, Perez could undermine the leadership's stranglehold on the closed-list ballot. Elective leadership positions would allow Perez to use resources to cultivate party leaders loyal to him, rather than to the CEN and the state-level party bosses. Given that leaders had exclusive control of nominations, successful cultivation of a new elected leadership would allow Perez to wrest control of nominations from the existing leadership. Finally, as Crisp (2000) points out, Perez continued to create consultative commissions designed to formulate policy with heavy private sector participation. Although this choice is consistent with both a clientelist adjustment and collective policy reform, the latter seems implausible, given the Venezuelan context. It had long been argued that the institutionalized participation of privileged members of civil society was one of the features that had made the Venezuelan system so inefficient and resistant to change. If Perez really was trying to implement collective goods reform, why maintain the structure that had coddled the vested interests that had benefited from ISI? The choice to maintain the structure yet change the players is far more consistent with a clientelist adjustment.

The view that Perez aimed to enact a clientelist adjustment and supplant the dominant parties as the only players that could deliver is consistent with what was seen as Perez's long-standing ambition and political acumen up to the point of his second administration. Is it plausible that a politician who had won two presidential elections, who was extremely popular with the citizenry, and who had accomplished political reforms that many others had advocated but that no one else could attain would make the elemental error of failing to adequately prepare the population for the needed economic reforms? I argue that it is more plausible that Perez did not make this mistake. He understood that in achieving a clientelist adjustment that would at least seriously damage the leading parties' reputation for delivering, far more formidable than public opposition would be the opposition from the elites within his own and the other major party. He calculated that the costs of failing to lay the groundwork with the citizenry would be outweighed by the benefits of taking the party elites by surprise. With this interpretation of events, Perez did not suddenly become a clumsy politician who bungled the obvious, but instead was the same savvy player who understood where his real opposition resided.

This explanation also sheds light on the motivation behind the major parties' response to the crisis. Why did political leaders who had been lauded as exceptional stewards of Venezuelan democracy become so inept and resistant to what all viewed as needed reforms? There is a great deal of documentary evidence of the exceptional skills and flexibility of Venezuelan elites (Levine 1973). Why did they become so rigid and hidebound after only one generation? These parties were clearly losing their ability to win the approval of the voters.[33] Why would they not enact some of the political reforms that would enhance their party's responsiveness to voters rather than hark back to old formulas that many now viewed as partly responsible for the system's failure to adapt to changing conditions? Would a leadership who took these steps not be rewarded with electoral success, and also with renewed support within their own party? Would the party that enacted these reforms not be able to champion itself as the mature party adapting Venezuelan democracy to modern realities, and thus reap electoral gains?[34]

As was discussed in Chapter 4, if elections were driven by provision of national collective goods policy, then reforms that made the leadership more accountable to the rank and file, or loosened their grip on candidate selection in favor of the public, would have increased parties' responsiveness to voters' preferences for policy goods. But if structural conditions meant the dominance of clientelistic strategies, party leaders making such choices would not in fact be adapting their party in order to be more electorally competitive, but instead would be weakening their electoral competitiveness by relinquishing their monopoly control over the reputation for delivering. Any reform that relinquished control of positions with authority over resources (the party leadership positions and nominations for congressional seats) in favor of some kind of vote with an uncertain outcome would weaken the party's ability to maintain its reputation for delivering. This explanation suggests that Venezuelan elites might still be exceptionally skilled and conciliatory. What changed were not leadership qualities but the strategies that would be effective in maintaining a reputation for delivering clientelist benefits in crisis-plagued Venezuela.

33. Crisp (2000, 176) provides an excellent concise description of rising abstention in the 1980s.

34. Many have argued that this was in fact the intent of political reforms adopted in 1989 and 1993. For a discussion of these reforms and why they omitted key changes that would have made the parties more representative, see Chapter 4.

This explanation is also consistent with the leaderships' repeated attempts to renew a pact rather than enact reforms that would decentralize internal party decisions and nominations. The return to the formula of a pact was not simply a nostalgic attempt to return to the glory days of old. The formula had the potential to solve the critical problem of how to adjudicate the costs of the clientelist adjustment. If agreements could have been forged on fair burden-sharing in adjusting to the crisis, it could have been a formula for maintaining the dominance of the major parties while enacting a clientelist adjustment. In short, the two major parties were not ignoring the crisis; they were attempting to use the mechanisms that had effectively adjudicated resource distribution in times of abundance to adjudicate resource distribution in a time of scarcity.

Finally, this explanation helps make sense of the paradox that the major parties turned against their only member to take the crisis seriously and attempt needed policy changes, and why more well-formulated alternatives were not forthcoming if the problem was Perez's ineptness. If parties were competing in the provision of policy goods, it is difficult to explain why one of two outcomes did not occur. Why did Perez's party not either take credit for being the first to provide a serious response, or if Perez's approach actually was simply too drastic, why did the leadership or some other prominent members of the party not offer an alternative?

If parties are competing to provide clientelistic benefits, we can make sense of this omission. The AD and COPEI moved to crush Perez because the major parties were the owners of the clientelist networks in Venezuela, and in impeaching Perez they were moving to safeguard their reputation for delivering. The AD calculated that they were better off with continued crisis rather than supporting a "reform" that was designed to seize their long-held position as the only agent capable of delivering to AD's constituency in a clientelistic system. Moreover, no other alternative leadership emerged because they had nothing to gain by proposing reforms. The rank and file in centralized clientelistic systems are most likely to preserve their position and improve their career prospects by keeping a low profile and maintaining their ties to the party with the incentive and ability to maintain that reputation. Rank-and-file members had nothing to gain from proposing alternative reforms unless they were willing to take on the Herculean task of enacting a clientelist adjustment and wresting control over the reputation for delivering from the existing party elites. Perez was perhaps one of the few willing to contemplate such an undertaking. He had long been seen as one of the most ambitious and entrepreneurial politicians in Venezuela, one who had consistently been advocating changes that would reduce the power of the small circle of party leaders (CEN). It is quite plausible that he saw the decade-old unanswered crisis as his critical opportunity to reshape who managed clientelism in Venezuela.

Policy Change Without Collective Goods Reform in Contemporary Venezuela: Chávez's Clientelist Adjustment

I have argued that if structural conditions continued to favor the clientelistic equilibrium in crisis-plagued Venezuela, the new winners who will prevail in the wake of the collapse of the old system will be the ones who discern how to reorganize clientelism in the context of the new constraints. In this section I will argue that Chávez has largely succeeded in such a reorganization of clientelism where Perez failed. What explains why Chávez has prevailed?

First and foremost, Chávez organized support among the military before he attempted to challenge the existing elites. Chávez's initial political organization was the MBR-200, originally a clandestine organization of dissident officers formed in 1983 by junior officers who were among the first graduates of the reformed National Military Academy (Academia Militar de Venezuela). Like military officers in Argentina and Brazil in the postwar period, young Venezuelan officers received courses on development, nationalism, and Marxism from the academy. In addition, salaries for military officers, traditionally among the highest in Latin America, had eroded throughout the 1980s and 1990s, which also created a climate open to critiques of the existing system (Trinkunas 2002). This military backing gave Chávez a level of clout that Perez was unlikely to have been able to match. As a creation of the dominant parties, Perez had an appeal and support that were inextricably linked to that system. Although he attempted to make an end run around the constraints of the system, when the dominant parties turned decisively against him, Perez had little to fall back upon. Chávez, however, began outside the system, and he had the backing of an important group that could wield force in his favor.

Second, Chávez built his clientelistic adjustment around a repudiation of neoliberal reform policies, whereas Perez was attempting to restructure clientelism while at the same time implementing a macroeconomic adjustment. The goal of Perez, as a creature of the existing parties, was to renew the viability of the existing system, albeit under his tutelage and with a distinct development-policy orientation. As an outsider, Chávez could combine a repudiation of neoliberal reforms with a rejection of the failed political system. With this strategy, he could more effectively court groups that had been excluded from the previous regime. Appealing to the former Venezuelan Communist Party and defeated guerrilla groups was a strategy much less likely to pay off for Perez. In addition, Chávez's outsider status allowed him to create a new, and as discussed in Chapter 3, very ingenious, narrative that cloaked his clientelistic reorganization in pseudodemocratic legitimacy.

Third, Chávez was the beneficiary of a significant increase in oil prices, as discussed in Chapter 2. It was only with the near doubling of government revenues beginning in 2004 that Chávez began to consolidate his position with nationwide programs such as the *misiones,* the *consejos comunales,* and workers' cooperatives. These resources may well make it possible for Chávez to completely outbid and eradicate the vestiges of the old clientelistic system, by replacing municipal and state governments with the *consejos.*

Finally, it is important to highlight Chávez's considerable political skill. As discussed in previous chapters, he has shrewdly discerned how he can imbue his clientelist reorganization with democratic legitimacy, by emphasizing how it will do away with sclerotic party and administrative bureaucracies that he argues are not the machinery of representation but instead an impediment to citizen participation. Chávez has also adroitly resurrected the anti-imperialist, anti-U.S. narrative and coupled it with attempts to reinvigorate OPEC as a force constraining the great powers. In this case once again, Chávez is the accidental beneficiary of U.S. foreign policy during his tenure, but he has certainly exploited it effectively. Finally, as discussed in previous chapters, Chávez clearly recognizes some of the key sources of inefficiency in clientelistic regimes and is shaping his reorganization accordingly. Thus, the replacement of multiple levels of government with one territorial unit (*consejos comunales*) for linking citizens to government, the replacement of multiple political parties with one party under his control, and the restructuring of the legislature all facilitate the management of mutual exclusivity of support and the ability to efficiently buy votes.

Chávez has rejected neoliberal reforms in favor of what he calls a policy to implement twenty-first-century socialism. To date Chávez's nationalizations have been limited to highly visible foreign firms, mostly in the oil sector, and large infrastructural industries such as telecommunications. The creation of worker-owned businesses and agricultural cooperatives remain a work in progress, and except for the invasion and takeover of some land in more rural areas, Chávez has yet to challenge domestic capital directly. It is unlikely that he will attempt to nationalize all industry. As the popular press has noted, his policies have not exactly been bad for many private business owners ("The Rise of the 'Boligarchs'" 2007). It seems more likely that his plan is to require that any company doing business assist Chávez in building his clientelistic network, as discussed in Chapter 4.

In comparison with those of the previous regime, Chávez's policies have actually reduced incentives for economic efficiency, and they are destined to founder on the same shoals as those of the ISI program. Policies that simply reduce incentives for efficiency, such as the creation of workers' cooperatives, will bleed resources from the government that are needed to prop up these operations. As long as oil revenues hold out, Chávez can concentrate on creating new clientelistic networks through such programs. But if demand grows and resources do not keep pace, Chávez increasingly will be forced to rely on confiscation of resources to maintain clientelism. Land invasions and demands to renegotiate international contracts or face nationalization are examples of such tactics. And once resort to confiscation becomes an important component of the strategy, this accelerates the onset of crisis in several ways. First, such policies typically rapidly reduce investment and create black markets. Moreover, once a clientelist is forced to resort to confiscation as a source of new resources, often what had previously been a hands-off policy toward domestic capital and asset owners who do not support the clientelist must be turned into a policy that directly attacks these powerful players and alters the balance of ins and outs in the clientelist system. Such moves are likely to invite increasingly confrontational resistance to the regime.

Weaknesses in Chávez's new clientelistic organization are already apparent. He is now employing the time-honored tools of deficit spending and of price and foreign exchange controls in an attempt to limit the effects of the disequilibria created by his policies. High oil prices will ease the maintenance of this system, but there is virtually no scenario in which such a set of policies can be maintained indefinitely. As the demands from new groups and from existing clients inevitably grow, Chávez will have to find new sources of resources, or he will face increasing opposition to his regime. If oil prices decline, a crises that invites a new restructuring of clientelistic networks is almost certain.

Policy Reform in Brazil, 1989–2006: Effective Development Policy Despite Weak Institutions

Policy makers in Brazil in the early 1990s faced a crisis remarkably similar to the one of the early 1960s, including accelerating inflation, external payments imbalance, an inefficient bureaucracy, and an underfunded and exclusionary social security system that created an internal debt of monstrous proportions. Yet unlike in the earlier period, in which the legislative response exacerbated the crisis, the contemporary Congress has addressed pressing public policy issues with cumulative reform. Two of the most striking features of this reform are that, first, a set of interests quite similar and numerically more powerful to those that opposed reform in the 1960s also vigorously opposed the reforms in the current period and, second, the administration's commitment to basic reforms has not varied with its ideological orientation.

Collor, elected president in 1989 and impeached in 1992, reformed trade policy and some aspects of public administration. Franco, who had been Collor's vice president and who finished out Collor's term, laid the foundation for macroeconomic stability through tax increases, initial privatization, and reprogramming federal transfers to the states. Cardoso, who was elected to two terms, in 1994 and 1998, succeeded in conquering inflation through banking reform, federal control of state and municipal finances, wage restraint in the public sector and in the minimum wage, extensive privatization, reform of the private sector pension system, and other important measures. Lula, the current president, elected in 2002 and reelected in 2006, implemented the first phase of public sector pension reform, as well as judicial reform and bankruptcy law reform.

Cumulative progress on basic structural reforms in each successive administration, despite alternation in power between rightist, center-right, and leftist governments, suggests that these reforms reflect something more fundamental than the policy preferences of the winning coalition. Constancy in pursuing these basic reforms despite considerable change in the ideological position of the winning coalition reflects a seismic shift that is independent of ideological or program commitments. These ongoing reforms signal a change in electoral incentives to reward the provision of basic public goods and broad policy outcomes such as sustained growth. The shift from clientelistic to policy-based voting means that any viable electoral contender, regardless of ideological stripe, must credibly commit to basic reforms aimed at eliminating major obstacles to renewed growth.[35]

Trade and exchange-rate policy were initially liberalized under Collor. Mercosul was created and tariff rates were substantially reduced. Although Mercosul has not played a prominent liberalizing role since Argentina's currency crisis of 2001, the level of protectionism practiced under its auspices is dramatically lower than in the postwar period (Lyne 1999). Exchange-rate policy was initially dictated by its use as the anchor for the macroeconomic stabilization plan begun under Franco (to be discussed next). Since 1999, when the government was forced off the peg used for the Real Plan, exchange rates have been determined by market forces. Thus, although Brazil's commercial policy is not a strictly neoliberal one of the Chilean variety, Brazil's blueprint for renewing growth is clearly based on improving efficiency and productivity through competition.

Macroeconomic stabilization was the next major reform begun under Collor's vice president, Franco, in 1993 (Collor was impeached in December 1992). The Real Plan, directed by Franco's finance minister, Cardoso, was successful in virtually eliminating inflation. As with postwar stabilization plans, the Real Plan was subject to great pressure by all of the same players: labor ministers, representing wage earners; Congress, representing bureaucrats; the military; and government agencies that previously had the ability to distribute credit freely.[36] Despite this pressure, however, the executive response has been markedly different from that of the earlier period.

Both the Cardoso and Lula governments insisted that any increase in the minimum wage or civil servant salaries be compatible with keeping inflation in check. Perhaps the most important new discipline in the national executive is related to the debts with the states. Refinancing of state and local government deficits has been strictly curtailed, a practice that was com-

---

35. Some readers might argue that international pressures have dictated a common neoliberal program across different administrations. This is implausible for several reasons. First, similar constraints held in the earlier period—politicians simply chose to ignore them. Thus, Brazil broke a number of agreements with the International Monetary Fund (IMF) in the earlier period, and was ultimately unable to raise funds in private capital markets by the late 1950s. Kubitschek, president from 1956 to 1960, tried to raise new capital with an ultimately unsuccessful campaign to convince American pension plans to invest in Brazil. Second, most observers concur that Lula's party, the PT, chose to publicly commit to maintain the basic parameters of the IMF agreement forged by the Cardoso administration before the 2002 elections because this was necessary to winning support from moderate voters. For an excellent discussion of why international pressures are not sufficient to explain policy reforms, see also Weyland 1996b.

36. For details, see Lyne 1999.

mon in the previous period and in previous administrations. As an example of the behavior that was de rigueur before the Real Plan, between 1987 and the final negotiation between Cardoso and the state governments in 1997, state debt had been renegotiated with the federal government on highly favorable terms twelve times. In 1997, however, for the first time, the federal government required changes at the state level that would guarantee continued solvency in return for federal assistance. States were required to make fiscal adjustments and privatize assets, in particular, the state-owned banks, which were often used to finance state budget deficits. Despite intense and continuing pressure from governors and from the state-level congressional delegations, both Cardoso and Lula have held firm and refused to consider any renegotiations of the 1997 deal.

Unlike in the postwar period, both Cardoso and Lula have fired officials who publicly advocated policies inimical to the maintenance of macroeconomic stability. In the Cardoso administration, the minister of development; the director of the National Development Bank; and the director of Petrobras, the largest state-owned enterprise, were dismissed for speaking publicly against the Real Plan (Estado de Sao Paulo 1999, 2000a). Both presidents have appointed and maintained the same finance minister and have defended him against all attacks both within and outside government.[37] Lula's sacking of Carlos Lessa, a figure who was widely viewed as more interested subsidizing national industry than in maintaining low inflation, from the National Development Bank (Banco Nacional de Desenvolvimento Economico e Social [BNDES]) in the fall of 2004 provided a clear signal that government policy would favor anti-inflation measures above all. In other words, the executive, operating under the same statutory rules as in the previous period, has exercised his right to appoint and dismiss executive officials in order to structure rewards and punishments to achieve compliance with its electorally advertised policy: stabilization and structural reform.

The executive has also acted to both reduce the excessive cost of the state bureaucracy and reformulate internal reward structures to promote development goals. Reform completed in early 2000 allowed the firing of civil servants for poor job performance, allowed distinct pay scales in different agencies and branches of government, and created internal promotion criteria that would no longer require a public civil service exam for vertical

---

37. Lula's finance minister, Palocci, resigned in March 2006, in order to avoid tainting Lula's likely reelection bid with the ongoing investigation into charges of bribery and campaign finance irregularities (see below).

internal advancement. The reforms also limited municipal, state, or federal bureaus' personnel expenditures to 60 percent of revenues; placed a cap on salaries; and prohibited remunerating any civil servant at a rate higher than that received by the president of the Republic (Estado de Sao Paulo 1998a; Secretaria de Administracao Federal 1993).

These reforms move the bureau from a mechanism for providing excludable benefits, insulating resource streams (life tenure for employees, special rigged exams for internal promotion, personnel expenditures often exceeding revenues), and dampening bidding wars (requirement for one pay scale throughout the bureau regardless of job type) to one in which political authorities can reward bureaucratic behavior consistent with achieving desired collective policy goals. As with the stabilization plans, these reforms were vehemently opposed by government employees organized into powerful unions. In the new law defining three types of functions as exclusively governmental (diplomacy, justice, and security), which conferred special tenure, pay, and advancement criteria on those fulfilling these crucial functions, the president also vetoed the twenty-seven additional types of service that congresspeople had added in an attempt to maintain special privileges for a vast range of government employees. He also vetoed an attempt to reinstitute the practice of giving temporary employees permanent status without having passed a civil service exam (Estado de Sao Paulo 2000b).

By the early 1990s, although Brazil's social security programs were not quite as exclusionary as in the earlier period, they were every bit as regressive and fiscally disastrous. The two dominant programs are a system for public sector employees (the Regime Jurídico Único [RJU] system) and one for those employed in the private sector (Regime Geral de Previdência Social [RGPS]). If state and municipal-level plans are included, the total social security deficit was 6 percent of GDP in 1999, and without reforms, direct costs were projected to rise to 14 percent of GDP by 2030 (Kay 2001). Among the problems regularly cited were regressive rules governing eligibility, contributions and benefits, failure to link contributions to benefits, the minimal service requirements for some groups (generally only five years for the highest paid), the ability to accumulate benefits from more than one position, the lack of a minimum age, and the practice of conferring 100 percent of final salary (Estado de Sao Paulo 1998b). While there were glaring inequalities within the systems, the most dramatic were across the two: the average pension in the private system was 1.9 times the minimum wage, whereas in the public system it was 12.9 (Kay 2001).

The Cardoso administration attempted reforms in both systems, but its legislation reforming the public system was subsequently declared unconstitutional by the Supreme Court. Its lasting contribution to pension reform was a significant overhaul of the private system that included a transition program for those already within the system and new criteria for contributions and benefits for all new entrants. In the new system, for those currently entering the work force, a "social security factor," which takes into account age, level of benefits paid in, and life expectancy at retirement will be used to calculate the level of benefits and ensure that they are commensurate with contributions. The progressivity of financing has been further improved by reducing monthly contributions for those in the lowest income categories, while increasing them for those in the middle and highest categories, while the deficit has been addressed partly by increasing the time of contribution for all workers by 20 percent. These changes are projected to contain what was already a deficit of 0.9 percent of GDP in 2000 to 1.6 percent in 2020 (Kay 2001).

To achieve this, a number of the most extreme privileges, and the most actuarially unsound features of the system, were abolished: the accumulation of benefits from different positions was eliminated, and the maximum level of benefits that any one beneficiary can receive was capped. Finally, some progressivity in benefits paid out was also introduced: those who earn up to twelve hundred reais a month (roughly one thousand dollars), will receive 100 percent of their salary in retirement. But for those above this maximum, their retirement pay is subject to gradual reductions, with the minimum set at 70 percent of active salary for those with the highest incomes (Estado de Sao Paulo 1998b).

Cardoso's social security changes were subject to some of the most virulent opposition of any of his reforms, in the streets, in the Congress and in the courts. This is not surprising, given that he was attempting to reduce the highly concentrated benefits and highly diffuse costs of the system (Arnold 1990). As would be expected in a policy-based system with candidate-centered electoral law, to pass the reform Cardoso had to dole out considerable specialized benefits to powerful veto players (Tsebelis 1995; Shugart and Carey 1992).[38] What remains a stark difference from the earlier period is that his reforms did in fact dramatically improve progressivity, inclusivity, equity of benefits, and progressivity and actuarial soundness of financing,

---

38. For a good summary of the deals Cardoso struck to pass the reform of the private system, see Kay 2001.

whereas in the earlier period what made it through Congress exacerbated all the existing shortcomings.

The Lula government took up the other urgently needed reform of the public sector system upon entering office. It achieved a historic reform of the public sector system, as well as a few new changes to the private sector system. The most dramatic change was the creation of a cap on benefits at twenty-four hundred reais (approximately two thousand dollars) for both the private and the public system. This meant dramatically reducing what public servants had previously received (100 percent of final salary) and slightly increasing the benefit for the private sector, in comparison with the Cardoso reform. The Lula government also introduced many of the same reforms as had previously been achieved in the private sector system into the public system, including prohibiting accumulation of benefits, contributions tied to benefits, and one of the most controversial changes—a tax on the pension benefits of current recipients. As many analysts have pointed out, the initial government proposals were subject to intense opposition, and lobbying in the Congress altered one of the key provisions: current workers retained the right to retire at full salary, and the cap on benefits went into effect only for new entrants. Once again, this is not surprising in a system with highly candidate-centered electoral law. Nevertheless, simulations of the effect of the reforms indicate that they reduced the implicit debt of the public sector system by about 20 percent, an achievement, as the authors note, unparalleled in any other social security reform (Souza et al. 2004).

Beginning in late 2004, the Lula government became mired in a series of scandals, involving a campaign finance controversy, accusations of illegal use of funds from state-owned enterprise, and allegations that deputies from (mostly) small right-wing parties in the government coalition were paid to vote with the government. While these scandals are lamentable, they do not support the claim that little has changed in contemporary Brazil. They also do not support an argument that the Brazilian system remains clientelist and that legislators have no concern for national policy. The most critical point to note in assessing the import of these scandals is the purpose of the most important and pervasive one, in which bribes were allegedly paid to legislators. These bribes were not designed to enrich individuals or to distribute favors to groups, but to implement the most important collective goods policy reform since the Fiscal Responsibility Law and other reforms that underpinned the Real stabilization plan.

The macroeconomic stability achieved in 1994 was certain to be short lived in the absence of a series of structural reforms to reduce the unsustainable claims on the national treasury and to free up more general tax revenue for investment in basic public goods. Two of the reforms for which the Lula government allegedly engaged in bribery were absolutely crucial in this regard. Unlike Cardoso, Lula succeeded with two changes to the social security system that were absolutely critical in putting the Brazilian state on long-term sound financial footing, as discussed above. Lula passed legislation requiring taxation of retirees' income and ending the extremely generous system of unfunded benefits for public servants.

This scenario is far more consistent with a system undergoing a transition from clientelism to policy-based voting than with one in which clientelism reigns and legislators have no concern for national level policy. In a transition from clientelism to a policy-based system, parties interested in winning national elections must adopt some kind of modus vivendi with vestigial clientelists. Although Cardoso was never found to participate in systematic bribery schemes, his government certainly made many accommodations to the most influential remaining clientelist during his administration, Antônio Carlos Magalhães. Yet as in the case of the Lula government, these accommodations were made in the service of passing collective policy reforms that would ultimately help to undermine clientelism.

In sum, the active opposition of powerful interests in every phase of these reforms rules out the possibility that they were made possible through some crisis-induced societal consensus. At the same time, given Brazil's candidate-centered electoral law, it is not surprising that some of these powerful interests were successful in altering the reforms to their advantage. What remains indisputable, however, is that despite a very similar crisis, nearly identical institutions, and more powerful vested interests, in stark comparison with the earlier period, each administration since the return to full democracy in 1989 has proceeded with reform. Unlike in the previous period, every government has succeeded in strengthening the Brazilian state's capacity to supply basic public goods and promote sustainable economic development.

Conclusion

The case studies in this chapter allow us to draw some important general conclusions about policy choice. First, in clientelist systems, institutions alter the efficiency of clientelist organization, rather than altering the balance of national versus locally targeted collective goods provided, as is the case in policy-based systems. Centralized institutions such as those employed in pre-Chávez Venezuela more effectively control bidding wars, in comparison with decentralized institutions such as those in place in postwar Brazil. As we have seen, despite employing diametrically opposed institutions, leaders in these two countries adopted very similar 1s1 policies that reduced social welfare in a very similar fashion.

Second, crisis is not a sufficient condition for collective goods policy reform. Once we recognize that the same electoral process can produce two distinct equilibria, each with its own electoral logic, we can move away from the flawed perspective that pre-crisis choices were simply dysfunctional, and that all that is needed to correct wrongheaded policies is sufficient demonstration of their failings. Both the original "dysfunctional" policies as well as the response to crisis are driven by how structural conditions shape voters' choices and the equilibrium electoral strategies. Thus we coined a new term to connote the policy changes that are designed to adjust clientelism to a resource crisis, and showed how this perspective provides considerable insight into Chávez's choices. The case of contemporary Brazil illustrated the alternative response to crisis—if crisis also means structural conditions are altered such that collective policy provision becomes the equilibrium strategy, then politicians will adopt collective goods reform.

Third, the theory of policy choice presented in this chapter allows us to think more carefully about the role of development orientation. In the contemporary Brazilian case of transition from clientelism to policy-based politics examined here, a program of inward-oriented development with a high level of state intervention was replaced with a more outward-oriented policy and a reduced state role, but this was the less significant change. The key determinant of whether democratic accountability functions to drive politicians to adopt effective collective goods policy is not the inward or outward orientation of development policy. It is electoral constraints that will drive politicians to keep a close eye on the social welfare implications of their policies, regardless of their development orientation.

This is consistent with the empirical demonstration that not all inward-oriented policy is doomed to failure and that not all outward-oriented policies are ensured of success (Huber 2003). Liberalizing policies that apparently introduce more market discipline can simply be a means to reorganize clientelist networks to adjust to new resource realities. Governments can license import firms and distribute export opportunities to their supporters just as they reserved the domestic production opportunities for their supporters. And since liberalizing policies are often essential for renewing international resource flows, liberalizing policies may actually increase the resources available for building clientelist networks. One critical implication is that in order to differentiate between systems that have made the shift from direct to indirect exchange, we cannot rely on indicators such as level of international trade flows or measures of privatization of state-owned firms. To differentiate democracies with effective accountability from those that will be fatally compromised by clientelism, we need more systematic and unique indicators of the two equilibria similar to the micro measures developed in Chapter 2, as well as more systematic cross-national data collection on these and additional measures.

Conclusion

Roughly a half century ago, the Social Science Research Council sponsored a large-scale study of the new postwar democracies that emerged from the second wave of democratization in Latin America, Asia, and Africa. These studies thoroughly demonstrated and nearly unanimously concluded that two of the central institutions of democratic politics, parties and interest groups, could not be understood through the lens of the reigning theories developed to study the advanced industrial democracies. Now, in the middle of the third wave of democratization, much of political behavior and choice in developing democracies continues to be characterized only negatively, in terms of how patterns in these countries fail to conform to the predictions of leading theories and how the protagonists' choices lead to dysfunctional outcomes.

These studies were only one portion of a large body of work by area and development scholars that has long emphasized that structural conditions have a powerful impact on the effective functioning of democratic accountability. Yet the current positive theory of elections and accountability, even in its latest incarnation as the new institutionalism, excludes such considerations. In developing the theory of the voter's dilemma, I have endogenized structural variables to a more general theory of voting and elections.

When structural conditions make widespread offers of valuable clientelistic benefits possible, voters cannot ignore asymmetry of excludability between clientelistic and collective goods, and the central collective choice problem of democratic accountability is most accurately characterized as a prisoner's dilemma. Under these conditions, voters of any income level and in any institutional environment will have a strong incentive to relinquish their statutory right to pass judgment on overall policy and trade their vote in quid pro quo exchange. I contend that herein lie the roots of the democracy-development paradox. If most voters are compelled by structural conditions and the logic of the voter's dilemma to trade their vote in a clientelistic exchange, then elections are nullified as a force for disciplining the social welfare consequence of politicians' policy choices. Under these conditions, politicians who fashion a development policy that maximizes benefits that can be exchanged in a quid pro quo will win elections. Politicians who reduce quid pro quo benefits in the interest of improving the welfare effects of development policy will lose elections. In Chapter 6 I showed how this logic provides an electorally based theory of the apparently irrational self-defeating choices that characterized most of the postwar ISI programs across the developing world. Under certain structural conditions, the voter's dilemma shows how individual and collective rationality diverge and, thus, why voters and politicians are compelled to make choices that lead to disastrous collective outcomes. In Chapters 3, 4, and 5, I showed how the theory of two electoral equilibria could also explain critical behavioral and institutional choices that precede policy promulgation, including party electoral and legislative behavior, party internal design, and legislative organization. In sum, the clientelistic electoral equilibrium that emerges from endogenizing structural conditions to the current positive theory of voting and elections provides a theory of both institutional and policy choice in democracies that are currently very poorly understood.

When structural conditions reduce the value of the clientelistic benefits that politicians can offer to negligible for most voters, then these voters can essentially ignore asymmetry of excludability between the two choices and vote for collective goods. The voter's dilemma highlights that it is only when a sufficient number of voters reach this point to tip the electoral equilibrium to favor collective goods provision at the national level that the assumptions that undergird the current positive theory of elections, and all the work that builds upon it, holds. To put it another way, the assumption that nonpoor voters have an incentive to vote for collective goods is a restrictive, not a universally valid, one. The assumption that the same prisoner's dilemma that plagues spontaneous collective goods provision does not plague the delegation of collective goods provision to elected leaders is a restrictive, not a universally valid, one. The conclusion that the central collective choice problem of democratic accountability is one of coordination as commonly assumed also only applies under these restrictive structural conditions.

Changes in structural conditions that reduce the value of the clientelistic offer to negligible for most voters do not alter the basic prisoner's dilemma structure of the problem, but they do dramatically reduce the costs that individuals face in contributing to the collective good of effective democratic accountability. The theory of the voter's dilemma thus accounts for the democracy-development paradox, not with failures to converge on similar effective solutions to the same basic coordination problem across democracies, but rather with an elaboration of how the problem can under some structural conditions effectively resemble a prisoner's dilemma, and under others a coordination problem.[1] Endogenous solutions to the social choice problems inherent in democratic government, such as those that have emerged in contemporary Brazil discussed in this book, are possible when structural conditions render electoral accountability as essentially a coordination problem among voters. But when structural conditions yield a prisoner's dilemma, electoral accountability, like any other strategic interaction so characterized, is not amenable to endogenous solutions.

This provides a much more plausible explanation for why a few democracies of the third wave, such as Brazil, have now embarked on a path of moderate and incremental, yet permanent, structural reform, than the notion that Cardoso and Lula are somehow endowed with a pragmatism that most leaders in developing democracies lack.

In this book I have focused primarily on building and testing a more general theory of voting choice that yields these two equilibrium electoral strategies. This theory has the advantage of rooting political behavior and choice in *both* advanced industrial *and* developing democracies in the imperatives of electoral competition. As such, it can explain why despite vigorous electoral competition in most developing democracies, politicians and parties repeatedly fail, over long periods, to organize in a fashion that would facilitate voters' ability to hold them responsible for collective goods provision. This theory not only provides new insight into political behavior and organization, but also provides a logic to the policy choices in developing democracies that otherwise appear simply dysfunctional and irrational. The possibilities for future development and testing of the theory are myriad. But this does not exhaust the insights gleaned from the recognition of the voter's dilemma.

Roughly a half century ago, William Riker challenged scholars of democracy to more carefully examine whether it is actually possible to reach democratic ends through democratic means. He called for using the analytic tools for studying democratic means, the theory of social choice, to probe how

---

1. I have not discussed cultural theories such as those developed by Putnam (1994) in this book, but I believe that this is an accurate if very oversimplified casting of the basic cultural argument. Putnam does not specify exactly the nature of the collective action problem that somehow does get solved spontaneously in society and in the voting booth in Northern Italy, but not in Southern Italy, but I believe that it is accurate to say that he views it as the same collective action problem in both the North and the South.

collective decision making could facilitate or obstruct democratic ends. As he noted, it was fruitless to pursue such ends through democratic means if our analysis of collective decision making demonstrated that it was logically impossible to reach such ends through democratic means. The voter's dilemma must surely be counted as a profound obstacle to reaching a central democratic goal, the provision of collective goods, through democratic means. It is arguably one of the most invidious for democracy yet uncovered. Unlike in much of the work on social choice and democratic outcomes, the voter's dilemma is completely independent of the specifics of process. As I have shown, under certain structural conditions, no amount of change to the specific rules can reduce or eliminate the problem the voter's dilemma raises for reaching democratic ends. This is of course extremely delicate ground on which to tread, as failure of democratic means can and often is used to justify other forms of government that have many other undesirable qualities. Yet as Riker pointed out, knowledge, rather than willful ignorance, is certainly a better climate in which continue to search for harmony in means and ends.

Perhaps as an antidote to overzealous condemnation of democratic means based on the voter's dilemma, it is important to note that the collective choice problem embodied in the voter's dilemma, despite its name, does not even depend on voting! Structural conditions that make widespread clientelistic offers viable precludes procuring collective goods under *any* system of delegation of authority to political leaders. The *social choice* itself is the source of the problem. It is a problem inherent in political authority itself, whether that authority is selected by democratic or other processes. And just as the theory of electoral competition derived from the voter's dilemma shed considerable light on political behavior and choice in developing democracies, a theory of clientelistic competition in different types of authoritarian regimes, particularly the theory relating to problems of efficiency and bidding wars, stands to illuminate patterns of politics in nondemocratic regimes—a terrain that to date is largely unexplored.

Just as with the current positive theory of voting and elections in democracies, one recent highly ambitious work that seeks to build a unified theory of political incentives across all regime types similarly fails to recognize how clientelism can short circuit accountability (Bueno de Mesquita et al. 2003). These scholars build a general theory of accountability based on the size of the winning coalition (the ruler's core supporters that receive private goods), and the size of the selectorate (those who can exercise choice for the leader but receive only public goods). According to the theory, as the size of the selectorate grows, political leaders are forced to provide more collective goods and fewer private goods (pork and rents). The obvious implication is that democracies will provide more public goods and have better records of economic growth than autocracies. Yet this theory cannot explain why so many democracies with large selectorates such as India and Indonesia in Asia, and Nigeria in Africa have such dismal records of public goods provision. Moreover, this theory cannot explain why democracies with similar-size winning coalitions and selectorates can have such dramatic differences in growth, income per capita, and public goods provision. A theory of political accountability that endogenizes structural conditions, and therefore demonstrates how clientelism can dramatically alter the real size of the selectorate, can explain these anomalies.

APPENDIX I: ANALYZING ROLL CALL VOTES IN THE BRAZILIAN FEDERAL CHAMBER OF DEPUTIES

There are significant differences in the quality of the data from the earlier and later periods. The electronic voting records for the current period (beginning with the first session of the Forty-ninth Congress, inaugurated in 1991) are publicly available online at http://www.camara.gov.br/Internet/plenario/votacao.asp. In addition to the individual votes, party leadership recommendations for rank-and-file voting are also published with the electronic voting records.

For the earlier period, no record of leadership recommendations exists, and the data is more precarious. The data was entered from the published records from the *Diario do Congresso* from the period. Although this record provides a comprehensive picture of roll call voting for the period, slightly less than 1 percent of the recorded votes could not be determined because of document decay.

The procedure for separating out the votes on which I calculated Rice index, index of likeness, and party votes was as follows. First, I removed any votes from the raw data that did not reach a quorum. Following Carey (2007), I did not use any arbitrary threshold of unanimity for excluding votes. Instead, I did a separate weighting of the Rice index for each vote, using Carey's measure of closeness. In the current period, the Rice indices weighted by closeness for government and opposition coalitions are nearly identical to the unweighted Rice indices. In the earlier period, however, the Rice indices weighted by closeness are somewhat lower than the unweighted numbers. Thus, using Carey's weighting procedure to calculate Rice indices strengthens both the argument about the earlier period that parties did not present voting records that could inform a public reputation and the argument about a marked change in the current period as a result of a shift to collective goods competition. For the figures, see Lyne 2005. The tables with the numerical data are available from the author upon request.

In the current period, we have considerably more information about parliamentary strategy. One of the key parliamentary maneuvers used in the

Brazilian Chamber of Deputies is to deny a quorum in which to conduct a vote. This is indicated both in the party leadership recommendations, when the party recommends "obstrução," and it is recorded in the deputy's action with an O. This parliamentary maneuver clearly complicates the calculation of traditional measures of unity and divisiveness. When the party leadership instructs their members to "obstruct," most deputies leave the floor and their action is recorded as an O, but often a few deputies remain on the floor and cast a vote, which is recorded as Yes or No. A calculation of the typical Rice index of |% Yes–% No| for the given party can thus be highly misleading in the case in which the party's leadership recommends obstruction. Consider two possible scenarios. First, one in which only two deputies out of a party of, say, fifty remain on the floor, and one votes yes and the other votes no, while the remaining forty-eight obstruct. Second, one in which all fifty members of the party obstruct, and none vote yes or no. The Rice index in the former case will be recorded as 0 and in the latter case as either 0 or null. Clearly the traditional Rice index in these cases is not capturing the relevant behavior we wish to capture—the degree to which the party is unified in achieving its parliamentary goals.

I addressed this problem by calculating an alternative measure of unity in these cases in which the leadership instructs its membership to obstruct. In these cases I substituted a measure that pits the number of deputies registering obstruct against the number of deputies voting yes on the bill. In this way I substitute the measure of yes versus no votes for an alternative that attempts to capture the degree to which the rank and file is acting in a unified fashion to carry out the leadership's directive.

It should be noted that a further complication means that this measure understates the degree of unity. Some deputies who are obeying the leadership and do not appear on the floor are typically registered as absent (*F* for *falta*) rather than as obstructing (*O* for *obstrução*). Discussions with the general secretary of the Mesa Diretora (Governing Board) of the Câmara dos Deputados revealed that there was no consistent way to distinguish an absence from an obstruction (Mozart Vianna de Paiva and Fernando Sabóia Vieira, interviews with the author, Brasilia, Brazil, July 11, 2002). Since some deputies who are following the leadership's wishes will be registered as absent and thus are not included in the calculation, the measure is a lower bound for the degree of unity within the party. The Lula I–VII cabinets were the cabinets with enough opposition obstruction recommendations to have a significant impact on the calculations, and for these cabinets, in the case of the opposition coalition only. In Table 18, for the Lula I–VII cabinets on roll call votes and party votes (see following paragraph), the modified measure of unity for the opposition coalition is listed first, with the standard Rice index listed in parentheses.

The use of the parliamentary tactic of obstruction also complicates calculations of party votes. If we count only those votes in which at least 50 percent of the members of the parties in opposition vote explicitly yes when the government votes no, or no when the government votes yes, then we are undercounting the instances in which the opposition is acting in a unified fashion to thwart the legislative will of the government. Once again, I calculate both standard party votes and an alternative measure that takes obstruction dynamics into account. The top-row entries providing the Rice index on party votes for the opposition during the Lula I–VI governments are calculated using the modified criteria for identifying party votes as follows. To gain a more accurate view of when the opposition is able to act in a unified fashion, I included all standard party votes as well as those votes in which at least 50 percent of the members of all parties in the opposition obstruct the government at the same time that at least 50 percent of the members of all parties in government vote yes or no on a bill. Once again, this measure certainly undercounts the number of votes on which the opposition acts cohesively to thwart the legislative will of the government, because on some votes in which the leadership instructs obstruction, some members of the opposition parties who are actually obstructing are recorded as absent. If enough members who are actually obstructing are counted as absent so as to lower the number obstructing below the majority, then this vote will not be counted as a party vote when in fact it should be. But since we cannot determine whether any absence is actually an action in concert with the will of the party leadership, I do not count them, but count only those votes in which at least 50 percent of all voting members of opposition parties officially register obstruction.

APPENDIX II: DISTRIBUTION OF PERKS IN THE BRAZILIAN FEDERAL CHAMBER OF DEPUTIES

I. Party Loyalty

The more comprehensive data available in the current period means that measures of party loyalty across the two periods differ. Since party leadership recommendations are publicly available in the current period, we can measure party loyalty very precisely. I designated a vote as loyal if the rank and file voted exactly as the leadership recommended when the leadership recommended a vote of "yes," "no," "abstention," or "obstruction." Party loyalty scores were calculated as simply the percentage of time the deputy voted as the leadership recommended. In all the analysis in this book, I used a party loyalty score for all votes with the given party in the previous legislature as the independent variable used to predict dependent variables in the current legislature (committee assignment, receipt of budget funds, committee presidency).

II. No Leadership Recommendation, Absences

If there was no recorded leadership recommendation, or the leadership recorded *L,* meaning that the rank and file was free to vote as it pleased (*liberado* in Portuguese), then I excluded these votes from the calculations. I measured loyalty both with absences not counted as a vote against the leadership, and with absences counted as a vote against the leadership.

III. Party Switching and Freshmen

Party switching and freshman status introduce some complications in the calculation of party loyalty scores. When a legislator switched parties within a legislature, and therefore voted with more than one party, I calculated a party loyalty score for each party for which the deputy was a member. I chose the party loyalty score for the given deputy with the party associated with the dependent variable of interest (party conferring committee seat or presidency, party releasing budget funds). If the deputy had no record of voting with a party in the relevant legislature because of either switching or freshman status, I substituted either (1) his or her loyalty rate for his former party in the first case or (2) the average loyalty rate for his or her party caucus in the appropriate (previous year's) legislature. In general, these substitutions do not introduce serious problems into the analysis. Desposato (2006b) has found that party switchers vote with their new party with the same frequency that they voted with their old party. The substitution of average caucus loyalty scores for freshmen deputies with no voting record was necessary for only roughly 7 percent of the observations (30 percent of deputies in one out of every four legislative sessions).

IV. The Period 1945–1964

In the earlier period, we do not have recommendations of the party leadership. For the earlier period I calculated party loyalty scores on the basis of how the majority of the party voted. One other possible method would be to infer the leadership position by how the party leader in the legislature voted, as Cox and McCubbins (1993) do for the U.S. case. I investigated this possibility but concluded for several reasons that this approach would be highly misleading. First, as is argued in Chapter 4, the leadership was not concerned with how the rank and file voted because credit-claiming in clientelist systems with candidate-centered electoral rules is a function of the individual deputy's prowess in obtaining and distributing benefits. Perhaps reflecting this, the data on the identity of the legislative party leaders for each party is seriously incomplete. There is no information on party leaders for any of the six major parties except the UDN until the second session of the Second Congress (52.2) beginning in 1952. Moreover the party leaders themselves were frequently absent (once again perhaps reflecting the alternative imperatives of clientelist competition). For the period in which a PDC leader is identifiable, the leadership did not vote on 50.1 percent of the votes. The same figure for the PSD is 30.6 percent, the UDN 48.2 percent, the PTB 34.2, the PSP 40.3, and the PR 47.8. If we combine these absences with the period in which no leader is identifiable, we have no information about leadership votes in the UDN for 48.2 percent of roll calls; for the PDC, 65.2

percent; for the PSD, 46.2 percent; for the PTB, 49.3 percent; for the PSP, 55.4; and for the PR, 62.9 percent. An attempt to calculate party loyalty by how the leadership voted would thus dramatically reduce the number of roll calls in the analysis. Corroborating these findings, the monographic work and expert opinion on this period unanimously report that legislative party leaders were not important players within the party.

We also have no measure of absences for the earlier period. Since deputies frequently vacated their seats to take other positions, it is difficult to tell whether they were in fact absent for a vote, or not occupying the seat for any given vote, so I calculated loyalty scores based only on recorded votes.

REFERENCES

Abranches, Sergio Henrique. 1978. "The Divided Leviathan: State and Economic Policy Formation in Authoritarian Brazil." Ph.D. diss., Cornell University.
Agor, Weston H., ed. 1971. *Latin American Legislatures: Their Role and Influence.* New York: Praeger.
Aldrich, John H. 1995. *Why Parties? The Origin and Transformation of Party Politics in America.* Chicago: Chicago University Press.
Aldrich, John H., and David Rhode. 2001. "The Logic of Conditional Party Government." In *Congress Reconsidered,* 7th ed., edited by Lawrence C. Dodd and Bruce I. Oppenheimer. Washington, D.C.: Congressional Quarterly.
Alexander, Robert J. 1964. *The Venezuelan Democratic Revolution.* New Brunswick: Rutgers University Press.
———. 1977. "Caudillos, Coroneis, and Political Bosses." In *Presidential Power in Latin American Politics,* edited by Thomas V. DiBacco. New York: Praeger.
Almond, Gabriel A. 1956. "Comparative Political Systems." *Journal of Politics* 18 (3): 391–409.
Almond, Gabriel A., and James S. Coleman, eds. 1960. *The Politics of Developing Areas.* Princeton: Princeton University Press.
Ames, Barry. 1987. *Political Survival: Politicians and Public Policy in Latin America.* Berkeley and Los Angeles: University of California Press.
———. 1994. "The Reverse Coattails Effect: Local Party Organization in the 1989 Brazilian Presidential Election," *American Political Science Review* 88 (1): 95–111.
———. 1995a. "Electoral Rules, Constituency Pressures, and Pork Barrel: The Bases of Voting in the Brazilian Congress." *Journal of Politics* 57:324–43.
———. 1995b. "Electoral Strategy Under Open-List Proportional Representation." *American Journal of Political Science* 39:406–33.
———. 2001. *The Deadlock of Democracy in Brazil.* Ann Arbor: Michigan University Press.
Amorim Neto, Octavio. 1998. "Of Presidents, Parties, and Ministers: Cabinet Formation and Legislative Decision-Making Under Separation of Powers." Ph.D. diss., University of California, San Diego.
———. 2002. "Presidential Cabinets, Electoral Cycles, and Coalition Discipline in Brazil." In *Legislative Politics in Latin America,* edited by Scott Morgenstern and Benito Nacif. New York: Cambridge University Press.
———. 2006. "The Presidential Calculus. Executive Policy Making and Cabinet Formation in the Americas." *Comparative Political Studies* 39:415–40
———. 2007. "Algumas conseqüencias políticas de Lula: Novos padrões de formação e recrutamento ministerial, controle de agenda e produção legislativa." In *Instituições Representativas no Brasil: Balanco e Reformas,* edited by Jairo Nicolau and Timothy J. Power. Belo Horizonte: Editora UFMG.

Amorim Neto, Octavio, Gary Cox, and Mathew D. McCubbins. 2003. "Agenda Power in Brazil's Camara dos Deputados, 1989–98." *World Politics* 55:550–78.
Amorim Neto, Octavio, and Fabiano G. M. Santos. 2001. "The Executive Connection: Presidentially Defined Factions and Party Discipline in Brazil." *Party Politics* 7:213–34.
———. 2003. "The Inefficient Secret Revisited: The Legislative Input and Output of Brazilian Deputies." *Legislative Studies Quarterly* 28 (4): 449–79.
Amsden, Alice. 1989. *Asia's Next Giant: South Korea and Late Industrialization*. Oxford: Oxford University Press.
Anderson, Charles W. 1967. *Politics and Economic Change in Latin America*. San Francisco: D. Van Nostrand.
Armijo, Leslie Elliot. 2001. "Democratic Inclusion and Macroeconomic Moderation: A Theory." Paper presented at the annual meeting of the American Political Science Association, San Francisco, August–September.
Arnold, R. Douglass. 1990. *The Logic of Congressional Action*. New Haven: Yale University Press.
Baron, David P. 1994. "Electoral Competition with Informed and Uninformed Voters." *American Political Science Review* 88 (1): 33–47.
Barro, R. J. 1973. "The Control of Politicians: An Economic Model." *Public Choice* 14:19–42.
Barry, Brian. 1970. *Sociologists, Economists, and Democracy*. London: Collier-Macmillan.
Bartolini, Stefano. 2002. "Electoral and Party Competition: Analytical Dimensions and Empirical Problems." In *Political Parties: Old Concepts and New Challenges*, edited by Richard Gunther, José Ramón Montero, and Juan J. Linz. Oxford: Oxford University Press.
Bates, Robert H. 1999. *Open Economy Politics: The Political Economy of the World Coffee Trade*. Princeton: Princeton University Press.
———. 2001. *Prosperity and Violence: The Politicial Economy of Development*. W. W. Norton.
Beatriz, Malva. 1999. "Sistema partidário e governabilidade nos tres premeiro anos do governo Fernando Henrique Cardoso." Master's thesis, University of Brasilia.
Becker, Gary. 1983. "A Theory of Competition Among Pressure Groups for Political Influence." *Quarterly Journal of Economics* 98 (August): 371–400.
Benevides, Maria Victoria de Mesquita. 1976. *O governo Kubitschek*. Rio de Janeiro: Paz e Terra.
———. 1981. *A UDN e o Udenismo: Ambiguidades do liberalismo Brasileiro (1945–1965)*. Rio de Janeiro: Paz e Terra.
Berelson, Bernard, Paul F. Lazarfeld, and William N. McPhee. 1954. *Voting: A Study of Opinion Formation in a Presidential Campaign*. Chicago: University of Chicago Press.
Bergsman, Joel. 1970. *Brazil: Industrialization and Trade Policies*. London: University Press for O.E.C.D.
Bezerra, Marcos Otávio. 1999. *Em nome das "bases": Política, favor e dependência pessoal*. Rio de Janeiro: Relume Dumará.
Bhagwati, Jagdish. 1978. *Anatomy and Consequences of Exchange Control Regimes*. Cambridge, Mass.: National Bureau of Economic Research.

Bhagwati, Jagdish, and T. N. Srinivasan. 1975. *India*. New York: National Bureau of Economic Research.

Binder, Sarah A. 1997. *Minority Rights, Majority Rule: Partisanship and the Development of Congress*. New York: Cambridge University Press.

Brambor, Thomas, William Roberts Clark, and Matt Golder. 2006. "Understanding Interaction Models: Improving Empirical Analysis." *Political Analysis*, 14 (1): 63–82.

Bremmer, Ian. 2006. "Lula's Silver Lining." Slate.com, September 29. http://www.slate.com/id/2150544/.

Bridges, Amy. 1984. *A City in the Republic: Antebellum New York and the Origins of Machine Politics*. New York: Cambridge University Press.

Buchanan, James M., Robert D. Tollison, and Gordon Tullock, eds. 1980. *Toward a Theory of the Rent-Seeking Society*. College Station: Texas A&M University Press.

Bueno de Mesquita, Bruce, James D. Morrow, Randolph Siverson, and Alastair Smith. 2001. "Political Competition and Economic Growth." *Journal of Democracy* 12 (1):58–72.

Cain, Bruce, John Ferejohn, and Morris Fiorina. 1987. *The Personal Vote*. Cambridge, Mass.: Harvard University Press.

Canache, Damarys. 2007. "*Chavismo* and Democracy in Venezuela." Paper presented at the symposium "Prospects for Democracy in Latin America," University of North Texas, April 5–6.

Cardoso, Fernando Henrique. 1973. *O modelo político Brasileiro*. Sao Paulo: Difusao Europeia do Livro.

Carey, John M. 1996. *Terms Limits and Legislative Representation*. New York: Cambridge University Press.

———. 2007. "Competing Principals, Political Institutions, and Party Unity in Legislative Voting." *American Journal of Political Science* 51 (1): 92–107.

Carey, John M., and Matthew Soberg Shugart. 1995. "Incentives to Cultivate a Personal Vote: A Rank Ordering of Electoral Formulas." *Electoral Studies* 14 (4): 417–39.

Carey, John M., and Gina Yannitel Reinhardt. 2004. "State-Level Institutional Effects on Legislative Coalition Unity in Brazil." *Legislative Studies Quarterly* 29 (1): 23–47.

Carroll, Royce, Gary W. Cox, and Mónica Pachón. 2004. "How Parties Create Electoral Democracy." Paper presented at the 2004 annual meetings of the American Political Science Association, Chicago, September 1–4.

Carroll, Royce, and Mona Lyne. 2006. "Rent-Seeking, Pork Barreling and Clientelism: Integrating the Study of Political Market Failure." Paper presented at the annual meeting of the American Political Science Association, Philadelphia, August 30–September 3.

Chandra, Kanchan. 2004. *Why Ethnic Parties Succeed: Patronage and Ethnic Headcounts in India*. Cambridge: Cambridge University Press.

Chang, Ha-Joon. 2003. "The East Asian Model of Economic Policy." In *Models of Capitalism: Lessons for Latin America,* edited by Evelyne Huber. University Park: Pennsylvania State University Press.

Cheibub, José Antonio, and Adam Przeworski. 1999. "Democracy, Elections, and Accountability for Economic Outcomes." In *Democracy, Accountability, and Representation,* edited by Adam Przeworski, Susan C. Stokes, and Bernard Manin. New York: Cambridge University Press.

Ciccariello-Maher, George. 2007. "Venezuela's PSUV and Socialism from Below." http://www.venezuelanalysis.com/articles.php?artno=2003.
Cohen, Roger. 2008. "New Day in the Americas." *New York Times*, January 6.
Collier, Ruth Berins, and David Collier. 1991. *Shaping the Political Arena*. Princeton: Princeton University Press.
Combellas, Ricardo. 1985. *COPEI: Ideologia y liderazgo*. Caracas: Editorial Ariel.
Cooper, Joseph, and David W. Brady. 1981. "Institutional Context and Leadership Style: The House from Cannon to Rayburn." *American Political Science Review* 75:411–25.
Cooper, Joseph, David W. Brady, and Patricia A. Hurley. 1977. "The Electoral Basis of Party Voting: Patterns and Trends in the House of Representatives." In *The Impact of the Electoral Process*, edited by Louis Maisel and Joseph Cooper. Beverly Hills, Calif.: Sage.
Coppedge, Michael. 1994a. *Strong Parties and Lame Ducks: Presidential Partyarchy and Factionalism in Venezuela*. Stanford: Stanford University Press.
———. 1994b. "Venezuela: Democratic Despite Presidentialism." In *The Failure of Presidential Democracy: The Case of Latin America*, edited by Juan J. Linz and Arturo Valenzuela. Vol. 2. Baltimore: Johns Hopkins University Press.
———. 1995. "Partidocracia and Reform in Comparative Perspective." In *Venezuelan Democracy Under Stress*, edited by Jennifer McCoy, Andrés Serbin, William C. Smith, and Andrés Stambouli. New Brunswick, N.J.: Transaction.
Corrales, Javier. 2002. *Presidents Without Parties: The Politics of Economic Reform in Argentina and Venezuela in the 1990s*. University Park: Pennsylvania State University Press.
Cox, Gary. 1987. *The Efficient Secret: The Cabinet and the Development of Political Parties in Victorian England*. Cambridge: Cambridge University Press.
Cox, Gary, and Keith T. Poole. 2002. "On Measuring Partisanship in Roll-Call Voting: The U.S. House of Representatives, 1877–1999." *American Journal of Political Science*, 46 (3): 477–89.
Cox, Gary, and Francis M. Rosenbluth. 1995. "The Structural Determinants of Electoral Cohesiveness: England, Japan, and the United States." In *Structure and Policy in Japan and the United States*, edited by Peter F. Cowhey and Mathew D. McCubbins. Cambridge: Cambridge University Press.
Cox, Gary C., and Mathew D. McCubbins. 1993. *Legislative Leviathan: Party Government in the House*. Berkeley and Los Angeles: University of California Press.
———. 2001. "Political Structure and Economic Policy: The Institutional Determinants of Economic Policy Outcomes." In *Presidents, Parliaments, and Policy*, edited by Stephan Haggard and Mathew D. McCubbins. New York: Cambridge University Press.
———. 2005. *Setting the Agenda: Responsible Party Government in the U.S. House of Representatives*. Cambridge: Cambridge University Press.
Crisp, Brian F. 1997. "Presidential Behavior in a System with Strong Parties: Venezuela 1958–1995." In *Presidentialism and Democracy in Latin America*, edited by Matthew Soberg Shugart and Scott Mainwaring. Cambridge: Cambridge University Press.
———. 1998. "Lessons from Economic Reform in the Venezuelan Democracy." *Latin American Research Review* 33 (1): 7–41.
———. 2000. *Democratic Institutional Design: The Powers and Incentives of Venezuelan Politicians and Interest Groups*. Stanford: Stanford University Press.

Crisp, Brian F., Daniel H. Levine, and Juan Carlos Rey. 1995. "The Legitimacy Problem. In *Venezuelan Democracy Under Stress,* edited by Jennifer McCoy, Andrés Serbin, William C. Smith, and Andrés Stambouli. New Brunswick, N.J.: Transaction.

Cruz-Saco, Maria Amparo, and Carmelo Mesa-Lago. 1999. *Do Options Exist? The Reform of Pension and Health Care Systems in Latin America.* Pittsburgh: University of Pittsburgh Press.

D'Araujo, Maria Celina. 1996. *Sindicatos, carisma e poder: O PTB de 1945–65.* Rio de Janeiro: Fundacao Getúlio Vargas.

de Soto, Hernando. 2001. *The Mystery of Capital: Why Capitalism Triumphs in the West and Fails Everywhere Else.* New York: Basic Books.

Desposato, Scott. 2001. "Institutional Theories, Social Realities, and Party Politics in Brazil." Ph.D. diss., University of California, Los Angeles.

———. 2006a. "How Informal Electoral Institutions Determine Brazilian Legislative Politics." In *Informal Institutions and Democracy: Lessons from Latin America,* edited by Gretchen Helmke and Steven Levitsky. Baltimore: Johns Hopkins University Press.

———. 2006b. "Parties for Rent? Careerism, Ideology, and Party Switching in Brazil's Chamber of Deputies: *American Journal of Political Science* 50 (1): 62–80.

Doring, Herbert, ed. 2001. *Parliaments and Majority Rule in Western Europe.* New York: St. Martin's Press.

Dornbusch, Rudiger, and Sebastian Edwards, eds. 1991. *The Macroeconomics of Populism in Latin America.* Chicago: University of Chicago Press.

Downs, Anthony. 1957. *An Economic Theory of Democracy.* New York: Harper and Row.

Drake, Paul. 1996. *Labor Movements and Dictatorships: The Southern Cone in Comparative Perspective.* Baltimore: Johns Hopkins University Press.

Ellner, Steve. 1994. "The Deepening of Democracy in a Crisis Setting: Political Reform and the Electoral Process in Venezuela." *Journal of Interamerican Studies and World Affairs* 35 (4):1–42.

———. 1996. "Political Party Factionalism and Democracy in Venezuela." *Latin American Perspectives* 23 (3): 87–109.

Erickson, Kenneth P. 1977. *The Brazilian Corporative State and Working-Class Politics.* Berkeley and Los Angeles: University of California Press.

Erie, Steven P. 1990. *Rainbow's End: Irish-Americans and the Dilemmas of Urban Machine Politics.* Berkeley and Los Angeles: University of California Press.

Estado de Sao Paulo. 1998a. "Acordo permitirá promulgar emenda." May 22.

———. 1998b. "As idas e vindas da reforma da Previdencia." November 6.

———. 1999. "Reuniao ministerial irá tentar recuperar folego do Avanca Brasil." September 8.

———. 2000a. "Calabi é demitido da presidencia do BNDES." February 23.

———. 2000b. "FHC sanciona lei do emprego público com 2 vetos." February 23.

European Union Election Observation Mission, Presidential Elections Venezuela 2006. 2006. *Preliminary Statement.* http://www.eueomvenezuela.org/pdf/EUEOM_Venezuela_Presidential eElection_2006_Preliminary_Statement.pdf.

Evans, C. Lawrence, and Walter J. Oleszek. 1996. *Congress Under Fire: Reform Politics and the Republican Majority.* Houghton Mifflin.

Evans, Diana. 2004. *Greasing the Wheels: Using Pork Barrel Politics to Build Majority Coalitions in Congress.* Cambridge: Cambridge University Press.
Evans, Peter B. 1979. *Dependent Development: The Alliance of Multinational, State, and Local Capital in Brazil.* Princeton: Princeton University Press.
———. 1995. *Embedded Autonomy: States and Industrial Transformation.* Princeton: Princeton University Press.
Evans/McDonough. 2006. "Venezuelan Political Climate: Registered Voters; Presentation of Results." Evans/McDonough. Consultores 30.11. November 29. http://www.evansmcdonough.com.
Fearon, James D. 1999. "Electoral Accountability and the Control of Politicians: Selecting Good Types Versus Sanctioning Poor Performance." In *Democracy, Accountability, and Representation,* edited by Adam Przeworksi, Susan C. Stokes, and Bernard Manin. New York: Cambridge University Press.
Ferejohn, John. 1974. *Pork Barrel Politics: Rivers and Harbors Legislation, 1947–1968.* Stanford: Stanford University Press.
———. 1986. "Incumbent Performance and Electoral Control." *Public Choice* 50:5–25.
———. 1999. "Accountability and Authority: Toward a Theory of Political Accountability." In *Democracy, Accountability, and Representation,* edited by Adam Przeworski, Susan C. Stokes, and Bernard Manin. Cambridge: Cambridge University Press.
Ferreira, Francisco H. G., Phillippe G. Leite, and Martin Ravallion. 2007. "Poverty Reduction Without Economic Growth? Explaining Brazil's Poverty Dynamics, 1985–2004." Policy Research Working Paper 4431, World Bank, Development Research Group.
Figueiredo, Argelina, and Fernando Limongi. 1998. "Relacao Executivo-Legislativo no Presidencialismo Multipartidário: Os regimes de 46 e 88." Paper presented at the twenty-second annual meeting of ANPOCS, Caxambu, Minas Gerais, Brazil, October.
Figueiredo, Argelina Cheibub, and Fernando Limongi. 2000. "Presidential Power, Legislative Organization, and Party Behavior in Brazil." *Comparative Politics* 32:151–70.
Fiorina, Morris, and Roger Noll. 1979. "Majority Rule Models and Legislative Elections." *Journal of Politics* 41:1081–104.
Forero, Juan. 2007. "Venezuela Tries to Create Its Own Kind of Socialism." *Washington Post Foreign Service,* August 6, A12.
Fox, Jonathan. 1994. "The Difficult Transition from Clientelism to Citizenship. Lessons from Mexico." World Politics 46 (2): 151–84.
Furtado, Celso. 1965. "Political Obstacles to the Economic Development of Brazil." In *Obstacles to Change in Latin America,* edited by Claudio Veliz. Oxford: Oxford University Press.
———. 1970. *Economic Development of Latin America: Historical Background and Contemporary Problems.* Cambridge: Cambridge University Press.
Garman, Christopher, Stephan Haggard, and Eliza Willis. 2001. "Fiscal Decentralization: A Political Theory with Latin American Cases." *World Politics* 53 (2): 205–36.
Geddes, Barbara. 1991. "A Game Theoretic Model of Reform in Latin American Democracies." *American Political Science Review,* 85 (2): 372–92.
———. 1994. *Politicians' Dilemma: Building State Capacity in Latin America.* Berkeley and Los Angeles: University of California Press.

Geddes, Barbara, and Artur Ribeiro Neto. 1992. "Institutional Sources of Corruption in Brazil." *Third World Quarterly* 13:641–61.
Gerber, Elizabeth R. 1999. *The Populist Paradox: Interest Group Influence and the Promise of Direct Legislation.* Princeton: Princeton University Press.
Gil, Federico. 1966. *The Political System of Chile.* Boston: Houghton Mifflin.
Graham, Lawrence S. 1968. *Civil Service Reform in Brazil: Principles Versus Practice.* Austin: University of Texas Press.
Grayson, George. 2000. "Mexico." In *Latin American Politics and Development,* edited by Howard J. Wiarda and Harvey F. Kline. 6th ed. Boulder, Colo.: Westview Press.
Greenfield, Sidney M. 1972. "Charwomen, Cesspools, and Roadbuilding: An Examination of Patronage, Clientage, and Political Power in Southeastern Minas Gerais." In *Structure and Process in Latin America: Patronage, Clientage, and Power Systems,* edited by Arnold Strickon and Sidney M. Greenfield. Albuquerque: University of New Mexico Press.
Groseclose, Tim, and James M. Snyder, Jr. 2000. "Estimating Party Influence in Congressional Roll-Call Voting." *American Journal of Political Science* 44 (2): 193–211.
Gudin, Eugenio. 1956. "Multiple Exchange Rates: The Brazilian Experience." *Economia Internazionale,* August.
Haggard, Stephan. 1990. *Pathways from the Periphery: The Politics of Growth in the Newly Industrializing Countries.* Ithaca: Cornell University Press.
Haggard, Stephan, and Mathew D. McCubbins, eds. 2001. *Presidents, Parliaments, and Policy.* New York: Cambridge University Press.
Hagopian, Frances. 1996. *Traditional Politics and Regime Change in Brazil.* Cambridge: Cambridge University Press.
Hawkins, Kirk. 2003. "The Logic of Linkages: Antipartyism, Charismatic Movements, and the Breakdown of Party Systems in Latin America." Ph.D. diss., Duke University.
Hippólito, Lúcia. 1985. *De raposas e reformistas—o PSD e a experiencia democrática brasileira (1945–64).* Rio de Janeiro: Paz e Terra.
Hirschman, Albert O. 1963. *Journeys Toward Progress: Studies of Economic Policy-Making in Latin America.* New York: Twentieth Century Fund.
———. 1971. *A Bias for Hope: Essays on Development and Latin America.* New Haven: Yale University Press.
Huntington, Samuel P. 1968. *Political Order in Changing Societies.* New Haven: Yale University Press.
Huber, Evelyne, ed. 2003. *Models of Capitalism: Lessons for Latin America.* University Park: Pennsylvania State University Press.
Inglehart, Ronald. 1990. *Culture Shift in Advanced Industrial Society.* Princeton: Princeton University Press.
Instituto Brasileiro de Geografia e Estatístico [IBGE]. 2003. "Estatisticas do século XX."
Jaguaribe, Helio. 1958. *Condições institucionais do desenvolvimento.* Rio de Janeiro: Instituto Superior de Estudos Brasileiros.
Jervis, Robert. 1978. "Cooperation Under the Security Dilemma." *World Politics* 30:167–214.
Joskow, Paul L., and Roger G. Noll. 1981. "Regulation in Theory and Practice: An Overview." In *Studies in Public Regulation,* edited by Gary Fromm. Cambridge, Mass.: MIT Press.

Kahil, Raouf. 1973. *Inflation and Economic Development in Brazil, 1946–63.* Oxford: Oxford University Press.

Kang, David. 2002. *Crony Capitalism: Corruption and Development in South Korea and the Philippines.* Cambridge: Cambridge University Press.

Karl, Terry Lynn. 1982. "The Political Economy of Petrodollars: Oil and Democracy in Venezuela." Ph.D. diss., Stanford University.

———. 1997. *The Paradox of Plenty: Oil Booms and Petro-States.* Berkeley and Los Angeles: University of California Press.

Kaufman, Robert R. 1967. *The Chilean Right and Agrarian Reform: Resistance and Modernization.* Washington D.C.: Institute for the Comparative Study of Political Systems.

———. 1974. "The Patron-Client Concept and Macro-politics: Prospects and Problems" *Comparative Studies in Society and History* 16 (3): 284–310.

———. 1990. "How Societies Change Developmental Models or Keep Them: Reflections on the Latin American Experience in the 1930's and the Postwar World." In *Manufacturing Miracles: Paths of Industrialization in Latin America and East Asia,* edited by Gary Gereffi and Donald L. Wyman. Princeton: Princeton University Press.

Kay, Stephen J. 2001. "Brazil's Social Security Reform in Comparative Perspective." Prepared for delivery at the 2001 meeting of the Southern Political Science Association, Atlanta, November 7–10.

Keck, Margaret. 1992. *The Worker's Party and Democratization in Brazil.* New Haven: Yale University Press.

Kenworthy, Eldon. 1970. "Coalitions in the Political Development of Latin America." In *The Study of Coalition Behavior: Theoretical Perspectives from Three Continents,* edited by Sven Groennings et al. New York: Holt, Rinehart and Winston.

Key, V. O., Jr. 1949. *Southern Politics in State and Nation.* New York: Knopf.

Kiewiet, Roderick D., and Mathew D. McCubbins. 1991. *The Logic of Delegation: Congressional Parties and the Appropriations Process.* Chicago: University of Chicago Press.

King, Gary, Robert Keohane, and Sidney Verba. 1994. *Designing Social Inquiry: Scientific Inference in Qualitative Research.* Princeton: Princeton University Press.

Kitschelt, Herbert. 2000. "Linkages Between Citizens and Politicians in Democratic Polities." *Comparative Political Studies,* 33 (6–7): 845–79.

Kitschelt, Herbert, and Steven Wilkinson, eds. 2007. *Patrons, Clients, and Policies: Patterns of Democratic Accountability and Political Competition.* New York:. Cambridge University Press.

Kornblith, Miriam. 1995. "Public Sector and Private Sector: New Rules of the Game." In *Venezuelan Democracy Under Stress,* edited by Jennifer McCoy, Andrés Serbin, William C. Smith, and Andrés Stambouli. New Brunswick, N.J.: Transaction.

Kornblith, Miriam, and Daniel H. Levine. 1995. *Venezuela: The Life and Times of the Party System.* In *Building Democratic Institutions: Party Systems in Latin America,* edited by Scott Mainwaring and Timothy Scully. Stanford: Stanford University Press.

Kramer, Gerald H. 1971. "Short-Term Fluctuations in U.S. Voting Behavior: 1896–1964. *American Political Science Review* 65:313–143.

———. 1983. The Ecological Fallacy Revisited: Aggregate- Versus Individual-Level Findings on Economics and Elections, and Sociotropic Voting. *American Political Science Review* 77:92–111.

Krueger, Anne O. 1974. "The Political Economy of the Rent-Seeking Society." *American Economic Review* 64:291–303.

Landé, Carl H. 1973. "Networks and Groups in Southeast Asia: Some Observations on the Group Theory of Politics." *American Political Science Review* 67:103–27.

Lavareda, Antonio. 1991. *A democracia nas urnas: O processo partidário eleitoral Brasileiro*. Rio de Janeiro: Rio Fundo Editora.

Leff, Nathaniel H. 1967. "Export Stagnation and Autarchic Development in Brazil, 1947–62." *Quarterly Journal of Economics* (May): 286–301.

———. 1982. *Underdevelopment and Development in Brazil*. Vol. 1, *Economic Structure and Change, 1822–1947*. Boston: Allen and Unwin.

Lemarchand, Rene. 1972. "Political Clientelism and Ethnicity in Tropical Africa: Competing Solidarities in Nation Building." *American Political Science Review* 66:68–90.

Lemarchand, Rene, and Keith Legg. 1972. "Political Clientelism and Development: A Preliminary Analysis." *Comparative Politics* 4:149–78.

Leoni, Eduardo, Carlos Pereira, and Lúcio Rennó. 2004. "Political Survival Strategies: Political Career Decisions in the Brazilian Chamber of Deputies." *Journal of Latin American Studies* 36 (1): 109–30.

Lesova, Polya. 2007. "Dow Jones Eliminates Venezuela from Its Indexes." *Market Watch* 3/28/07. http://www.marketwatch.com/news/story/dow-jones-eliminates-venezuela-its/story .aspx?guid=%7B0C73D1E3-CE18–472E-95C4–57D4B1158CA7%7D.

Levine, Daniel H. 1973. *Conflict and Political Change in Venezuela*. Princeton: Princeton University Press.

———. 1978. "Venezuela Since 1958: The Consolidation of Democratic Politics." In *The Breakdown of Democratic Regimes: Latin America*, edited by Juan J. Linz and Alfred Stepan. Baltimore: Johns Hopkins University Press.

Levine, Daniel H., and Miriam Kornblith. 1995. "Venezuela: The Life and Times of the Party System." In *Building Democratic Institutions: Party Systems in Latin America*, edited by Scott Mainwaring and Timothy Scully. Stanford: Stanford University Press.

Lewis-Beck, Michael S. 1988. *Economics and Elections: The Major Western Democracies*. Ann Arbor: University of Michigan Press.

Lijphart, Arend. 1990. *Democracies: Patterns of Majoritarian and Consensus Government in Twenty-one Countries*. New Haven: Yale University Press.

Little, I. M. D., Tibor Scitovsky, and Maurice Scott. 1970. *Industry and Trade in Some Developing Countries: A Comparative Study*. Oxford: Oxford University Press.

Lima, Olavo Brasil de, Jr. 1980. *The Brazilian Multi-party System: A Case for Contextual Political Rationality*. Ann Arbor, Mich.: University Microfilms International.

Limongi, Fernando, and Argelina Cheibub Figueredo. 1995. "Partidos Políticos na Câmara dos Deputados: 1989–1994." *Dados* 38:497–525.

Linz, Juan J., and Arturo Valenzuela. 1994. *The Failure of Presidential Democracy*. Vols. 1–2. Baltimore: Johns Hopkins University Press.

Lohmann, Susanne. 1998. "An Information Rationale for the Power of Special Interests." *American Political Science Review* 92 (4): 809–27.

Lotta, Raymond. 2007. "Hugo Chavez Has an Oil Strategy . . . but Can This Lead to Liberation?" *Revolution* (Revolutionary Communist Party, U.S.A.), July.

"Lula's Leap: The Economist Talks to Brazil's President." 2006. *Economist*, March 2.

Lupia, Arthur, and Matthew D. McCubbins. 1998. *The Democratic Dilemma: Can Citizens Learn What They Need to Know?* New York: Cambridge University Press.

Lyne, Mona. 1999. "The Voter's Dilemma and Electoral Competition: Explaining Development Policy and Democratic Breakdown in Developing Democracies." Ph.D. diss., University of California, San Diego.

Lyne, Mona M. 2005. "Parties as Programmatic Agents: A Test of Institutional Theory in Brazil." *Party Politics* 11 (2): 193–216.

———. 2006. "Beyond the Presidential-Parliamentary Debate: An Electoral Theory of Legislative Conflict and Cooperation." Paper prepared for delivery at the annual meeting of the American Political Science Association, Philadelphia, August 30–September 3.

———. 2007. "Rethinking Economics and Institutions: The Voter's Dilemma and Democratic Accountability." In *Patrons, Clients, and Policies: Patterns of Democratic Accountability and Political Competition*, edited by Herbert Kitschelt and Steven Wilkinson. Cambridge: Cambridge University Press.

———. 2008. Proffering Pork: Party Reputation Building in the Brazilian Legislature." *American Journal of Political Science* 52 (2).

Lyne, Mona M., and Heather Hawn. 2007. "How Weak States and Strong MNCs Make Competitive Politicians: A Clientelist Model of Developing Country Policy Choice." Paper prepared for delivery at the annual meeting of the Midwest Political Science Association, Chicago, April 12–15.

Lyne, Mona M., Daniel Nielson, and Michael J. Tierney. 2003. "Runaway Agents: Multimember Principles and Delegation." Paper presented at the annual meeting of the American Political Science Association, Philadelphia, August.

Macario, Santiago. 1964. "Protectionism and Industrialization in Latin America." *United Nations Economic Bulletin for Latin America* 9 (1): 61–102.

Magee, Stephen P., William P. Brock, and Leslie Young. 1989. *Black Hole Tariffs and Endogenous Policy Theory*. Cambridge: Cambridge University Press.

"The Magic of Lula: What Brazil's Scandal-Tarnished President Should Do with a Second Chance." 2006. *Economist*, March 2.

Mainwaring, Scott. 1992. "Brazilian Party Underdevelopment in Comparative Perspective." *Political Science Quarterly* 107:677–708.

———. 1995. "Brazil: Weak Parties, Feckless Democracy." In *Building Democratic Institutions: Party Systems in Latin America*, edited by Scott Mainwaring and Timothy Scully. Stanford: Stanford University Press.

Mainwaring, Scott P. 1999. *Rethinking Party Systems in the Third Wave of Democratization: The Case of Brazil*. Stanford: Stanford University Press.

Mainwaring, Scott, and Anibal Perez-Linán. 1997. "Party Discipline in Multiparty Systems: A Methodological Note and an Analysis of the Brazilian Constitutional Congress." *Legislative Studies Quarterly* 22:471–93.

Mainwaring, Scott, and Timothy Scully, eds. 2005. *Building Democratic Institutions: Party Systems in Latin America*. Stanford: Stanford University Press.

Malloy, James M. 1977. "Authoritarianism and Corporatism in Latin America: The Modal Pattern." In *Authoritarianism and Corporatism in Latin America*, edited by James M. Malloy. Pittsburgh: University of Pittsburgh Press.

———. 1979. *The Politics of Social Security in Brazil*. Pittsburgh: University of Pittsburgh Press.

Martz, John D. 1964. "Dilemmas in the Study of Latin American Political Parties." Journal of Politics 26 (3): 509–31.

———. 1966. *Acción Democrática: Evolution of a Modern Political Party in Venezuela*. Princeton: Princeton University Press.

———. 1977. *Venezuela: The Democratic Experience*. New York: Praeger.

Mayhew, David. 1974. *The Electoral Connection*. New Haven: Yale University Press.

———. 1991. *Divided We Govern: Party Control, Lawmaking, and Investigations, 1946–1990*. New Haven: Yale University Press.

McQuerry, Elizabeth. 2001. "Banking on It: Increased Foreign Bank Entry into Brazil." *EconSouth* 3 (3).

Menges, Constantine. 1966. "Public Policy and Organized Business in Chile: A Preliminary Analysis." *Journal of International Affairs*, 20.

Morgenstern, Scott. 2003. *Patterns of Legislative Politics: Roll Call Voting in Latin America and the United States*. New York: Cambridge University Press.

Morgenstern, Scott, and Benito Nacif, eds. 2001. *Legislative Politics in Latin America*. New York: Cambridge University Press.

Morgenstern, Scott, and Richard F. Pottoff. 2004. "The Components of Elections: District Heterogeneity, District-Time Effects, and Volatility." *Electoral Studies* 24:17–40.

Mueller, Dennis C. 1989. *Public Choice II: A Revised Edition of Public Choice*. Cambridge: Cambridge University Press.

Myers, David J. 1995. "Perceptions of a Stressed Democracy: Inevitable Decay or Foundation for Rebirth?" In *Venezuelan Democracy Under Stress*, edited by Jennifer McCoy, Andrés Serbin, William C. Smith, and Andrés Stambouli. Miami: North-South Center.

Naim, Moisés. 1993a. "The Launching of Radical Policy Changes, 1989–91." In *Venezuela in the Wake of Radical Reform*, edited by Joseph S. Tulchin with Gary Bland. Boulder, Colo.: Lynne Rienner.

———. 1993b. *Paper Tigers and Minotaurs: The Politics of Venezuela's Economic Reforms*. Washington, D.C.: Carnegie Endowment for International Peace.

Navarro, Juan Carlos. 1995. "In Search of the Lost Pact: Consensus Lost in the 1980's and 1990's." In *Venezuelan Democracy Under Stress*, edited by Jennifer McCoy, Andrés Serbin, William C. Smith, and Andrés Stambouli. New Brunswick, N.J.: Transaction.

Nicolau, Jairo Marconi. 1998. *Dados eleitorais do Brasil*. Rio de Janeiro: Revan: IUPERJ-UCAM.

Nielson, Daniel L. 2003. "Supplying Trade Reform: Political Institutions and Trade Policy in Middle-Income Democracies." *American Journal of Political Science* 47 (3): 470–91.

North, Douglass C. 1990. *Institutions, Institutional Change, and Economic Performance*. Cambridge: Cambridge University Press.

North, Douglass C., and Robert Paul Thomas. 1973. *The Rise of the Western World: A New Economic History*. Cambridge: Cambridge University Press.

Nunes Leal, Victor. 1977. *Coronelismo: The Municipality and Representative Government in Brazil*. New York: Cambridge University Press.

O'Donnell, Guillermo. 1979. *Modernization and Bureaucratic-Authoritarianism: Studies in South American Politics.* Berkeley and Los Angeles: University of California Press, International and Area Studies.

———. 1988. "States and Alliances in Argentina, 1956–76." In *Toward a Political Economy of Development: A Rational Choice Perspective,* edited by Robert Bates. New York: Cambridge University Press.

———. 1994. "Delegative Democracy." *Journal of Democracy* 5 (1): 55–69.

Olson, Mancur. 1982. *The Rise and Decline of Nations.* New Haven: Yale University Press.

Papakostas, Apostolis. 2001. "Why Is There no Clientelism in Scandinavia? A Comparison of the Swedish and Greek Sequences of Development." In *Clientelism, Interests, and Democratic Representation,* edited by Simona Piattoni. Cambridge: Cambridge University Press.

Peltzman, Sam. 1976. "Toward a More General Theory of Regulation." *Journal of Law and Economics* 21:211–40.

Pereira, Carlos, and Bernardo Mueller. 2000. "Uma teoria de preponderância do executivo: O sistema de commisões no legislativo Brasileiro." *Revista Brasileira de Ciências Socias* 15 (43): 45–67.

Pereira, Carlos, and Lúcio Rennó. 2001. "O que é que o reeleito tem? Dinâmicas político-institucionais locais e nacionais nas eleições de 1998 para a Câmara dos Deputados." *Dados* 44 (2): 323–62.

Piattoni, Simona. 2001. "Clientelism in Historical and Comparative Perspective." In *Clientelism, Interests, and Democratic Representation,* edited by Simona Piattoni. Cambridge: Cambridge University Press.

Popkin, Samuel L. 1991. *The Reasoning Voter: Communication and Persuasion in Presidential Campaigns.* Chicago: University of Chicago Press.

Powell, John Duncan. 1970. "Peasant Society and Clientelist Politics." *American Political Science Review* 64 (June): 411–25.

———. 1971. *Political Mobilization of the Venezuelan Peasant.* Cambridge: Harvard University Press.

Prebisch, Raul. 1963. "Towards a Dynamic Development Policy for Latin America," New York: United Nations.

Przeworksi, Adam, Bernard Manin, and Susan Stokes, eds. 1999. *Democracy, Accountability, and Representation.* New York: Cambridge University Press.

Putnam, Robert D. 1993. *Making Democracy Work: Civic Traditions in Modern Italy.* Princeton: Princeton University Press.

Pye, Lucien W. 1958. "The Non-Western Political Process." *Journal of Politics* 20 (3): 468–86.

Ramseyer, J. Mark, and Francis McCall Rosenbluth. 1993. *Japan's Political Marketplace.* Cambridge: Harvard University Press.

Ranis, Gustav. 1990. "Contrasts in the Political Economy of Development Policy Change." In *Manufacturing Miracles: Paths of Industrialization in Latin America and East Asia,* edited by Gary Gereffi and Donald L. Wyman. Princeton: Princeton University Press.

Rasmusen, Eric. 1989. *Games and Information: An Introduction to Game Theory.* Cambridge, Mass.: Basil Blackwell.

"The Rise of the 'Boligarchs.'" 2007. *Economist,* August 7.

Roberts, Kenneth M. 1995. "Neoliberalism and the Transformation of Populism in Latin America: The Peruvian Case." *World Politics* 48 (1): 82–116.

———. 2003. "Social Correlates of Party System Demise and Populist Resurgence in Venezuela." *Latin American Research Review* 45 (3): 45–57.
Rocha, Antonio Sérgio Carvalho. 1995. "O Congresso nacional no processo orçamentário pós-Constituente (1988–93): Retomando o 'poder sobre as finanças'?" Master's thesis, University of São Paulo.
Rhode, David W. 1990. "The Reports of My Death Are Greatly Exaggerated: Parties and Party Voting in the House of Representatives." In *Changing Perspectives on Congress*, edited by Glenn R. Parker. Knoxville: University of Tennessee Press.
———. 1991. *Parties and Leaders in the Postreform House*. Chicago: University of Chicago Press.Rohter, Larry. 2007. "Antônio Carlos Magalhães, Brazil Politician, Dies at 79." New York Times, July 21.
Romero, Simon. 2007. "Political Clashes Shake Venezuela's Strained Oil Industry." *New York Times*, July 23.
Roth, Guenther. 1968. "Personal Rulership, Patrimonialism, and Empire Building in the New States." *World Politics* 20 (2): 194–206.
Samuels, David. 2000. "Concurrent Elections, Discordant Results: Presidentialism, Federalism, and Governance in Brazil." *Comparative Politics* 33:1–20.
———. 2003. *Ambition, Federalism, and Legislative Politics in Brazil*. New York: Cambridge University Press.
———. 2006. "Sources of Mass Partisanship in Brazil." *Latin American Politics and Society* 48 (2): 1–27.
Santos, Fabiano. 2002. "Parties and Committees in the Coalition Presidential System." *Dados* 45 (2): 237–64.
Santos, Fabiano, and Lúcio Rennó. 2004. "The Selection of Committee Leadership in the Brazilian Chamber of Deputies." *Journal of Legislative Studies* 10 (1): 50–70.
Santos, Wanderley Guilherme dos. 1986. *Sessenta e quatro: Anatomia da crise*. São Paulo: Vértice.
Sartori, Giovanni. 1986. "The Influence of Electoral Systems: Faulty Laws or Faulty Method." In *Electoral Laws and Their Political Consequences*, edited by Bernard Grofman and Arend Liphart. New York: Agethon.
———. 1994. "Neither Presidentialism nor Parliamentarism." In *The Failure of Presidential Democracy*, edited by Juan Linz and Arturo Valenzuela. Baltimore: John Hopkins University Press.
Scheiner, Ethan. 2005a. *Democracy Without Competition in Japan: Opposition Failure in a One-Party Dominant State*. Cambridge: Cambridge University Press.
Schmidt, Steffen W., Laura Guasti, Carl H. Landé, and James C. Scott., eds. 1977. *Friends, Followers, and Factions: A Reader in Political Clientelism*. Berkeley and Los Angeles: University of California Press.
Schmitt, Rogerio. 1999. "Coligacoes eleitorais e sistema partidário no Brasil." Ph.D. diss., Instituto Universitario [IUPERJ], Rio de Janeiro.
Schmitter, Phillipe C. 1971. *Interest Conflict and Political Change in Brazil*. Stanford: Stanford University Press.
———. 1974. "Still the Century of Corporatism?" *Review of Politics* 36 (January): 85–131.
Scott, James C. 1969. "Corruption, Machine Politics, and Political Change." *American Political Science Review* 63 (4): 1142–58.
———. 1972. "Patron-Client Politics and Political Change in Southeast Asia." *American Political Science Review* 66 (March): 91–113.

Scott, Robert. 1966. "Political Parties and Policy-Making in Latin America." In *Political Parties and Political Development*, edited by Joseph LaPalombara and Myron Weiner. Princeton: Princeton University Press.

Scott, Robert E. 1970. "Political Parties and Policy-Making in Latin America. In *Political Parties and Political Development*, edited by Joseph LaPalombara and Myron Weiner. Princeton: Princeton University Press.

Secretária de Administração Federal. 1993. *Estrutura e organização do poder executivo: Administração pública Brasileira*. Brasília: Centro de Documentação, Informação, e Difusão Graciliano Ramos.

Sheahan, John. 2002. "Alternative Models of Capitalism in Latin America." In *Models of Capitalism: Lessons for Latin America*, edited by Evelyne Huber. University Park: Pennsylvania State University Press.

Shugart, Mattew S. 1992. "Leaders, Rank and File, and Constituents: Electoral Reform in Colombia and Venezuela." *Electoral Studies* 11 (1): 21–45.

Shugart, Matthew S., and John M. Carey. 1992. *Presidents and Assemblies: Constitutional Design and Electoral Dynamics*. Cambridge: Cambridge University Press.

Shugart, Matthew S., and Stephan Haggard. 2001. "Institutions and Public Policy in Presidential Systems." In *Presidents, Parliaments, and Policy*, edited by Stephan Haggard and Mathew D. McCubbins. Cambridge: Cambridge University Press.

Shugart, Matthew S., and Marten P. Wattenberg. 2001. *Mixed-Member Electoral Systems: The Best of Both Worlds?* Oxford: Oxford University Press.

Sinclair, Barbara. 1983. *Majority Leadership in the U.S. House*. Baltimore: Johns Hopkins University Press.

———. 1995. *Legislators, Leaders, and Lawmaking: The U.S. House of Representatives in the Postreform Era*. Baltimore: Johns Hopkins University Press.

Skidmore, Thomas E. 1967. *Politics in Brazil, 1930–1964*. New York: Oxford University Press.

———. 1977. "The Politics of Economic Stabilization in Postwar Latin America." In *Authoritarianism and Corporatism in Latin America*, edited by James M. Malloy. Pittsburgh: University of Pittsburgh Press.

Snyder, James M., and Tim Groseclose. 2000. "Estimating Party Influence on Congressional Roll Call Voting." *American Journal of Political Science* 44 (2):193–211.

Snyder, James M., and Michael M. Ting. 2002. "An Informational Rationale for Political Parties." *American Journal of Political Science* 46 (1): 90–110.

Soares, Gláucio, A. D. 1973. *Sociedade e política no Brasil*. São Paulo: DIFEL.

———. 2001. *A democracia interrompida*. Rio de Janeiro: Fundação Getúlio Vargas.

Sola, Lourdes. 1982. "The Political and Ideological Constraints to Economic Management in Brazil, 1945–63." Ph.D. diss., University of Oxford.

Souza, André Portela, Hélio Zylberstajn, Luís Eduardo Alfonso, and Priscilla Matias Flori. 2004. "Fiscal Impacts of Social Security Reform in Brazil." In *Anais do XXXII Encontro Nacional de Economia* [Proceedings of the Thirty-second Brazilian Economics Meeting] with number 138, edited by Associacao Nacional dos Centros de Pósgraduacao em Economia [Brazilian Association of Graduate Programs in Economics]. http://econpapers.repec.org/paper/anpen2004/138.htm.

Souza, Maria do Carmo Campello de. 1976. *Estado e partidos políticos no Brasil (1930–1964)*. São Paulo: Editora Alfa-Omega.

———. n.d. "Federalismo no Brasil: Aspectos políticos-institucionais do federalismo (1930–1964)."
Stigler, George J. 1971. "The Theory of Economic Regulation." *Bell Journal of Economics and Management Science* 2 (1): 3–21.
Stokes, Susan C. 2000. "Rethinking Clientelism." Paper presented at the Twenty-second International Congress of the Latin American Studies Association, March 16–18, Miami, Florida.
———. 2001. *Mandates and Democracy: Neoliberalism by Surprise in Latin America.* New York: Cambridge University Press.
———. 2005. "Perverse Accountability: A Formal Model of Machine Politics with Evidence from Argentina." *American Political Science Review* 99 (3): 315–25.
———. 2006. "Do Informal Rules Make Democracy Work? Accounting for Accountability in Argentina." In *Informal Institutions and Democracy: Lessons from Latin America*, edited by Gretchen Helmke and Steven Levitsky. Baltimore: Johns Hopkins University Press.
———. 2007. "Is Vote-Buying Undemocratic?" In *Elections for Sale: The Causes and Consequences of Vote Buying*, edited by Fredric C. Schaeffer. Boulder, Colo.: Lynne Reiner.
Stokes, Susan, and Luis Fernando Medina. 2007. "Monopoly and Monitoring: An Approach to Political Clientelism." In *Patrons, Clients, and Policies: Patterns of Democratic Accountability and Political Competition*, edited by Herbert Kitschelt and Steven Wilkinson. Cambridge: Cambridge University Press.
Strikon, Arnold, and Sidney Greenfield, eds. 1972. *Structure and Process in Latin America: Patronage, Clientage, and Power Systems.* Albuquerque: University of New Mexico Press.
Strøm, Kaare. 1990. *Minority Government and Majority Rule.* New York: Cambridge University Press.
———. 2000. "Delegation and Accountability in Parliamentary Democracies." *European Journal of Political Research* 37 (3): 261–89.
Sustar, Lee. 2007. "Chavez and the Meaning of Twenty-first-Century Socialism: Where Is Venezuela Going?" *International Socialist Review* 54. http://www.isreview.org/issues/54/Venezuela.shtml.
Taylor-Robinson, M. 2006. "Do the Poor Count? Democratic Institutions and Accountability in a Context of Poverty."
Thorp, Rosemary, and Laurence Whitehead. 1979. *Inflation and Stabilization in Latin America.* New York: Holmes and Meier.
Tribunal Superior Eleitoral. 1945. *Dados estatisticos.* Vol. 1, *Eleições Federais e Estaduais.* Rio de Janeiro: Tribunal Superior Eleitoral.
———. 1950. *Dados estatisticos.* Vol. 2, *Eleições Federais e Estaduais.* Rio de Janeiro: Tribunal Superior Eleitoral.
———. 1955. *Dados estatisticos.* Vol. 3, *Eleições Federais, Estaduais e Municipais, realisadas no Brasil em 1952, 1954 e 1955, e em confronto com os anteriores.* Rio de Janeiro: Tribunal Superior Eleitoral.
———. 1963. *Dados estatisticos.* Vol. 5, *Eleições Federais, Estaduais realisadas no Brasil em 1960 e em confronto com os anteriores.* Rio de Janeiro: Tribunal Superior Eleitoral.
———. 1964. *Dados estatisticos.* Vol. 6, *Eleições Federais, Estaduais realisadas no Brasil em 1962 e em confronto com os anteriores.* Rio de Janeiro: Tribunal Superior Eleitoral.

———. 1966. *Dados estatisticos*. Vol. 4, *Eleições Federais, Estaduais realisadas no Brasil em 1958, e em confronto com os anteriores*. Rio de Janeiro: Tribunal Superior Eleitoral.

Trinkunas, Harold A. 2002. "The Crisis in Venezuela's Civil-Military Relations: From Punto Fijo to the Fifth Republic." *Latin American Research Review* 37 (1): 41–76.

Tsebelis, George. 1995. "Decision Making in Political Systems: Veto Players in Presidentialism, Parliamentarism, Multicameralism, and Multipartyism." *British Journal of Political Science* 25 (3): 289–325.

U.S. Department of Energy. 2004. *Energy Information Administration, Country Analysis Briefs: Venezuela*. June. www.eia.doe.gov.

Valenzuela, Arturo. 1977. *Political Brokers in Chile: Local Government in a Centralized Polity*. Durham, N.C.: Duke University Press.

Venezuela Information Office. 2006. "A Mission to End Poverty: State-Sponsored Social Programs in Venezuela."

Verdier, Daniel. 1994. *Democracy and International Trade*. Princeton: Princeton University Press.

Vianna, S. B. 1987. *Política econômica no segundo governo Vargas (1951–54)*. Rio de Janeiro: BNDES.

Wade, Robert. 2003. *Governing the Market: Economic Theory and the Role of Government in East Asian Industrialization*. Princeton: Princeton University Press.

Weingast, Barry R. 1997. "The Political Foundations of Democracy and the Rule of Law." *American Political Science Review* 91 (2): 245–63.

Weingrod, Alex. 1977. "Patrons, Patronage, and Political Parties." In *Friends, Followers, and Factions: A Reader in Political Clientelism*, edited by Steffen W. Schmidt, Laura Guasti, Carl H. Landé, and James C. Scott. Berkeley and Los Angeles: University of California Press.

Weyland, Kurt. 1996a. *Democracy Without Equity: Failures of Reform in Brazil*. Pittsburgh: Pittsburgh University Press.

———. 1996b. "Risk Taking in Latin American Economic Restructuring: Lessons From Prospect Theory." *International Studies Quarterly* 40 (2): 29–52.

INDEX

accountability vacuum, 11–12, 16–17, 23 n. 4, 170–71, 177, 211. *See also* democratic accountability
   Brazilian, 149–50, 156, 161, 173–74
   party behavior related to, 100, 144, 148–49
   Venezuelan, 144, 151–55, 163, 165, 173–74
advanced industrial democracies, 8–13. *See also* developing democracies
   democratic accountability in, 3, 12
   electoral politics in, 13, 39–40, 57 n. 50, 75, 261
   legislative organization in, 176
   public goods provision in, 8–9, 23 n. 4, 24
   study of, 34 n. 23, 259
Advisory Council of the Presidency of the Republic (Venezuela), 224
agendas, legislative. *See also* legislators/legislatures
   Brazil, 176–87, 196–207
   control of, 18, 136, 175–208
   Venezuela, 186–87, 204
agriculture, 66, 219 n. 10, 248
alliances. *See* coalitions
Almeida, José Américo de, 119
Ames, Barry, 89, 129, 132, 139 n. 29, 173
Amorim Neto, Octavio, 151 n. 3, 200, 206 n. 15
Amsden, Alice, 56
Anderson, Charles W., 177 n. 1, 230 n. 22
ant vote, 81
Argentina, 70 n. 12, 235 n. 27, 250
   democracy in, 4, 6, 15, 61
asymmetry of excludability, 4–5, 12 n. 11, 31–33, 35 n. 25, 61, 259–60. *See also* benefits, excludability of; clientelist goods, excludability of; collective goods, excludability of; policy-based goods, excludability of

balance of payments, 73, 209, 212, 214–17, 234, 249
Bank of Brazil, 80, 238 n. 30
barriers to entry, 43, 122–23, 195
Bates, Robert H., 27 n. 11
benefits. *See also* clientelist goods; collective goods; policy goods
   delivery of, 64, 74–82, 87, 90 n. 27, 136
   excludability of, 14, 26–27, 252
   trading votes for, 121, 235, 238
Bergsman, Joel, 213, 214–15, 237, 238 n. 30
Bhagwati, Jagdish, 238 n. 30
bicameralism, Brazilian, 10, 65
bidding wars for votes, 46, 59, 127, 230 n. 22, 262. *See also* reservation price of voters; vote buying
   minimizing, 49, 52, 156–57, 160, 168–69, 233, 236 n. 28, 239–40, 256
bloc voting, 14 n. 12, 55 n. 47, 81, 87–88, 159–61, 236 n. 28
Bornhausen, Jorge, 144 n. 31
Brady, David W., 104–5
Brambor, Thomas, 134
Brazil
   accountability vacuum in, 149–50, 173–74
   bloc voting in, 14 n. 12, 81, 87–88, 236 n. 28
   candidate-centered electoral laws, 14, 19, 85, 87–89, 129, 147, 151 n. 3, 217, 253–54, 255
   democracy in, 15, 61, 102, 162, 255
   institutional theory applied to, 10, 11, 12, 19
   municipalities, 89–91
   1964 coup, 59 n. 52, 66, 102
   Old Republic, 156
   partisan tides in, 82–87
   policy issues in, 65–66

Brazil (*continued*)
  political party behavior in, 99–109, 115–18
  population, 69
  voting patterns in, 68–72, 87–93, 97
Brazil, contemporary
  budget formation in, 158–60, 170–73
  crisis response in, 19, 68, 147–48, 249–55, 256
  legislative organization in, 18, 136, 196–208
  policy-based voting in, 16, 170–71
  political party behavior in, 8, 102–3, 127–45
  reforms in, 1–3, 7–8, 21–23, 209–11, 224–26, 244–55, 261
Brazil, postwar
  collapse of democracy in, 3, 4, 6
  crisis response in, 23, 68, 99, 209–10, 219–34, 239–40
  decentralization in, 49, 148, 173–74, 177–85, 192–94, 256
  intraparty unity in, 122, 149–51
  ISI in, 19, 70, 118–22, 123, 209, 212–34
  legislative organization in, 186, 187, 192–94, 199
  party behavior in, 103–9, 118–22, 144–45, 154–55
  policy-based voting in, 7–8
  quid-pro-quo voting in, 16
  vote monitoring in, 80–82
Brazilian Democratic Movement (MDB, Movimento Democrático Brasileiro), 103
Brazilian Democratic Movement Party (PMDB, Partido do Movimento Democrático Brasileiro), 102, 103, 139, 143, 173
Brazilian Labor Party (PTB, Partido Trabalhista Brasileiro), 100
  cabinet memberships, 107, 109
  committee presidencies, 193
  party alliances, 109 n. 7, 137, 160
  rise of, 101, 180–81
  voting records, 120–21
Brazilian Progressive Party (PPB, Partido Progresista Brasileiro), 173. *See also* Democratic Social Party (PDS, Partido Democrático Social)

Brazilian Social Democracy Party (PSDB, Partido da Social Democracia Brasileira), 102, 103, 139, 143, 171, 173
Bremmer, Ian, 21
Brizola, Leonel, 22 n. 2, 91, 92, 101, 103
Buarque, Cristovam, 22 n. 2
Buchanan, James M., 26, 27 n. 11
Budget Committee (Brazil), 158–60, 170–72, 174, 178–81, 184, 194, 197
budgets
  balancing, 71, 211, 232, 251
  control of, 95, 113, 158, 189, 193, 198–99, 222
  inflation and, 71
  public health, 28
  Venezuela, 185–86, 195
bureaucracies
  Brazilian, 1, 3–4, 66, 161, 220, 222, 249, 251–52
  professional, 12, 23 n. 4, 30, 52
  Venezuelan, 67, 127, 186
Bush, George W., 190 n. 10
businessmen, 13, 26

cabinets, composition of
  Brazilian, 104, 107–9, 134–36, 205–6, 220 n. 11
  Venezuelan, 112–13, 122–23, 186
CACEX. *See* Bank of Brazil
Café Filho, Joao Fernandes Campos, 107, 205, 206
  stabilization program of, 220, 221 n. 14
Caldera, Rafael, 111, 152, 225
candidate-centered electoral laws, 10, 83, 85, 234. *See also* Brazil, candidate-centered electoral laws; party-centered electoral laws
  legislative organization and, 153, 192
  party organization and, 47–49, 116–17, 118, 144, 149–50
candidato nato rule, 156 n. 9
capital, 51–52, 54, 217 n. 8, 218. *See also* production, capital-intensive
capitalism, 13, 71
carbon vote, 81
Cardoso, Fernando Henrique. *See also* Real Plan

cabinet of, 134, 203
reforms by, 1, 21, 249, 252–53, 261
Carey, John M., 128 n. 23, 134, 150–51 n. 3, 198
Chamber of Deputies (Brazil), 158–60, 171, 178–85, 197–99, 222, 249
Chamber of Deputies (Venezuela), 94–95, 152
Chapa Branca faction, 119
Chávez, Hugo, 21–23. *See also* Venezuela, under Chávez
　clientelist networks of, 72–74, 76, 79–80, 100, 125–27, 148, 168, 195, 209, 210, 246–48
　dissolution of political parties by, 17, 18, 95, 100, 111, 148, 167, 173–74, 246–48
　intermediation system of, 124–27, 144, 167–68
　land takeovers by, 69 n. 9, 248
　reforms by, 2–3, 7–8, 67, 152–53, 196, 207, 210–11, 225, 246–48
　vote monitoring by, 78–79
Chile, 14 n. 12, 82, 250
Christian Democratic Party (PDC, Partido Democrata Cristao), 100, 101, 109, 138, 142, 143, 144
citizen-government links, 124–27
citizen voters, 55, 56
Clark, William Roberts, 134
class-based representation, 32, 238–39
Cleofas, Joao, 119
clientelist-based electoral strategy, 23–62, 70 n. 11, 165, 173–74. *See also* competition, clientelist; politics, clientelist; structural conditions, clientelist
　appeals to voters, 115–16, 118, 142
　Brazilian, 254–55
　centralized *vs.* decentralized, 4–7, 239–46
　crisis response, 8, 210–11, 226–29, 239–46
　direct *vs.* indirect exchange under, 23–29
　endogizing, 115, 124
　legislative organization, 175–76, 188–96, 203–5
　party organization, 46–50, 49, 87, 165, 168, 173–74
　policy-based strategy *vs.*, 13–14, 56–57, 75, 126
　policy choice and, 18–19, 49–50, 64 n. 2, 255–56
　poverty-based theory of, 8–15, 23 n. 4, 36, 37–38
　rejecting, 33–35, 51–52, 60–61, 69, 74, 96, 121, 210, 229–30, 233–34
　reorganization of, 125–27, 167–69
　shift from, 88–89, 91, 127–29, 134, 136, 176, 203, 249–50, 255, 256
　strategic interaction theory of, 36–37
　Venezuelan, 72, 124, 209, 242–48
　vote monitoring and, 77, 79, 80–82
　voters' preferences for, 4, 55, 82–97
clientelist goods, 21–62, 245
　delivering, 63, 122, 151 n. 3, 195, 204, 207, 230
　excludability of, 27, 31–33
　votes exchanged for, 4–7, 53, 67, 117, 123–24, 166, 227, 238, 259
clientelist networks, 117–18, 161. *See also* Chávez, Hugo, clientelist networks of
　Brazilian, 80–82, 92, 118–22, 161, 174, 194
　individualist, 19, 49, 156, 192
　restructuring, 210–11, 229–34, 240–46, 256–57
　Venezuelan, 162
client producers, 55, 58, 232–33
Clinton, Bill, 190 n. 10
closed-list proportional representation (PR), 17, 45 n. 35, 76, 93, 147–55, 162–66, 174, 243. *See also* open-list proportional representation (PR)
club goods, 26 n. 10
coalitions, 59, 233–34. *See also* majorities
　Brazilian, 128–34
　electoral, 85 n. 24, 86, 90 n. 27, 136–43, 262–63
　governing, 104–9, 111–15, 123–24, 178–79, 199
　legislative, 65, 132, 134, 150, 203–7
　voter, 31, 55 n. 47, 105
coffee exports, 219 n. 10
collective accountability, 4, 30–33, 60, 62, 229. *See also* democratic accountability

collective action, 4, 22, 29, 33, 122–23, 192–93, 230, 261
  legislative organization for, 192–93
  organizing for, 43, 195
  among voters, 82
collective goods, 12, 21–62, 175, 259–63. *See also* locally-targeted collective goods; nationally-targeted collective goods
  clientelist-based, 4–7, 16, 19
  crisis response and, 229–34
  excludability of, 5, 27–28, 34, 36, 44, 61
  by legislators, 103–4, 187–92, 207–8
  policy-based, 19, 226–29
  political parties' reputation for, 17, 47–49, 153, 160, 207–8, 260–62
  reforms in, 7–8, 187, 233–34, 243, 245–48, 254–55, 256
  voters' preferences for, 10, 64–65, 97, 162, 170, 210–11, 229, 260
collective-individual goals. *See* individual-collective goals' alignment
Collor, Fernando, 134, 200, 203, 249, 250
Common Minimum Program, 220 n. 11
competition
  clientelist, 75, 122, 125, 160–68, 174–75, 189, 194–96, 200, 204, 210, 230 n. 22, 235–38
  electoral, 19, 55, 59, 136, 142, 152, 227, 261–62
  government-opposition, 16, 40–43, 104–5, 107, 109, 111, 115, 134–36, 140–42, 144, 190, 192, 196–97
  policy-based, 39–49, 148, 156, 226–29, 242, 245
Confederation of Venezuelan Workers (CTV, Confederación de Trabajadores de Venezuela), 225
consejos comunales (community councils), 17, 76, 80, 126–27, 247
Constitution and Justice Committee (Brazil), 178, 179–82, 184–85, 193, 197
Cooper, Joseph, 104–5
COPEI Political Electoral Independent Organization Committee (Comité de Organización Política Electoral independiente), 111, 114, 123, 195, 241, 245
  decline of, 2, 100, 152, 166 n. 10, 167, 242
  dominance of, 67 n. 5, 76, 77, 207, 231
  National Accord and, 224
  National Committee of, 153, 163, 186
  Pact of Punto Fijo and, 94, 95, 110, 169
Coppedge, Michael, 95, 113, 123, 147 n. 1, 163 n. 18, 187, 194
COPRE Presidential Commission for the Reform of the State (Comisión Presidencial para la Reforma des Estado), 113 n. 11, 164, 223
Cox, Gary, 28, 45, 49, 57 n. 50, 83, 105, 187, 190, 199, 200, 206 n. 15
credit claiming, 84 n. 22, 117, 120–21, 122, 173, 204
crisis. *See also* Brazil, contemporary, crisis response in; Brazil, postwar, crisis response in; import substitution industrialization policies (ISI), crisis in; Venezuela, pre-Chávez, crisis response in
  debt, 54, 68, 217
  responses to, 8, 10–11, 18–19, 60, 210, 219–55, 256
Crisp, Brian F., 94, 95, 113–14, 153, 165, 195, 217 n. 8, 243
Cruzado stabilization program, 83
currency
  devaluations, 2, 67 n. 5
  stabilizations, 12, 23 n. 4, 30, 83

daddy industries, 213 n. 2, 215, 237
debt
  Brazilian, 249, 250, 254
  crisis of, 54, 68, 217
  international, 65, 67, 70
decentralization, 48, 87, 193, 232–33, 243
decision-making. *See* legislators/legislatures, organization of
democracies, 11–13, 18, 63 n. 1, 124, 187, 259–63. *See also* advanced industrial democracies; developing democracies; single-party democracies

democracy-development paradox, 8–15, 38, 211, 226, 259–62
  causes of, 3–4, 24, 57
democratic accountability, 3–15, 60–62. *See also* accountability vacuum; collective accountability
  collective choice problem of, 256–57, 259–63
  effective, 145, 150, 153
  electorally-based theories of, 24, 96, 121, 209
  as prisoner's dilemma, 29–39, 75 n. 15
  short-circuiting, 49–50, 57
  in Venezuela, 22, 113 n. 11
Democratic Action (AD, Acción Democrática)
  decline of, 2, 84, 100, 152, 167, 242
  dominance of, 67 n. 5, 76, 77, 96, 231, 245
  legislative activities, 114, 153, 187, 207
  National Accord and, 224
  National Executive Committee (CEN), 153, 154, 163, 165–66, 186, 243, 246
  organization of, 76–77, 122–23, 195
  Pact of Punto Fijo and, 94, 95, 110, 169
democratic centralism, 154, 163, 174
Democratic Labor Party (PDT, Partido Democrático Trabalhista), 171, 206
Democratic Social Party (PDS, Partido Democrático Social), 102, 103, 140 n. 30
Democratic Social Party (PDT, Partido Democrático Social), 102, 171
dependency theory. *See also* labor, division of
de Soto, Hernando, 27 n. 11, 35 n. 24
Desposato, Scott, 140
developing countries
  delivery of votes in, 25, 35, 81–82
  democratic accountability in, 8–15
  economic reform in, 54, 59, 231
  ISI policy in, 27 n. 11, 209, 212, 215, 235 n. 26, 236 n. 28
developing democracies. *See also* advanced industrial democracies
  accountability vacuums in, 23 n. 4, 211–12

  legislative organization in, 175, 176–77, 185, 190 n. 9
  political theory in, 34 n. 23, 40, 259
  voters' choices in, 34, 261–62
development policies. *See* economic development
dominance scores, candidates', 89–93, 159, 160–61, 163, 171, 173, 183 n. 5
Dutra, Gaspar, 107, 119 n. 15, 206
  stabilization program of, 220, 221

economic development, 16, 18–19, 51–62, 69, 209–57, 260. *See also* developing countries; import substitution industrialization program (ISI); industrialization; macroeconomic stabilization
  Brazilian, 8, 66, 121, 255
  democratic accountability and, 3–4, 8–9, 11–15
  failures of, 3, 13, 59, 147, 177
  quid-pro-quo incentives for, 56 n. 49, 58
Economics Committee (Brazil), 179, 180–81, 184
economy
  agricultural, 42
  domestic, 51, 238
  government intervention in, 211–12, 216
  liberalization of, 53–54, 224, 256–57
  reforms of, 6, 231, 248
education, 38, 51
elections, 67–72, 76–77, 88–95, 103–4, 168, 259. *See also* equilibrium electoral strategies; laws, electoral; secret ballots; single-*tarjeta* (single-card) vote
electoral accountability, 9–10, 36, 67, 209
electoral performance, 6
  legislative organization and, 181, 184–85, 194–96
  party organization and, 158, 160–61, 163, 171–72, 174
electoral sanctions, 3–4, 7–9, 15–16, 31–33, 32, 154
electoral strategies, 5, 24, 118. *See also* equilibrium electoral strategies; re-election strategies

elites, ruling, 59, 69 n. 9, 96, 127, 194, 225, 243–44, 246. *See also* oligarchies, regional
Ellner, Steve, 166 n. 10
employment, 26, 51, 52, 61–62, 79, 80–81. *See also* jobs; unemployment
Eneas, Cameiro, 22 n. 2
entrepreneurial producers, 35 n. 25, 55, 56, 58
equilibrium electoral strategies, 5–8, 9 n. 6, 23 n. 4, 29–49, 148, 256–57, 260–63. *See also* clientelist-based electoral strategy; policy-based electoral strategy; quid-pro-quo-based electoral strategy
  crisis response and, 210–11
  single, 203
  Venezuela, 93–97
Evans, Peter B., 235 n. 26
exchange
  clientelist, 4–7, 53, 67, 117, 123–24, 166, 227, 238, 259
  direct, 12–14, 19, 33, 35, 37, 41, 77, 81–82, 117, 126 n. 19, 162
  direct *vs.* indirect, 23–29, 63 n. 1, 145, 257
  electoral, 30–32
  indirect, 44, 49, 129
  policy-based, 88, 121–22
  quid-pro-quo, 25–28, 49, 61, 82, 236, 259–60
  of votes, 12, 30, 49, 117, 121
exclusion, 6–7, 35, 37–39, 64, 77. *See also* asymmetry of excludability; mutual exclusivity
executive branch of government. *See* cabinets, composition of; legislators/legislatures; presidentialism/presidents
exports, 53–54, 59, 231, 256
  Brazilian, 119, 156, 219 n. 10
  manufactured, 212–15, 218, 234, 236

federal deputies. *See* Chamber of Deputies (Brazil); Chamber of Deputies (Venezuela); legislators/legislatures
federalism, 10, 65
Ferejohn, John, 12, 24, 26, 28, 33
feudal land system, 55 n. 45, 119

Fifth Republic Movement (MVR, Movimiento V [Quinta] República), 111, 152–53, 166
Figueirado, Angelina, 136, 139
Fiscal Emergency Fund (FEF, Fundo de Emergencia Fiscal), 198–99
foreign exchange. *See also* investment, foreign
  Brazilian, 119, 219 n. 10, 250
  Venezuelan, 73, 216, 217 n. 9, 238 n. 30
Foreign Relations Committee, (Brazil), 179, 193
franchise. *See* voters/voting
Franco, Itamar, 134, 203, 249, 250

Garotinho, Anthony, 22 n. 2, 92
Geddes, Barbara, 66
goals, alignment of, 46–50, 147–74
Golder, Matt, 134
Gomes, Ciro, 22 n. 2
Goulart, Joao, 101, 107, 108, 109 n. 7, 206 n. 15
  stabilization program of, 220, 221
government, 29–30, 95–96. *See also* budgets; bureaucracies; competition, government-opposition party; legislators/legislatures; presidentialism/presidents
  interventions by, 53–54, 55 n. 45, 56, 59, 211–12, 216, 231, 256
  legislative opposition to, 129, 190, 192
  policy choices of, 95–96, 209–57
governors, direct election of, 154 n. 6, 242–43
Graham, Lawrence S., 222
growth. *See* economic development
Guidelines for a National Accord (Venezuela), 224

Haggard, Stephan, 153, 235 n. 26
high-income voters, 12, 14 n. 12, 15, 33, 59, 61
Homeland for All Party (PPT, Patria para Todos), 167
Hurley, Patricia A., 104–5
hyperinflation, 68, 70, 73–74. *See also* inflation

imports, 53–54, 73, 216
import substitution industrialization policies (ISI), 27 n. 11, 61, 70–71, 83, 118–23, 156, 234–39, 256
  crisis in, 19, 209, 210–11, 219–34, 239–46
  failure of, 147, 218–19
  flaws in, 7, 210, 211–19, 235, 248, 260
income, 15, 38. *See also* high-income voters; low-income voters; middle-class voters; poverty
  distribution of, 6, 51–52, 56, 211
  threshold of, 57, 59, 233
  voting behavior based on, 7, 13–14, 30, 32, 69
incumbent advantage, 8 n. 5, 40–43, 164, 190, 192
index of likeness, 105, 107, 132
India, 71
individual-collective goals' alignment, 46–50, 147–74
Indonesia, 54 n. 42
industrialization, 13. *See also* import substitution industrialization policies (ISI); production
  Brazil, 3, 66, 119, 156, 161
  Venezuela, 114
infant-industry policies, 7, 19, 209, 212–18, 235–38
inflation, 67–68, 70, 73–74
  Brazil, 3, 65, 220, 221–22, 249
  reduction of, 1, 26, 71, 250, 251
infrastructure, 29 n. 13, 30
institutionalist theories, 9, 29, 229. *See also* new institutionalism
  of crisis response, 231, 233–34
  democratic accountability and, 3, 32
  of electoral rules, 19, 43 n. 33, 47
  of political party behavior, 136, 145, 147–50, 227
  regarding roll call votes, 129, 132, 134
Institutional Revolutionary Party (PRI) Mexico, 232 n. 23
interest groups, 14 n. 13, 30 n. 17, 34 n. 23, 50, 235 n. 26, 259
  state-corporatist, 25, 32, 56, 80–81, 88, 161, 236, 238–39
International Monetary Fund (IMF), 250 n. 35

interparty divisiveness, 104–7, 116–18. *See also* parties, political
  Brazil, 118–22, 150
  Venezuela, 111–15, 122–24
intraparty unity, 104–7, 116–18. *See also* parties, political
  Brazil, 118–22, 136, 143–44, 149, 150
  Venezuela, 111–15, 154
investment, 58–59, 72, 254
  foreign, 193–94
  industrial, 2, 212–15, 218, 235, 237, 248

Japan, 37, 38, 151 n. 3, 212
Jimenez, Perez, 110
jobs, 65, 67, 232. *See also* employment; labor unions
  lack of, 71–72, 209
  providing, 52, 69, 126 n. 19, 215, 236
  trading votes for, 14 n. 12, 19, 33, 35, 53, 55 n. 45, 58, 81
justice systems, 1, 35, 38, 53. *See also* Constitution and Justice Committee (Brazil)

Kaldor-Hicks criteria, 227 n. 17
Kang, David, 214 n. 4
Karl, Terry Lynn, 113
Kaufman, Robert R., 235 n. 27
Kenworthy, Eldon, 176–77, 190 n. 9, 196, 199
Keohane, Robert, 63
King, Gary, 63
Kitschelt, Herbert, 26, 54 n. 43, 63 n. 1, 64 n. 2, 83, 114, 238 n. 30
Krueger, Anne O., 26, 27 n. 11
Kubitschek, Juscelino, 83, 107–9, 180, 206 n. 15, 250 n. 35
  stabilization program of, 119, 220, 221

labor, division of, 56, 235 n. 26
labor unions, 26, 30 n. 17
  Brazil, 101
  jobs provided by, 52, 236 n. 28
  Latin America, 71–72, 80–81
  state-corporatist, 32, 156
Lacerda, Carlos, 206 n. 15
land, 42
  Chávez's takeovers of, 69 n. 9, 248
latifundista system, 55 n. 45, 119

Latin America
  development in, 70
  exports from, 156
  labor unions in, 71–72, 80–81
  legislative organization in, 180
  liberalization in, 54 n. 43
  politics in, 230 n. 22
  private property in, 69 n. 9
  reforms in, 224
Laverda, Antonio, 66
laws, electoral, 11, 34, 116–17, 136. *See also* candidate-centered electoral laws; party-centered electoral rules
legislators/legislatures. *See also* agendas, legislative; coalitions, legislative; parties, political; rank-and-file party members
  Brazil, 88–93, 118–22, 128–34, 175–87, 254
  crisis response by, 220–23, 239–40
  election of, 32 n. 20, 76, 88–93, 94, 136–42, 155–61
  executive relations, 9, 11, 34, 116–17
  organization of, 18, 175–208, 227, 260
  party behavior in, 104–7, 109, 111–12, 114–18, 128–34, 151, 188–89, 200
  policy goods provided by, 103–4, 153–54, 157
  reelection strategies, 48, 170 n. 22
  Venezuelan, 151–55, 247
  voting patterns of, 163, 171–72, 184
Leoni, Eduardo, 134
Lessa, Carlos, 251
Liberal Front Party (PFL, Partido da Frente Liberal), 102, 103, 139, 143, 144, 172–73
liberalization, economic, 53–54, 224, 256–57
licensing, 55 n. 45, 56, 61
Lijphart, Arend, 43 n. 33
Limongi, Fernando, 136, 139
Lincoln, Abraham, 22 n. 3
locally-targeted collective goods, 10–11, 55, 255–56. *See also* nationally-targeted collective goods; pork-barrel goods
  delivery of, 5, 34, 38, 116–18, 170–71
  nonexcludable, 88–89, 173
  receipt of, 18, 24–25, 28, 35, 149

United States, 26
  voting influenced by, 151 n. 3, 158
low-income voters, 12–13, 15, 34, 35, 61
loyalty
  party, 13, 18, 148, 157–61, 171–72, 174, 181, 183–85
  voter, 77–78
Lula da Silva, Luiz Inácio
  cabinets of, 134, 144 n. 31, 200, 203, 206
  reforms by, 1–2, 21–22, 66 n. 4, 249, 251, 254, 261
  scandals surrounding, 1, 254–55
Lusinchi, Jaime, 223
Lyne, Mona M., 235 n. 26

macro conditions, 64, 69, 70
macroeconomic stabilization, 65, 177, 178 n. 2, 188–89, 199, 220–21, 249–51, 254–55. *See also* Real Plan
Magalhaes, Antonio Carlos, 40, 144, 172, 255
Mainwaring, Scott, 102 n. 2, 138 n. 28
majorities, 1, 4, 35 n. 24, 43, 176–96
manufacturing. *See* exports, manufactured; industrialization; production
Mayhew, David, 206 n. 15
mayors, election of, 154 n. 6
MBR-200 (Revolutionary Bolivarian Movement 200), 246
McCubbins, Mathew D., 28, 45, 49, 83, 105, 187, 190, 199, 200, 206 n. 15
means tests, 25 n. 8, 27
mercantilism, 27 n. 11
Mercosul, 250
Mesa Diretora, Brazil, 178, 197
Mexico, 43 n. 34, 232 n. 23
middle-class voters, 13, 14 n. 12, 32, 51–52
Middle East, 59, 61, 72
middle-income democracies, 23 n. 4
military. *See also* Brazil, 1964 coup
  governments of, 40, 68, 70, 198, 215 n. 5, 250
  legislature and, 102–3, 220
  reforms by, 110, 125
  Venezuela, 246
  vote monitoring by, 79

misiones sociales. *See* social missions (*misiones sociales*)
mobilization, political, 70 n. 11, 230 n. 22
modernization theories, 6, 12, 15, 62
Movement for Socialism (MAS, Movimiento al Socialismo), 152, 166, 224
multiparty system, 140, 142
municipalities, Brazilian, 89–91, 159–61, 173
mutual exclusivity, 43–44, 169, 247, 252

Naim, Moisés, 216–17, 238 n. 30
National Commission on Costs, Prices, and Salaries (Venezuela), 223
National Democratic Union (UDN, Uniao Democrática Nacional), 100
  cabinet participation, 108
  committee memberships of, 179, 180–81, 183, 193
  electoral performance, 102 n. 2, 118–22, 160–61
  party alliances, 101, 107, 109 n. 7, 206 n. 15
nationalization, 53, 125–26, 235 n. 27
  Chávez's, 2, 247–48
nationally-targeted collective goods, 23 n. 4, 145, 227, 255–56
  cabinet positions related to, 136
  delivery of, 9–10, 34, 83, 115, 116–20, 129, 149–50
  elections influenced by, 5–6, 173, 244
  policy for, 11, 55, 124
  receipt of, 24–25, 35
National Renewal Alliance Party (ARENA, Associacao Renovadora Nacional, 103
natural resources, 53, 58, 61
neoliberalism, 224, 242, 246–47, 250
New Deal (U.S.), 42 n. 32
new institutionalist theory, 65, 259
  clientelism and, 8–15, 83–84
  of collective goods provision, 5–6, 24
  of legislative organization, 203
  of open-list PR, 10, 170
  of party organization, 111, 147 n. 1, 149–50, 153
North, Douglass C., 11, 212 n. 1

O'Donnell, Guillermo, 6, 15, 61, 70–71
oil revenues, 43 n. 34, 58, 59, 61, 225 n. 16, 231
  control of, 42, 195
  foreign exchange and, 216–17
  Venezuela, 2–3, 7, 72–73, 96, 122–23, 125–27, 168, 231, 247–48
oligarchies, regional, 100–101, 119, 161, 193. *See also* elites, regional
open-list proportional representation (PR), 10, 17–18, 49, 65. *See also* closed-list proportional representation (PR)
  legislative organization and, 192
  party organization and, 147–50, 155–61, 170–72, 174
opposition parties, 164, 206 n. 15. *See* competition, government-opposition; parties, political, opposition
Organization of Petroleum Exporting Countries (OPEC), 72, 247

Pact for Reform (Venezuela), 223–24
Pact of Punto Fijo, 94, 110–15, 122–25, 169, 186, 220 n. 11
Palocci, Antonio, 251 n. 37
parliamentarism, 9–10, 11. *See also* legislators/legislatures
particularism, 23–29, 49, 50
parties, political, 259. *See also* coalitions; rank-and-file party members; reputations, party
  behavior patterns, 99–147, 164, 227
  crisis response, 243–45
  leadership of, 154–66, 170–74, 177–78, 184, 197–98, 233
  loyalty patterns, 13, 18, 148, 157–61, 171–72, 174, 181, 183–85
  opposition, 136, 164, 197, 206 n. 15
  organization of, 12, 13, 17, 45–49, 140, 142, 147–74, 227, 243, 247, 259–61
  policy-based appeals, 16, 42, 86, 143, 172
  reforms by, 240–42
  switching, 77–78, 100, 134, 140–42
  voting records, 117, 120–22, 187–92, 204, 206–8
partisan tides, 64, 82–87

party-centered electoral laws, 9–11, 19, 83–84, 94, 111, 153, 217. *See also* candidate-centered electoral laws
  crisis response and, 234
  legislative organization and, 153, 192
  party organization and, 47–49, 117–18, 144, 147 n. 1, 149–50, 217
patronage, 23 n. 5, 25, 27, 222, 242
pelegismo, 80 n. 19
Pereira, Carlos, 134
Perez, Carlos Andrés, 84
  attempts at reform, 110–11, 210, 220, 224–25, 240–47
  impeachment of, 2, 223, 225, 241, 245
Perón, Juan Domingo, 235 n. 27
platforms. *See* parties, political, policy-based appeals
pluralist political systems, 124
policy-based electoral strategy, 46–47, 54–60, 82–97. *See also* competition, policy-based; structural conditions, policy-based
  appeals to voters through, 99–146
  Brazil, 7, 147–49, 196–99, 209, 211, 255
  clientelist-based strategy, 13–14, 56–57, 75, 126
  crisis response, 143, 165, 173–74, 210–11, 226–27
  democratic accountability and, 31, 145, 161, 170
  incentives for, 17–19, 51–52
  legislative organization, 175–76, 188–92, 194–96, 204
  party-centered electoral laws and, 10, 153
  responsiveness of, 154–57, 165, 173, 253
  risks of, 7–8, 32
  shift to, 60–61, 88–89, 91, 97, 127–29, 134, 136, 172, 176, 200, 203, 249–50, 255, 256
  vote monitoring, 74–75, 77, 79
  voters' preferences for, 25–27, 49–50, 64–65, 95, 145, 154–56, 162–66, 173–74, 206–7, 239–40, 244
policy choice, 16, 18–19, 49–50, 64 n. 2, 70–71, 209–57, 259–63

policy goods, 27, 31–33, 244
  delivering, 39–40, 82, 100, 121, 149, 160, 170, 187–92, 196, 198–99, 204, 206–8
  demand for, 66, 67, 128, 142
  excludability of, 163
  voter preferences for, 239–40, 244
policy-making. *See* legislators/legislatures, organization of
politicians. *See also* rank-and-file party members
  access to resources, 55–56, 57, 60
  accountability of, 3–4, 9, 25, 33, 66
  behavior of, 53, 64
  clientelistic, 39
  goals of, 40, 170 n. 22
  goods provided by, 36, 66, 82
  policy choices of, 13, 260–61
  populist, 22 n. 2
politics
  behavior in, 16–17, 117
  Brazilian, 8
  clientelist, 15, 23–62, 83, 87, 163, 187, 237, 242
  electoral, 62, 113 n. 9, 115, 160
  exclusionary, 31, 190, 192, 230 n. 22
  institutions and, 11–13
  policy-based, 43–44
  quid-pro-quo, 15, 57
pork-barrel goods, 37, 44, 57, 84 n. 22, 115 n. 13, 129, 145, 173, 234, 262. *See also* locally-targeted collective goods; particularism
poverty, 2, 3, 6, 29
  as clientelist theory, 8–15, 23 n. 4, 36, 37–38
presidentialism/presidents, 9–10, 32 n. 20
  Brazil, 65, 88–93, 104, 129, 171, 193, 197–200, 222
  committee, 178–86, 193–94, 196–97, 203–4
  legislative powers of, 150 n. 3
  Venezuela, 2, 11, 18, 113
  voting for, 32 n. 20, 76, 88–92, 94–95
price supports. *See* subsidies
prisoner's dilemma, 4, 6–7, 14 n. 12, 29–39, 75 n. 15, 259–61. *See also* voter's dilemma

private assets, 61, 69–70, 69 n. 9
private rate of return, 212 n. 1
privatization, 224, 249
production, 2, 7, 53–59, 61–62, 235 n. 27
  capital-intensive, 19, 209, 212–18, 235–38
  manipulation of, 33, 35 n. 24
Progressive Social Party (PSP, Partido Social Progresista), 100, 101, 109, 120, 137, 160
property rights, 35, 69 n. 9, 233 n. 24
  control of, 42 n. 31, 53, 56
  efficient, 4, 12, 23 n. 4, 30
proportional-representation systems, 46–47. *See also* closed-list proportional-representation (PR); open-list proportional-representation (PR)
protectionism, 26–27, 53–54, 234–35, 237. *See also* subsidies
  high, 212–18, 238, 250
  levels of, 19, 209
public goods. *See* clientelist goods; collective goods; policy goods
public opinion, 16, 64–67, 97, 241
public policy, 28, 235
  Brazilian, 8, 49, 249
  democratic accountability and, 3–4
  legislative organization and, 18, 117, 177, 185–87
  parties' reputations for, 14 n. 13, 26, 63, 117
  Venezuelan, 10–11, 111, 113, 217
  voter preferences for, 9–11, 16, 58, 65
Putin, Vladimir, 69 n. 9
Putnam, Robert D., 14 n. 12, 261 n. 1
Pye, Lucien W., 14 n. 13

Quadros, Janio, 101 n. 1, 220, 221 n. 14
Quércia, Orestes, 22 n. 2
quid-pro-quo-based electoral strategy, 16–17, 54–60, 200, 259–63
  appeals to voters through, 99–146
  delivering, 39–49, 83, 88, 123–24, 207
  exchange according to, 25–28, 49, 61, 82, 236, 259–60
  incentives for, 51–52, 53
  legislative organization, 189

maximizing, 209–57
networks of, 90 n. 27
party organization according to, 87
policy reputations and, 115–24
rejection of, 32, 36
Venezuela, 118–22
vote buying with, 30, 58
voters' preference for, 4, 7, 13–16, 33, 66, 96

Ramos, Nereu, 107–8
Ranis, Gustav, 235 n. 26
rank-and-file party members. *See also* parties, political
  access to resources, 87
  behavior of, 147–50, 165
  bidding wars among, 162–63
  control of, 44–48, 118, 153–54, 160, 166, 174–75, 188, 244–45
  electoral appeal of, 16, 17, 230 n. 22
  voting records of, 132, 171–73
Rasmussen, Eric, 29
rational-choice institutionalists, 9
Real Plan, 66 n. 4, 83, 250, 251, 254
reelection, strategies, 42, 43, 48, 134, 157. *See also* electoral strategies
reform, 230–31. *See also* Brazil, contemporary, reforms in; Chávez, Hugo, reforms by
Reinhardt, Gina Yannitel, 134
Rennó, Lúcio, 134
rent/rent seeking, 262. *See also* locally-targeted collective goods; particularism
  clientelist, 37, 44, 57
  policy-based, 115 n. 13, 211–12, 234, 235 n. 26, 238 n. 30
Republican Democratic Union (URD, Unión Republicana Democrática), 94, 110
Republican Party (PR, Partido Republicano), 100, 101, 102 n. 2, 137, 138, 160, 179
Republican Progressive Party (PPR, Partido Progresista Republicana). *See* Democratic Social Party (PDS, Partido Democrático Social)
reputations
  for delivering, 210, 226, 231–32, 239–46

reputations (continued)
  party, 17, 45–46, 49, 82–84, 87, 118–22, 148, 157, 188, 189, 200, 206–8
  personal, 45, 88, 140, 148, 157, 163, 170, 204
  policy, 44, 82, 103–4, 111–24, 127–43, 147–74, 198–99
reservation price of voters, 63–64, 72, 74, 88, 210, 229–30, 233–34. *See also* bidding wars for votes; vote buying
resources
  access to, 55, 57, 117, 122–23, 160, 195, 204–5, 207, 239
  candidate *vs.* party-centered, 47–48
  centralized *vs.* decentralized, 48–49, 122–24, 148
  constraints on, 227 n. 17, 229–34, 240–46, 256–57
  control of, 18, 41–43, 56, 84, 136, 156, 166, 248
  distribution of, 50, 78, 87, 95–96, 119–20, 125–27, 129, 156, 168–69, 187–92, 226–27, 229
  government, 185–87, 193
  natural, 53, 58, 61
  supply of, 7, 53–54, 58–61, 63–64, 67–68
  Venezuelan, 72–74
  for vote buying, 157–58, 163–64
rewards, 45–46, 49, 57 n. 50
Rice index, 105, 132
Riker, William, 261–62
roll call votes, 105–7, 128–34, 181, 183–84, 200
roll rates, 190, 199–207
Rosales, Manuel, 168
rural voters, 13
Russia, privatization in, 54 n. 43

Salgado, Plinio, 91
Samuels, David, 139 n. 29, 170 n. 22, 173
Santos, Fabiano, 151 n. 3, 206 n. 15
Santos, Wanderly Guilherme dos, 102 n. 2
Sardinia, 27 n. 11
Sarney, José, 83, 200
Sartori, Giovanni, 99, 107

Scandinavia, 62
Schmitter, Phillippe C., 14 n. 13, 80
Scott, Robert, 177 n. 1
secret ballots, 75 n. 15, 77, 151 n. 3
sectoral clientelism, 27, 56 n. 49. *See also* quid-pro-quo-based electoral system
seniority, 158, 171, 173, 181, 184–85
Shugart, Matthew S., 150 n. 3, 151 n. 3, 153, 165, 198
single-member districts, 154 n. 6, 165, 247
single-party democracies, 23 n. 4, 37–38, 167–69
single-*tarjeta* (single-card) vote, 17, 44 n. 35, 76–77, 149, 154, 174
Soares, Gláucio A. D., 102 n. 2
social choice, 261–63
Social Democratic Party (PSD, Partido Social Democrático), 100–101
  cabinet memberships, 107, 119
  committee memberships, 178–79, 183–84
  decline of, 102, 180–81
  legislative majority held by, 193
  party alliances, 109 n. 7, 138, 160–61, 178–79
  voting records, 120–21
socialism, 61
  Venezuelan, 2, 19, 247–48
Social Legislation Committee (Brazil), 179, 193
social missions (*misiones sociales*), 125–26, 247
Social Pact (Venezuela), 223
social rate of return, 213 n. 1
social safety nets, 233 n. 24
social security, 81, 234 n. 24
  Brazil, 1, 3, 66, 220, 221–23, 249, 252–53, 255
social welfare, 28–29, 50, 214, 236, 256, 259–60. *See also* welfare-enhancing policies
South Korea, 56 n. 48, 71, 212, 213, 214 n. 4
stabilization programs. *See* balance of payments; macroeconomic stabilization; Real Plan
standards of living, 7, 19, 57, 60, 69, 218, 223, 236

state. *See* government
stencil vote, 81
Stokes, Susan C., 12 n. 11, 14 n. 12, 35 n. 25
structural conditions, 51–54, 57 n. 50, 63, 97, 259–62. *See also* debt, international; inflation
 clientelist, 19, 31–32, 36, 115, 121–25, 142–45, 148, 151 n. 3, 157, 161–63, 166, 189, 194, 210–11, 230 n. 22, 236, 242, 244, 246
 democratic accountability and, 4–8, 13, 60–62, 259
 endogenizing, 6, 260, 263
 for exports, 219 n. 10
 measuring, 67–75
 policy-based, 30, 50–60, 71–72, 127–28, 226–29
 quid-pro-quo, 42, 48, 50–60
 reforms in, 254–55
 voters' choices shaped by, 14 n. 12, 15, 211, 229, 256
subsidies, 7, 61, 156, 212, 214–17, 231–32, 235–36. *See also* import substitution industrialization policies (ISI); protectionism
suplentes (substitutes), 158 n. 14
supply-demand factors, 29 n. 16, 39, 51–60, 63–64, 67–78, 142, 219 n. 10
support
 electoral, 16, 43–44, 64
 legislative, 192
 mutually exclusive, 232–34
 political, 27, 139
 worker, 239
surveys, 64 n. 2

Taiwan, 56 n. 48, 71, 212, 213
tariffs. *See* protectionism
taxes, 38, 53, 126, 156, 221, 231, 249
technology, new, 56 n. 49, 57 n. 50
Thomas, Robert Paul, 212 n. 1
Tollison, Robert D., 26, 27 n. 11
trade, 45, 53, 216–17, 219 n. 10. *See also* import substitution industrialization policies (ISI)
 Brazil, 1, 249, 250
trienio, 110

trumping resources, 41–43, 166. *See also* oil revenues
 control of, 75, 83–84, 93, 96–97, 162, 192–93, 195
Tullock, Gordon, 26, 27 n. 11
two-party systems, 140, 151

underdevelopment. *See* economic development, failures of
unemployment, 71–72, 209
United Nations Economic Commission for Latin America (ECLA), 213, 234–35
United Socialist Party of Venezuela (PSUV, Partido Socialista Unido de Venezuela), 18, 80, 111, 167, 168
United States, 155 n. 8, 212
 candidate-centered electoral laws, 151 n. 3
 locally-targeted collective goods, 26, 38
 machine politics in, 35, 42 n. 32, 45
 Venezuelan opposition to, 247

Vargas, Getúlio, 42 n. 32, 100, 101, 107, 161, 205, 206
 industrialization by, 83, 119, 156, 180
 stabilization program of, 220, 221
Venezuela
 democracy in, 6, 20, 73, 111, 113 n. 9, 124, 151–55, 186 n. 6, 187, 194, 240
 institutionalist theory applied to, 10–12, 19
 ISI in, 7, 19, 209–10, 214–34
 political party behavior in, 99, 115–18, 122–24
 public opinion in, 66–67
 structural variables in, 72–74
 voting patterns in, 16, 93–97
Venezuela, pre-Chávez
 centralization in, 48–49, 173, 255–56
 collapse of democracy in, 2, 4, 15
 crisis response in, 23, 67 n. 5, 99, 109–11, 147–48, 151, 240–45
 decentralization in, 162–66, 186–87, 193, 195, 207, 243
 economy, 3, 10–11, 48
 electoral reforms in, 148, 151 n. 4, 174
 legislative organization in, 175, 185–87, 203

Venezuela (*continued*)
  party behavior in, 109–15, 144, 171
  party-centered electoral laws in, 94, 111, 217
  vote monitoring in, 76–78
Venezuela, under Chávez, 11, 21–23. *See also* Chávez, Hugo
  crisis response in, 147
  legislative organization in, 196, 207
  party-centered electoral laws, 153
  party organization in, 110, 144, 166–69
Venezuelan Communist Party (PCV, Partido Comunista de Venezuela), 167
Venezuelan State-owned Oil Company (PDVSA, Petróleos de Venezuela), 79, 126
Verba, Sidney, 63
vetoes, mutual, 18, 27, 29 n. 14, 175–208, 227
  Brazil, 19–94, 196–207
  Venezuela, 193–96
vote buying, 17–18, 38. *See also* bidding wars for votes; exchange, of votes; reservation price of voters; votes, cost of
  Brazil, 68–70, 84
  efficient, 45–62, 147–74, 185, 194, 247
  quid-pro-quo, 42, 58
  Venezuela, 77, 162–63
vote monitoring, 64, 74–82, 87, 97
voter-politician links, 4, 13, 175, 217
  clientelistic, 16, 63–64
  democratic accountability and, 30–32, 34
  direct, 5, 74, 94, 117
  indirect, 5, 16, 44, 94
voter's dilemma, 4–5
  clientelism and, 37–38
  democratic accountability and, 15, 29–39, 125
  logic of, 6, 50–54, 71, 115, 142, 144, 229
  policy implications of, 69, 226
  provision of goods and, 21–62
  theory of, 57, 63–64, 75, 259–63
voters/voting. *See also* clientelist-based electoral strategy, voters' preferences for; policy-based electoral strategy, voters' preferences for; quid-pro-quo electoral strategy, voters' preferences for
  appeals to, 40–44, 99–146, 151 n. 3, 174, 204
  clientelist goods linked to, 27, 32, 35 n. 25, 229
  delivery of, 28, 56, 78, 81–82, 89, 93, 227
  democratic accountability and, 60–62, 153
  effects of party switching on, 14 n. 12, 82–97, 140–41
  ex officio, 161, 236 n. 28
  illiterate, 69–70, 81
  income influences on, 7, 12–15, 30, 32–35, 51–52, 59, 61, 69
  measuring, 63 n. 1, 64–65
  for nonexcludable goods, 36
  party, 105, 132, 134, 142–44, 148, 175
  personalist, 89, 145, 150, 170–72
  pooling, 85 n. 24, 86, 90 n. 27
  risks in, 59–60
  structural conditions' influence on, 256
  theories of, 23, 162, 165, 173–74, 259, 261–62
  variables of, 16
vote swings, 85–87

Wade, Robert, 56
wage control, Brazil, 220–21, 249, 250
Weingrod, Alex, 27 n. 11
welfare-enhancing policies. *See also* social welfare
  collective goods and, 26, 28, 226–27
  electoral constraints on, 8–9, 19
  improvement in, 214, 218, 237
  reduction of, 50, 70, 211–12
Wilkinson, Steven, 63 n. 1, 64 n. 2
worker-owned cooperatives, 2, 125–26, 247–48
Workers' Party (PT, Partido dos Trabalhadores), 1, 22, 86, 102, 143, 198, 250 n. 35. *See also* Lula da Silva, Luiz Inácio
working-class voters, 13, 14 n. 12, 32, 52, 238–39